HENSLOWE'S ROSE

HENSLOWE'S ROSE
The Stage & Staging

Ernest L. Rhodes

The University Press of Kentucky

The drawings in plates 16, 18, 19, 20, 21, and 22
are by Heddi Siebel.

Publication of this book was assisted by
the American Council of Learned Societies
under a grant from the Andrew W. Mellon Foundation.

ISBN: 0–8131–1305–9

Library of Congress Catalog Card Number: 73–80466

A statewide cooperative scholarly publishing agency
serving Berea College, Centre College of Kentucky,
Eastern Kentucky University, Georgetown College,
Kentucky Historical Society, Kentucky State University,
Morehead State University, Murray State University,
Northern Kentucky State College, Transylvania University,
University of Kentucky, University of Louisville, and
Western Kentucky University.

Editorial and Sales Offices: Lexington, Kentucky 40506

For Carolyn
"in lieu of many ornaments"

Contents

Plates follow page   66

Plates

Preface

THE IDEA for this book grew out of my experience in designing and building a set for Shakespeare's *Twelfth Night* shortly after I became the technical director of the Guignol Theater of the University of Kentucky in 1950. The stage shown in the De Witt sketch of the Swan, limited as it is to two openings for use by the actors (plate 5), seemed to me inadequate for the presentation of the plays of Shakespeare and his contemporaries. Moreover, the various attempts of scholars to explain how the stage of the Swan could have been changed by the use of curtains or the addition of another door to accommodate those plays were unconvincing. At the time, I assumed there were other extant pictures of Shakespearean stages than the one drawn by Arend Van Buchell in 1596 from a sketch or a report by his friend Johannes De Witt. Only Inigo Jones's design for the Cockpit Theatre at Whitehall could be found. This was a drawing made in 1628 or 1629, at least twelve years after Shakespeare died. Perhaps, I reasoned, the sketch of the Swan was inaccurate and a close examination of the plays given at that theater might throw some light on Shakespearean staging conditions. I found only one extant play that was known to have been given at the Swan—Middleton and Dekker's *Chaste Maid in Cheapside*, printed in 1630, or about thirty-four years after the De Witt sketch was made. By tracing the movement of the actors about the stage, I concluded that the *Chaste Maid* could have been presented on the stage of the Swan as it is depicted in the De Witt sketch. Joseph Quincy Adams's suspicion that the Swan "may have been provided with a stage that could be removed so as to allow the building to be used on occasions for animal-baiting" (*Shakespearean Playhouses*, p. 165), suggested to me the possibility that the De Witt sketch might be an atypical rather than a typical Shakespearean stage.

Not long after I began graduate work in English at the University of Kentucky in 1952, Professor Thomas B. Stroup introduced me to George F. Reynolds's *Staging of Elizabethan Plays at the Red Bull Theater: 1605–1625*. Continuing as technical director of the Guignol, I maintained an interest in staging and decided to write my doctoral dissertation on the staging of Elizabethan plays at the Rose theater. I tried to apply the methodology of Professor Reynolds's work on the Red Bull to my study of the plays of Henslowe's Rose. Assembling all the pictures, documents, and plays that could be related immediately and directly to the Rose, I "blocked" the plays, that is, traced the movement of the actors about the stage. I concluded that those plays required for presentation a stage encompassed on three sides by walls provided with a total of five openings for use in coming onto the stage and leaving it. This conclusion was reached inductively. The stage as I envisioned it was shown in a sketch facing the first page of my dissertation, which was completed in 1958 and accepted in 1959.

Since 1959, my research has been directed toward an attempt to show that the three walls around the stage of the Rose were indeed provided with five openings onto the stage, and that this fact is important to an understanding of the plays of Shakespeare and his contemporaries. I have encountered two obstacles: first, no pictorial evidence was known that supported my findings; and second, since the De Witt sketch of the Swan has been the only picture we have of a stage in use while Shakespeare lived, that sketch has become encrusted with authority and given a degree of immunity from criticism that verges on sanctity. Although E. K. Chambers, Allardyce Nicoll, and many other reputable scholars have questioned or boldly challenged the importance of the sketch as evidence about the Shakespearean stage, the authority of the Van Buchell drawing prevails.

Dr. Frances A. Yates's discovery of the stage engravings in Robert Fludd's *Ars Memoriae* followed by her 1966 publication of them in *The Art of Memory* (pp. 336–37) provided pictorial evidence about the Shakespearean stage which supports some of the conclusions that I reached in 1958 about the stage of the Rose. Three of the Fludd engravings (my plates 6, 7, and 8) show stages encompassed on three sides by walls. Two of the engravings (plates 7 and 8) show an opening centered in the wall at the rear of the stage with an opening in each of the walls at the side of the stage. Finally,

Fludd's "Sequitur figura vera theatri" (plate 8) shows five openings arranged in three walls encompassing the stage almost precisely as I have shown them (plate 9) in my "Elevation View Rose Theater," facing page 1 of my dissertation. My work is also supported by, and in turn, I think, supports Miss Yates's suggestion "that the London public theatres, including the Globe, were an adaptation of the ancient theatre as described by Vitruvius, made within John Dee's sphere of influence, with its particular appeal to the middle and artisan classes" (*Theatre of the World*, p. xii). Although I have corresponded with Dr. Yates and she may be generally aware of the nature of my work, she has not seen this book and is not responsible for the inferences I have drawn from her work. I should, however, acknowledge here a gracious act on her part that has saved me from some difficulty that bears directly upon this book.

While I was examining an enlarged photograph of the stage of the *Theatrum* in a vignette from the 1616 title page of Ben Jonson's *Workes*, I noticed that a portion of the facade of the stage which could be seen was distinctly Vitruvian (plate 10). E. K. Chambers, I recalled, had observed that although the *Theatrum* "may be merely a bit of classical archeology," it "appears to have the characteristic Elizabethan hut" (*ES* 2:520). I formed the theory that the stage in the vignette was perhaps drawn from Elizabethan or Jacobean theaters and I proposed this theory in a paper which I sent to several scholars interested in Elizabethan staging—including Dr. Yates. She responded promptly, indeed immediately, with a photograph of an engraving, *Theatrum Marcelli*, which is printed here, I believe, for the first time since it was published in 1579 (plate 11). The engraving is from Antonio Lafreri's *Speculum Romanae Magnificentiae*, which Miss Yates explains is "a description, with engravings, of famous buildings in Rome, amongst them the Theatre of Marcellus." A comparison of the 1579 Lafreri engraving (plate 11) with the vignette from the title page of Jonson's *Workes* (plate 10) indicates that the engraving is the source, or closely related to the source, of the Jonson *Theatrum*. The Lafreri engraving, of course, pretty well demolishes my theory about the origin of the stage in the *Theatrum*.

I have not attempted here to explore the possible connection between the Rose and the Theater of Marcellus, a connection suggested by the fact that a playwright who sometimes worked for Henslowe, Ben Jonson, illustrated his *Workes* with a copy derived from Lafreri's engraving, *Theatrum Marcelli*. It should be noted, however, that Margaret Beiber reports in her *History of the Greek and Roman Theater* (p. 184) that the Theater of Marcellus was completed by Augustus in 11 B.C. Elsewhere (p. 186) she says "The form of the theaters built in the late republican and Augustan periods must be the one which Vitruvius Pollio . . . knew when he described, in about 16–13 B.C., the Roman theater . . . and recommended it for imitation." In other words, we now know that Jonson knew in 1616, through the Lafreri engraving, of a Renaissance version of a Vitruvian theater. Moreover, it seems likely, from what we know about Jonson's classical interests, that the Lafreri engraving was copied and put in its prominent place on the title page of the *Workes* to illustrate the playwright's idea of what the theater should be rather than to show what it was actually like. In the absence of pictorial evidence that can be related directly to the Rose theater, I have decorated the facade of my reconstructed stage with details taken from the Jonson *Theatrum*. I show it as one of Henslowe's playwrights may have thought it should ideally have been in 1616, the year Shakespeare died. By providing me with a photograph of the *Theatrum Marcelli*, Dr. Yates has prevented my claiming that the stage of the Rose was possibly quite like the facade of the stage in the *Theatrum* in a vignette on the title page of Jonson's *Workes*. I am sincerely appreciative of her kind help.

My debts to those who have helped with this book are many, and one of them is to the people of my country who made it possible for me to continue my education through veterans' benefits at the conclusion of World War II. This book is being published with the help of a generous grant from the American Council of Learned Societies; I am as pleased to have been selected for aid by that organization as I am grateful for the assistance. Also, the opportunity for work on this book has been regularly made available to me by Old Dominion University in Norfolk, Virginia, and financial aid has come through its Research Foundation. I am indebted for courteous help to a number of people in the Research Foundation directed by Provost Clifford L. Adams.

Scholars whose works and ideas I have used are given credit at the appropriate places, and I have mentioned something of Professor George Fulmer Reynolds's influence on this book. Shortly before he died, this great scholar wrote me a friendly and encouraging letter about my work. I shall always be proud to have known him through that brief association.

I am indebted to a number of people and institutions who have provided me with the pictures I use. Most of those pictures were obtained years ago, and often those who sent me the pictures did not identify themselves. Even so, I should like to thank them and the institutions they represent. The official sources of the several pictures I use are given in my list of illustrations.

The model illustrating my findings about the stage of the Rose (plate 1) was developed with the assistance of three of my former students. The first version was built by Phillip L. Verell who spent an entire summer on the project. The late Michael L. Taylor built a second version from material used in the first. The present model was built from the second by still another former student, my colleague William R. Duffy. I want also to acknowledge here the help I received from professors Frederick W. Culpepper, Jr. and Zeb C. Cummings III, of the Industrial Arts Education Department of Old Dominion University and three of their students, James R. Doyle, Richard L. Edwards, and Leo Maxwell Gibbs, Jr. They worked on the models, made drawings and photographs, and advised me on a number of problems that I could not have solved without their knowledge. I also received the same kind of help and advice from my sons Stanley Homer Rhodes and Lloyd Mason Rhodes.

Several friends have either typed or read one of the versions of this book as it developed, and I am truly grateful for their help and interest. The first in point of time was a fellow graduate student and now Professor Nancy Riffe of Eastern Kentucky University, Richmond, Kentucky. The second was Charles O. Burgess, who has since become Provost of Old Dominion University. Others include Professor Louise DeVere of the department of English, Augusta College, Augusta, Georgia, and Mrs. Mabel McLane of Portsmouth, Virginia, who typed two different versions and a part of a third. The present version has been read and corrected by Mary Beverley Dabney of Norfolk, Virginia.

The several sketches by Heddi Siebel, illustrating the use of parts
of the stage of the Rose (plates 16 and 18–22) were originally con-
ceived and set down by Jean Bowman of Norfolk, Virginia.

J. Leeds Barroll of the University of South Carolina, Charles B.
Lower of the University of Georgia, and George Walton Williams
of Duke University, three colleagues interested in the Shakespearean stage, have given generously and patiently of their time and
knowledge. Professor Lower read two different versions of the
manuscript and provided me with voluminous comment on count-
less points. Professor Williams has given many hours to going over
this work with me chapter by chapter. Many specific suggestions
made by these two excellent scholars and good friends have become
a part of this book. Even so, both have frequently disagreed with
assumptions that I have made and some of the conclusions that I
have reached. They must, of course, be absolved completely of all
responsibility for any errors that may be found in this work.

Professor Thomas B. Stroup, of the University of Kentucky,
who directed my graduate work and my dissertation, has been
involved in this book at every step in its development. My debt to
him as a student and later as a colleague can never be paid, but I
freely acknowledge it here. Moreover, I should like to absolve him
of all responsibility for errors in this work. It may, however, be
difficult to grant him complete absolution. As he must himself
realize, he is the shaping force of this work and indeed my profes-
sional life.

Finally, I acknowledge proudly my association with and my
indebtedness to still another colleague, my wife, Professor Carolyn
Hodgson Rhodes, without whose encouragement and understanding I could never have completed this work.

Introduction

HENSLOWE'S ROSE is probably the most important theater in our literary history, excepting, of course, the 1599 Globe. Yet it has not been studied as a theater or as a stage in its own right. This lack of interest is easily explained, for the Rose faded in the shadow of Shakespeare's Globe on the Bankside in the spring of 1603 and has remained figuratively in the shadow of the Globe since then. Even so, William Shakespeare, Ben Jonson, and most of the well-known playwrights of the period had a hand in writing plays that were presented at the Rose.[1] Many of these plays must be included in any anthology that purports to represent the best drama of the period. And the most famous actor of the day, Henslowe's son-in-law Edward Alleyn, probably appeared on the stage of the Rose in the roles of Orlando, Barabas, Tamburlaine, and Doctor Faustus. The Rose then is a Shakespearean playhouse whose stage and staging practices are worthy of study because of the playwrights who wrote for it, the actors who performed there, and the quality of the plays presented.

Studies of individual theaters, such as this study of the Rose, were advocated by Professor George F. Reynolds in his doctoral dissertation in 1905; his work on the Red Bull, which deals specifically with evidence related to the staging of plays at that theater between 1605 and 1625 was published in 1940. He points out that his study bears upon all Renaissance staging because it demonstrates the necessity for a reexamination of some of our theories about that stage and the way it was used. Reynolds says that his book "offers such a re-examination with stricter methods of procedure and severer checks on conclusions. Instead of studying plays chosen to prove some special point or thesis, it considers all the evidence offered by an objectively selected group of plays."[2] Chambers, in 1923, noted in his *Elizabethan Stage* that "the ideal method would have been to study the staging of each theatre separately, before coming to any conclusion as to the similarity or diversity of their arrangements."[3] The need for more studies like the one made by Reynolds and those advocated by Chambers is voiced by Allardyce Nicoll: "The already existent inquiries into particular, as opposed to general, problems have been seen to have yielded matter of prime interest. We need more of these, conducted with the most rigorous selectivity. Each theatre and its plays should have their appropriate volume."[4]

I am indebted to Professor Reynolds's work on the Red Bull theater for an attitude and an approach; I attempt here to consider all the evidence offered by an "objectively selected" body of material about the stage of the Rose and the way it was used in presenting plays. I divide my sources of evidence, as Professor Reynolds does, into three groups which I have labeled for convenience as pictures of the Rose, documents of the Rose, and plays of the Rose.

I proceed upon the assumption that Dr. Frances A. Yates is correct in her suggestion that "the London public theatres, including the Globe, were an adaptation of the ancient theatre as described by Vitruvius, made within John Dee's sphere of influence, with its particular appeal to the middle and artisan classes."[5] I will argue from evidence in the pictures, documents, and plays of the Rose that the stage in Henslowe's theater was a Vitruvian adaptation, similar in detail to the scale model reconstructed as plate 1 (see also Appendix D). I believe it had to have five openings in its walls to meet the demands placed on it by plays known to have been given for Henslowe. And on the basis of what I can find out about the way the stage was used, the practices followed at the Rose may be described as a fusion of medieval stagecraft (including its classical antecedents) with an Elizabethan adaptation of the Vitruvian stage—an adaptation that did not use perspective scenery as it was developed in Italy by Serlio.

Dr. Glynne Wickham shows in his work on the early English stage that "the mediaeval theatre grew up under the shadow of its Greek and Roman forbears and it was to this past that it turned for enlightenment and instruction with ever increasing vigour from the twelfth century to the sixteenth."[6] Elsewhere in the same work (*EES*, vol. 2, pt. 1, p. 8) he argues that "the so-called 'mansion staging' or *décor simultané* of the Middle Ages was imported intact into the first permanent theatres of Elizabethan London; that it survived in the public theatres with some modifications occasioned by increasingly adroit use of the tiring-house wall (its doors, its recesses, its windows) until these theatres were closed in 1642."

I find that the tiring-house wall of the Rose, which was integrated into the framework of the theater building, provided a fixed scenic background—the *frons scaenae* of a Vitruvian-Shakespearean stage. It could not be taken down or carried away to indicate changes in the place of the action in the play. Its gates, the penthouse above the gates, and a gallery at each side of the penthouse may be equated in play after play of the Rose with the mansions of medieval staging. And to the extent that these elements of the tiring-house wall were fixed and were used in the same way that medieval mansions were used, the staging at the Rose may be described in E. K. Chambers's term as "synchronous" (*ES* 3:88).

However, as Wickham observes (*EES*, vol. 2, pt. 1, p. 9), "We must try to visualize the stage-craft of the period 1576–1660 and beyond as essentially homogenous—traditional, emblematic techniques of mediaeval invention undergoing various slow modifications." I argue that the manner in which plays were presented at the Rose, and particularly the way in which stage properties were handled, show clearly the "traditional, emblematic techniques of mediaeval invention undergoing various slow modifications." I find properties such as thrones, clouds, a rainbow, and an eagle were lowered from a hut above the stage; other large stage properties including such items as trees and animals were pushed up through a trap from under the stage; still others, stage pieces such as beds, thrones, tombs, and arbors were thrust out through the openings at each side of the gates in the tiring-house wall (the two discovery spaces). I also find in the plays of the Rose that large stage pieces such as hearses and chariots were sometimes carried or drawn onto the stage through two more openings—one in each of the walls located at the sides of the stage. These stage properties—emblems and modified medieval mansions, lowered, pushed up, thrust out, carried, or drawn onto the stage through fixed openings—were frequently used, with the dialogue, to indicate a change in the place of the action of the play as well as to add to visual enjoyment. Whenever these emblems were brought onto the stage or taken off to designate change in the place of the action, the practices at the Rose may be described by E. K. Chambers's term as "successive" staging (*ES* 3:88).

Obviously, many of the practices followed in presenting plays at the Rose were those we generally associate with the Shakespearean theaters, practices giving Shakespearean drama one of its distinctive qualities. I believe those practices develop, flower, as a result of the imaginative handling of routine theatrical problems arising from the fusion of medieval stagecraft (including its classical antecedents) with an Elizabethan adaptation of the Vitruvian stage.

The pictures of the Rose consist of two maps, six engravings, two sketches, and six woodcuts (Appendix A), all of which are contemporary, or seem to be derived from sources contemporary, with the Rose. These pictures show something of both the exterior and the interior of a theater. Unfortunately the two maps (Norden's maps of 1593 and of 1600) and the engraving *Civitas Londini* (plates 2, 3, and 4) offer contradictory evidence about the shape of the building. It appears as round in the maps and as polygonal in the engraving—in which Norden set his revised map of 1600. And none of the pictures of the Rose, regardless of the degree of certainty with which they can be related to that theater, provides details about the shape of the stage or the arrangement of the wall or walls separating the stage from the rest of the theater.

Pictorial evidence, however, figures prominently in most of the longer studies made of the Elizabethan stage since George Reynolds's work in 1940. John Cranford Adams, for example, attempts to reconstruct the first Globe on the theory that the characteristics of the stage in the theater may be deduced from the fact that Visscher's picture shows the outside of the theater as an octagonal structure.[7] C. Walter Hodges endeavors "to bring together a collection of evidence, and especially of pictures related to the subject which . . . will create a visual impression of the style and manner of the London theatre in the time of Shakespeare."[8] Richard Southern relies heavily upon the sketch of the Swan (plate 5) to illustrate how far "it seems justifiable to go in reconstructing a practical Elizabethan theatre upon the evidence at present available to us."[9]

Despite the warning of Nagler in 1958 that "it is only with certain reservations that we can take De Witt's Swan as a picture of a typical Elizabethan theatre,"[10] the authority of the sketch increased, and it became generally accepted during the 1960s as the only satisfactory picture of a stage in use during Shakespeare's life. Leslie Hotson employed the drawing, describing it as the "unfinished de Witt sketch of the Swan," to support and explain details in his "in-the-round" staging theory.[11] Glynne Wickham concludes his "survey of the architectural precedents for Elizabethan playhouse design" by accepting "De Witt's sketch of the Swan Theatre at its face value without modification, interpolation or any other unwarranted change" (*EES* vol. 2, pt. 1, p. 204). And Richard Hosley in "The Origins of the So-called Elizabethan Multiple Stage," expresses his "belief that the Swan Playhouse, as recorded in the famous De Wit or Van Buchel drawing, is not only typical of Elizabethan public playhouses but also capable of accommodating the production of nearly all extant Elizabethan plays."[12] Andrew Gurr says that "Of all the pieces of evidence which can help us to fill in the details of the picture of public playhouses, incontestably the most important is Arend van Buchell's copy of de Witt's sketch of the interior of the Swan."[13]

T. J. King studies 276 plays written between 1599 and 1642 along with nine facades "generally accepted as pictorial and architectural evidence concerning the English pre-Restoration stage."[14] He introduces his work, published in 1971, with the statement that his central aim "is to seek positive correlations between the external evidence, as provided by contemporary architecture and pictures of early English stages, and the internal evidence, as provided by the texts of plays first performed in the years 1599–1642" (p. 1). King finds such "positive correlations" between the nine facades and "the nucleus of the textual evidence" provided mainly by "eighteen extant playhouse documents, including promptbooks, manuscripts dependent on playhouse copy, and printed plays with manuscript prompter's markings" (p. 4). In other words, he finds that the texts of the plays indicate that they could be acted with commonplace properties in front of the unlocalized facades shown in the extant pictorial evidence.

Professor King includes with his nine facades the drawings by

Inigo Jones for the remodeled Cockpit-in-Court, 1628–1629, show-ing five openings in the wall encircling the stage. King does not, however, include any of the pictures of stages discovered by Miss Frances Yates.[15] Nor does he discuss her suggestion that "the London public theatres, including the Globe, were an adaptation of the ancient theatre as described by Vitruvius, made within John Dee's sphere of influence, with its particular appeal to the middle and artisan classes."

The most interesting of the five pictures of stages discovered by Miss Yates in Robert Fludd's *Ars Memoriae* (1619) was the "Thea-trum Orbi" (plate 6). Miss Yates called the engraving to the atten-tion of Robert Bernheimer and he identified it in 1958 as a stage set up in a tennis court by English actors traveling in Germany.[16] She published all five of the pictures in 1966 in her book *The Art of Memory*, where they were reproduced between pages 336 and 337 as plates 16, 17, 18a, and 18b. Drawing details from the De Witt sketch of the Swan, she identified the "Theatrum Orbi" as a picture of Shakespeare's second Globe (*Art of Memory*, pp. 342–67) and illustrated her findings with a "sketch of the stage of the Globe Theatre based on Fludd," appearing between pages 352–53 as plate 20. In a 1966 article in *Shakespeare Studies*, I. A. Shapiro identified the "Theatrum Orbi" as the stage of the Blackfriars.[17] The follow-ing year both a reply by Miss Yates and a review of the controversy about the identification of the engraving were carried by *Shakespeare Studies*.[18] Herbert Berry, the reviewer, argues that "the engravings show no actual theatre," and suggests that they are "a melange which is generally continental."[19]

The identification of the Fludd engraving with a particular thea-ter is of less importance to this study than Miss Yates's discovery of the five engravings and her theory growing out of the discovery. The engravings provide pictorial evidence suggesting that the out-of-doors public theaters were of two kinds. The first kind was the amphitheater, or animal-baiting ring—the multipurpose game- or playhouse with a removable platform stage backed by a wall or a booth containing two doors.[20] The Fludd engravings show two such stages (*Art of Memory*, plate 16). The Van Buchell sketch of the Swan shows such a multipurpose baiting ring and playhouse (plate 5). And the contract for the Hope (Greg 3:20) describes it as a

"Plaiehouse fitt & convenient in all thinges, bothe for players to
playe In, And for the game of Beares and Bulls to be bayted in . . .
[with] A fitt and convenient Tyre house and a stage to be carryed or
taken awaie, and to stande uppon tressels good substanciall and
sufficient for the carryinge and bearinge of suche a stage."

The second kind of out-of-doors public theater suggested by the
Fludd engravings (plates 6, 7, and 8) is the Vitruvian theater with a
permanent stage enclosed on three sides by walls as in Palladio's
Teatro Olimpico, built in 1584 (plate 12) and in the Roman theater
at Orange (plate 13).

Miss Yates's discovery of the Fludd engravings and her theory
that the London public theaters of Shakespearean England were
adaptations of the ancient theater described by Vitruvius provide
an answer to a problem that has long discomforted historians of the
stage: Van Buchell's sketch of the Swan (for many years believed
the only contemporary picture extant of the inside of a Shakespearean playhouse) shows a stage which is inadequately equipped for
the presentation of many of the plays of Shakespeare and his
contemporaries. Bernard Beckerman, for instance, observes, "All
sorts of ingenious explanations, that the hangings were not in place
or that a stage width curtain was added for performance, have been
offered, but the fact remains: the Swan, as it is depicted in the
drawing, unaltered, could not have accommodated the Globe
plays."[21] And I concluded some years ago from evidence provided
mainly by the plays given at the Rose that they required a stage
encompassed by three walls which had a total of five openings (plate
9).[22]

Miss Yates's discovery of the engravings and her theory about the
Vitruvian antecedents of the Shakespearean playhouse has stimu-
lated scholarship of prime importance to an understanding of the
stage and the staging of Renaissance drama. For example, Richard
Charles Kohler reports, "An exact mathematical correspondence
has been discovered between the data for the Fortune and the
Vitruvian geometric scheme, a more concrete connection between
Roman principles and English practice than has heretofore been
revealed."[23] In short, Miss Yates's work and the scholarship growing out of it enable me to illustrate my findings about the staging
and the stage of the Rose with a model and floor plans of the stage.

Because I have elected to illustrate my findings with a model (plate 1) and diagrams (plates 14 and 15), I have set up a Vitruvian plan for the Rose (plate 17) and used some of the dimensions given in the contract for the Fortune to fill in missing details. I picture the stage as extending to the middle of the yard as specified in Henslowe's contract for the Fortune. I show it encompassed by three walls as in three of the stage illustrations in Robert Fludd's *Ars Memoriae* (plates 6, 7, and 8). And finally, I show it with a total of five openings, located and arranged as in the Teatro Olimpico (plate 12) and in the Roman Theater at Orange (plate 13) from which Palladio's theater was derived.

In the absence of pictorial evidence that can be related immediately and directly to the Rose, I have decorated the facade of Henslowe's stage with details drawn from the stage of the *Theatrum* in the vignette on the title page of the 1616 edition of Ben Jonson's *Workes*. I believe the *Theatrum* embodies Jonson's concept of what the Shakespearean playhouse should have been. That concept, I can now report, was apparently based in part on an extant Renaissance engraving of the Theater of Marcellus. Doctor Yates has kindly provided me with a picture of the theater, *Theatrum Marcelli*, taken from Antonio Lafreri's *Speculum Romanae Magnificentiae* of 1579, a description, with engravings, of famous buildings in Rome. The Lafreri engraving is either the source of the Jonson vignette or very closely related to that source, as a comparison of the two, reproduced as plate 10 and plate 11, will indicate.

The documents of the Rose form the second source of evidence about the stage and staging of the Rose. The material Reynolds describes (p. 30) as "contemporary contracts, descriptions, and allusions outside of the plays," provides more details than the pictures of the Rose. Most of the documents described by Foakes and Rickert as "the chief source for theatrical history between 1590 and 1604," Philip Henslowe's *Diary* and the fragments and manuscripts associated with it, are related immediately and directly to the Rose.[24] And most of the entries in his *Diary* usually concern either this theater, which he built in 1587 and, in effect, operated from 1592 to 1603, or the Fortune, which he built in 1600 to replace the Rose. The Henslowe documents provide specific information about the extant plays of the Rose: the authors who wrote them, the costumes and properties used to stage them, the dates of performances, the frequency with which they were repeated, the money they earned for Henslowe, and many similar details nowhere else available in such quantity about any of the plays of theaters of the Shakespearean period.

Heretofore this wealth of information, which I call "documents of the Rose," has been employed mainly to piece out, by analogy, the details about Shakespeare's theater or to support some theory about the stage in that theater and its practices.[25] Consequently, much of the material that I am using, authoritative material related immediately and directly to the stage of the Rose theater, will be familiar to the historian of the stage.

Included in the Henslowe material are two documents that cannot be labeled as "documents of the Rose": the contracts for the Fortune and for the Hope. I use details from these contracts for the construction of the model and diagrams when such details cannot be found in authoritative sources. Obviously no claim can be made that they are precise for the Rose.

The third source of evidence about the stage of the Rose and its practices is the repertory of plays presented there. Before the evidence they offer is considered, the plays must be identified and classified according to the degree of certainty that the extant texts represent the actual production of the piece at the Rose.

Drawing heavily from and frequently contesting points made by Frederick Gard Fleay,[26] the late Sir Walter W. Greg worked through the entries in Henslowe's *Diary* identifying approximately 280 plays—most of which have been lost (2:148–235). About 230 of those plays were presented at the Rose between 1592 and 1603 by six different companies that appeared there: Lord Strange's men, Earl of Sussex's men, Queen's and Sussex's men together, Admiral's men, Admiral's and Lord Pembroke's men together, and Worcester's men. Chambers contested many of Greg's identifications and vigorously opposed most of those made by Fleay (*ES* 3:201–518, and 4:1–55). And Chambers himself made some tentative identifications of extant plays with entries in the *Diary* which have not been generally accepted. He suggests, for instance, "The

Comedy of Errors might quite well be 'the gelyous comedy' produced as a new play by Strange's on 5 January 1593 . . . I am not sure that it was not" (*Facts and Problems* 1:310). In brief, the identification of extant plays with entries in the *Diary* is not a matter upon which authorities are in complete agreement.

Eighty-nine extant plays or fragments of plays have sometimes been identified with the Rose theater by Greg, Chambers, and others (Appendix A, "Plays of the Rose"). Of these eighty-nine plays, however, I find only forty-three extant in texts that may be associated with production of the plays at the Rose. And following (with some modification) Reynolds's system of classifying the plays according to the degree of certainty with which their extant text may be associated with production on a particular stage (*Red Bull*, p. 5), I find sixteen that can be classified as a-plays.

One may speak of a-plays as "certainly" representing production at the Rose. As Reynolds puts it for his study (p. 5), the list of a-plays "includes those plays of which the evidence is of unquestionable reliability. Those are the plays which we have good reason to believe were given at the Red Bull in the years we are concerned with, and whose texts may reasonably be taken as representing their performance there."

Twenty-seven extant texts of plays identified with the Rose have been classified as b-plays, as "probably" representing production at that theater. In his study of the Red Bull, Reynolds says (p. 5), "The B list consists of those plays which were probably, but not surely, given at the Red Bull, and also those plays surely given there but whose texts as we have them may not represent Red Bull performances."

Reynolds's c-list is made up of plays "only possibly connected" with the Red Bull in the years in question. And he concludes that they are "of little or no authority" for the Red Bull (p. 51). Forty-six of the eighty-nine plays that have sometimes been identified with the Rose have been placed in the c-list and are given no further consideration in this study because their connection is so tenuous as to make the evidence they may have about the stage "of little or no authority" for Henslowe's playhouse (Appendix A).

The sixteen a-plays and the twenty-seven b-plays, forty-three in all, make up the repertory of extant plays of the Rose. The history of each play in the repertory is traced and the work of the several scholars who have identified the plays, especially that of Greg and Chambers, has been employed to link the plays in the repertory to the Rose. Likewise, the textual scholarship, especially that of Greg, Fredson Bowers,[27] and Wilfred Jewkes,[28] has been drawn upon to establish the authority of the extant texts as containing reliable evidence about the stage of the Rose and its practices (Appendix A).

The textual and stage histories of the plays in the repertory are quite complex, in part because of the many companies that played for Henslowe; consequently, I have further divided the sixteen a-plays and the twenty-seven b-plays into subgroups according to the degree of certainty with which the extant texts of those plays appear to be representative of production at the Rose theater (Appendix A, "Plays of the Rose").

The principal reason for classifying the plays according to the reliability of the evidence they may contain about the stage is, of course, to provide a check on conclusions—to avoid unreasonable claims for evidence drawn from plays "of little or no authority." The danger of making such claims is avoided by excluding the c-plays from this study. Even so, I have retained the rest of the system to document the apparent difference in the reliability of a-plays "surely" given at the Rose and b-plays "probably" given there, or else "surely" given there but extant in a text only "probably" representative of the performance of that work for Henslowe. Actually I have found, as did Reynolds in his study of the Red Bull (p. 187), that the scheme "finally comes to less than one would expect." For all practical purposes there is no discernible difference in the kinds or the clarity of the evidence in the two lists. The evidence does, however, speak with varying degrees of clarity about details related to the stage of the Rose and its practices, regardless of whether that evidence is derived from plays in the a- or the b-list. A play in the a-list, for example, may offer testimony that merely suggests the validity of a particular point, whereas a play in the b-list may provide evidence that clearly indicates the validity of the same point. Consequently, I have modified Reynolds's system still further in an attempt to show whether the evidence drawn from the plays is "suggestive evidence" or "indicative evidence." As I use the terms, "suggestive evidence" merely prepares one to accept the validity of details and is useful only when it is employed cumulatively with other evidence. "Indicative evidence" tends to prove, within reasonable limits, the validity of details. It should be emphasized, therefore, that the words "suggest" and "indicate" are in this study given distinct and precise meanings.

A Note on Practices

WHERE LINES have been numbered consecutively in plays, as in those issued by the Malone Society, references are made to lines, and the abbreviations "l" for line and "ll" for lines are dropped. Act and scene divisions are usually ignored.

Where references must be made to signatures, the abbreviation "sig." has been dropped as well as "r" for recto. A reference to signature C2 recto, for example, will be cited as "C2," while a reference to signature C2 verso will be cited as "C2v."

The Elizabethan "s," "f," "i," "j," "u," "v," and "w" have been silently shifted into modern dress; otherwise I quote passages as I find them, without the use of "*sic*."

Abbreviations

EES	Glynne Wickham, *Early English Stages 1300 to 1600*, 2 vols. in 3 (London: Routledge and Kegan Paul; New York: Columbia University Press, 1963–72)
ES	E. K. Chambers, *The Elizabethan Stage*, 4 vols. (Oxford: Clarendon Press, 1923)
JEGP	*Journal of English and Germanic Philology*
MSR	*Malone Society Reprint*
PMLA	*Proceedings of the Modern Language Association*
RES	*Review of English Studies*
SQ	*Shakespeare Quarterly*
SS	*Shakespeare Survey*
SSt	*Shakespeare Studies*
TLS	*Times Literary Supplement*

1

The Theater Building

THE ROSE theater owed its name, according to Chambers (2:405), to the fact that it was built on property that had been, "as recently as 1547–48, a rose garden."[1] The use made of the property before Philip Henslowe built his theater there is of some importance: one may assume, for instance, that if the plot had been used for growing roses, it was sufficiently well drained and solid to permit some excavation below the stage for a "cellarage"—if such excavation was indeed necessary.

Henslowe obtained the site through a lease dated 24 March 1585, in which the property is described, in Greg's abstract of that lease (3:1), as "all that her messuage or Tennement then Called the little rose with Twoe gardens to the same adioyninge sett lienge and beinge in the parrishe late Called Saincte margarette in Southworke in the county of Surry." The property can be located more closely by a lease dating from Henry VIII's reign (Greg 2:25–26 n.2) which refers to "a Tenement Called the Rose on the east Sid" of the tenements called "the barge the bell and the Cocke" lying between the Thames on the north and Maiden Lane on the south. Chambers (2:405–06) quotes Rendel as saying that the "little rose" was just east of the still-existing Rose Alley. Chambers places the Rose, in relation to its two future neighbors on the Bankside, "in the Liberty of the Clink midway between . . . the Globe on the east and the Hope on the west."

The site of the playhouse itself is precisely located by an extant contract of partnership between Henslowe and John Cholmley, a "grocer of London," for financing, building, and operating upon "all that pcell of grownde or garden plotte Contayninge in lenghe and bredthe sqare every waye ffoorescore and fourteene foote of assize. . . . a Playehowse now in framinge" (Foakes and Rickert, p. 304).

Norden's 1593 map of London (plate 2) confirms the details about the location of the Rose that are contained in the Henslowe-Cholmley agreement by showing "The playhouse" on the Bankside in approximately the center of the "little Rose" estate, east of Rose Alley and north of Maiden Lane.[2] Southeast of the theater, near the corner formed by the junction of a hedgerow and Maiden Lane, is a long narrow structure that must have been the "small teñte" assigned to Cholmley (Foakes and Rickert, p. 305). The "messuage or Tennement then Called the little rose" seems to be the larger building at the corner of the property southwest of the theater. "The Beare howse"—that is, the Beargarden—is shown in this map as north and west of the Rose in 1593.

Cholmley's "small teñte" apparently disappeared from the Bankside before 1600 when Norden revised his earlier map, although the "messuage or Tennement" is still standing (plate 3).[3] Of unusual interest, however, is the appearance of Shakespeare's Globe, built in 1599, just across Maiden Lane to the south and east of the Rose. Thus, all the reliable evidence about the location of the Rose is confirmed by a contemporary map published in 1593. This map is in turn verified by a revision that puts the Rose in its precise place, near the junction of Rose Alley and Maiden Lane, and shows it in 1600 to be the middle theater in a group of three theaters—the Beargarden, the Rose, and the Globe—lying in a line running approximately southeast from the Thames.[4]

The deed of partnership between Henslowe and Cholmley sets 10 January 1587 as the earliest date to be associated with the Rose, for Greg (2:43) satisfactorily disposes of the suggestion that the Rose or a theater on the site of the Rose may have existed as a place of public entertainment prior to 1587.

Plays may have been given at the Rose as early as 29 October 1587; a letter from the Privy Council bearing that date (Greg 2:44) calls the attention of the Justices of Surrey to the fact that regulations prohibiting plays on Sunday were not being observed "espiciallie within the Libertie of the Clincke." The Rose was apparently the only public playhouse in existence there in 1587. C. W. Wallace, in an article in the London *Times* (30 April 1914), says that the records of the Sewer commission for Surrey mention the Rose as "new" in April 1588.

The most important date in the history of the Rose is marked by an entry in the *Diary* (Foakes and Rickert, p. 16): "In the name of god A men 1591 [1592] beginge the 19 of febreary my lord stranges meme A ffoloweth 1591 [1592]." Immediately below this note Henslowe records, "Rd at fryer bacune the 19 of febreary . . satterdaye . . xvii^s iii^d." Thus, although plays may have been given at the Rose as early as 1587, certainly performances were given there on 19 February 1592 and thereafter.

It is not known exactly when playing stopped at the Rose. Although the Admiral's men left there to take over the Fortune during the summer or early autumn of 1600, two or possibly three companies were at the playhouse for short stays after this. Pembroke's men presented two plays there in October of 1600, and Worcester's men were there from August 1602 until playing was stopped in the spring of 1603 by the death of Elizabeth. Worcester's men returned to the Rose on 9 May 1603 but apparently left shortly afterwards; their return is followed by only one entry in the *Diary*. According to C. W. Wallace in the London *Times* (30 April 1914, p. 10), Henslowe was amerced for the Rose on 4 October 1605 and reported that the property was "out of his hands." The Sewer Records of 14 February 1606 listed the property as in the hands of one Edward Box, of Bread Street, London. The last reference to the Rose theater in the Sewer Records, according to Wallace, was dated 25 April 1606 when it was described as "the late playhouse in Maid lane." Although this entry seems to terminate the history of the theater, I shall have occasion to refer later to evidence suggesting the possibility that the building may have been standing as late as 1622.

SIZE AND SHAPE OF THE ROSE

Two contemporary references to the Rose as "little" and as "smal" must be considered before one can come to a conclusion about the size of the theater. As the original lease shows, the property on which it was built took its name from a "messuage or Tennement then Called the little rose" (Greg 3:1). Several properties in and about London were called the Rose, and Greg (2:43) suggests that it may have been to distinguish it from the others that the property

Henslowe leased was called the "little rose." Thus the reference to the "little rose" was not necessarily an allusion to the size of the theater.

The second reference to the Rose which might indicate that it was small is found in the prologue to *Fortunatus* (b-1):

> And for this smal Circumference must stand
> For the imagind Sur-face of much land,
> Of many kingdomes, and since many a mile
> Should here be measurd out: our muse intreats
> Your thoughts to helpe poore Art.

There is little reason for concluding that this allusion to the "smal Circumference" of the Rose indicates that the theater was small in comparison with other Elizabethan playhouses. Like the familiar speech of the chorus at the beginning of *Henry V*, the prologue to *Fortunatus* seems merely to emphasize the scope of the action of the play by contrasting its vastness with the theater in which the play was being presented.

Firsthand testimony about the size of the Rose is included in De Witt's "Amphitheatres in London" (1596), which is quoted in part from J. Q. Adams's translation (*Shakespearean Playhouses*, p. 167):

There are four amphitheatres in London [the Theatre, the Curtain, the Rose, and the Swan] of notable beauty, which from their diverse signs bear diverse names. In each of them a different play is daily exhibited to the populace. The two more magnificent of these are situated to the southward beyond the Thames, and from the signs suspended before them are called the Rose and the Swan. . . . Of all the theatres, however, the largest and the most magnificent is the one of which the sign is a swan, called in the vernacular the Swan Theatre; for it accommodates in its seats three thousand persons.

According to De Witt, then, the Rose was not as large or as "magnificent" as the Swan; it was, however, more "magnificent" than the Curtain and the Theatre.

The difference in cost between the Rose and the Fortune indicates that the Rose was larger than the Fortune. According to the contract for the construction of the Fortune (Foakes and Rickert, pp. 306–10), Peter Street was to receive £440 for building the

theater, and he had to furnish the material. The partnership agreement between Henslowe and John Cholmley for the construction
and operation of the Rose (Foakes and Rickert, pp. 304–06) shows
that Cholmley's share in the project was £816—almost twice the
amount that was paid for the Fortune. Greg believes this sum of
£816 represents the capital invested in the partnership, in effect, the
cost of building the Rose.[5] If the Rose cost almost twice as much as
the Fortune, the Rose was probably the larger building. If so, the
Rose had to be more than eighty feet in diameter; Henslowe specified in the contract for the Fortune (Foakes and Rickert, p. 307)
that the building "conteine ffowerscore foote of lawfull assize
everye waie square wthoute."

The actual diameter of the Rose is given, I believe, in the
Henslowe-Cholmley partnership agreement (Foakes and Rickert,
pp. 304–06). I interpret the agreement as limiting Cholmley's
interests in the three parcels of land making up the "little rose"
property[6] to two plots of ground, those occupied by the "small
teñte"[7] and by the playhouse; and the dimensions of those plots
were rigidly fixed by the walls of the buildings that stood on them.
The origin of the plots is not stated in relation to any known
reference point or landmark on the property—except the walls of
the buildings. Thus one can account for provision in the agreement granting Cholmley rights-of-way across Henslowe's property to the "small teñte": "free . . . passage . . . as well by and
throughe the alley there called Rosse Alleye. . . . As allso in
and by and throughe the waye leadinge into the saide mayden
Lane." Thus, also, one can account for the provision binding
Cholmley to bear an equal share in maintaining the "brigges
wharff[es] and all other the ways and brygges now leadinge
. . . into onto and from the saide pcell of grownde" on which
the playhouse stood. Thus, finally, one can account for the provision in which Henslowe assures his partner of exclusive right
to do business, to sell bread and drink "in or about the saide pcell
of grownde," that is, inside or outside the theater walls.

As I understand the contract, the measurements of "all that pcell
of grownde or garden plotte Contayninge in lenghe and bredthe
sqare every waye ffoorescore and fourteene foote of assize little
more or lesse" were determined by the outside dimensions of the

"playe howse now in framinge and shortly to be ereckted and sett uppe upone the same grounde or garden plotte." The theater building, which appears to have been circular, is represented in my model as being ninety-four feet in diameter.

The excessive cost of the Rose, as compared with the cost of the square Fortune, suggests that the Rose was not only large but circular.[8] Also, the large sums Henslowe spent for repairs and additions to the Rose may be explained in part by assuming a circular shape for the playhouse, which would have demanded more intricate and expensive carpentry than an obviously polygonal or rectangular structure. He records an expenditure of £103.2.8 for repairs and additions to the theater before Strange's men began to act there in February 1592 (Foakes and Rickert, p. 13) and then paid another £108.19.00 for more repairs and additions during Lent in 1595 (Foakes and Rickert, p. 7). Thus the cost of this work over a period of only three years was almost half as much as the total cost of building the Fortune.

The extant maps and engravings of the Rose offer evidence about the shape of the building, but it is sometimes contradictory. Authorities disagree about the identification of the theaters shown on the Bankside.[9] Some authorities believe that the Rose is the circular building in the foreground of the Hondius view (1610) and in several engravings related to it, which possibly include Delaram's view (1615–24), the view on the title page of Holland's *Herwologia Anglica* (1620), and the inset found on the title page of Sir Richard Baker's *Chronicle* (1643) (plates 23–25 and 27). J. Q. Adams asserts in his *Shakespearean Playhouses* (p. 146 n. 1) that "the circular building pictured in these maps has been widely heralded as the First Globe, but without reason; all the evidence shows that it was the Rose." Shapiro (*SS* 1:31–33), on the other hand, thinks that the Globe, not the Rose, is the circular theater represented in the foreground of the engravings related to the Hondius view, engravings which he believes may be derived from a common original drawn sometime after the Rose was pulled down in about 1605.

One cannot dismiss the possibility that the Rose is represented by the circular theater in the foreground of the Hondius group; if the putative original engraving from which the group was derived antedates 1600, then the Rose, not the Globe, would have to be the theater shown. Moreover, the Rose has to be the building shown in the foreground if the prototype of the Hondius group was made while both theaters were standing. If this is true, the engravings simply do not include enough of the Bankside to show the Globe, located according to Greg (2:56) "some couple hundred of yards southeast of the Rose." In each of the engravings a portion of the theater in the foreground is obscured by the border of ornamentation superimposed upon the Bankside portion of the view. If the Rose was still standing when the original engraving was made, then the Globe was not included in the view.

It cannot be said with certainty that the Rose was torn down or otherwise destroyed before the Hondius view itself was set into the map of Great Britain engraved for John Speed's *Theatre of the Empire of Great Britain* in 1611. The reference to the Rose in the Sewer Records as the "late playhouse in Maid lane" (C. W. Wallace, London *Times*, 30 April 1914, p. 10) may suggest that the theater building was torn down by 25 April 1606, but it can scarcely be taken as conclusive proof of the destruction of the building. The problem of determining the exact date of the disappearance of the Rose from the Bankside is complicated by an undated couplet quoted by Chambers (2:410) from Rendle's *Bankside* 15 that "In the last great fire/ The Rose did expire," as well as by Malone's unverified assertion (*Variorum* 3:56) that the Rose was in use "for the exhibition of prizefighters" after 1620, and finally by the puzzling fact that Alleyn paid one shilling in tithe "dew for ye rose" in 1622 (Greg 2:44). Opposed to the evidence that the Rose was standing after 1620 is Visscher's view (about 1616) in which only one theater appears in the neighborhood where both the Globe and the Rose were known to have been situated from 1599 to 1606. It is possible that a single theater in the drawing represents the location of more than one theater. Nevertheless, one may conclude that the round building in the foreground of the Hondius group of engravings may be the Rose; however, one cannot use with confidence the evidence these pictures may contain about the Rose.

E. K. Chambers says of the Rose (2:409) that "if the maps can be trusted, it was octagonal." He believes it is shown in the Delaram engravings "but not in any later views except those of the Merian group, where it appears, flagged, but unnamed, on the river edge"

(2:410). I. A. Shapiro, however, does not find the Rose among the theaters in Delaram's engraving, which he identifies as the Globe, the Beargarden, and the Swan. Chambers was not aware of another engraving showing an octagonal Rose in a recently recovered view of London, *Civitas Londini*, dating from 1600 (plate 4). This engraving, Shapiro thinks, is incorrect in its depiction of the theaters on the Bankside as polygonal structures, and he shows that this incorrect engraving is the source from which the Merian group is derived (*SS* 1:25–37). "Unless further independent evidence of polygonal theaters of the Bankside can be found," he says, "we shall be justified in discounting that of *Civitas Londini*."[10] If Shapiro is correct, we may set aside Chambers's identifications of the Rose as the octagonal structures in the Delaram and Merian engravings and reject as inaccurate the octagonal Rose shown in *Civitas Londini*.

Shapiro's case for the circular shape of the theaters on the Bankside is based primarily on Norden's map of 1593 and a revision of that map, made in 1600, set into the *Civitas Londini*. The map of 1593 shows two circular theaters on the Bankside, "The Beare howse," that is, the Beargarden, and "The play howse," which is clearly Henslowe's Rose. Four circular theaters are shown and labeled in the revision: "The Swone" or the Swan, "Bearegard" or the Beargarden, "The Star," which is the Rose, and "The globe," that is, Shakespeare's first Globe. Shapiro says (*SS* 1:27) that

Norden's reputation as an expert surveyor and cartographer should in any case encourage one to trust a map inscribed "Joannes Norden Anglus descripsit," and in fact its representation of Southwark is consistent with every other piece of reliable evidence we have. Moreover, the prominence of the Beargarden and the Playhouse (Henslowe's Rose) in the foreground invites scrutiny, and makes any obvious inaccuracy here unlikely.

The *Civitas Londini* was done "By the industry of Jhon Norden. Cum privil. R. Ma," that is to say, supervised by him. The contradiction in the shapes of the theater as they appear in the panorama and the map Norden set into the engraving is explained by Shapiro (*SS* 1:30):

The prominence of Sir Nicholas Moseley's name and arms suggests that *Civitas Londini* was intended to commemorate him and his mayoralty. If so, he may have arranged for an already existing panorama to be brought up to date, just as Norden's maps of 1593 have been brought up to date. Even if the whole had been supervised by Norden there would be nothing surprising in his passing this panorama, for much of it is so obviously purely conventional and "artistic" that he would probably consider it unnecessary that its details should be correct. Another possibility is that Norden had drawn a view of London from the "statio prospectiva" shown on the tower of St Mary Overie . . . and that for the Southwark foreground the engraver had had to supplement Norden's view from sources now unknown, or memory, or imagination, or a mixture of these.

The force of Shapiro's explanation is dramatically revealed when one compares the Bankside section of *Civitas Londini* (plate 4) with the same section in Norden's maps of 1593 and 1600 (plates 2 and 3). If one follows Shapiro and rejects *Civitas Londini* as unreliable, the only pictorial evidence that remains about the shape of the Rose is found in Norden's two maps, made while the theater, apparently a circular building, was standing.

THE OUTSIDE OF THE ROSE

Henslowe's theater, "The play howse," is shown in Norden's map of 1593 as a round unthatched shell, without a hut above the stage, flagstaff, or flag—the hallmarks of a flourishing Elizabethan public playhouse. Several entries in the *Diary* show that early in 1592 Henslowe made payments to a thatcher and purchased a mast—possibly for use as a flagstaff. The Rose appears to be a flourishing playhouse, complete in all respects, in Norden's revised map of 1600.[11] One may infer from these facts that the first map, published in 1593, was drawn before the additions indicated by the *Diary* were made to the Rose and that the revised map of 1600 shows these additions. We have seen that the evidence provided by these maps and the Henslowe material is consistent about the location of the Rose. The extent to which these maps and this Henslowe material corroborate and illuminate a number of other details about the Rose further confirms the accuracy and validity of the Norden maps. With Norden's reliability established, I shall attempt to piece together from the maps and Henslowe's documents the few remaining details they seem to provide about the theater and the property on which it was erected.

The building from which the Rose took its name, that "messuage or Tennement then Called the little rose" (Greg 3:1), is shown in both of Norden's maps at the southwest corner of the property near the junction of Rose Alley and Maiden Lane. Since the structure is not mentioned in the Henslowe-Cholmley agreement, Greg (2:45) believes it was excluded from the partnership and reappears under the heading of "the Rosse Rent[es]" in Henslowe's accounts for 1603 (Foakes and Rickert, p. 247). It is also mentioned again in 1603 in the "Memorandom . . . consernynge the tackynge of the leace a new of the littell Roosse" in which Henslowe was "to bestowe a hundred marckes upon [the] buildinge" (Foakes and Rickert, p. 213). We do not know what became of the building after 1603 or what specific use was made of it. Perhaps J. Q. Adams is correct in his conjecture (*Shakespearean Playhouses*, p. 143) that Henslowe leased the building as a brothel—"for this was the district of the stews." And perhaps the structure was still standing in 1622 and is referred to in connection with the one shilling Alleyn paid in tithe "dew for ye rose" (Greg 2:44). Regardless of what eventually happened to the building, it is shown in both maps and its existence after 1600 is confirmed by the *Diary*. It cannot be the "small teñte" assigned to Cholmley "to keepe victualinge in"; that structure shown in the map of 1593, at the southeast corner of the property, does not appear in the revised map of 1600.

Some connection may exist between the disappearance of the "small teñte" and of Cholmley, who is not heard of again after 1587 except for the words "Cholmley when" scribbled on a page at the beginning of the *Diary*, "in 1592 at the earliest" (Greg 2:45). The partnership, as Greg points out (2:44), was to run till the spring of 1595 and was to Henslowe's advantage so long as the profits were below £204 a year. Cholmley could not have realized much from the venture prior to 1592, if indeed he remained active in the enterprise until that time; his profits, according to the agreement with Henslowe, were to come from half the admissions and from the sale of "breade o^r drinke" and other refreshments in and about the theater. They depended upon a flourishing theater. Aside from the possibility that a few plays may have been given at the Rose in 1587, we have no record of playing there until the *Diary* records the performances beginning in 1592. Moreover, if Norden's first map can be relied upon, the theater was not completed before then. Cholmley's "small teñte" may have been left behind just long enough after the grocer's exit to be included in Norden's map of 1593 before it too disappeared.

Nine entries in the *Diary* (Foakes and Rickert, pp. 9–12) show payments made to "the thecher" for work done, almost certainly, before 19 February 1592, when Strange's men began playing at the Rose. These entries include:

Itm pd unto the thecher . . . . .vii[s]
Itm pd unto the thecher . . . . .xx[s]
Itm pd unto the thechers man . . . . .iii[s]
Itm pd unto the thecher . . . .
Itm pd unto the thecher . . . . .x[s]
Itm pd the thecher . . . . .v[s]
Itm pd the thecher . . . . .x[s]
Itm pd the thecher . . . . .v[s]
Itm pd unto the thecher a bondell of lathes . . . . .xii[d]

A "thechers man" is mentioned, so at least two men were employed part of the time on the job for which Henslowe paid about 61 shillings. However, one of the entries does not show the amount paid and another reveals that "a bondell of lathes" worth twelve pence was given in lieu of wages. Although it is difficult to say how much time was required to thatch the theater, it could not have been a mere repair job. Several entries in the *Diary* (Foakes and Rickert, p. 10), show that workmen received from ten pence to fourteen pence for a day's work. If a single thatcher was paid a comparable wage, say a shilling a day, the job would have taken at least 61 days. Five of the eight payments to "the thecher" were made in multiples of five shillings, and two other payments total ten shillings; such payments lead one to conjecture that the thatcher, who seemingly furnished the materials and his own assistant or assistants, was paid five shillings a day. If this is reasonable, then the job of thatching the Rose took two or three men about twelve days. Surely the entire building was thatched at this time.

The most prominent addition made to the Rose in 1592 was the hut. Henslowe seems to have been considering the erection of this structure over the stage early in 1592, for among the items he records as expenses charged against the playhouse at that time is an "itm pd for A maste . . . xii^s" (Foakes and Rickert, p. 10), which may be identified with a flagstaff that appears above the hut in Norden's revised map.

Glynne Wickham believes that what is "really significant" about these additions to the Rose is that they are confined to the area of the stage and tiring-house. He suggests, and it is indeed an attractive idea, that the additions indicate a deliberate change of policy in Henslowe's mind: "In effect this change spells the translation of the house from a gamehouse that could be hired by actors for stage plays into a playhouse for a resident company that could still be used for games if not needed by actors."[12] The consequence of this change in policy, Wickham continues (p. 61), "was heavy capital expenditure on the wholesale remodelling of the tiring-house area including the installation of heavens, loft and ceiling above the tiring-house, complete with flag-pole to crown the work. These are the additions incorporated in Norden's map of 1600."

In any case, Norden's maps and the Henslowe material are remarkably consistent about many of the additions made to the outside of the Rose between the time the first map was drawn in 1592 and the time of its revision in 1600. One interesting addition about which the *Diary* and *Papers* do not provide information is the flag shown atop the hut in the revised map of 1600. We know that flags were an important adjunct of the Shakespearean playhouse. The De Witt sketch shows a flag bearing a swan and Henslowe records (Foakes and Rickert, p. 215) that he "Layd owt for the company [Worcester's men] the 4 of September 1602 to bye A flage of sylke the some of . . . xxvi^s 8^d." While nothing is recorded about the first flag that flew above the Rose, Norden's mistake in naming the theater "The Stare" suggests that the flag he saw had emblazoned upon it a rose similar to the Tudor rose, and that in the distance it appeared to the map-maker to be a multipointed star.

Norden's maps are not entirely clear about a number of details concerning the outside of the building. For instance, the hut is not shown sharply enough for one to be certain which way it faced or to determine how much of the theater it actually covered. Beyond the fact that the building is shown as circular in both maps and that its shape may account for Henslowe's numerous purchases of "lathes," "lathe naylles," "sand," and "lyme" (Foakes and Rickert, pp. 7 and 9–13), to repair parts of the outside walls which probably were of plaster, little appears in the maps to indicate the material from which the outside walls of the Rose were constructed.

Of the remaining details about the outside of the Rose, it should be noted that in both maps a single rectangular opening is shown, which is in the theater wall at the ground level facing Maiden Lane and presumably represents an entrance to the building. Above this opening, in the map of 1600, appears a row of four evenly spaced rectangular openings representing windows in the second story of the building. Only three such openings are shown in the map of 1593; the place where the fourth should appear is obscured by a shadow. The single row of windows in each of the maps suggests that the stage had but two levels and a hut. Because the problem of determining the number of levels in the playhouse stage involves evidence contained in the plays staged there, I shall consider that problem later and summarize here the conclusions I have reached, mainly from the Henslowe material and Norden's maps, about the location, dates, size, and shape of the theater and the property.

It appears, then, that Philip Henslowe leased on 24 March 1585 three adjoining parcels of land known as the "little rose" estate, situated on the Bankside east of Rose Alley and north of Maiden Lane. On 10 January 1587 he entered into a partnership with John Cholmley to finance the construction of a large circular theater which I believe was about ninety-four feet in diameter. The theater does not seem to have been completed until Strange's men began playing there 19 February 1592, for the building was not thatched until about that date. The hut, flagstaff, and flag were probably not added until after the middle of June 1592. The building seems to have been constructed of timber with a plastered exterior. Playing stopped at the theater sometime during May 1603 and by 25 April 1606 the Rose is described in the Sewer Records as "the late playhouse" in Maiden Lane. Several puzzling references suggest, however, that the Rose may have been standing as late as 1622.

With this information as a background, I move from the outside of the Rose to the inside in attempting to reconstruct the stage of the playhouse from evidence contained primarily in the plays given there between 1592 and 1603.

2

The Trapdoor

THE SHAKESPEAREAN public theater was a little universe, a micro-
cosm, a representation in wood and plaster of the heavens above,
the world below, and hell beneath.[1] In reconstructing the little
world that was the stage of the Rose, we may as well begin with a
part of the world that fascinated the Elizabethan: the ground on
which he walked and the ever-present openings in it that led to hell.
And while we are at the entrance to it, we can consider hell itself.

The existence of at least one trapdoor in the floor of the stage of
the Rose may be established by some thirty-two episodes in fourteen plays—three a-plays and eleven b-plays. At the same time the
difficulties in using evidence provided by plays may be illustrated:
the plays surely representative of production at the Rose, the three
a-plays, do not give us as many details about the trap as some of the
b-plays. Two of the a-plays indicate that there was a hole in the floor
of the stage of the Rose. The dialogue in *Titus Andronicus* (a-4)
indicates that an actor falls into a "lothsome pit" and that another
falls into the same hole trying to pull him out of it (D4–E1). A
similar incident occurs in *Look about You* (a-4) when John and
Faukenbridge both fall into a hole and are robbed by Skinke
(2043–70). Neither incident is elaborated by stage directions, although a stage direction in *The Four Prentices of London* (b-8) indicates
that a corpse is brought onto the stage and buried (C2): "*Enter a
Coarse after it Irishmen mourning, in a dead March: to them enters Eustace,
and talkes with the chiefe mourner, who makes signes of consent, after buriall
of the Coarse, and so Exeunt.*" It is reasonable to conclude from the
dialogue in the two a-plays and the stage direction in the b-play that
there was actually a hole in the floor of the stage at the Rose theater.

The following episode from a third a-play, *A Knack to Know a
Knave*, suggests, though it does not clearly indicate, that an actor
comes onto the stage through a hole in the floor. Dunston, a
magician, decides to use his powers to call up a devil (1582–83): "*As-*

moroth ascende, veni Asmoroth, Asmoro[t]h veni. En[t]er the Devill." One simply cannot be sure from this episode whether the devil entered through a hole in the floor in response to the command "ascende" or came onto the stage through an opening in a wall in response to Dunston's "veni." However, other plays of the Rose contain episodes involving the use of magic and indicating that supernatural beings come onto the stage through a trapdoor in the floor of the stage and leave through the same place, as in *The Silver Age* (b-2) (H1v): "*Earth riseth from under the stage. . . . Earth sinkes.*" In *Alphonsus of Aragon* (b-6) stage directions read (951–70): "*Rise Calchas up in a white Cirples and a Cardinals Myter. . . . Calchas sinke downe where you came up.*" In *The Brazen Age* (b-2) a stage direction reads (H4v): "*Gallus sinkes, and in his place riseth a Cocke and crowes.*" A large property is brought onto the stage through the trap according to a stage direction in *A Looking Glass for London* (b-6) (517–25): "*The Magi with their rods beate the ground, and from under the same riseth a brave Arbour.*" Elsewhere in the same play (1230–31): "*a flame of fire appeareth from beneath, and Radagon is swallowed.*" In *Edward I* (b-9) are presented two related episodes (H2v and H3v) which were so sensational that they were described on the title page of the play as "the sinking of Queene Elinor, who suncke at Charing-crosse, and rose againe at Potters-hith, now named Queene-hith." It may be concluded from the several episodes cited here that a trapdoor was present in the floor of the stage of the Rose, that it was used sometimes as a pit or a grave, and that often actors representing supernatural beings used it for their entrances and exits.

It must be pointed out that one cannot be sure that a trap was used every time a supernatural being "*enters*" or "*appears.*" Reynolds believes (p. 187), "The same version, so far as stage directions go, may have been presented in different ways." Elsewhere, Reynolds reports (p. 188) that an "examination of all the plays given in a definite period at a single theater [the Red Bull, 1605–25] shows—not what one might expect, a series of customary stagings for similar scenes, but rather the opposite—that similar scenes were often staged differently. After all, why not? We like variety ourselves." Keeping in mind that not all episodes involving magic and the appearance of supernatural beings necessarily call for the use of a trap, we can come to some conclusions about the trap at the Rose by

looking at the thirty-two episodes that suggest or indicate the use of
such a door in the floor of the stage.

It is significant that Beckerman finds only seven instances in the
plays of the Globe (p. 92) in which traps are used, and that four of
these occur in one play, *The Devil's Charter*. Twenty-nine of the
thirty-two instances in which a trap may have been employed at the
Rose involve the use of magic and the appearance of supernatural
beings, if we may include the Queen's sinking and her rising in
Edward I. The middle of 1595 saw the end of the vogue for magicians such as Faustus and Friar Bacon. At any rate, no plays calling
for devils to enter or evil mortals to go out through traps seem to
have been added to the repertory of the Rose after *Edward I*, an old
play, was given there on 29 August 1595. Of course many of the
plays in which the trap was used to stage episodes involving magic
and the supernatural continued to be presented. *Faustus* (b-5),
for example, held on at the Rose until 13 October 1597. And
Heywood's Hercules plays, *The Silver Age* (b-2) and *The Brazen Age*
(b-2) were revived there in 1598. Our association of traps with the
appearance of devils on the Shakespearean stage may possibly stem
from the well-known woodcut on the title page of the 1616 quarto of
Faustus. However, the evidence this woodcut offers about the stage
and the staging practices of the Rose is of doubtful value (Appendix
A, "Pictures of the Rose"). The use of the trapdoor is also implied
and its effectiveness attested in a story of an incident involving the
appearance on stage of devils during a performance of *Faustus* at
Exeter. In one of the versions reported by Chambers (3:423–24) "as
Faustus was busie in his magicall invocations, on a sudden they
[i.e., the players] were all dasht, every one harkning other in the
eare, for they were all perswaded, there was one devell too many
amongst them; and so after a little pause desired the people to
pardon them, they could go no further with this matter; the people
also understanding the thing as it was, every man hastened to be
first out of dores." Although a trapdoor could have been employed,
it may be said again that the episode could have been just as effective
if the "one devell too many amongst them" had entered through a
door.

Professor Reynolds points out in his study of the Red Bull that
two plays, *The Golden Age* and *The Silver Age*, seem to require more

than one trap.[2] The stage direction in *The Golden Age* (b-2) (K2v) reads, *"Enter at 4 severall corners the 4 winds: Neptune riseth disturbed."* Apparently the business with the winds created an effect that prompted Heywood to repeat it in a slightly different version in *The Silver Age* (b-2) (K2v): *"Hercules sinkes himselfe: Flashes of fire; the Divels appeare at every corner of the stage."* Reynolds observes (p. 91): "The 'winds' and the 'divels' 'enter' or 'appeare' at the corners of the stage, a normally not very useful place for a trapdoor; also 'enter' and 'appeare' instead of 'rise' cause some doubt. Perhaps the actors scrambled up over the edge of the stage." Or perhaps they entered through openings in walls encompassing the stage—openings near enough to the four corners of the stage to allow the winds and devils to move to the corners quickly. In any case, these two are the only extant plays of the Rose in which it is suggested that more than one trapdoor was needed.

The demands placed upon the single trapdoor that was in the floor of the main stage of the Rose and the effectiveness with which it was employed suggest that it was located near the center of the stage; in the absence of more specific evidence, it has been placed there in the floor plan, Stage Level, of Henslowe's Rose theater (plate 14), which represents my own reconstruction of Henslowe's stage.

The plays provide more evidence about the width of the trapdoor than they do about its location. It had to be wide enough to accommodate *"a brave Arbour"* which the stage directions indicate was thrust up from *"under the ground"* in *A Looking Glass for London* (b-6) (517–25). And, as the dialogue indicates in *The Silver Age* (b-2) (G4v), it had to accommodate Pluto and Proserpine in Pluto's "brass-shod wagon" drawn by at least a pair of devils who were his "Coach-steeds, and their traces altogether." There is also the *"Buls head"* which *"appeares"* in *The Brazen Age* (b-2) (B3): *"When the Fury sinkes, a Buls head appeares. . . . He* [Hercules] *tugs with the Bull, and pluckes off one of his horns. Enter from the same place Achelous with his fore-head all bloudy."* The use of a trap is suggested in *Friar Bacon* (b-4) (1191–280) in the contest between the magicians: *"Bungay conjures and the tree appeares with the dragon shooting fire,"* and *"Hercules appeares in his Lions skin."* The contest ends when Bacon commands Hercules to "Vanish the tree and thou away with him," and a stage direction reads *"Exit the spirit with Vandermast and the Tree."* It may be argued from the evidence provided by these four b-plays that the trap was probably involved in staging a number of the episodes in which large properties were brought onto the stage and taken away. A trap about three and one-half feet wide could have served, and I have represented it as of that width in the diagram illustrating my findings (plate 14).

Little can be offered as evidence showing the length of the trap other than the burial episode in *The Four Prentices of London* (b-8) (C2), which indicates that the trap had to be about six feet long to accommodate a corpse. Some indication of the length of the trap may develop, however, from a consideration of the manner in which it was operated. Greg notes in his *Editorial Problem in Shakespeare* (p. 39) a stage direction in the prompt book for Massinger's *Believe as You List*, 1631, which reads *"Gascoine: & Hubert below: ready to open the trap-door for Mr. Taylor."* So far as I know this is the only allusion to the actual manner in which a trapdoor was operated in a Renaissance theater, and of course it has no authority as evidence about the Rose. It is of interest, however, because the plays of the Rose show that the trap was operated from underneath the Stage. For example, in *The Silver Age* (b-2) Pluto gives a cue for opening the trap underneath the stage when he says (G4v), "Cleave earth, and when I stampe upon thy breast/ Sinke me." The magi in *A Looking Glass for London* (b-6) (522) likewise are signaling for the trap to be opened by someone under the stage when they *"with their rods beate the ground."* Furthermore, the phrasing of speeches indicates that the trapdoor always moves downward, not upward. In the example above from *The Silver Age*, Pluto calls out "Cleave earth." The queen in *Edward I* (b-9) (H2v) says, "Gape earth and swallow me"; the earth obliges, and a few lines later the queen's daughter exclaims, "Oh she is suncke, and here the earth is new closde up againe." The evidence shows that the trap was apparently opened by someone below the stage, and that it always opened in a downward direction. This information encourages one to speculate further about the way the trap was operated.

In *The Silver Age* (b-2) (G4v), where a stage direction calls for two people in a chariot drawn by at least two others to sink below the stage, it would seem that the trap had to be much longer than a grave, at least twelve feet in length; one suspects it was even longer. In any case, the number of men required to lower a platform three and one-half feet wide and twelve feet long loaded with a chariot and four people rules out the possibility that it was lowered bodily to the ground by men beneath the stage. Although a machine of some kind might have been used, no evidence has been found to support such a conclusion. On the other hand, the requirements for the chariot's descent could have been met by a platform, wide enough and long enough to accommodate the chariot, Pluto and Proserpine, and the "Coach-steeds, and their traces altogether," if the platform was hinged at one end and propped up or securely fastened at the other when it was not in use. One man, or at most two men, could have loosened and lowered the unhinged end of the platform to the floor of the basement to provide a ramp down which Pluto's chariot could have easily rolled. Actors walking up the ramp would have appeared to be rising from out of the earth (plate 16) as Medea describes the army that sprang from dragon's teeth in *The Brazen Age* (b-2) (G2v):

> Already from beneath
> Their deadly pointed weapons gin to appear,
> And now their heads, thus moulded in earth,
> Streightway shall teeme.

Likewise, actors walking down the ramp would have appeared to be sinking into the earth. Moreover, a trapdoor capable of being used as a ramp to provide for the descent of Pluto in his chariot would have provided space enough, when lowered, for thrusting up such large stage properties as a tree or a *"brave Arbour."*

Most of the details about the size and shape of hell beneath the stage at the Rose must be left as conjecture. All that the evidence indicates is a space beneath the stage, high enough and wide enough to permit people to move about and handle large stage properties, such as Pluto's chariot and a *"brave Arbour."* This space extended under the stage from the trap to another opening in the floor somewhere behind the wall dividing the main stage from the tiring-house. For example, a stage direction in *The Silver Age* (b-2) (K2v–K3) shows that an actor sinks through a trap, goes presumably under the floor of the stage, emerges behind the main stage wall, and reenters through a door onto the main stage: *"Hercules sinkes himselfe: Flashes of fire; the Divels appeare at every corner of the stage with severall fireworkes. The judges of hell, and the three sisters run over the stage, Hercules after them."* Beyond this, we know little about hell at the Rose.

3

The Stage of the Rose Theater

THE HEIGHT OF THE STAGE

THE STAGE of the Rose had to be high enough above the ground to permit the actors and stagehands to move about beneath the stage with speed and ease sufficient to maintain the proper pace of the play. Excavation was possible because the Rose, according to Chambers, was built on land originally used for growing roses, and one can assume that it was well-drained and solid enough to permit some digging below the surface without the risk of running into mud and water.[1] If the cellar of the Rose was excavated at all, it was probably not more than a foot or so below the level of the yard, just enough to provide a little headroom and working space. Excavation, however, would have been expensive, and no evidence exists to show that it was done. Moreover it was apparently unnecessary. Hodges believes that "an outdoor stage for a standing audience" in the pre-Shakespearean street theater "would tend to be a high one, about level with the top of a man's head." This characteristic, he suggests, was probably continued in at least some Shakespearean playhouses.[2]

One might be inclined to follow Hodges and assume that the stage of the Rose was about level with the top of a man's head, if it could be established that "groundlings" always stood to watch plays at that theater. I did not, however, find a single reference to indicate that they stood at the Rose. On the contrary, I did find in five plays a total of eight direct appeals to the audience to be seated (Appendix C, "Seats for the Audience"). For instance, the presenter asks the audience to be seated in one of the first plays given there, *The Battle of Alcazar* (b-4) (30): "Sit downe and see what hainous stratagems these damned wits contrive." Again in the same play, about thirty-three lines later, the presenter urges the audience to "sit you and see this true and tragicke warre."

In each instance, the appeals to the audience to be seated, or to remain seated, are made by a chorus, or by an actor functioning as a chorus. In each instance the appeals are made at the beginning of the play or, as in the plays *Captain Stukley* (a-3) (L3) and *The Downfall of Robert* (a-2) (I2v), at points where a break in the action occurs and the chorus appears to provide links between action past and action to follow. Finally, although it is possible that these requests were directed only to a part of the audience, nothing appears in any of the appeals to suggest that they were directed to a particular group, or that a particular group, such as the spectators in the yard, were excluded.

These appeals to the audience to be seated are, of course, puzzling in view of Chambers's positive assertion (2:527) that "spectators in the yard always stood." He supports his assertion with references to several documents and plays, but none of them are related to the Rose; only Platter's report of 1599 (2:364–65) and *Hamlet* are even contemporary with Henslowe's playhouse. Chambers's references, in fact, do little more than show that groundlings did exist and that playwrights and others often spoke of them contemptuously as, for instance, "the understanding, grounded, men," or as "the understanding gentlemen o' the ground." The frequent use of the word "understanding" in these jibes at the intelligence and taste of the groundlings may, obviously, be taken as a pun pointing to the fact that they were quite often on their feet during the presentation of a play. Eight appeals made to the audience to be seated during the performances of five plays at the Rose indicate that it was difficult to get the groundlings to sit down and stay down; however, the pun on the word "understanding" with reference to groundlings "standing under," that is, standing below the level of the floor of the stage, can hardly be taken as evidence that they always stood or were expected to stand throughout the performances of plays at the Rose.

The theory that groundlings always stood may have originated from the account of Thomas Platter of Basle, who visited three theaters in London in the fall of 1599.[3] He observes that "anyone who remains on the level standing pays only one English penny: but if he wants to sit, he is let in at a further door, and there he gives another penny." Platter's rather detailed account of the plays at the two theaters and his most specific description of the seating arrangements suggest that they are particular to the arrangements at the Curtain or the Globe or both.

Another possible basis for the theory that groundlings always stood may be pictures in which people are shown standing around scaffoldlike platform stages to witness executions and performances in street theaters. Hodges supports this theory. Yet, significantly, one of the pictures he uses to illustrate it, the "Woodcut from Parabosco's *Il Pellegrino*, 1552" (*Globe Restored*, p. 39), shows a play in progress on a Serlio-like stage witnessed by an audience that may or may not be standing. In fact, none of the pictures usually cited as showing the Shakespearean stage can be offered as positive evidence that groundlings always stood. They are not shown in the yard in the De Witt sketch of the Swan, nor are they present in the vignette from the 1640 title page of *Messalina*. Moreover, it can be argued from the details in the vignette from the title page of *Roxana*, 1632, and the frontispiece to *The Wits, or Sports upon Sport*, 1662, that these pictures show the audience seated. The pictorial evidence is not convincing.

Apparently spectators stood in the yard to watch plays given at the theaters attended by Platter, probably the Globe and the Curtain. Moreover, the several jibes at "the understanding, grounded, men" that Chambers notes are persuasive. Chambers's assertion (2:527), however, that "Spectators in the yard always stood," ought to be qualified in view of the appeals made to the audiences to be seated at the Rose. While groundlings stood in some theaters, it cannot be assumed that they were expected to stand in the yards of all of them. Whether they were expected to stand or sit depended, I think, upon the height of the stage in the particular theater.

The average Elizabethan Englishman, judging by those unfortunate enough to lie in one of the common plots used for the burial of plague victims in London, was five feet five and three-quarters inches tall.[4] The stage in the out-of-doors Shakespearean public playhouse attended by this average Englishman would have been about five feet six inches high, or higher, if he stood in the yard and was able to see the action. If the stage had been any lower, the man in the yard would have found himself trying to watch the play through the heads and shoulders of those standing in front of him. The only way he could have seen the play would have been for all those in the yard to sit down. Thus I explain the several appeals at the beginning of the plays of the Rose urging the audience to be seated: the stage was not high enough for everyone in the yard to stand and see the action.

In the absence of evidence indicating that seats were provided in the yard, I believe that the spectators were expected to sit directly on the ground, on rushes, or perhaps on stools they brought with them. Allowing a few inches for the difference in the heights of the Elizabethan and the modern audience, I estimate the minimum height of the stage of the Rose as four feet and six inches. If it had been much lower, the groundlings would have had difficulty in seeing the stage—even from a sitting position;[5] and Henslowe would have been forced to dig a cellar under the stage to provide headroom for the actors and stage hands who worked there.

I estimate the maximum height of the stage as five feet six inches, on the basis that there would have been no reason for appeals to the audience to be seated if it had been higher. Vitruvius says (5.6) "The height of the stage is not to be more than 5 feet, so those who are seated in the orchestra can see the gestures of all the actors."[6] I show the stage in my drawings and model as five feet high.

THE WALLS AROUND THE STAGE

The pictures of the Rose show very little of the walls around the stage and indicate little or nothing about the shape or the size of the stage. Two pictures, one on the 1616 title page of *Faustus* (plate 34) and another on the 1630 title page of *Friar Bacon* (plate 35), both show a wall at the rear of the stage containing a window and supporting a bookshelf. These pictures, however, have only a possible connection with the stage of the Rose (Appendix A, "Pictures of the Rose") and cannot be relied upon.

Several plays of the Rose suggest that the facade consisted of three walls. *David and Bathsheba* (b-9), for instance, begins with a stage direction following the speech of the Prologus: "*He drawes a curtaine, and discovers Bethsabe with her maid bathing over a spring: she sings and David sits above vewing her.*" If Bathsheba remained within the area in which she was discovered, then David, sitting above, had to be at one side of the stage in order to see her. If Bathsheba was revealed in an opening at one side of the stage, then David could have been placed in the gallery behind the stage. In either case, the staging of incidents in which action, presumably in a discovery area, is viewed from above suggests that the wall at the rear of the stage was flanked by walls at each side of the stage. An incident in *The Brazen Age* (b-2) (H2v–I3), in which Venus and Mars are trapped in Vulcan's net and "*All the Gods appeare above, and laugh*," may possibly have been staged in a manner similar to that in which the opening scene of *David and Bathsheba* was presented. A third incident of this kind occurs in *The Silver Age* (b-2) (I4–K1), when Juno and Iris watch Jupiter descend to make love to Semele. Here a stage direction reads: "*Juno and Iris plac'd in a cloud above.*" In *The Spanish Tragedy* (a-3) two groups of actors are above the stage to watch Hieronimo's play. During the play-within-a-play, Hieronimo "*shewes his dead sonne*" (3045), hanging in an opening before which he earlier "*knocks up the curtaine*" (2909).

While the episodes in which players overlook action on the main part of the stage suggest the presence of walls flanking a wall at the rear of the stage, these episodes do not indicate with certainty that such flanking walls were present. The players watching from above could have been in a gallery in the second or third story of the auditorium. Also, it seems likely that many episodes beginning in discovery spaces spill out onto the main part of the stage, even episodes like the one in which Hieronimo "*shewes his dead sonne.*" In the episode in which Juno and Iris watch Jupiter descend to make love to Semele in *The Silver Age* (b-2) (I4–K1), for example, it is clear that she is "*drawne out in her bed,*" and thus may have been visible from a vantage point high in the back wall.

An allusion to "flinty bulwarkes" and two corners of the stage in *I Henry VI* (b-8) (2.1) suggests that the stage of the Rose was enclosed by three walls. The passage containing these allusions begins with the entrance of the English forces under Talbot to attack a French stronghold. They bring scaling ladders and Talbot speaks.

> Let us resolve to scale their flinty bulwarkes.
> *Bed*. Ascend Brave Talbot, we will follow thee.
> *Tal*. Not altogether: Better farre I guesse,

That we do make our entrance severall wayes:
That if it chance that one of us do faile,
The other yet may rise against their force.
Bed. Agreed; Ile to yond corner.
Bur. And I to this.
Tal. And heere will Talbot mount, or make his grave.

A complicated bit of stage business in *The Four Prentices of London* (b-8) also suggests that walls flank the stage (I2v): *"The Christians are repulst. Enter at two severall dores, Guy and Eustace climbe up the wals, beate the Pagans, take away the crowns on their heads, and in the stead hang up the contrary Shields, and bring away the Ensignes, flourishing them severall wayes."* Guy and Eustace are brothers who must not for the sake of the plot be aware of each other or of each other's exploits in this scene. Consequently, they must enter at different places, "at two severall dores" and climb two different walls, walls that flank the stage unless "wals" means a single wall and the brothers scale it at opposite sides of the stage.

The evidence contained in two pictures of the Rose that may show the inside of that theater, those on the title pages of *Faustus* and *Friar Bacon*, is not conclusive about the wall or walls that divided the stage from the tiring-house. Nor is the evidence provided by one play in the a-list and five in the b-list.

In the absence of evidence about the wall or walls of the stage in Henslowe's playhouse, I shall proceed upon the assumption that Miss Frances Yates is correct in her theory "that the London public theatres . . . were an adaptation of the ancient theatre as described by Vitruvius" (*Theatre of the World*, p. xii). In following Miss Yates, I am also following Alardyce Nicoll who said in 1957 that a prototype for the permanent Shakespearean playhouses "suggests itself in the kind of theatre best exemplified in Palladio's Teatro Olimpico . . . based on the type of theatre which has been preserved at Orange."[7] In my reconstruction of the stage of the Rose (plates 1, 14, and 15), I show it as a rectangular platform that extended to the center of the yard. I show it enclosed by three walls as in the Roman playhouse at Orange, and in the Renaissance version of it by Palladio, and in the Fludd stage illustrations discovered by Miss Yates (plates 6, 7, and 8).

THE SIZE OF THE STAGE

The documents of the Rose do not provide specific measurements for the stage. I have, therefore, used some of the measurements given in the contract for the Fortune in reconstructing the stage of the Rose. I make no claim that these measurements are precisely accurate; they are, however, suggestive and illustrative in providing a visual background for the presentation of my conclusions about the way plays were staged at the Rose.

Richard Charles Kohler has discovered an "exact mathematical correspondence" between the data for the Fortune and the Vitruvian geometric scheme.[8] Since Henslowe built both the Rose and the Fortune, it is reasonable to suppose that he may have followed the Vitruvian plan in building the earlier theater. In this case, we can determine the width and depth of the stage and locate the openings in the walls encompassing the stage if we can determine the figure Henslowe took to be the inside diameter of the Rose. I have argued (chapter 1) that the overall diameter of the Rose was ninety-four feet.[9] If we assume that the exterior wall of the building was eighteen inches thick, then the inside diameter of the Rose would have been ninety-one feet.

A Vitruvian plan to obtain measurements for the reconstruction of Henslowe's theater (plate 17) may be set up by drawing a circle on a scale representing the inside diameter of the Rose as ninety-one feet, and drawing within that circle four equilateral triangles whose vertexes touch the circumference at equal intervals.[10] If the plan was followed rigidly, the stage of the Rose would have been twenty-two feet and nine inches deep and forty-five feet and six inches wide, that is, one-fourth as deep and one-half as wide as the inside diameter of the building. I use these dimensions in my scale model and floor plan (plates 1 and 14).

4

Five Openings in the Walls

I HAVE found in tracing the movement of the actors about the stage in the plays of the Rose that the stage shown in the De Witt sketch of the Swan simply could not have accommodated the pieces presented in Henslowe's theater. Most of the plays required three openings in the stage wall or walls. Some certainly had to have at least four openings and a few seem to me to have required five.

There is nothing new about the idea that the stage shown in the drawing of the Swan was inadequately equipped for the presentation of many Shakespearean plays; for the past fifty years scholars have regularly pointed out that these plays often require more than the two doors shown in the sketch of the Swan. Richard Hosley, who believes that the Swan was a "typical" Elizabethan playhouse "capable of accommodating the production of nearly all extant Elizabethan plays,"[1] concludes that "probably there were three rather than two doors" in the wall behind the stage of the Globe.[2] And, as we have noted, Bernard Beckerman says that "the Swan, as it is depicted in the drawing, unaltered, could not have accommodated the Globe plays."[3]

E. K. Chambers suggested in his reconstructions of a square and an octagonal theater in 1923 that the Shakespearean playhouse was provided with five openings (*ES* 3:84–85). He says (p. 100): "We have already had some hint that three may not have been the maximum number of entrances. If the Elizabethan theater limited itself to three, it would have been worse off than any of the early neo-classic theatres based upon Vitruvius, in which the *porta regia* and *portae minores* of the scenic wall were regularly supplemented by the *viae ad forum* in the *versurae* to right and left of the *proscenium*." In 1959 Allardyce Nicoll suggested that "it would appear that we have to accept as the most reasonable, effective and practical interpretation of the phrase 'pass over the stage' a movement from yard to platform to yard again."[4] Thus Nicoll posits the use of the opening labeled in the Swan drawing as *ingressus*, with a similar opening on the opposite side of the building, to provide that playhouse with a total of four openings for use in presenting plays. A year later, J. W. Saunders suggested the use of "wing accesses" at the Globe, providing that playhouse with five openings for use in presenting plays.[5] Robert M. Wren argued in 1967 that "the Blackfriars theater had a five-entry, architectonically-segmented facade stage, markedly unlike the Swan or any reconstruction based on the Swan."[6]

The crux of the problem created by the Swan drawing is discussed by Nicoll, who points out that the stage directions in Shakespearean plays "sometimes confirm and sometimes contradict the type of stage indicated by the de Witt drawing."[7] Nicoll moves on to argue that

from these stage directions, therefore, we have fundamentally to alter our conception of the open-air public playhouse. We must imagine a round or rectangular theater, set with galleries for the spectators, a large raised stage in the centre of the pit or *orchestra*, backed by a wall, no doubt decorated architecturally with one large and two small openings, perhaps two more doors in side walls, a roof over the stage, supported on elaborately carved and painted pillars, windows above from which spectators may gaze or actors speak.

Nicoll concludes that "almost at once a prototype suggests itself in the kind of theatre best exemplified in Palladio's Teatro Olimpico . . . . based on the type of theatre which has been preserved at Orange."[8]

Nicoll, of course, anticipates Miss Yates's discovery of the Fludd engravings and her theory that Vitruvius's ideas referred to in John Dee's preface to *Euclid* (1570) passed to the middle and artisan classes who later built and operated the public out-of-doors playhouses in London (*Theatre of the World*, pp. xi–xii). Miss Yates's theory points to the possibility that Henslowe or his workmen were acquainted with the Vitruvian plan of the theater and used it in building or altering the Rose. Moreover, Kohler's article, "The Fortune Contract and Vitruvian Symmetry" (*SSt* 6:311), demonstrates Henslowe's acquaintance with the Vitruvian plan. Even so, Henslowe's knowledge and use of the plan does not prove that he followed it to the extent that he required that five openings be cut in the walls of the stage. Actually, Vitruvius allows for adjustments, "additions" or "deductions" in "the planning of theatres."

> The architect must observe in what proportions symmetry must be followed, and how it must be adjusted to the nature of the site or the magnitude of the work. . . . and whatever else occurs to compel us to depart from proportion in the interest of convenience. . . . it will not be inappropriate to make slight additions or deductions, provided this is done with taste and so as to avoid a clumsy effect.[9]

My conclusion that there were five openings in the walls encompassing the stage of the Rose does not proceed deductively from the probability that Henslowe was acquainted with the Vitruvian plan or used it. Rather, I concluded inductively in 1958 (before I had seen Nicoll's 4th edition of *The Development of the Theatre* or became aware of Miss Yates's discovery and her theory) that the plays given at the Rose had to have a stage provided with three openings in the wall at the rear of the stage and an opening in each of the walls that flanked the stage.[10] The conclusion I reached about the number and location of the openings in the walls of the Rose in 1958 was illustrated at that time (plate 9). That conclusion has since gained the support of one of the Fludd engravings discovered by Miss Yates and published in 1966 in her *Art of Memory* as plate 18b. This engraving (my plate 8) was labeled by Fludd as "Sequitur figura vera theatri," which Miss Yates translates as "the figure of a true theatre" (p. 353). It shows five openings in the walls, three in the wall at the rear of the stage and one in each of the walls at the sides.

Since I need not argue here that at least three openings are required for the presentation of most Shakespearean plays, I shall turn to a consideration of the plays of the Rose that seem to require four and in a few cases five openings in the walls of the stage. Among these plays are *The Golden Age* (b-2) (K2v), which contains a stage direction reading "*Enter at 4 severall corners the 4 winds,*" and *The Silver Age* (b-2) (K2v), in which "*the Divells appear at every corner of the stage.*" A third play, *The Four Prentices of London* (b-8), also contains a stage direction which suggests the use of four openings (I3): "*Enter at one dore Robert and Charles, they meete Eustace with his Trophee: Enter at another dore Godfrey* [,] *Tancred, they meet Guy with his Trophee.*" The dialogue which follows this stage direction indicates that the two meetings occur at the same time on separate parts of the stage. The plot requires that Guy and Eustace enter at separate doors and that each be unaware of the existence and exploits of each other and of their other brothers, Charles and Godfrey, who enter "*at one dore*" and "*at another dore.*" For the purposes of the plot four openings are needed.

An episode in *Fortunatus* (b-1) in which four openings, and possibly a fifth, are plainly indicated (5.1.168–74) may be sufficient to indicate their use without tracing the action through a number of complicated scenes.[11] The episode begins when Andelocia regains possession of his magic hat, makes a wish, and flies away with Agripyne. The courtiers spring to action:

> *Orle.* Mount every man upon his swiftest horse.
> Flie severall waies, he cannot bear her farre.
> *Gall.* These paths weele beate. *Exeunt Galloway and Orleans.*
> [Through door no. 1]
> *Linc.* And this way shall be mine.
> [Through door no. 2]
> *Cornw.* This way, my Leige, Ile ride
> [Through door no. 3]
> *Athelst.* And this way I:
> No matter which way, to seeke miserie. *Exit Athelstane.*
> [Through door no. 4]
> *Longa.* I can ride no way, to out-runne my shame.
> *Montr.* Yes, Longaville, lets gallop after too.
> *Exeunt.*
> [Possibly through door no. 5]

The evidence showing four openings on the stage of the Rose should not be undervalued. If we accept as valid Kernodle's finding that the facade of the Elizabethan stage "was primarily a center-nucleus, center-accent form," then the use of four openings may be taken as implying the presence of a fifth opening.[12]

A stage direction in *Englishmen for My Money* (a-2) suggests that five openings may have been used to begin a scene played in the Exchange: "*Enter Pisaro, Delion the Frenchman, Vandalle the Dutchman, Aluaro the Italian, and other Marchants, at severall doores.*" To insist that five openings were used to begin this scene, however, would be to interpret the meaning of "severall" rather rigidly. In fact, the evidence for five openings that emerges when one traces the action in the plays is more conclusive than any that can be found in any single stage direction.

Two instances occur in *I Henry VI* (b-8) (2.1 and 3.2) in which the use of five openings is suggested. The action in the first of these two scenes may be traced here to illustrate the way these openings were sometimes employed; it begins with a stage direction: *"Enter a Sergeant of a Band, with two Sentinals,"* apparently from the "Court of Guard" near the gates leading into the besieged town of Orleans. The sergeant and the men part after speaking half a dozen lines, the sergeant returning to the court of guard outside the town. Plainly, two openings are required for posting the guard, and a third may be postulated as representing the gates of Orleans. A fourth opening is necessary for the action which follows immediately: *"Enter Talbot, Bedford, and Burgundy, with scaling Ladders: Their Drummes beating a Dead March."* Talbot and his forces cannot enter from the places through which the French have just made their exits because no alarm has yet been given to make known the presence of the attacking Englishmen. The English scale the wall at three different places; as soon as they have gained the walls, a stage direction tells us *"The French leape ore the walles in their shirts."* The stage direction continues, *"Enter Severall ways, Bastard, Alanson, Reignier, half-ready, and halfe unready,"* which indicates that the French leaders enter at three different openings. These openings can be associated with the besieged town of Orleans and may be identified as: 1) the main gates into the town, 2) an opening leading to the court of guard, and 3) an opening on the opposite side of the stage from the court of guard through which the two sentinels made their exit at the beginning of the scene. The French leaders mill about the town from which they have been expelled and after speaking twenty-five lines they flee from an English soldier, a battlefield scavenger, who comes on stage through a fourth opening—presumably the same one that Talbot and his men used earlier when they entered to attack Orleans. In their flight the French obviously cannot run back into the town from which they have fled. Nor does it seem likely that they would run over the battlefield scavenger to flee in the direction from which he came. They had to flee through a fifth opening. The scavenger picks up the clothing left by the French and goes out to end the scene—one suspects through the place used by the French to escape, the fifth opening. It would have been as much out of character for him to enter the town as it would have been for him to have come on stage from there. He belongs to a dishonorable crew which includes such fellows as Dericke and John Cobler in *The Famous Victories* (b-3) (F4v); in fact he is as near to the scene of the fighting as he has ever been, or will ever get, when he enters bringing up the rear, one might say, and frightening away the already beaten enemy.

The second instance in *I Henry VI* (b-8) (3.2) is not as strong as the first in its suggestion that five openings were used, but it provides a most important detail which was not clearly shown in the scene in which the English take Orleans. This second instance locates quite definitely the "gates" to besieged places and shows that they were practical—that is, capable of being opened and closed. Like the first, this scene is played before a stronghold, a besieged city. It begins: "*Enter Pucell disguis'd, with foure Souldiers with Sacks upon their backs.*" Pucell locates the scene: "These are the Citie Gates, the Gates of Roan." The fact that the gates are capable of being opened and closed is indicated by one of the soldiers who says: "Therefore we'le knock." According to a stage direction they "*Knock,*" and a few lines later are permitted to enter the city. Two openings are obviously used for this action; and since the scene is played before a stronghold, Pucell and her soldiers cannot have entered from a place associated with "Roan," but must have come through an opening leading from some distant place. Likewise, the French soldiers who come on stage as soon as Pucell enters the "Citie Gates" must also come from some distant place. This second group of French soldiers discuss plans to gain entrance to "Roan":

> *Bastard:* Here entered Pucell and her Practisants:
> Now she is there, how will she specifie?
> Here is the best and safest passage in.
> *Regi.* By Thrusting out a Torch from yonder Tower
> Which once discern'd, shewes that her meaning is,
> No way to that (for weaknesse) which she entred.
> *Enter Pucell on the top, thrusting out a Torch burning.*

The French soldiers outside of "Roan" then leave the stage to enter the town through the place Pucell has detected as being suitable for an entrance. Almost immediately Talbot's forces flee from the city through either the "Gates of Roan" or the flanking entrance on the opposite side of the gates through which the second French force has just entered. Thus three openings are used in staging this scene from *I Henry VI:* 1) the entrance Pucell uses at the beginning of the scene, 2) the "Gates of Roan," and 3) the opening used by the second group of French soldiers as they leave the stage for the place through which they are to enter "Roan." A fourth opening is suggested, I believe, by the flight of Talbot's forces from "Roan." It does not seem likely that they fled in the direction from which the French originally came.

If we consider all the evidence provided by the two scenes from *I Henry VI* (2.1 and 3.2) we may entertain the idea that five openings were required to stage them: 1) the centered practical "Gates of Roan" and Orleans in the back wall, 2) the two entrances in the back wall flanking the "Gates of Roan" and leading to other entrances into the besieged places, and 3) the two openings in the side walls leading to distant places.

Several other plays include action suggesting the presence of five openings.[13] It would be tedious to trace all these relevant episodes in detail. I shall attempt to show in the chapters that follow the kinds of openings found on the stage of the Rose, their location, their uses, and their characteristics; in my discussion of the discovery spaces (chapter 7) I shall carefully trace the action in the massacre scene (323–543) of *The Massacre at Paris* (b-3) because it not only shows five openings but it also shows the author exploiting these openings for dramatic purposes.

The five openings with which I shall be concerned in the next three chapters are 1) "the gates," centered in the wall at the rear of the stage and provided with two practical doors—capable of being closed to bar intruders, 2) the "one doore" and "the other doore" located in the walls flanking the rear wall, and 3) two discovery spaces which flanked "the gates" and were sometimes referred to as the court of guard, the curtains, or the porter's lodge.

The exact location of the five openings in my model and my floor plan of the stage (plates 1 and 14) has been determined according to the Vitruvian plan. This was done by drawing a line from the center of the theater through the apices of each of the five triangles behind the stage (plate 17). The points at which these five lines intersect the lines representing the boundary of the stage locate the centers of the five openings (that is, doors) in the walls encompassing the stage.[14]

5

The Gates

THE ACTION in fifty-four episodes found in twenty-four different plays of the Rose begins in one of the "doores" (sometimes two separate doors) and focuses on "the gates" or in some instances a practical door.[1] The movement of the actors about the stage in these episodes enables us to locate and describe the most prominent of the openings on the stage at the Rose—"the gates," double doors centered in the wall at the rear of the stage, as in Robert Fludd's "Theatrum Orbi" (plate 6).

The first scene of *Titus Andronicus* (a-4) contains an episode that locates the doors (plate 18). The action begins with a stage direction: "*Enter the Tribunes and Senatours aloft: And then enter Saturninus and his followers at one dore, and Bassianus and his followers, with Drums and Trumpets.*" It is quite clear that the opposed factions enter at different doors. They are competitors for election by the "Tribunes and Senatours" to the office of "Romes Emperour." Saturninus and Bassianus clamor at the gates for admission to the "Senate house" and are addressed by Marcus Andronicus from above. Finally they are admitted:

> *Saturninus*. Open the gates and let me in
> *Bassianus*. Tribunes and me a poore Competitor.
> *They goe up into the Senate house.*

Perhaps another episode from a less well known play, *John a Kent* (b-7) (777–882), will be sufficient to demonstrate that the episode just considered from *Titus Andronicus* is not peculiar to that play. The episode begins with dialogue: "*S. Griffin*. Silence, me thinkes I heare sweet melodie,/ And see he sets the Castell gate wyde ope" (777–78). A stage direction in the margin at the right of Griffin's speech reads: "*Musique whi[le] he opens the doore.*" An actor comes on stage from one side and exits into the castle (780): "*Ffrom one end of the Stage enter an antique. . . . exit into the C[astle].*" A second actor comes onto the stage from the other side (799–810) and exits into the castle: *"Ffrom the other end of the Stage, enter another antique, as the first. . . . exit into the castell."* Two more "Antiques" come on stage, one through a trap and one *"out of a tree, if possible it may be,"* and they also go into the castle, after which Cumber follows (848): *"Exit into the Castell, & makes fast the dore."* The action which has taken place is then discussed by Gosselen (877–82):

> Didst thou not first set ope the Castell gate?
> and then from sundry places issued foorth,
> the skipping antiques, singing severall songs,
> as loovers use, that have endurde some wrongs?
> And when they all were entred at the gate,
> thou followedst, seeming then to barre it fast.

The gate is tested by those outside the castle (893) and found to be fastened: *"John.* The gate is fast my Lordes, bound wth such charmes as very easily will not be undoone." A stage direction in the margin at the right of this speech reads: *"He tryes the doore."* A few lines later (900) a stage direction calls for a person inside the castle to appear on the walls: *"Enter John a Cumber on the walles lyke John a Kent."* The scene ends after some conversation between those outside the castle and the people on the walls.

The episodes above from *Titus Andronicus* and *John a Kent* show in the dialogue and stage directions a pattern of stage movement that is characteristic of twenty-seven "besieging episodes" found in thirteen plays of the Rose (Appendix C, "The Gates").

Of course, not all these besieging episodes taking place before a stronghold originate with action in two flanking doors; more often these scenes originate with a single force moving from only one opening to attack a stronghold represented by the gates. Otherwise the pattern of action in these scenes is the same as it is in the scene from *Titus* and from *John a Kent:* the attackers seek admission and the defenders appear on the walls where they talk to or fight with the attackers. Sometimes the attackers are repulsed, as in *George a Green* (b-3) (273–379); sometimes they are successful, as in *Edward I* (b-9) (D3). In any case, these episodes have so many common characteristics that one may classify them together and be quite sure that they all indicate, first, the presence of the gates located in the rear wall and, second, the presence of at least one opening flanking the gates on each side of the stage. Moreover, the frequency with which besieging episodes are found in plays given for Henslowe indicates that the gates used in staging them were a permanent part of the facade rather than a "separate structure" of some kind such as Professor Reynolds thinks (*Red Bull*, pp. 76, 85, 133, 148, 155–56, and 189) may have been used at the Red Bull theater.

In a few instances the gates were opened at the Rose to reveal a discovery space. This seems to have been the case in *The Brazen Age* (b-2) where a practical door first represents the gates of Troy (E3v–F2) and later is used as the place in which the golden fleece and its terrible guards are kept (G2–G2v). In the same play, the gates may represent the entrance to the cave in which, or before which, Venus and Mars are caught in Vulcan's net (H2–I3). It seems likely that the gates were also employed in *Alphonsus of Aragon* where a stage direction reads (1246–48): "*Let there be a brazen Head Set in the middle of the place behind the Stage, out of the which, cast flames of fire, drums rumble within, Enter two Priests.*"

The location of the gates and the uses made of them suggest something about the characteristics of the door and the opening. For instance, the central location indicates that the gates, simply for artistic reasons, were placed before the largest opening on the stage. Kernodle says: "As we discovered in examining the habits of medieval painters and designers. . . . the center accent led to the development of the conventionalized façade, the pattern for the Flemish and Elizabethan public theatres."[2]

The use made of the gates to represent entrances to strongholds and the possibility that the opening may have served on occasion as a discovery space suggest also that the door was actually a large double door with two sections that opened out and onto the stage. If the golden fleece episode and the Venus-Mars net scene in *The Brazen Age* (G2–G2v and H2–I3) were presented in the center opening, the door, or double doors, must have swung out and away from the "*Two firey Buls . . . the Dragon sleeping,*" and from the couch on which Venus and Mars were caught, in order to clear these properties which had to be as near as possible to the front of the opening in order to be seen.

Other evidence shows that the gates were provided with double doors that opened onto the main stage. In *The Death of Robert* (a-2), when King John calls to Bruce on the walls to open the gates to Windsor Castle, Bruce replies (L2): "I will not ope the gates, the gate I will:/ The gate where thy shame, and my sorrow sits." Bruce then opens a shutter before a window above the stage and shows his dead mother and brother. The distinction Bruce makes between the "gates" to Windsor Castle and the "gate" to the window indicates that the gates were provided with double doors. The fact that these double doors probably opened out onto the main stage is strongly suggested in *Captain Stukley* (a-3) where the action in a scene played before the gates (D3–D3v) is later described (D4) as taking place at "the North gate that opens toward the Fewes."

The indications that the gates were provided with practical double doors and that these opened out onto the main stage, permitting "discovery" episodes to be presented, enable one to hazard an opinion about the size of the opening. Perhaps it was as much as eight feet wide and nine or ten feet high. I show it in my model as eight feet wide and nine and one-half feet high.

The use made of the gates, particularly in besieging episodes, strongly suggests that one of the gates was provided with a hole or grille of some kind through which people could carry on a conversation. In *Captain Stukley* (D3 and D3v) a person inside the castle of Dundalke coughs and is heard by those outside the gates, and in *I Henry VI* (b-8) (3.2) Pucell talks to the "Watch" inside the gates of "Roan."

One could assume that all of the openings on the main stage of the Rose were equipped with practical doors, if for no other reason than to protect the building and the property stored in the tiring-house areas from the weather. It is perhaps surprising, therefore, to find that the opening centered in the wall at the rear of the stage, and representing the gates, seems to be the only one provided with practical doors that were unquestionably used in staging plays at the Rose. Aside from the twenty-seven besieging episodes, the plays of the Rose contain only thirteen episodes in which the use of a practical door is clearly indicated and fourteen more in which the use of such a door is suggested (Appendix C, "Practical Doors"). This assumes that a practical door is suggested or indicated every time someone *"knocks within"* or *"enters and knocks"* at an opening representing the entrance to a house, room, cave, or similar place. Considering the very large number of entrances to and exits from such places, the instances are indeed few—twenty-seven in all. Among these are at least five instances in which the practical door may be clearly identified with the center door. The door to Lelio's house in *Knack to Know an Honest Man* (b-3) is the focal point for the action in four scenes (2, 5, 9, and 15) and one of these (scene 9) is very much like a besieging episode at the gates before a stronghold: Gnatto speaks through a grate from within Lelio's house and An-netta and Lucida appear on the balcony and speak to the besiegers trying to force the door centered in the wall at the rear of the stage. In *The Blind Beggar of Alexandria* (b-3) (1020–80), the count knocks *"within"* and carries on a conversation for about sixty lines, presumably through a grate in a door. He is finally admitted onto the main stage and exits from there. This door may be identified with the gate in the center of the stage, which was provided with a grate.

In most cases in which a practical door is demanded by the stage directions and dialogue, it can be located rather clearly in the center of the wall at the rear of the stage. In a few instances, as in *The Massacre at Paris* (b-3) (417–535), where it is suggested that three practical doors are used in succession, a careful examination of the stage business will show that two of these openings were apparently provided with curtains. I have found no instance in the plays given at the Rose theater in which it is clearly shown that actors simul-taneously enter or leave the stage through two different practical doors. If practical doors were ever used in any but the center opening for the presentation of plays at the Rose, the occasions were rare. I show practical doors in the center opening used as gates to strongholds, but omit them from the other openings on the main stage in my diagrams and model of the Rose.

In summary then, I have argued that fifty-four episodes found in twenty-four plays of the Rose (Appendix C, "The Gates," and "Practical Doors") indicate that the stage was provided with a set of double doors like those in Fludd's "Theatrum Orbi" (plate 6). Centered in the wall at the rear of the stage, they were a permanent part of the stage and represented the gates to cities, castles, abbeys, the Tower of London, and the homes of noble persons such as Sir

John Oldcastle. They may, I think, be equated with the *porta regia* of the Vitruvian theater. I find nothing in the Henslowe material or in the plays of the Rose to suggest that "the gates" were represented by some kind of a removable structure, as Reynolds posits in his work on the Red Bull (p. 188). I think it is clear from the stage directions and the dialogue in the plays of the Rose that the gates were real, rather than fictive. They were present, and I shall argue that they were flanked by a pair of openings in the wall at the rear of the stage which were provided with curtains (chapter 7: The Discovery Spaces). These discovery spaces may be equated with the *portae minores* and it is possible that they were provided with practical doors as well as curtains. The evidence at our disposal is simply not enough for us to hazard a guess, since only about one of every five plays given at the Rose is extant. I am inclined, therefore, to assign to the gates the few instances in plays of the Rose in which practical doors are required. Indeed, the gate mentioned in the dialogue of *John a Kent* (b-7) (893–94) is described by a stage direction in the margin as "the doore." John reports, "The gate is fast my Lordes, bound wth such charmes, as very easily will not be undoone. *He tryes the doore.*"

Although I am not sure whether the discovery spaces, the Shakespearean adaptation of the *portae minores*, were provided with practical doors that were sometimes used with curtains in staging plays at the Rose, I am rather confident that neither curtains nor practical doors were ever employed in the "one doore" and "the other doore" in presenting plays there. It is to these openings, the Shakespearean *viae ad forum*, in the walls that flanked the wall at the rear of the stage that I shall now turn.

6

One Door and the Other Door

ALLARDYCE NICOLL pointed out in 1957 that "there are many [stage] directions which indicate entries or exits by the 'ends' of the stage."[1] Certainly a theater with openings in walls at each end of the stage seems to be necessary for the presentation of a number of plays of the Rose which call for entrances "*at one doore . . . at the other doore*" or "*at either end*" or "*on the one side . . . on the other part,*" as well as directions calling for actors to "*pass over the stage.*"

In his article "Passing Over the Stage" (*SS* 12:47–55), Nicoll suggests the use of the "*ingressus*" with a similar opening on the other side of De Witt's Swan theater as necessary "for the effective carrying-out of a dignified 'passage over the stage.'" J. W. Saunders has offered "two alternative methods by which wing access could have been provided" in his "Staging at the Globe, 1599–1613" (*SQ* 11:401–25). He says that he has "tried, without complete success, to avoid downright commitment to any one theory" about the stage of the Globe; the two diagrams (pp. 422–25) illustrating his conclusions both show stages provided with five openings. Nicoll, in attempting to reconcile the evidence presented by the sketch of the Swan with the demands made upon the stage by Shakespearean plays, envisions the De Witt drawing with a total of four doors. Two of them, however, are not clearly indicated, and the sketch would have to be revised to incorporate them as elements used in the presentation of plays. For one thing, steps leading from the stage down into the yard would have to be provided on both sides of the platform, or else runways of some kind would have to be constructed from the platform to the "*ingressus.*"

Fortunately, as we have seen, new light has been directed upon the Shakespearean stage by Miss Frances Yates's discovery of five pictures of stages in Fludd's *Ars Memoriae*, among which are pictures of two stages (plates 7 and 8) whose sides are enclosed by walls —each provided with openings.[2] The discovery of these pictures, including two with platform stages (as in the De Witt sketch of the Swan), and the now controversial "Theatrum Orbi,"[3] supports the supposition that no two Shakespearean playhouses were exactly alike. But more important, I think, the Fludd drawings and Miss Yates's *Theatre of the World*, growing out of her discovery of those drawings, has directed our attention to the Vitruvian antecedents of some Shakespearean playhouses. We may now entertain the information provided by many extant plays that they were presented on a stage whose sides or ends were both enclosed by walls, each containing an opening that was frequently designated as a door and used regularly by actors coming onto the stage and leaving it.

Stage directions in plays of the Rose point to the existence of two openings that were regularly designated as doors (Appendix C, " 'One Doore' and 'the Other Doore' "). *Titus Andronicus* (a-4) contains such a direction (C1v) which reads:

Enter the Emperour, Tamora   *Enter at the other doore*
and her two sonnes, with the   *Bascianus and Lavinia,*
Moore at one doore.   *with others.*

It is possible that other openings were also designated as doors in stage directions like the one in *Faustus* (b-5) (1489) reading "*Enter at several dores, Benvolio, Fredericke, and Martino.*" Here it appears that three actors come onto the stage through three openings and that the openings are designated as doors. A stage direction in the prologue to *The Four Prentices of London* (b-8) designates three openings as doors: "*Enter three in blacke clokes, at three doores.*" And there is a stage direction in *Englishmen for My Money* (a-2) (393–94) that calls for four persons and "other Marchants" to enter at "severall doores": "*Enter Pisaro, Delion the Frenchman, Vandalle the Dutchman, Aluaro the Italian, and other Marchants, at severall doores.*" In this instance it is possible that five openings are used and designated as doors. However, only two openings were regularly designated as doors, and references to action beginning or ending in openings "*on one side*" or "*the other side,*" or "*at either end,*" or "*at the further end of the stage*" show that these two "*doores*" were located in walls flanking the stage (Appendix C, " 'One Side' and 'the Other Side' ").

Convincing evidence about the location of the "*doores*" in walls flanking the stage at the Rose is contained in the episodes and scenes found in the plays given at Henslowe's theater. For instance, a common episode in these plays is the procession—found in all of the plays presented at the Rose. I count 388 processions in the 689 scenes in these plays, and I am positive that many more processions were used than are specifically indicated by the stage directions.[4]

In any case, it is evident that the processions in the plays given at the Rose had access to two entrances on opposite sides of the stage, because two processions often entered and met[5] as in *John a Kent* (b-7) (137–40). *"Enter at one doore Ranulphe Earle of Chester, Oswen his son[n] young Amery, Lord Mortaigue, wth them the Countesse, her daught[er] Marian, and fayre Sidanen. At another doore enter the Earles [of] Pembrooke, Moorton and their trayne."* Furthermore, processions sometimes marched across the stage, apparently entering at one door, passing across the stage, and leaving through the door opposite the one used for the entrance. In *The Spanish Tragedy* (a-3) (210–29) such a procession must have pleased the playwright or the company so much that it was repeated:

> *The Armie enters, Balthazar between Lorenzo*
> *and Horatio captive.*
> *King.* A gladsome sight, I long to see them heere.
> *They enter and passe by.*

A few lines later the king commands, "Goe let them march once more about these walles . . ." and they *"Enter againe."* Twice in *The Shoemakers' Holiday* (a-2) (1.1.235 and 5.3.1) processions also march across the stage.

The many processions in the plays of the Rose show that there were doors "at either end" of the stage and that these doors were used regularly by groups that passed across the stage in some kind of order.

The kinds of uses made of the doors located "at either end" of the stage are worth some attention. These doors were employed in such a way that most of the scenes in plays of the Rose can be classified according to one of three patterns of action originating in the doors. One or both of the doors are used in 237 scenes that follow a "slanting" pattern of action. These scenes include 40 set before a stronghold, 19 inside a stronghold, 119 at court, 53 before a house, and 6 before a cave. The action in these scenes begins in one and sometimes both of the openings at the side of the stage and slants across the stage to focus itself on some part of the stage or some stage property placed before or near an opening in the wall at the rear of the stage, in a movement similar to that of besieging episodes.[6]

The forty scenes set before strongholds and the nineteen scenes set inside them are little more than besieging episodes in which the action begins in one or both of the openings at the side of the stage and slants towards the wall at the rear of the stage to focus on the gates, as in the opening scene of *Titus Andronicus* (a-4). The scene in *The Golden Age* (b-2) (H1) which is set inside the "Darrein Tower" is perhaps one of the clearer examples of the movement inside strongholds. It begins with a procession: *"Enter foure old Beldams, with other women."* After a time *"The 'larme bell rings:*

> 3. *Beld.* The larme bell rings
> It should be K. Acrisius by the sound of the clapper.
> 4. *Beld.* Then clap close to the gate and let him in.
> *Enter Acrisius.*

If I have correctly located "the gates" as a permanent part of the stage centered in the wall at the rear of the stage, the beldams entered through "one doore" or "the other doore." As is characteristic of the pattern of action followed in these scenes, the gates are identified (we know from the situation that they are the gates at the entrance to the "Darrein Tower" and that the beldams are inside that place). The opening used for the entrance of the beldams is not identified. Nor is the opening identified through which they leave the stage at the end of the scene. All one can do is to assume that the opening or openings used by the beldams to come onto the stage and to leave it lead to places inside "Darrein Tower." One of the significant characteristics of the movement of actors upon the stage of the Rose is that the opening through which they come onto the stage and the one they use to leave it is almost never designated as leading to a specific place.

The use of one and occasionally both of the doors at the side of the stage is characteristic of the slanting pattern of action in 119 court scenes. Here the action normally begins with a processional entrance and focuses upon a throne. Setting aside, for the moment, the question of whether the throne was placed on stage or in a discovery space, one may hold that it was located between at least two flanking openings. In *Look about You* (a-4) (76–81), a stage direction shows such an arrangement. "*Sound Trumpets, enter with a Harrald on the one side, Henry the second Crowned, after him Lancaster, Chester, Sir Richard Faukenbridge: on the other part, K. Henry the Sonne crowned, Herrald after him; after him Prince Rich. John, Leyster, being set, enters fantasticall Robert of Gloster in a gowne girt: walkes up and downe.*" Here two processions enter from opposite sides of the stage and all of the royal persons, except "*fantasticall Robert of Gloster,*" are seated: "*Old K.* Why doth not Gloster take his honoured seate?" Certainly this dialogue and the stage direction that precedes it indicate that the king was seated on a throne located between flanking openings through which the action moved onto the stage to focus on the throne. Although in some cases the processions may pass across the stage before a throne, as noted earlier in *The Spanish Tragedy* (a-3) (224), where the king directs, "Goe let them march once more about these walles," in most court scenes it seems that the action begins in a door and focuses itself on the throne as it does in *The Downfall of Robert* (a-2) (1629–31): "*Enter John crowned, Queene Elianor, Chester, Salsbury, Lord Prior, sit downe all, Warman stands. Joh.* As Gods Vicegerent, John ascends this throne." In none of the instances cited are the openings in which the action begins and ends designated as leading to a specific place. The processions merely come from some unnamed point of origin and go offstage to some vague destination when the scene ends.

The fifty-three scenes staged before houses are akin to besieging episodes in which the gates are the focal point of the action. Quite often these scenes begin with a stage direction calling for an actor to enter and knock, as in *A Knack to Know an Honest Man* (b-3) (80–132) "*Enter Lelio with his sword drawen, hee knockes at his doore.*" The door at which Lelio knocks is carefully identified; it is his own. The opening he uses to come on stage is not designated; the place from which he comes can be anywhere.

Six scenes may be mentioned here as a part of the group of 237 scenes whose movement is like that in besieging episodes. These 6 scenes are set before caves, which may perhaps be identified with the gates or with a discovery space. An excellent example of the movement in scenes before caves is provided by the opening scene of *Look about You* (a-4) (1–15). Robert and a servant enter. Robert directs his servant: "Goe, walke the horses, wayte me on the hill,/ This is the Hermits Cell." Robert calls for the Hermit to "come foorth," and he does: *"Enter Skinke like an Hermit."* The place from which Robert comes is not indicated, but his destination is clearly specified as the "Hermits Cell"—represented presumably by the gates or a discovery space. The location of the "Hermits Cell" between flanking openings is indicated by the action in a subsequent scene (2081–87):

> *Ski*. Ile faine unto my cell, to my faire Lady,
> But John and Faukenbridge are at my heeles.
> And some od mate is got into my gowne,
> And walks devoutly like my counterfeite,
> I cannot stay to question with you now,
> I have another gowne, and all things fit,
> These guests once rid, new mate? Ile bum, Ile marke you.

Skinke apparently leaves the stage through a door opposite the one used for his entrance. He could not have fled in the direction from which he came because the men pursuing him enter almost immediately.

A simple pattern of action, similar to the movement of processions, is found in a second group consisting of 184 of the 689 scenes in plays of the Rose. Like processions, these scenes apparently begin in a door at the side of the stage and flow onto the stage. There they are developed through dialogue and intruded episodes of one kind or another. Finally they move offstage through the door opposite the one used for the entrance.

The fifty-three street scenes in plays of the Rose are representative of the processionlike scenes that begin in a door on one side of the stage and end by leaving through a door on the opposite side of the stage. In *The Spanish Tragedy* (a-3) (1488–507), for instance, the scene begins with a stage direction: *"Enter Boy with the Boxe."* We know from the dialogue in the preceding scene that the boy has come from Lorenzo's house. The boy stops on stage long enough to inspect the box and let the audience know it contains nothing. He says, "I must goe to Pedringano, and tell him his pardon is in this boxe"; and after commenting upon the situation, he leaves with a stage direction, *"Exit."* One can infer that the boy is on the street, somewhere between Lorenzo's house and the prison where Pedringano is being held; and that he is moving—from one locality to another.

Forty-five woodland scenes in plays given at the Rose also suggest movement across the stage. These scenes are localized only in a general way. In *George a Green* (b-3) (924–70) we find a processionlike entrance:

> *Enter Robin Hood, Mayd Marian, Scarlet,*
> *and Much the Millers sonne.*

The dialogue which follows suggests that the party is in the forest and indicates that preparations are being made for a journey through the woods (959–62):

> *Robin.* . . . Bend up your bowes, and see your strings
> be tight,
> The arrowe keene, and every thing be ready,
> And each of you a good bat on his necke,
> Able to lay a good man on the ground.

Robin Hood announces the destination of the party, and the actors apparently go out through the door opposite the one used at the beginning of the scene—the group is on its way (967–70):

> Then come on Marian, let us goe:
> For before the sunne doth show the morning day,
> I will be at Wakefield to see this pinner, George a Greene.
> *Exeunt omnes.*

I place in this group—with the street and woodland scenes—eighty-six scenes whose setting is only implied from something that is happening, or from something which precedes or follows. An example of these scenes, whose location is only "indicated generally" may be taken from *Friar Bacon* (b-4) (2010–73). The action begins with a direction: *"Enter a de[v]ill to Seeke Miles."* The devil apparently does not come on stage through a trapdoor because the direction calls for him to *"Enter,"* and he says, "Now Bacon hath raisd me from the darkest deepe,/ To search about the world for

Miles his man." The devil spies Miles: "See where he comes, Oh he is mine." A stage direction follows: *"Enter Miles with a gowne and a corner cap."* After some conversation, the agreeable Miles gets upon the devil's back to be transported to hell and the scene ends with a stage direction *"Exeunt roring."*

The 184 scenes considered in the second group have a common characteristic: this is movement interrupted by incidents that occur in settings whose location is suggested only in a very general or vague way. The movement itself—people going from one place to another—suggests that openings on opposite sides of the stage are used to represent the beginning and the end of that portion of the journey that the audience sees. The boy in *The Spanish Tragedy* (a-3) (1488–507), Robin Hood and his band in *George a Green* (b-3) (924–70), and Miles and the devil in *Friar Bacon* (b-4) (2010–73) are all on their way somewhere and all still have some distance to go before they reach their destination. In order to create and sustain the illusion of traveling, the actors in these scenes must enter on one side of the stage and leave on the other. And finally the settings in these 184 scenes are not localized. The opening through which they come onto the stage does not relate to any specified place nor does the one through which they leave.

A third group of scenes, sixty-five camp scenes and forty-four battlefield scenes, follows one of two patterns of action, both of which employ the *"one doore"* and *"the other doore."* Some of these scenes follow a pattern of action that is processionlike. Often in the camp scenes actors representing armies enroute to battle or to camp may enter at one door, pass across the stage, and leave at the other door. This seems to be the case in *Hamlet* in the ten-line Folio version of the scene beginning with the stage direction *"Enter Fortinbras with an Armie"* (4.4.2734–44). Sometimes in the battlefield scenes the victors assemble on stage or enter in a procession at one door and leave apparently at another as in *I Henry VI* (4.7.2330–31):

> *Char.* . . . And now to Paris in this conquering vaine,
> All will be ours, now bloody Talbots slaine. *Exit.*

Most of the camp scenes and the battlefield scenes follow a pattern of action which is "excursionlike." Frequently in these scenes a group of actors representing an army will enter at one opening, discuss their situation, and then withdraw to their camp. In *Sir John Oldcastle* (a-1) (1600–1604), the king is advised that the enemy is moving towards his position and says: "Let us withdraw, my Lords, prepare our troopes,/ To charge the rebels, if there be such cause." In *Captain Stukley* (a-3) (K3–L1v) the "excursionlike" pattern of Shakespearean stage battles may be traced. The action begins with the confrontation of two armies entering *"at either end"* of the stage: *"Two Trumpets sound at either end: Enter Mully hamet and Antonio."* A few lines later Sebastian and Mully Mahamet enter to support Antonio. And then *"Enter Abdelmeleck and his traine"* to support Mully Hamet. After boasting and taunts, the confrontation ends:

> *anto.* . . . Proud abdelmeleck, kneele and beg for grace.
> *abbel.* Then proud Sebastian I deny all meanes.
> *Maha.* Therefore Mahamet and Sebastian farewell.

From the dialogue it is apparent that the two forces withdraw through the openings "at either end" of the stage, that is through "one doore" and "the other doore."

The last word of the confrontation between the two forces as they withdraw from the stage is followed by a single stage direction *"Excursions."* This term is defined thus in the *Oxford English Dictionary*: "The action of running out or forth" . . . *Mil.* a sally, sortie, raid—1701." Thus the pattern of movement in this scene of confrontation between forces "at either end" of the stage develops into a stage battle with those forces apparently issuing out of the openings into which they have just withdrawn, engaging in swordplay and then withdrawing again.

The stage direction *"Excursions"* is followed on the next line by another stage direction indicating that the *"Excursions"* are over and that the battlefield scene has shifted to a camp scene.

> *Enter Sebastian antonio, avaro and Stukly*
> *In counsell together.*
> *Sebast.* Advise us Lords if we this present night,
> Shall pass the river of Mezaga here,
> Upon whose [sudzy] banks our tents are picht,
> Or stay the morning Fresh approaching sun.

This camp scene ends with Sebastian advising his forces that he has given orders to his "pyoners" to

> make our passage smother through the forde
> And least they loyter we ourselfe in person
> Will overlook them that by ten aclocke,
> Within yonder plaine adjacent to Alcazar,
> The lot of happy fortune may be cast,
> Come Lordes and each unto his severall charges
> *Muly.* Bravely resolvd, myselfe will follow you.
> . . . .
> *Exeunt.*
> *The Trumpets sounding to the Bataile. Enter*
> *abdelmeleck and sebastian, fighting: after them*
> *againe, Muly Mahamet, and Muly hamet: then*
> *antonio: with some other passing away, then they*
> *retired back, abdelmeleck alone in the battell.*

The dialogue with which the camp scene ends suggests that the actors left the stage through an opening opposite the one used for the entrance. But this is not clear. The action in the battlefield scene that follows is clear, however, and it shows the use of openings "at either end" of the stage. "*Antonio: with some other passing away, then they retired back, abdelmeleck alone in the battell,*" may be interpreted as follows: Antonio and another person run across the stage and leave through an opening opposite the one they used to come onto the stage. Then they reenter, pursued by Abdelmeleck, and flee from the stage through the opening they used when they ran across the stage to begin the episode. Abdelmeleck pauses and speaks several lines "*alone in the battell*"; that is, alone on the stage, the battlefield.

The remaining 159 of the 689 scenes in plays of the Rose do not follow a discernible pattern of action.[7] I find little in them that throws light on the way doors were used. Most of these scenes have interior settings, are precisely located, and as a rule do not contain much vigorous physical action.

The use made of the "*one doore*" and "*the other doore*" at "*one side*" and "*the other side*" of the stage for presenting 388 processions and other actions occurring in 530 scenes—more than three-fourths of the scenes in the plays of the Rose—indicates much about those openings.

The doors had to be wide enough to allow two men to march abreast in the many armies that entered and crossed the stage. In one instance, in *The Spanish Tragedy* (a-3) (210–11), they had to accommodate three men walking side by side: "*The Armie enters, Balthazar between Lorenzo and Horatio Captive*." Furthermore, the doors had to be wide enough to accommodate such stage properties as Bajazeth's cage in *I Tamburlaine* (b-6) (D5), Tamburlaine's chariot in *II Tamburlaine* (b-6) (K4), the "canopie" under which the king and queen walk in Longshank's coronation procession in *Edward I* (b-9) (C2), and the "hurdle" on which David is drawn across the stage on his way to be executed in the same play (H4v).

The frequent use of the doors in the presentation of stage battles indicates that they had to be high enough to permit the passage of soldiers with muskets, spears, halberds, and flying banners. Possibly the soldiers could have carried their weapons at "trail arms" and have dipped their colors to come onto the stage and go off, but this seems unlikely because specific directions are given in a few instances for them to do these things—indicating exceptions to the general practice. In *The Massacre at Paris* (b-3) (1583–86), for example, "*They march out with the body of the King, lying on foure mens shoulders with a dead march, drawing weapons on the ground*."

Perhaps the best indication of both the height and width of the doors is found in the stage direction referred to earlier in *Edward I* (b-9) (C2) which calls for the entrance of "*the King and Queene under a Canopie*." It is difficult to conceive of this effect being staged with the grace and dignity demanded of a representation of a coronation procession unless an adequate opening at least seven and one-half feet high and five feet wide was provided.

Although all of the openings in the walls around the stage seem, at times, to have been referred to as doors, I have been concerned in this section with "*one doore*" and "*another doore*" located "*at either end*" of the stage. The frequency with which they were used for entrances from and exits to generally undesignated places precluded their use to represent openings to specified places, such as gates to cities or castles and doors to houses, rooms, chambers, studies, or cells. If the two "*doores*" were provided with curtains, they had to be pushed back while playing was in progress to accommodate the more than 388 processions and some 530 scenes which began "*at one doore*" and usually ended in "*another doore.*" If these openings had practical doors—and I find nothing to show that they did—one may infer that they were swung back and fastened against the wall while the play was in progress.

The two "*doores*" placed "*at either end*" of the stage of the Rose (plate 19) were akin to the openings used by the Venerable Bede's "spearwa," just as the stage and the facade of the theater were akin to the room and the walls through which the bird flitted. These two "*doores*" at the Rose represented the finite limits to man's view of the parade of life as it moved before the many places perched on the crust of hell, yet under the shadow of the heavens, passing through the little world that was the stage of the Rose.

7

The Discovery Spaces

PROFESSOR Richard Hosley begins his article "The Discovery-Space in Shakespeare's Globe" (*SS* 12:35–46) by attacking the concept of an "inner stage" and in effect disposing of it with the observation "there is no unambiguous evidence whatsoever for an Elizabethan 'inner stage' "(p. 36).

Hosley finds that discoveries at the Globe are "few and infrequent." They are "primarily shows of persons or things themselves inherently interesting. They are never (as in the proscenium-arch theater) conveniences for the sake of arranging furniture out of sight of the audience." They "do not involve any appreciable movement within the discovery-space, the discovered player . . . being discovered as it were *en tableau* and subsequently leaving the discovery-space for the stage." In addition, the "texts afford no sign of closing the discovery-space after a discovery, presumably because it was automatically and unobtrusively closed" (pp. 44–45).

Hosley concludes that the discovery space at the Globe was "equipped with a curtain or curtains. . . . was off stage, or outside and somehow distinct from the main playing-area. . . . and . . . need not have been deeper than 4 ft. or wider than 7 ft." (p. 46).

Hosley does not seem to be concerned with Reynolds's idea that discoveries may have involved "a curtained framework easily removable . . . to provide a discoverable space on the Swan stage" (*Red Bull*, p. 132). Nevertheless, this idea persists, and as recently as 1962 Beckerman has said of the "enclosure," his term for the discovery space (p. 87): "Though I tend to believe that the enclosure was permanent, it could very well have been temporary, provided there were hidden access to it." It is just possible for a tent to have been erected on the stage of the Rose in *Edward I* (b-9) and the queen discovered in it: "*The Queenes Tent opens, shee is discovered in her bed*" (F1). However, there is nothing in the stage directions or dialogue to indicate how the tent was placed on the stage of the Rose theater.

Professor Hosley observes (p. 46) that "it is perhaps inexact to speak of a single discovery-space at the Globe, for an action in *The Devil's Charter* requiring discoveries . . . in two separate places suggests that there were (or could be) at least two." Certainly this is the case at the Rose where I find that the gates were sometimes swung open to effect discovery as in *The Brazen Age* (b-1)(G2–G2v). There is also an episode in *The Death of Robert* (a-2) (2775–80) in which a shutter of some kind is opened above the stage to discover a Senecan tableau. Thus far, the points I would make about the discovery spaces at the Rose are substantially the same as Hosley makes in his article about the Globe.

Hosley posits his findings on the theory that "the Globe discovery-space was behind an open doorway in the tiring house wall (usually we may suppose, the middle doorway of three) essentially similar to the doorways in the Swan drawing and fitted with hangings as in the *Wits* frontispiece or the *Roxana* vignette" (p. 46). I contend, however, that there were two more openings in the walls encompassing the stage of the Rose, one on each side of the gates in the wall at the rear of the stage. They were provided with curtains and ought to be carefully distinguished from the "*one doore*" and "*other doore*" located in the walls on the "*one side*" and "*the other side*" of the stage. The "*one doore*" and the "*other doore*" were used regularly for exits to and entrances from undesignated places. On the other hand, I believe the fourth and fifth openings were employed as exits and entrances leading to and from clearly designated places such as studies, caves, porter's lodges and courts of guard; they served as alleys, and as unimportant corridors inside houses, taverns, and the courts of kings. I argue in chapters 15 and 16 that the fourth and fifth openings were employed regularly for storing properties behind curtains and moving them unobtrusively onto the stage and taking them from the stage, often without directions or reference either to the properties or to the curtains. Finally, the fourth and fifth openings were used occasionally, as the texts of extant plays show, for the discovery of persons or unusual properties such as Hieronimo's "dead sonne" in *The Spanish Tragedy* (a-3) (3043–46) or the hellmouth in *Faustus* (b-5) (2017). It is of course the few carefully documented episodes involving the use of curtains for discoveries that permit us to designate the fourth and fifth openings at the Rose as the two discovery spaces.

Chambers seems to be cautiously aware of the openings I call the two discovery spaces when he comments upon demands made by a number of plays for more openings than are provided in the sketch of the Swan. He notes that there are "certain scenes in which one *domus* will not suffice and two or possibly even three must be represented" (*ES* 3:98–100). Among the plays he cites as containing such scenes are several given at the Rose, including *The Blind Beggar of Alexandria* (b-3), *Sir John Oldcastle* (a-1), *Captain Stukley* (a-3), and *A Knack to Know an Honest Man* (b-3). Assuming that I have shown correctly in chapter 6 that the frequency of the use of the "*one doore*" and "*the other doore*" as entrances from and exits to unspecified places precluded their use as entrances and exits to clearly designated places, then Chambers is pointing to the fourth and fifth openings that I have labeled as the two discovery spaces. He concludes his discussion with a statement quoted earlier but worth repeating here (*ES* 3:100): "Possibly also entrances and exits by other avenues than the two scenic doors, which we infer from the Swan drawing, and the central aperture which we feel bound to add, are not inconceivable."

Reynolds finds that "sometimes, at least . . . there were surely two discoverable spaces on the stage at once" (p. 155), and he concludes that the plays of the Red Bull could have been given "on a stage structurally like that of the Swan, with the single important addition of a third door" (p. 188). He concedes that "the evidence available does not allow a positive answer as to whether there was a structural curtained space or not." Reynolds's conclusions illustrate the problem faced by scholars attempting to reconcile the sketch of the Swan with the demands made by Shakespearean plays upon it.

As we can see, then, scholars have long been aware of the demand made by the plays upon the stage in the Shakespearean playhouse for two discovery spaces; at the same time they have been uncomfortably aware of the fact that the Swan drawing, as it stands, does not provide openings enough to accommodate plays requiring two discovery spaces. The "inner stage" theory, however, has usually provided an explanation for scenes seemingly requiring two discovery spaces. Consider, for example, Fredson

Bowers's explanation for a decision in his edition (pp. 15–16) of an
a-play of the Rose, Thomas Dekker's *The Shoemakers' Holiday*:

With some trepidation I have altered the traditional numbering of acts and
scenes imposed upon undivided quartos, in part because in the conventional division the length of the various acts was highly uneven but more
especially because by usual numbering Jane in her shop (my III.iv) is
assigned as IV.i, followed immediately by the shoemakers in their shop
(my IV.i) as IV.ii. Since both scenes clearly must have employed the inner
stage, it seemed to me better to insert a hypothetical act interval between
them to allow time for changing the few necessary properties. It must be
admitted, however, that the difficulty in successive scenes without a break
could have been overcome if at some point in the first scene Jane had come
out to Hammon and the curtains had closed behind her.

The only distinguishing characteristic of the two discovery
spaces, the fourth and fifth openings onto the stage of the Rose, is
that they were provided with curtains capable of being opened and
closed. However, curtains are not mentioned or required every
time these openings were used. As a first step in showing that a
fourth and fifth opening existed and were used frequently as discovery spaces, I shall describe an episode in *Titus Andronicus* (a-4)
requiring a fourth opening, although no curtain is mentioned in the
episode. The action calls for the use of a tomb, apparently placed in
or before an opening on stage, and into this tomb a coffin is pushed
(A4v): "*They open the Tombe.*" The tomb is described (A3v) as "the
Monument of that Andronicy" and referred to by Titus (A4v) as
the "sacred Receptacle of my joyes,/ Sweete cell of vertue and
Nobilitie." These references to the tomb as a "Monument" and
"cell," coupled with the fact that the Admiral's Men had three
tombs in their inventory on 10 March 1598 (Foakes and Rickert, p.
319), indicate strongly that a stage property of some kind was used
in entombing one of Titus's sons (B1v) and later (C1) in the same
scene the body of "Noble Mutius." It would have been unlikely that
the tomb was placed over the trap and the body interred by pushing
it into the tomb and on down into the basement. The trap was
probably located near the center of the stage, and a large tomb
placed there would have blocked much of the action focused around
the gates. Finally, no provision is made for the removal of the tomb

after it is used, a fact which may indicate that it was placed just inside an opening in the wall at the rear of the stage and covered with a curtain at the end of the scene.

The scene in which the tomb is used begins with the stage direction: *"Enter the Tribunes and Senatours aloft: And then enter Saturninus and his followers at one dore, and Bassianus and his followers, with Drums and Trumpets."* Here it seems most likely that the doors on *"one side"* and on *"the other side"* of the stage are employed. The rivals, Saturninus and Bassianus, clamor at the gates, and are admitted (A4): *"They goe up into the Senate house."* Certainly the tomb which was opened (A4v) a few lines after Saturninus and Bassianus go up into the *"Senate house"* would have been an intolerable impediment if placed before the gates or the doors at each end of the stage.

The tomb is used again in the same scene for the interment of another of Titus's sons. After the tomb is used the first time: *"Sound Trumpets, and lay the Coffin in the Tombe"* (B1v), Saturninus is elected emperor. He apparently descends from the balcony and enters through the gates (B2v–B3) to thank Titus "for thy favours done,/ To us in our election this day." Mutius is killed by Titus a few lines later, and during the struggle Saturninus takes Tamora and her followers and goes back, apparently through the gates, to the *"Senate house"* (B3v): *"Enter aloft the Emperour with Tamora and her two sonnes and Aron the moore."* At B4v the party on the balcony leaves that place through a door somewhere behind the stage. Titus and his remaining sons inter Mutius with his brothers (C1): *"they put him in the tombe."* Almost immediately (C1v) two opposing forces come on stage through *"one doore"* and *"the other doore."*

Enter the Emperour, Tamora	*Enter at the other doore*
and her two sonnes, with the	*Bascianus and Lavinia,*
Moore at one doore.	*with others.*

Clearly, the tomb used twice for the interment of Titus's sons could not have been placed before the gates or before the doors at each end of the stage. One may hold that it was placed before a fourth opening, located between the gates and *"one doore"* or *"the other doore"* on *"one side"* of the stage or *"the other side."* And, more than likely, the tomb was placed behind a curtain and "discovered" with the stage direction (A4v): *"They open the tombe."*

A scene beginning in a "discovery space," a recessed place separated from the main stage by a curtain (the fourth opening), is sometimes followed by a second scene which also appears to have originated in another discovery space (the fifth opening). Perhaps the *"chaire"* Ely *"ascends"* in *The Downfall of Robert* (a-2) (45) was placed in a recessed area and discovered. The scene which follows (46–53) obviously requires a discovery space because Robin and Marian *"infolde each other, and sit downe within the curteines."* Successive scenes using discovery spaces may be found in *The Golden Age* (b-2) (B4 and C2) and in *The Shoemakers' Holiday* (a-2) (3.4 and 4.1).

Three episodes in *Edward I* (b-9) (D3, F1–F2, and G3) can be fitted together to show actors passing directly from one curtained discovery space to a second curtained discovery space (plate 20). In the first episode, Longshanks and his forces go out through a practical door (D3) to end the scene taking place before a stronghold: *"Lleul.* The gates are opened, enter thee and thine. . . . *Exeunt."* Thus, the center opening with its practical door obviously was present and used in a typical besieging episode. In a subsequent scene (F1), Edward goes to visit his queen and *"The Queenes Tent opens, shee is discovered in her bed."* The third episode (G3) begins with a stage direction: *"After the christening and mariage done, the Heraldes having attended, they passe over, the Bride is ledd by two Noble men, Edmund of Lancaster, and the Earle of Sussex, and the Bishop."* Gloster speaks:

let us now goe visit the King and Queene, and present their Majesties with their young Sonne Edward Prince of Wales. *Then all passe in their order to the Kinges Pavilion: the King sits in his Tent with his Pages about him.*

Edward receives his son and says:

Lords, let us visite my Queene and wyfe, whom we will at once present with a Sonne and Daughter honoured to her desire. *Sound Trumpets: they all march to the Chamber. Bishop speakes to her in her bed.*

The action moves from *"one doore"* or *"the other doore"* to a curtained space, and apparently continues past the gates to a second discovery space.

An effective way to illustrate the presence and use of the two discovery spaces is to trace the action in scene 5 in Marlowe's *Massacre at Paris* (b-3) in which all the openings on the main stage are used, and in addition the gallery is employed.[1] The scene begins at line 323 with a stage direction: *"Enter Guise, Anjoy, Dumaine, Gonzago, Retes, Montsorrell, and Souldiers to the massacre."* Gonzago takes a party and leaves the stage (347) to go to the Admiral's house, which we shall see was apparently located in the gallery: *"Exit Gonzago and others with him."* Anjoy, Guise, and Retes remain on the main stage and talk. Retes directs the attention of those on stage to the Admiral's house (353): "Look my Lord, ther's some in the Admirals house." A stage direction follows (355–56): *"Enter into the Admirals house, and he in his bed."* Anjoy directs those with him (357–58) to "come let us keep this lane, and slay his servants that shall issue out." Gonzago calls as he apparently enters onto the balcony (359): "Where is the Admirall?" Gonzago permits the Admiral a brief prayer (361–62): "Then pray unto our Ladye, kisse this crosse." According to a stage direction at the end of this speech, Gonzago stabs him. The Guise calls to Gonzago (364): *"Gonzago,* what, is he dead?" Gonzago replies, "I my Lord." The dialogue which follows (365–80) indicates that the Admiral's body is thrown down from the gallery to be identified by Guise and Anjoy on the stage:

Guise. Then throw him down
Anjoy. Now cosin view him well, it may be it is some other, and he escapte.
Guise. Cosin tis he, I know him by his look.
See where my Souldier shot him through the arm.
He mist him neer, but we have strook him now.
Ah base Shatillian and degenerate, cheef standard bearer to the Lutheranes,
Thus in despite of thy Religion,
The Duke of Guise stampes on thy livreles bulke.
Anjoy. Away with him, cut of[f] his head and handes.
And send them for a present to the Pope.

The Guise directs Mountsorrell (389) to "goe shoote the ordinance of[f]" to signal the start of the massacre: "The ordinance being shot of[f], the bell tolles." The Guise and his party *"Exeunt"* (399), and the massacre is under way.

The direction *"Exeunt"* (399) is followed by another direction (400): *"The Guise enters againe, with all the rest, with their Swords drawne, chasing the Protestants."* This action, which is akin to flight and pursuit in battlefield scenes, passes all the way across the stage and ends (405) with the stage direction *"Exeunt."* Here, then, the *"one doore"* and *"the other doore"* have been employed.

At line 406, *"Enter Loreine running, the Guise and the rest pursuing him."* Loreine is caught and stabbed to death at line 413 by Guise. Provision for the removal of the body is made in the dialogue (415–16): "Come dragge him away and throw him in a ditch. *Exeunt."*

The stage direction *"Exeunt,"* (416) is followed at line 417 by the stage direction: *"Enter Mountsorrell and knocks at Serouns doore."* This action involves a discovery space. Seroun's wife calls, apparently from within, to ask, "Who is that which knocks there?" When Mountsorrell answers that he is from the Duke of Guise, the wife, who seemingly does not come on stage, calls: "Husband come down, heer's one would speak with you from the Duke of Guise." At the next line (422) *"Enter Seroune."* Mountsorrell stabs him (435): *"Stab him."* No provision is made for removing Seroun's body from the stage when Mountsorrell leaves (436): *"Exit."* Nothing in the dialogue indicates that a door was opened or closed; it seems likely, therefore, that Seroun fled or fell back through the curtains before the discovery space as Mountsorrell stabbed him.

No time elapses between the stage direction calling for Mountsorrell to *"Exit"* (436) and another stage direction at line 437 reading *"Enter Ramus in his studie."* Here the action moves directly from one discovery space to a second discovery space. Moreover, the playwright varies the action in this episode. Taleus comes from within to report to Ramus that "The Guisians are hard at thy doore and meane to murder us: harke, harke they come,/ Ile leap out at the window." Taleus runs back into the discovery space and Ramus follows (449), urging "Sweet Taleus stay." A stage direction at line 450 says: *"Enter Gonzago and Retes,"* apparently through the discovery space, because they bring Taleus onto the stage with them (451–52). He is released because "he is a catholick." Line 457 reads: *"Enter Ramus." "Exit Taleus."* Ramus comes back onto the stage from within the discovery space. The Guise and Anjoy enter (464) and at line 503 Ramus is killed: *"Kill him."* No provision is made for the removal of Ramus's body, and again it seems that he was killed within the discovery space or else his body was pushed through the curtains after he was killed.

The final episode in the massacre is planned by Anjoy and Guise, who remain on stage before Ramus's study (514–20):

> *Guise.* . . . my Lord, could we devise,
> To get those pedantes from the King Navarre,
> that are tutors to him and the prince of Condy.
> *Anjoy.* For that let me alone, Cousin stay you heer,
> And when you see me in, then follow hard.
> *He knocketh, and enter the King of Navarre and*
> *Prince of Condy, with their schoolmaisters.*

Guise, who has concealed himself near or within the discovery space representing Ramus's study, enters (529): *"Enter Guise."* The King of Navarre and Condy leave the stage (532): *"Condy.* Come let us goe tell the King. *Exeunt."* At lines 534–35, Guise kills the "schoolmaisters." Anjoy, with others, removes the bodies from the stage: *"An.* Away with them both. *Exit Anjoy."* Anjoy's exit here is arranged to get him offstage for his entrance a few lines later in a new scene (544–77): *"Enter Anjoy, with two Lords of Poland."*

The last episode in the massacre, the killing of the "pedantes," involves the use of the practical door, the gates. Admittedly the stage direction does not show that a practical door is opened at line 519 with the entrance of the king of Navarre, Condy, and the "schoolmaisters." However, the entrance here is to the apartment of a king and a prince. It may be held that it was more impressive than the entrances to Seroun's house and to Ramus's study. The careful arrangements for the removal from the stage of all the victims except Seroun and Ramus indicate that these two fell, fled, or were pushed through curtains before discovery spaces when they died. The "pedantes" had to be removed from the stage because they died before the one practical door on stage and their bodies could not be disposed of as were the bodies of Seroun and Ramus. With the murder of the "pedantes" and the removal of their bodies from the stage, the massacre ends. The Guisians *"Exeunt"* at line 543 and the scene ends.

The development of scene 5, when considered from the view-point of dramaturgy, suggests that the author carefully and deliberately wrought it to take full advantage of the physical characteristics of the stage of the Rose on which *The Massacre at Paris* was first presented as a "ne" play between 25 and 31 January 1593, by Lord Strange's men (Foakes and Rickert, p. 20).

The massacre does not start until the leader of the Protestants, the admiral, has been slain and thrown down from his high place as a friend of the king. It is dramatically most effective and appropriate that the admiral be killed and thrown down from the gallery up to which the king went to see him (285–322). The care with which Anjoy and Guise inspect the body to be certain they have destroyed the "base Shatillian and degenerate, cheef standard bearer to the Lutheranes," and the fact that the signal for the massacre is not given until Guise and his followers are sure of the admiral's death attest his importance and power.

The massacre itself begins on the most common level with only general victims, "Protestants," who are chased across the stage, entering and leaving through the most common entrances onto and from the stage.

Loreine, a leader of the Protestants and one who styles himself as "a preacher of the word of God," is chased onto the stage through "*one doore*," caught, killed, and dragged off. The fact that he is identified, particularized, makes him more important in a dramatic sense than were the "Protestants" who were chased across the stage.

The murder of Seroun is staged before one of the two discovery spaces and is more dramatic than the murder of Loreine. Seroun is given a wife; he does not expect to be murdered and does not hesitate to come out and speak to someone sent by Guise; he asks to pray before he is killed and is stopped because he begins "O Christ my Saviour" instead of seeking "the intercession of some Saint"; he urges, "O let me pray unto my God," and is cut down with a curt reply and death: "Then take this with you. *Stab him*." Seroun is developed more fully than Loreine; and while he is apparently a Protestant, he is not shown as an active and defiant opponent of the Guisians as was Loreine. Seroun's murder is more vicious, more dramatic, than that of Loreine and it occurs before an opening that is less frequently used than the doors at "*either end*" of the stage, and therefore is dramatically a more important and effective place before which to stage an episode.

Ramus's murder before a second discovery space is as effectively placed on stage as is Seroun's murder in the preceding episode. However, Ramus's murder is much more dramatic. He could have escaped when he left the stage to prevent his friend Taleus from jumping out of a window; instead he returns when Taleus is captured. After Taleus, Ramus's intimate friend and a Catholic, is released, it appears as though Ramus will escape. Also Ramus reveals that he has a stipend from the king, which suggests that the murderers would not dare touch him. Countering the indications that Ramus may escape, and therefore creating suspense, is the development of the character of the Guisians during the episode. They are shown as degenerating from religious fanatics to common cutthroats: "Come Ramus, more golde, or thou shalt have the stabbe." Nothing appears to indicate that Ramus is an enemy of the Guisians. Ramus's last few seconds are spent, not in a prayer which, like Seroun's, might have offended the Guisians on religious grounds, but in a defense of his ideas about the *Organon*. Every circumstance touched upon in the episode indicates that Ramus may escape and should escape; when he is struck down, the executioners are revealed as vicious destroyers, envious of knowledge and drunk with blood: "*Anjoy.* Nere was there Colliars sonne so full of pride. *Kill him.*"

The people involved in the episode climaxing the massacre scene are the most important of all those thus far affected by the slaughter. They are the teachers and companions of the young king of Navarre and the prince of Condy. Moreover, the "pedantes" are characterized as above suspicion of Protestantism by Navarre's remark upon greeting Anjoy: "My Lord, they say that all the protestants are massacred." The "schoolmaisters" are killed without ever speaking, a fact which suggests that the playwright was intent upon characterizing them as innocent victims of a vicious killer: "Come sirs, Ile whip you to death with my punniards point. *he kils them.*" The most effective location for presenting this climactic episode was before the "gates," the practical door, centered in the wall at the rear of the stage of the Rose.

The fourth and fifth openings on the main stage, the two discovery spaces, may be identified with the door to Seroun's house and with Ramus's study. They are certainly identifiable with the *"Tent"* in *Edward I* (b-9) in which Longshanks's throne was placed and a second *"Tent"* in which his queen was discovered in a bed. They are identifiable also as Jane's shop and Hodge's shop in *The Shoemakers' Holiday* (a-2) (3.4 and 4.1); as the space in which Robin and Marian *"sit downe within the curteines,"* and the space before which or in which was placed the elevated *"chaire"* Ely *"ascends"* in *The Downfall of Robert* (a-2); and as the place before which a tomb was set in *Titus Andronicus* (a-4).

Although it is difficult to identify the two discovery spaces as passageways between the stage and the tiring-house, they seem to have been used frequently for that purpose. More than likely these spaces were also employed to represent unimportant rooms and corridors in the 86 scenes set inside the houses, the 12 scenes set inside taverns, and in the 119 scenes set in royal courts.

Many scenes, particularly those requiring a number of properties, apparently originate in a discovery space and move onto the stage without any mention being made of the curtains. Banquets, for instance, require more properties than any other kind of scene or episode that is regularly found in plays of the Rose. Some of the properties and methods of staging used may be indicated by directions and dialogue from *Patient Grissil* (a-1) (4.3):

Gwen. Rees, lay her table, and set out her fittailes, and preades, and wines, and ale, and peare, and salt for her guesse (1–2).
Enter Rice with a company of beggers: a Table is set with meate (12).
Gwen. Rees pring stooles, sid awl downe, Rees pring more meate (16–17).
Gwen. Rees fedge wine and peares enough, and fall to pegger, and eate awl her sheere (36–37).
A drunken feast, they quarrel and grow drunke, and pocket up the meate, and dealing of Cannes like a set at Mawe. Exit Rice (38–39).

The staging of this scene is typical of eighteen banquets given in plays at the Rose.[2] The banquets, as in the scene above and in *Faustus* (b-5) (1012), are usually brought in: *"A senit while the Banquet is brought in."* Those attending banquets regularly *"Enter"*; there is not a single instance of a banquet being "discovered" in the plays of the Rose. The properties involved are apparently numerous, and sometimes, as in the example cited from *Patient Grissil* or in *The Silver Age* (b-2) (H2–H3), as many as eleven people eat and drink together and end their carousing in "*A confused fray with stooles, cups & bowles.*" Though not a single banquet seems to have been staged behind the curtain line in a discovery space, there is good reason to believe that the banquets staged at the Rose passed through those openings onto the stage; except for the gates, the discovery spaces provided the shortest way from the place where the banquets were presumably prepared to the place where they were to be enjoyed. Also, the curtains before the discovery spaces provided convenient places behind which the properties could be assembled and through which they could be moved quickly onto the stage. The convenience of removing properties from the stage through these openings may also be noted.

If banquet scenes were staged in the manner I suggest, a number of scenes set in shops, studies, and similar places could have been presented in the same way. Curtains are not mentioned in the "Semsters shop" scene in *The Shoemakers' Holiday* (a-2) (3.4) which is regularly assigned to a discovery space by the "inner stage" theory. The properties for this scene could well have been brought onto the stage through a discovery space. The curtained opening would then become the entrance to the "Semsters shop." The action in this scene is brief and may be reconstructed as follows: "*Enter Jane in a Semsters shop working, and Hamond muffled at another doore, he stands aloofe. Ham.* Yonders the shop, and there my faire love sits." Hamond goes to Jane, who apparently rises and approaches him: "Sir, what ist you buy?" He indicates some rather small properties that could have been carried or perhaps worn by Jane: "this handkercher," "these ruffles," and "this band." During the scene, which runs for about 126 lines, Hamond proposes marriage and Jane tentatively accepts him before the "*Exeunt.*" One need not be concerned whether a curtain is actually opened to "discover" this scene. Jane and the properties that must be visible to the audience apparently have "spilled out" of the recessed area and onto the main stage. It can be assumed that "*Exeunt*" indicates that Jane left the stage and that the properties were removed through the curtained passageway used at the beginning of the scene. And in this particular instance, Hamond may well have accompanied Jane.

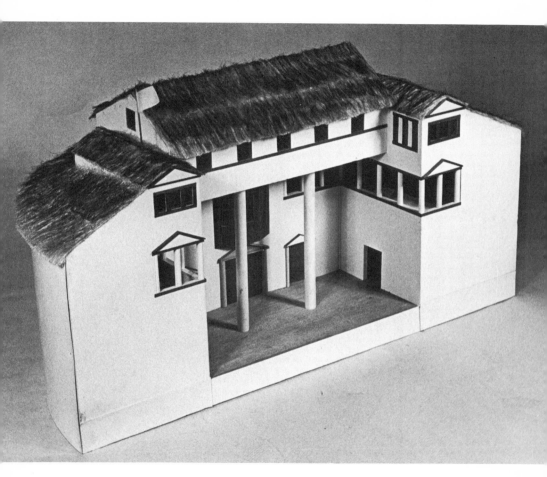

PLATE I
The stage of Henslowe's Rose theater
Model by William R. Duffy

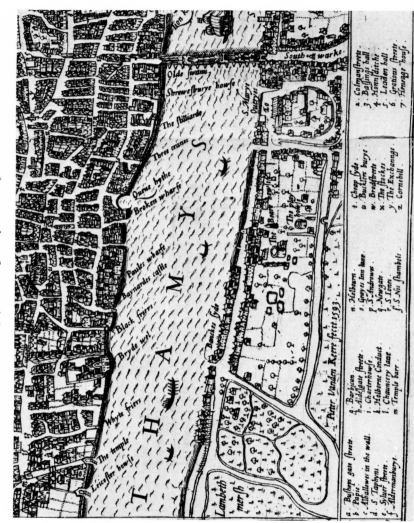

PLATE 2

Norden's map of London, 1593. The Rose is the round structure labeled "The play howse."

Courtesy of the Birmingham Reference Library

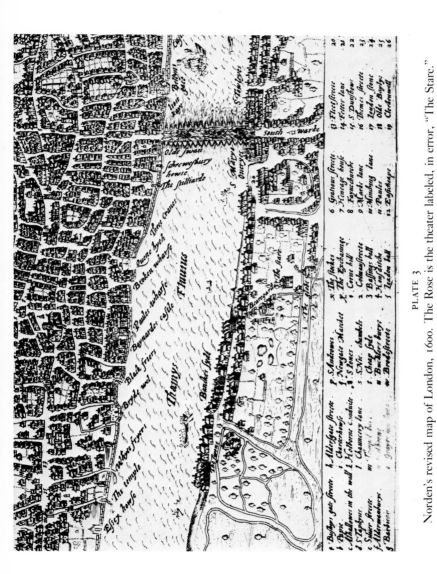

PLATE 3

Norden's revised map of London, 1600. The Rose is the theater labeled, in error, "The Stare."

Courtesy of the Royal Library, Stockholm, Sweden

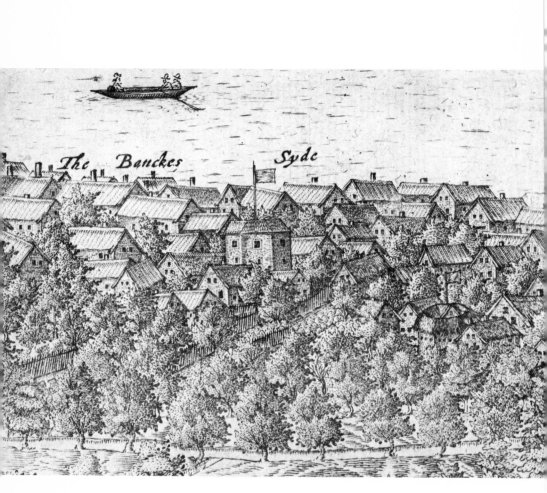

The Banckes Syde

PLATE 4
Civitas Londini, 1600. This section shows the Beargarden (in the center), then the Rose
and (in the lower right corner) the Globe.
Courtesy of the Royal Library, Stockholm, Sweden

Labels within the sketch: tectum; porticus; sedilia; orchestra; ingressus; mimorum ædes; proscænium; planties sive arena

PLATE 5

Arend Van Buchell's sketch of the Swan theater made from another sketch or possibly on the basis of a report by Johannes De Witt, who visited London for a few days in 1596.

Courtesy of the Bibliotheek der Rijksuniversiteit te Utrecht

PLATE 6
"Theatrum Orbi" from Robert Fludd's *Ars Memoriae*, 1619
By permission of the Folger Shakespeare Library, Washington, D.C.

PLATE 7
"Forma Theatri" from Robert Fludd's *Ars Memoriae*, 1619
By permission of the Folger Shakespeare Library, Washington, D.C.

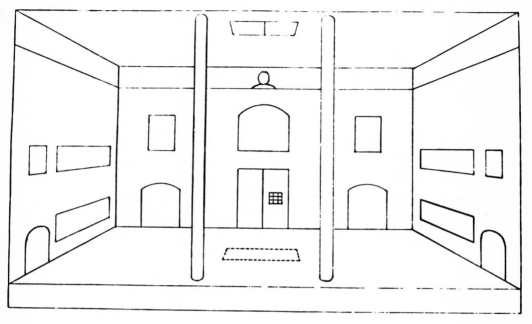

PLATE 9
Elevation view of the Rose

PLATE 10

"Theatrum," title page, *Workes of Ben Jonson*, 1616
By permission of the Folger Shakespeare Library, Washington, D.C.

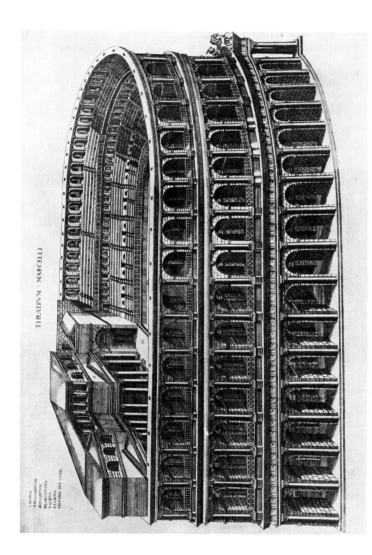

PLATE 11

"*Theatrum Marcelli*" from Antonio Lafreri's *Speculum Romanae Magnificentiae*, 1579

Courtesy of Dr. Frances A. Yates, the Warburg Institute, University of London

PLATE 12
Andrea Palladio's Teatro Olimpico, 1584

PLATE 13
The Roman theater at Orange

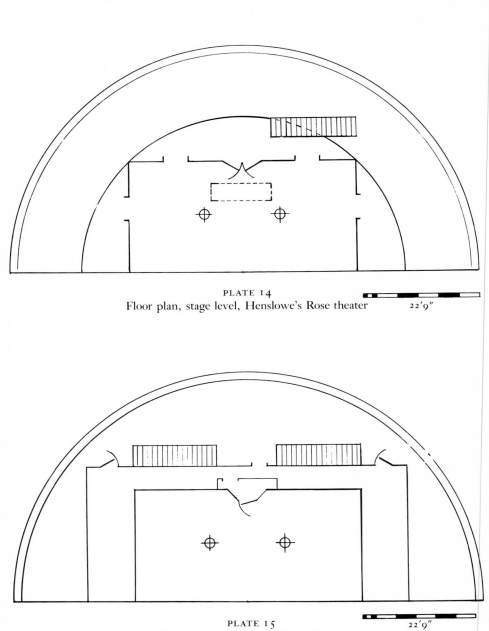

PLATE 14
Floor plan, stage level, Henslowe's Rose theater   22′9″

PLATE 15
Floor plan, gallery level, Henslowe's Rose theater   22′9″

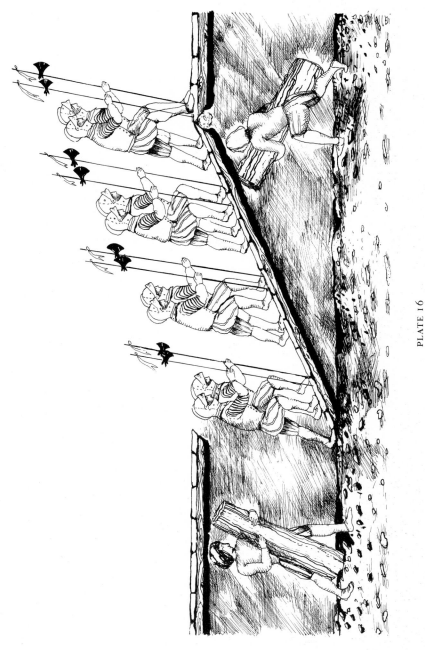

PLATE 16

The trapdoor. "Already from beneath/ Their deadly pointed weapons gin to appeare,/ And now their heads, thus moulded in the earth,/ streightway shall teeme." *Brazen Age*, G2v.

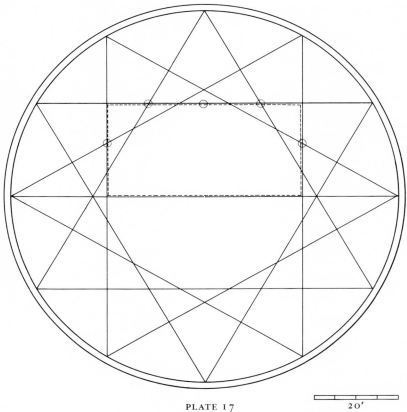

PLATE 17
Vitruvian plan for the Rose

20'

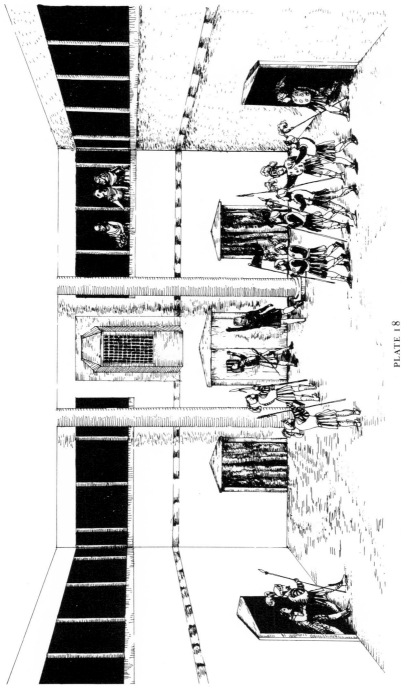

PLATE 18

"The gates," "one doore" and "the other doore," and the gallery. *Enter the Tribunes and Senatours aloft.*
And then enter Saturninus and his followers at one dore, and Bassianus and his followers, with Drums and
Trumpets. . . . Saturninus. Friends . . . Open the gates and let me in. / *Bassianus.* Tribunes and me a
poore Competitor. / *They goe up into the Senate house." Titus Andronicus,* A3–A4.

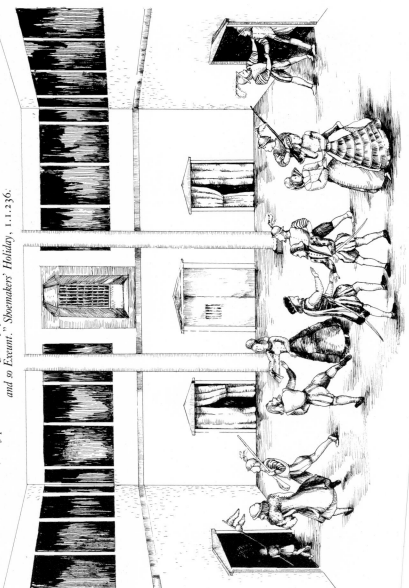

PLATE 19

"One doore" and "the other doore." "Sound drumme, enter Lord Maior, Lincolne, Lacy, Askew, Dodger, and souldiers, They passe over the stage, Rafe falles in amongset them, Firke and the rest cry farewel, &c. and so Exeunt." Shoemakers' Holiday, I.I.236.

PLATE 20

Two discovery spaces. *"The King sits in his Tent with his Pages about him. . . . Lords, Let us visite my Queene and wyfe. . . . Sound Trumpets: They all march to the Chamber. Bishop speakes to her in her bed."* *Edward I,* G3.

PLATE 21

The gallery, the window, and "the gates." "*Ki.* . . . Come downe young Bruse, set ope the castle gates. . . . *Br.* . . . I will not ope the gates, the gate I will:/ The gate where thy shame and my sorrowe sits./ See my dead mother, and her famisht sonne." *The Death of Robert*, 2770–77.

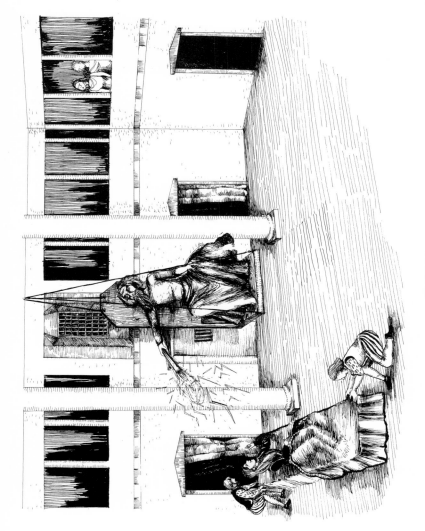

PLATE 22

"My lords Rome," the lift, and a discovery space. *"Juno and Iris plac'd in a cloud above.... Enter Semele drawne out in her bed.... Thunder, lightnings, Jupiter descends in his majesty, his Thunderbolt burning," Silver Age,* I4–I4v.

PLATE 23

Hondius view of London, 1610. It is possible that the Rose is represented by the circular theater
shown in this engraving inset into the map of Great Britain in John Speed's
Theater of the Empire of Great Britain
Courtesy of the British Museum

PLATE 24

Delaram's view of London, 1615–1624? The circular theater in the foreground may be the Rose.

Reproduced by gracious permission of her majesty the queen

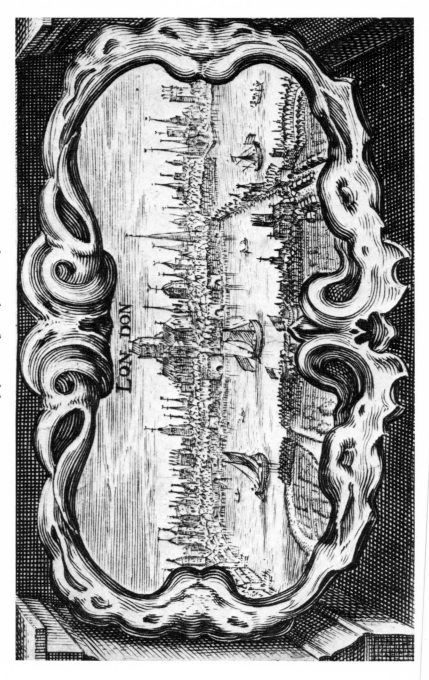

PLATE 25

Holland's *Herωologia Anglica*, title page, 1620. This engraving is related to those in the Hondius group. It is possible that the Rose is represented by the circular theater in the foreground.

Courtesy of the Birmingham Reference Library

PLATE 26

Bankside section from Merian's view of London, 1638. The Rose is represented here as the third theater from the left.

Courtesy of the London Topographical Society

PLATE 27

Baker's Chronicle, title page, 1643. This picture is related
to the Hondius view. The circular theater in the
foreground may represent the Rose.
Courtesy of the British Museum

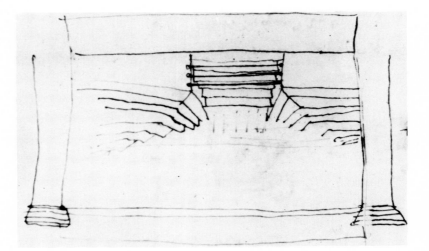

PLATE 28

Sketch on Henslowe letter, 28 September 1593. Dulwich
College MS. I.14.
Courtesy of the Governors of Dulwich College

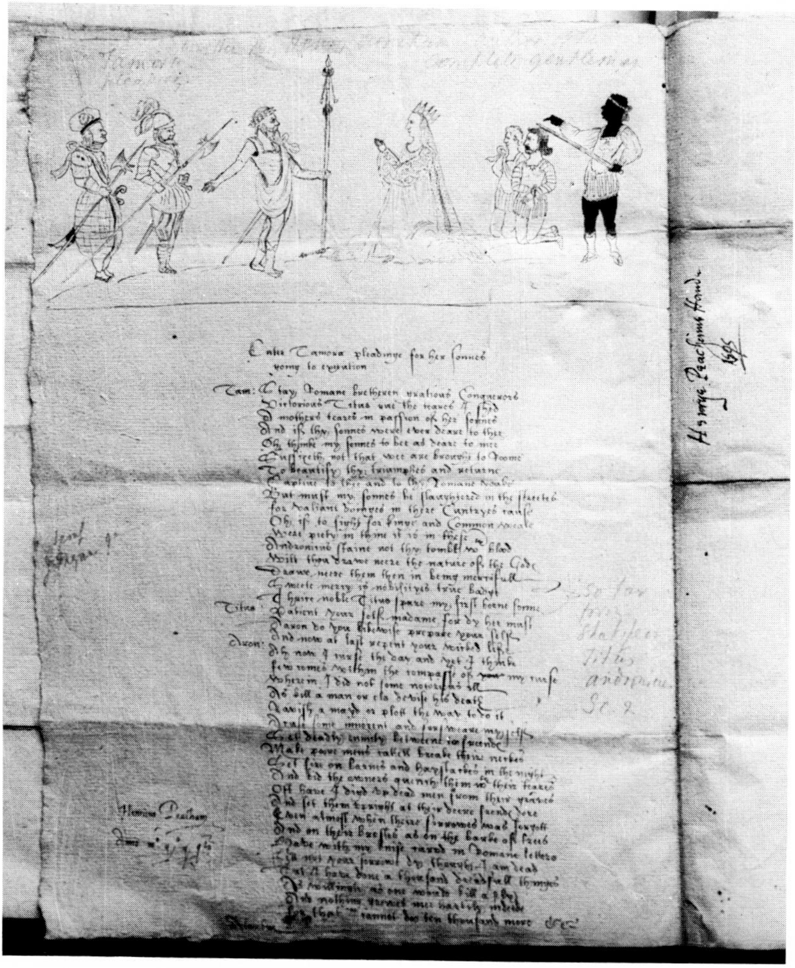

PLATE 29

Scene from *Titus Andronicus*, 1595

*Courtesy of Courtault Institute of Art; this picture is reproduced
with the permission of Lord Bath*

PLATE 30
Zenocrate from *Tamburlaine the Great*, 1597
Courtesy of the Henry E. Huntington Library

PLATE 31
Tamburlaine from *Tamburlaine the Great*, 1597
Courtesy of the Henry E. Huntington Library

The Spanish Tragedie

OR,

Hieronimo is mad againe.

Containing the lamentable end of *Don Horatio*, and
Belimperia; with the pittifull death of *Hieronimo*.

Newly corrected, amended, and enlarged with new
Additions of the *Painters* part, and others, as
it hath of late been diuers times acted.

LONDON,
Printed by W. White, and are to be sold by I. White
and *T. Langley* at their Shop ouer against the
Sarazens head without New-gate. 1615.

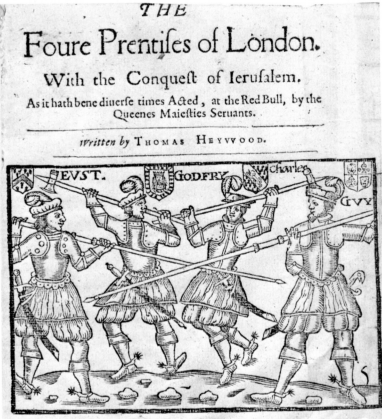

THE
Foure Prentiſes of London.
With the Conqueſt of Ieruſalem.

As it hath bene diuerſe times Acted, at the Red Bull, by the
Queenes Maieſties Seruants.

Written by THOMAS HEYVVOOD.

/ Printed at London for *I. W.* 1 6 1 5.

PLATE 33
Four Prentices, title page, 1615
Courtesy of the Bodleian Library

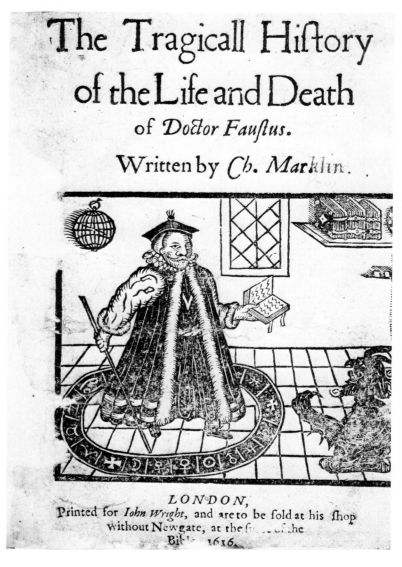

The Tragicall Hiſtory
of the Life and Death
of *Doctor Fauſtus.*

Written by *Ch. Marklin.*

LONDON,
Printed for *Iohn Wright*, and are to be ſold at his ſhop
Without Newgate, at the ſ.... of the
Bib... 1616.

PLATE 34
Faustus, title page, 1616
Courtesy of the British Museum

THE
HONORABLE
HISTORIE OF
FRIER *BACON*, AND
FRIER *BONGAY*.

As it was lately plaid by the Prince *Palatine* his Seruants.

Made by *Robert Greene*, Master of Arts.

LONDON,
Printed. by ELIZABETH ALLDE dwelling
neere Christ-Church. 1630.

PLATE 35
Friar Bacon, title page, 1630
Courtesy of the Bodleian Library

The scene (4.1) in *The Shoemakers' Holiday* (a-2) that follows the "Semsters shop" scene is almost identical. The basic pattern of the action is the same, and again it is a shop scene in which curtains are not mentioned. One can assume that it is placed in the discovery space opposite the one used for the "Semsters shop" in order to avoid confusion in stage traffic and in the minds of the audience. It is clearer in this scene that the properties were brought onto the main stage at the beginning of the scene. At least Hodge's order to the boy to "looke to the tooles" may be considered as a cue motivating the business of removing properties from the stage at the end of the scene with the actors' *"Exeunt."*

With the scenes that seemingly spill out of a discovery space and leave the stage through the same opening without express mention of curtains I believe one may identify a number of scenes in which a curtain is mentioned. The complicated scenes in *Friar Bacon* (b-4) (513–823, 1561–694, 1779–894) are staged in his "study" and in his "cell," which may be identified as the same place.

In one of these (1561–694) Bacon enters: *"Enter Frier Bacon drawing the courtaines with a white sticke, a booke in his hand, and a lampe lighted by him and the brasen head and miles, whith weapons by him."* At line 1600 Bacon directs "draw closse the courtaines Miles now for thy life,/ Be watchfull and *Here he falleth asleepe.*" An explanation for the movement in this scene is that Bacon and Miles come onto the stage through the curtains before a discovery space, bringing the properties used in this scene. Miles closes the curtains and he too goes to sleep. We can be reasonably sure from the dialogue mentioning a "post" and the stage direction in the margin (1612–14), *"Sit down and knocke your head,"* that Miles is on the main stage and that he bumps his sleepy head against a post or one of the columns supporting the heavens at the Rose. Although the two other scenes (513– 823, 1779–894) presumably occur in the same place as the "brasen head" scene, curtains are not mentioned. We may assign them, I believe, to scenes that spill out of the discovery spaces and are developed before those places regardless of whether curtains are mentioned or not.

The use made of the gates for discoveries has been commented upon in a previous section; I shall allude also, in sections that follow, to the possible use of the balcony and to a window on the balcony level that was opened to discover episodes. However, most of the discovery scenes that seem to call for the use of a curtain apparently were presented in one of the two discovery spaces on the main stage. Curtains are sometimes called for at the beginning of a scene, but rarely are they used to close a scene.[3] I have found only one instance, *II Tamburlaine* (b-6) (H2–H4v), in which a scene both begins and ends with stage directions calling for a curtain to be used: "*The Arras is drawne and zenocrate lies in her bed of state, Tamburlaine sitting by her: three Physitians about her bed, tempering potions. Theridimas, Techelles, Usumcasane, and the three sonnes.*" The scene ends with another stage direction: "*The Arras is drawne.*" Beds, however, are frequently brought onto the stage and taken from it. In *The Golden Age* (b-2) (I1v) Danaë is brought out: "*Enter the foure old Beldams, drawing out Dana's bed: she in it.*" Later (I2v) "*The bed is drawne in.*" In the same play (C2) a stage direction reads: "*Enter Sibilla lying in child-bed, with her child lying by her, and her Nurse, & c.*" Beds are "thrust out" in *The Silver Age* (b-2) (I4v) and, twice, in *The Massacre at Paris* (b-3) (300 and 355–56). It is not unreasonable to believe that the scene of Zenocrate's death developed as other scenes in the discovery spaces apparently developed: the curtain was opened, the bed thrust onto the stage, the scene was played around the bed; and when the scene ended, the bed was drawn in and the curtains closed.

In most cases in which a curtain is clearly called for, an episode follows, rather than a scene. These episodes are usually developed in one of two ways. During the action in a particular scene a curtain is sometimes opened to present a tableau, as in *The Spanish Tragedy* (a-3) (3045). Hieronimo apparently opens a curtain to discover the body of Horatio: "*He Shewes his dead sonne.*" Presumably Horatio's body remains behind the curtain line in a recessed area until the curtain is closed. Tableaux of this kind are not frequent in the plays of the Rose; they require a small space and it is actually not necessary that everyone in the audience have a clear view of them. The impact of tableaux did not depend completely upon their being clearly seen: the Rose was the theater in which "our muse intreats,/ Your thoughts to helpe poore Art."

A more common episode is one in which a curtain is opened to discover a tableau which "breaks" and "spills out" onto the stage. In

Fortunatus (b-1) (3.1.357) one finds a good example: "*Musicke sounding still: A curtaine being drawne, where Andelocia lies sleeping in Agripines lap, shee has his purse, and herselfe and another Lady tye another (like it) in the place, and then rise from him.*" Agripine speaks to Athelstane, who was on stage when the curtain opened. The lady who assisted Agripine exits after one line. After about thirty-five lines, Agripine and Athelstane leave the stage. They are quite aware of Andelocia, who is still in the place where he was discovered: "*Athelst. . . . Leave him, that when he wakes he may suspect,/ Some els has robd him.*" Shaddow then enters, apparently onto the main stage, and after about ten lines he sees Andelocia and wakens him. Similar episodes are found in scenes in which royal persons are discovered on thrones as in *The Death of Robert* (a-2) (923–30) and *David and Bathsheba* (b-9) (1911–67).[4]

The two discovery spaces that flanked the gates at the Rose were more like passageways than the single recessed area, "the inner stage," posited by J. C. Adams. Scenes were apparently never played behind the curtain line in these spaces, and the episodes that originated there usually "spilled out" and developed on the main stage. Although doors may have been placed in these openings, they do not seem to have been used in presenting the plays; consequently I do not show practical doors before these openings in my model or diagrams illustrating the Rose.

Some indication of the height of the discovery spaces is given by the elevated throne which appears in them in such plays as *The Downfall of Robert* (a-2) (45) and its sequel *The Death of Robert* (a-2) (925–66). In *I Tamburlaine* (b-6) (D5v) and *Faustus* (b-5) (895–905) a conqueror in each of these plays by Marlowe ascends to his throne by stepping on the back of an obviously defeated rival. Also the opening should have been as high as possible to provide light upon the tableaux set behind the curtain line in these spaces. I estimate the height of the discovery spaces as about eight and one-half feet, which would make them lower than the gates and higher than the doors at either end of the stage.

Allowing for such action as thrusting out beds, I estimate the width of the discovery spaces as about six feet, making them narrower than the gates and wider than the doors at each end of the stage.

8

Links between the Heavens and Hell

THE STAGE and the areas above it that were used for playing were linked by the facade, by the two columns supporting the heavens, and by stairs apparently located behind the facade. These three parts of the playhouse ought to be considered before we turn to the playing places above the stage.

It is more than likely that the Rose had three galleries for spectators, as did the Swan, the Fortune, the Hope, and presumably the Globe. In fact, the evidence for three galleries in the Elizabethan public theater is so well known that it need not be reviewed here. However, Professor John C. Adams's theory that these galleries fixed the number of levels in the facade of the Globe cannot be employed to explain the conditions at the Rose; though the Rose probably had three galleries, the facade which extended up from the floor of the stage to the underside of the platform that supported the heavens seems to have consisted of only two levels.

Adams assigns a "music-room" to the third level in the facade of his reconstruction of the Globe. It is unlikely, however, that such a room was needed at the Rose, where playing stopped in 1603; for, as Hosley points out, "interact music was peculiar to the private theaters, at least down to 1604."[1]

A third level could have been used in *I Henry VI* (b-8) (3.2) when Pucell enters *"on the top, thrusting out a Torch burning,"* or in *The Silver Age* (b-2) (I4) when Juno and Iris are *"plac'd in a cloud above,"* or in a number of similar incidents in which the playwright employs terms suggesting places high above the earth rather than indicating a specific level above the stage. However, there is not a single stage direction or anything in the movement of the plays of the Rose to indicate clearly that a third level was required.

Eight consecutive entries in Henslowe's *Diary* (Foakes and Rickert, p. 13) indicate that the facade of the Rose was limited to two levels:

pd for sellynge the Rome over the tyerhowsse . . . . .x^s
pd for wages to the plasterer . . . . .iiii^s
pd for sellinges my lords Rome . . . . .xiiii^s
pd for makenge the penthowsse shed at the tyeringe
howsse doore as foloweth pd for owld tymber . . . . .x^s
pd for bordes & quarters . . . . .xviii^s vi^d
pd for bordes . . . . .xiii^s vi^d
pd for naylles & henges & bowlltes . . . . .xix^s
pd the carpenters for wages . . . . .ix^s

The first three entries may be considered together, for they refer to wages paid for the preparation of rooms for plastering and for the actual job of plastering.[2] These rooms are on the same level, in the story over the tiring-house; for it is doubtful that "my lords Rome" would have been located in a third story, from which it would have been difficult to see and hear the plays. It is also doubtful that "my lords Rome" would have been located on the level with the main stage—the province of the gallants and their friends. One more point may be made about the first three entries: the work they refer to was extensive, costing Henslowe twenty-eight shillings—equal to wages paid to one man for about twenty-eight days of work.[3]

Because the eight entries are set apart from those that precede and those that follow, it is reasonable to infer that the entries are concerned with closely related projects: 1) the ceiling and plastering of the underside of the roofs (the ceilings) in the rooms over the tiring-house, and 2) the extension of those ceilings forward over the main stage in what Henslowe refers to as "makenge the penthowsse shed at the tyeringe howsse doore." Thus, as I interpret these entries, it may be concluded that the "penthowsse shed" was used by Henslowe as a term to describe the "shadow"—the platform supporting the heavens or the "cover" over the stage. And it may be further concluded that the facade, extending from the floor of the stage to the underside of the platform supporting the heavens, had but two stories: the story in which the tiring-house was located and the story containing "the Rome over the tyerhowsse."

It must be admitted that the meaning of the term "penthowsse shed at the tyeringe howsse doore" is not clear. It seems unlikely, however, that the "penthowsse shed" refers to an awninglike structure immediately above a door leading into the tiring-house from outside the theater. No such structure appears in the pictures of the outside of the Rose, and we have two reliable pictures showing a door at the side of the theater, which presumably leads into the tiring-house spaces: Norden's maps made in 1593 and in 1600 (plates 2 and 3).

It is also unlikely that the term "penthowsse shed" refers to an awninglike structure at a door leading from the stage into the tiring-house. In the first place, no such structure can be found in any of the extant pictures of Elizabethan theaters, unless one wishes to consider the awninglike projection in the vignette from the title page of *Messallina* (1640) as a "penthowsse shed." Moreover, the expenditure of seventy shillings for such items as "owld tymber," "bordes and quarters," "naylles & henges & bowlltes," and wages for carpenters for approximately nine days of work indicates that something more substantial than an awninglike structure was involved.[4]

The term "shed" is defined in the *Oxford English Dictionary* (from a 1481 citation) as "a slight structure built for shelter or storage or for use as a workshop, either attached as a lean-to to a permanent building or separate; often with open front or sides. The special purpose is indicated by a defining word prefixed, as *cow-*, *cart-*, *goat-*, *tool-shed*." The term "penthouse" is defined in the *Oxford English Dictionary* (from ca. 1325) as "a small building erected as a 'lean-to' to another . . ." and (from 1483) as "any smaller building attached to a main one."

It may be inferred that the special purpose of the "shed" was indicated by Henslowe when he prefixed "penthowsse" as a defining word. That is, the "shed" was a "structure built for shelter . . . with open front or sides" above the penthouse (a "smaller building attached to a main one"). The "penthowsse" itself was apparently a small structure like the one shown in "Theatrum Orbi" in Robert Fludd's *Ars Memoriae*. And like the one illustrating Fludd's work (plate 6), it was located above the door (the gates) leading from the main stage into the tiring-house.

The hut, which was erected on the platform that I have identified as "the penthowsse shed at the tyeringe howsse doore," was added at the Rose at about the time Henslowe made the entries referring to the "penthowsse shed." The eight entries follow one dated 13 April 1592. Greg (2:47–48) is of the opinion that they refer to work in connection with the opening of the Rose for Lord Strange's men in February 1592, but he is not certain whether the work was done before Strange's men came to the theater or while it was idle between 22 June and 29 December 1592. It is possible that the work on the hut was not completed until late in 1592, because Norden does not show a hut above the Rose in his map of the Bankside published in 1593. (He does show a hut above the building in his revised map published in 1600.)

Pictorial evidence indicates that the facade of the Rose had only two levels. Henslowe's playhouse appears in Norden's map of 1593 and in the revision made in 1600 as a round structure provided with a door, above which is a single row of windows.[5] The hut, which we know was placed above the stage, is shown in the map as being above the windows that presumably gave light and ventilation for the spaces located on a level with the "Rome over the tyerhowsse." If the tiring-house had been built with a third level, one would expect Norden to have included another row of windows giving light and air for that level. This he clearly does in his representation of the Bear Garden in the map of 1600.[6]

OBSTRUCTIONS ON THE STAGE

The only obstructions that seem surely to have been on the main stage of the Rose were two posts, presumably columns supporting the heavens (Appendix C, "Obstructions on the Stage"). Obstructions of some kind, perhaps a break or breaks in the back wall, are also suggested by overlooking-overhearing episodes contained in almost every play that was presented at the Rose theater.

The posts or columns are mentioned six times in four plays. In a comic incident in *Friar Bacon* (b-4) (1611–14), Miles is directed to *"Sit down and knocke your head"* against a post which is mentioned in the dialogue. Two columns seem to figure in two night scenes in *Englishmen for My Money* (a-2) (1654–61) and (1700–1702), in which two foolish men stumble around in the dark and on both occasions run into both of the columns, again referred to in the dialogue as posts. The same kind of scene occurs in *Two Angry Women* (a-2) (2249–51): "*Coom*. A plague on this poast, I would the Carpenter had bin hangd that set it up." In the *Spanish Tragedy* (a-3) a man is bound to a stake, presumably one of the columns, to be burned to death (1132). Later he is released (1169).

The suggestion is strong in *John a Kent* (b-7) that the columns supporting the heavens may have been used to represent trees. A tree is mentioned in several places (1026–30, 1133) and actors walk about a tree (1393). In one instance (835–36) the author suggests that an actor descend onto the stage from a tree, perhaps one of the columns, "*the fourth out of a tree, if possible it may be*." On the other hand, trees were placed on stage as in *Fortunatus* (b-1) (1.3.19) and in one instance in this play (4.1.67–92) a man climbs one of these trees. In short, all that can be determined about the uses made of the columns on stage is that people ran into them, were tied to them, and possibly climbed up or slid down them in some plays in which it is suggested that the columns were used to represent trees.

The possible uses made of the columns tell us little about their size or location, other than to suggest that they were not too large for a man to climb. The contract for the Fortune (Foakes and Rickert, pp. 306–10) likewise offers little information about the size of the columns except to indicate that the theater was approximately thirty-three feet high, from the ground to the underside of the hut, a fact which permits one to estimate that the columns at the Rose were about that high. The columns had to be large and strong, especially if only two of them were used to support the penthouse shed and the hut. I have arbitrarily scaled the columns in my model of the Rose (plate 1) to indicate that they were approximately twenty-four inches in diameter. I have also assumed that the columns at the Rose were round in this circular building because Henslowe is quite specific in the contract for the square Fortune "that all the princypall and maine postes of the saide ffr ame and Stadge forwarde shalbe square."

The location of the columns on the stage of the Rose was apparently determined by the location and the size of the hut that they supported. Norden's map of 1600 and *Civitas Londini* (plates 3 and

4) both show a structure that seems to have extended over the stage to the middle of the yard. The platform upon which the hut at the Fortune sat may have reached the middle of the yard, because the contract requires a "shadowe or cover over the saide stadge" and specifies that the stage extend "to the middle of the yarde." It may be argued that the platform and hut above it were, among other things, needed to protect the actors and their costumes.

I am inclined to believe, however, that the huts in the Norden map of 1600 and *Civitas Londini* (plates 3 and 4) may have been distorted by the tiny scale of the theater buildings shown in those pictures. The "shadowe or cover over the saide stadge" at the Fortune did not necessarily have to cover the entire stage and extend with the stage "to the middle of the yarde." It may be argued that a cover extending to the middle of the yard would have a tendency to cast too much of a shadow over the stage and make it difficult to see the actors' faces in the out-of-doors playhouse.

The De Witt sketch of the Swan shows a cover that reaches only to the center of the stage where it is supported by two columns (plate 5). In my model (plate 1) I show the largest of the three huts as a rectangular structure set on a level with the eves of the theater building and rising well above it. The large hut extends forward to about the middle of the stage and is supported by two columns set on a line and spaced at equal intervals, approximately fifteen feet and two inches from each other and from the nearest flanking wall.

Even though the evidence is silent about other obstructions on the stage of the Rose, the possibility must be noted that some kind of obstruction may have been present in or near the back wall and used for the fifty-eight overlooking-overhearing episodes that occur in twenty-eight plays.[7]

These overlooking-overhearing episodes must be distinguished from similar episodes such as those in which persons conceal themselves either by going behind "the arras," as Polonius does, or by getting "into the box tree," as Malvolio's tormentors do. We may reach some conclusion about the way these overlooking-overhearing episodes were presented and determine whether an obstruction was used in staging them by considering a typical episode of this kind, such as occurs in *The Shoemakers' Holiday* (a-2) (3.1.1–28). The action begins with the direction, *"Enter Lord*

Maior, and master Scotte," who have come "To be a witnesse to a wedding knot,/ Betwixt yong maister Hammon and . . . [Rose]" (1–3). The Lord Mayor says (4), "O stand aside, see where the lovers come." Then *"Enter Hammon, and Rose."* The young people speak several lines while the Lord Mayor and Scotte remain silent. Finally the observers speak to each other but are presumably not heard by Hammon and Rose (20–21). The young people continue their conversation until the observers make their presence known (29): "*L. Ma.* Why how now lovers, are you both agreede?"

In the episode just traced, the following pattern emerges, one common to many overlooking-overhearing episodes: the observers become aware of someone they intend to watch and then announce the fact, often in an aside if only one person is watching, using the term "*stand close,*" or, less frequently, as in the instance just considered, "*stand aside.*" The action and conversation of those who are watched is often interrupted by dialogue between the watchers, or by asides, but those observed are unaware of the watchers. The episode usually ends with the observers coming forward and making their presence known to the observed. This pattern is followed rather regularly in overlooking-overhearing episodes.

Obviously some convention allowed onlookers and listeners to be on stage unobserved by other characters. It is possible that some kind of obstruction, not now identifiable, was present and used in staging these episodes. It seems more likely, however, that the onlookers and listeners merely moved back on the cue of "*stand close*" or "*stand aside*" to a position from which they watched, listened to, and discussed the actions of others.

THE STAIRS

The stairs leading from the stage up to the gallery, and presumably providing access to other stairs leading to the hut, are specifically referred to in six plays of the Rose (see Appendix C, "The Stairs"); and their existence is suggested by references to the gallery and places above the stage in twenty-seven plays (see Appendix C, "The Gallery"); nevertheless, the evidence tells very little about the stairs, probably because they were located behind the walls of the stage.

The fact that the stairs were placed behind the walls is shown in a number of instances in which people in the gallery or on the walls talk to others on the stage and then announce that they will descend. During the time the actor on the wall descends, a person on stage often speaks about something that must not, for the sake of the plot, be overheard by the actor who is descending. For example, in *The Blind Beggar* (b-3) (370–74), Elimine, standing somewhere above the main stage, announces that she is descending:

> *Elimine*. . . . Ile meet thee straight.
> *Count*. Oh I thanke you I am much beholding to you,
> I sawe her in the tower and now she is come downe,
> Lucke to this patch and to this velvet gowne.
> *Enter Elimine and Bragadino A Spaniard following her*.

The "patch" and "this velvet gowne" that the count mentions are parts of his disguise about which Elimine must not be informed.

The stairs were readily accessible to the gates and apparently to at least one of the discovery spaces. In *Titus Andronicus* (a-4) (A3–A4), Saturninus and Bassianus clamor at the gates for admission to the *"Senate house,"* that is, the gallery, and are admitted: *"They goe up into the Senate house."* The case is similar in *John a Kent* (b-7) (847–908) which contains an episode calling for people to appear in the gallery after they have left the stage through the gates. In *The Death of Robert* (a-2) (3021–34), Bruce descends from the gallery and comes through the door representing the gates to Windsor Castle: "Of Windsor Castle here the keys I yield." In *The Golden Age* (b-2) (I1v), Jupiter apparently leaves through a discovery space to go up to Danaë in the gallery; he could not have used the gates because they represented the gates to the outside of the Fort of Brass. Of course he could have left the stage through a door at one side of the stage, but it seems more likely that he would have used a discovery space nearer the gates, from which place stairs leading to the gallery were clearly accessible.

The accessibility of the stairs to the gates and presumably to one or both of the discovery spaces is indicated by the speed with which actors descended from the gallery and entered onto the main stage. Bruce, for example, descends in *The Death of Robert* (a-2) (3026–34) during the time required for the delivery of eight lines; and, as was noted, he seems to have come onto the stage through the gates. Danaë is apparently brought into the gallery in her bed in *The Golden Age* (b-2) (I1v) and eleven lines are spoken while Jupiter leaves the stage (presumably through a discovery space), goes up the stairs, and enters to her in the gallery. Eleven lines are spoken as Titus descends to Tamora in *Titus Andronicus* (a-4) (I3v–I4), and three are delivered while Elimine comes down from the gallery to the main stage in *The Blind Beggar* (b-3) (370–74). One cannot be sure about the openings Titus and Elimine used when they come onto the stage. But they certainly used stairs located behind the walls of the main stage, and the stairs were readily accessible to the gates and to one or both of the discovery spaces.

9

The Places above the Stage

ALTHOUGH references are plentiful to the several places located above the stage and used in presenting plays at the Rose, those references yield little specific information about them beyond what can be gathered from their names: the gallery, the penthouse and the window, "my lords Rome," and the heavens.

Richard Hosley believes that Shakespeare's plays were "designed for production in a theatre having a gallery over the stage essentially similar to the Lords' room shown in the Swan drawing."[1] The plays given at the Rose required a raised place for playing that was located behind the stage and divided by a bay-window-like structure, a penthouse, attached to the wall of the stage just above the tiring-house doors, that is, "the gates." I find nothing to suggest that the gallery at the Rose and "my lords Rome" were identical. Hosley insists that "the gallery shown in the Swan drawing is not an 'upper stage' in the usual sense of that rather inappropriate and in some respects misleading term."[2] Certainly the several places for playing above the stage at the Rose should not be mistaken for independent stages. I know of no scene that is played completely from beginning to end in one of the places above the stage; regularly actors appearing above the stage are joined in action with players below them on the stage.

The principal place for playing on the level above the stage of the Rose was the gallery running along the back wall from one side of the stage to the other (plates 1 and 15). The gallery was used in twenty-seven plays given at the Rose to represent such places as: walls above a stronghold, or towers, or an upper room or chamber of some kind (see Appendix C, "The Gallery"). The gallery seems also to have been used to represent elevated places, as in *Two Angry Women* (a-2) where Mistress Barnes remarks, "Here Ile set my torch upon this hill." Of the several uses made of the gallery, one, its use in besieging episodes to represent the walls above a stronghold, is sufficient to show its location. Typically in besieging episodes the defenders come onto the walls (the gallery) and talk to those seeking admission at the gates. In *George a Green* (b-3) (295–99), for example, James seeks admission at the gates of Sir John a Barley's house, and then, *"Enter Jane a Barley upon the walles"* to deny his request. Two instances in which people appear on the walls in *John a Kent* (b-7) and refuse to admit others at the gates also occur (900–20 and 1447–88). And of course a besieging episode begins the action in *Titus Andronicus* (a-4) (A3). Clearly the gallery that is used in these episodes to represent walls must be located above the "gates" and between doors on *"one side"* and *"the other side"* of the stage.

Some indication as to the height of the gallery above the main stage is provided by references in the plays of the Rose to attempts to scale the walls—to climb up to the gallery from the main stage. In *A Knack to Know an Honest Man* (b-3) (995–96), Zepheron directs his soldiers: "If any shall attempt to scale these walls,/Assault him, and kill him if you can." In one instance it is suggested that a man did climb up to the gallery with the aid of "hooks," but this action in *The Jew of Malta* (b-5) (F1) is merely reported by Pilia-borza, who tells the "Curtezane" that "I Clamber'd up with my hooks" to the Jew's countinghouse. According to the dialogue and stage directions, the walls are scaled in *David and Bathsheba* (b-9). The action begins with David's enemies calling down from the walls (201–02), "If ye dare assay to scale this tower,/Our angrie swords shall smite ye to the ground." David's forces respond (220–28):

> *Joab*. Assault ye valiant men of Davids host,
> And beat these railing dastards from their dores.
> > *Assault, and they win the Tower, and Joab speakes above*
> Thus have we won the Tower, which we will keepe,
> Maugre the sonnes of Ammon, and of Syria.
> > *Enter Cusay beneath.*
> *Cus*. Where is lord Joab leader of the host?
> *Joab*. Here is lord Joab, leader of the host.
> Cusay come up, for we have won the hold. *He comes.*

Cusay speaks as he ascends to the gallery, apparently on a scaling ladder of some kind. Also, in *II Tamburlaine* (b-6) (K8) a stage direction reads "*Alarme, and they scale the walles.*" A stage direction in still another besieging scene, *I Henry VI* (b-8) (2.1), indicates that ladders were used to scale the walls: "*Enter Talbot, Bedford, and Burgundy, with scaling Ladders.*" The dialogue reveals that they scale the walls at three places.

Only one instance is found in the plays of the Rose in which people clearly descend from the walls directly onto the main stage. In *I Henry VI* (b-8) (2.1), "*The French leape ore the walles in their shirts.*" But this incident takes place immediately after the English forces have scaled the walls with ladders. It seems likely that the French left the walls by scrambling down the ladders that the English used in ascending the walls. Hercules is called upon in *The Brazen Age* (b-2) (L2) to come onto the stage, possibly from the gallery, but one cannot be sure just how this was done: "*Enter Hercules from a rocke above.*" In one instance, *Massacre at Paris* (b-3), a man is murdered in the gallery and his body is thrown down onto the main stage. Here, however, it seems that a dummy was used, for Guise says (375): "The Duke of Guise stampes on thy liveles bulke." Moreover, in a subsequent scene (592–93) they hang the murdered man on a tree:

> 2. . . . lets hang him herre upon this tree.
> 1. Agreede.   *They hang him.*

It is not likely that an actor would be called upon to withstand such treatment. It can be inferred from the instances mentioned that the gallery was probably too high above the main stage for actors to reach it except by ladder and that it was impossible for them to jump or to be dropped from that place without injuring themselves. The evidence does not provide specific information about the height above the main stage of the balcony level. I have therefore chosen again to use the figures found in the contract for the Fortune (Foakes and Rickert, pp. 306–10). According to the contract, the Fortune was placed on a foundation at least one foot above the ground and consisted of three stories: one twelve feet high, a second eleven feet high, and a third nine feet high. The theater reconstructed according to these figures, then, was thirty-three feet high—from the ground to the underside of the platform that supported the hut.

I have shown in chapter 3 that the height of the stage at the Rose was about five feet above the level of the ground. The facade that extended from the floor of the stage to the underside of the platform that supported the hut would thus have been about twenty-eight feet high. If the facade was limited to two levels, as seems likely, it is not unreasonable to assume that the floor of the gallery was about fifteen feet above the stage and that the distance from the floor of the gallery to the underside of the platform supporting the hut was about thirteen feet.

The physical characteristics of the gallery are suggested by a scene in *II Tamburlaine* (b-6) (K6v–K8). The scene begins with a stage direction (K6v): "*Enter the Governour of Babylon upon the walles, with others.*" The governor and Maximus each have a long speech; a stage direction then indicates (K7): "*Enter another kneeling to the Governour.*" The governor and "Another" each deliver speeches, after which a stage direction reads (K7v): "*Enter Theridimas and Techelles, with other Souldiers*" onto the main stage. After a few lines are exchanged between the governor and Tamburlaine's soldiers on the main stage, a stage direction indicates (K8): "*Alarme, and they scale the walles.*"

The first thing to note about this scene from *II Tamburlaine* is that only three people speak from the gallery, although the stage direction (K6v) indicates that the governor enters "with others." No instance was found in the twenty-seven plays using the gallery in which more than ten people appeared together in the gallery at the same time, this number appearing in *John a Kent* (b-7) (918–20). The next greatest number appearing together in the gallery is indicated by a stage direction in the same play (1447–48): "*John a Kent in his owne habit, denvyle, Griffin, Powesse, Evan, Countesse, Sydanen, Marian, and Shrimp on the walles.*" The fact that no more than ten people ever appear together in the gallery indicates, I believe, that it was a relatively narrow passageway.

A second point to note about the scene cited from *II Tamburlaine* is that physical action in the gallery is restricted. The one bit of movement provided for in the scene from *II Tamburlaine* is the entrance of "*another kneeling to the Governour.*" It is significant that in besieging episodes in which the walls of a stronghold are scaled the defenders never resist with vigor for very long. Perhaps the most vigorous action taking place in the gallery in any of the plays of the Rose is the murder of the admiral in *The Massacre at Paris* (b-3) (355–75). Here a bed is brought into the gallery and a wounded man, apparently represented by a dummy, is stabbed and thrown down to the stage. The largest properties used in the gallery were the beds in *A Massacre at Paris* and in *The Golden Age* (b-2).

Finally, the scene cited from *II Tamburlaine* indicates that the action takes place near the front of the opening. The governor on the walls of Babylon talks to Tamburlaine's soldiers on the main stage. This action is characteristic of all of the scenes played before strongholds but is not limited to those scenes. Abigall in *The Jew of Malta*, for example, talks to her father and *"Throwes downe bags."*

Except in a few instances as in *A Knack to Know an Honest Man*, in which the gallery serves as a passageway between upstairs rooms (1051–64, 1071–110), action in the gallery is directed towards the stage. Obviously a rail or wall of some kind was present along the front of the gallery to prevent the actors there from toppling into the midst of those on the stage with whom they talked. The fact that the action in the gallery regularly takes place near the front of the opening suggests, of course, that the gallery did not project out of the wall very far, if at all, and that the actors had to be near the front of the opening in order to be seen.

A familiar stage stunt, which is sometimes cited as evidence for the presence of a trapdoor in the floor of the gallery, indicates that the balustrade before the gallery was a solid wall or parapet. A reasonable explanation of what happens when Barabas is supposed to fall into the cauldron in *The Jew of Malta* (b-5) (K2) is to assume that he fell to the floor and, hidden by a solid wall before the gallery, crawled to stairs which he descended. The playwright effectively masks this business by providing that "A warning-peece shall be shot off from the Tower." The stage direction effecting this business reads: "*A charge, the cable* [for the supposed trap] *cut, A Caldron discovered.*" Certainly Barabas was given ample time, while the audience recovered from the shock of *"A charge"* being fired, to scramble down the stairs and climb into his *"Caldron"* before the trick was discovered. A solid wall at the front of the gallery, however, would have been required to mask this bit of stage trickery.

I have found no evidence to indicate that the gallery was provided with curtains. Danaë suggests in *The Golden Age* (I2v) to

Jupiter "for modesties chast law,/ Before you come to bed, the curtaines draw." The bed, it seems, is located in the gallery for this episode; and, in the absence of other evidence for curtains before the gallery, one may assume they were attached to the bed. In any event, *"The bed is drawne in"* immediately after Danaë makes her request.

THE PENTHOUSE AND THE WINDOW

In accordance with the principle of center nucleus accent, which Kernodle believes to underlie Elizabethan stage architecture, the gallery at the Rose had centered before it a penthouse.[3] This structure is mentioned by Henslowe (Foakes and Rickert, p. 13) in his reference to "makenge the penthowsse shed at the tyeringe howsse doore." The penthouse is, however, distinct from the "penthowsse shed," which was a "structure built for shelter . . . with open front or sides" above the penthouse (a "smaller building attached to a main one"). In other words, the "shed" was the platform on which the "hut" was erected, and the underside of the platform was that part of the stage often referred to as "the shadow" or "the covering." The penthouse was a bay-window-like structure located directly above the gates, as shown in Fludd's "Theatrum Orbi" (plate 6). Unlike the penthouse in the Fludd drawing, the one at the Rose (plate 1) had a hinged window facing the audience. This window is probably related to the entry in the *Diary* (Foakes and Rickert, p. 13): "pd for naylles & henges & bowlltes." Unfortunately the bottom portion of the leaf on which this item appears has been torn from the *Diary* and other possible entries containing details about the penthouse lost. In the absence of more specific details, I show the penthouse as a bay window with three sashes—one of which was hinged and swung out towards the audience (plate 21).

A hinged window that swung out towards the audience was used to stage such scenes as the one ending with a Senecan tableau in *The Death of Robert* (a-2) (2770–80). Several things may be learned about the penthouse and the window by tracing the action through the tableau in this Robin Hood play. Preparation for the scene begins with the entrance of Lady Bruce and Brand (1887). The woman is forced to enter a door and go up a set of stairs, "Goe in, goe in: its higher up the staires" (1894). Here a practical door is used because a stage direction (1921) specifies that *"Hee seemes to locke a doore."* Because the gates are the only doors on the stage of the Rose that were capable of being opened and shut, or locked, it may be concluded that Lady Bruce left the stage through the gates and after hesitating at the foot of the stairs went on up into the "tower," where she and her infant son were imprisoned and starved to death.

Further preparation for the tableau is made with the report of a messenger to King John (2224–32):

> Yoūg Bruse, my Lord, hath gotten Windsor castle,
> Slaine Blunt your Constable, and those that kept it:
> And finding in a tower his mother dead,
> With his young brother starv'd and famished:
> That every one may see the rufull sight,
> In the thick wall he a wide windowe makes:
> And as he found them, so he lets them be
> A spectacle to every commer by,
> That heaven and earth, your tyrant shame may see.

The scene ending with the Senecan tableau begins as a besieging scene with a stage direction (2735): *"Drum. Enter Chester, Mowbray, Souldiers: Lester, Richmond at an other* [door]: *Souldiers."* The action takes place before the gates of Windsor as King John indicates with his first speech following his entrance (2757), "To Windsor welcome, Hubert." Young Bruce enters above and King John calls to him (2768–70):

> Why stand ye Lords, and see this traitour pearcht
> Upon our Castles battlements so proude;
> Come downe young Bruse, set ope the castle gates.

Bruce replies (2776—78):

> I will not ope the gates, the gate I will:
> The gate where thy shame, and my sorrowe sits.
> See my dead mother, and her famisht sonne.

Eventually young Bruce agrees to open the gates to King John (3021–26):

I will come downe: but first farewell dear mother.
> *Kisse her.*

Farewell poore little George, my pretty brother.
Now will I shut my shambles in againe.
Farewell, farewell.
In everlasting blisse your sweete soules dwell.

This speech indicates that before Bruce descended, he went to the place where his dead mother and brother were sitting and (after kissing the mother and bidding his brother farewell) closed "the gate where thy [King John's] shame . . . sits." Seven lines are spoken on stage while Bruce descends, enters the main stage, and says to King John (3034): "Of Windsor Castle here the keys I yield."

This Senecan tableau indicates that the Rose theater had a place for acting, a room, located above the stage. This place, often referred to as a "tower," was accessible to the gallery and could also be reached by going through the gates (centered in the wall at the rear of the stage) and mounting stairs behind the wall of the stage. This place used to represent a tower was provided with a shutter that was capable of being opened to discover a person sitting or standing in an opening. Furthermore the place was large enough for an actor to walk around the person sitting in the chair, kiss him, and close the shutter—presumably from the inside. Every reference to "a window," or "the window," and to a place, such as a room, or a tower, above the main stage of the Rose (Appendix C, "The Penthouse and the Window") is consistent with what we know about the location of the penthouse, as Henslowe describes it (Foakes and Rickert, p. 13), "at the tyeringe howsse doore."

It may be illuminating to consider some of the instances in other plays of the Rose in which the penthouse and the window are apparently involved. In *The Jew of Malta* (b-5) (H3), Barabas says that Pilia-borza knows how to "climbe up to my Counting-house window." Bel-imperia, imprisoned in *The Spanish Tragedy* (a-3) in an upstairs room, shows herself *"at a window"* (1724), presumably the same window from which she earlier had dropped (1225) a letter to Hieronimo written in her own blood. Near the beginning of *A Looking Glass for London* (b-6) (150–60), Oseas the prophet is brought in (presumably into the penthouse) by an angel *"and set downe over the Stage in a Throne."* Oseas speaks at the end of the several scenes, a kind of chorus, until the angel returns (1824) and he is "taken away" (1846). *I Henry VI* (b-8) (1.4) contains a reference to a "Grate" in "this Turrets top" through which the English leader, Salisbury, looking down into the city of Orleans, is shot by a boy with a linstock.[4] Though the directions and dialogue are not as explicit as one might wish, it seems that the situation in *I Henry VI* may have been reversed in *A Massacre at Paris* (b-3) where a soldier shoots down onto the stage from the window (103–05):

> Stand in some window opening neere the street
> And when thou seest the Admirall ride by,
> Discharge thy musket and perfourme his death.

These orders are executed (227–29): "*As they are going, the Souldier dischargeth his Musket at the Lord Admirall.*"

Fortunatus (b-1) contains an incident which tells something about the size of the penthouse. Two men are taken (one at a time) and shackled together in stocks located above the stage in a place which is referred to as "yonder tower" (5.2.87), alluded to in the same scene (122) as "this prison," and described still later in the same scene (183) as "this towre." The men talk together and at least three men must be in the "towre" when the second is placed in the stocks.

The width of the window is indicated by action in *Faustus* (b-5) (4.2.1319–60) in which Mephistopheles apparently places "Two spreading hornes most strangely fastened/ Upon the head of yong Benvolio," who has fallen asleep with his head lolling outside of the window. The window is not wide enough for Benvolio to pull his head back inside once the horns have been placed there. Faustus finally directs Mephistopheles to "remove his hornes" (1360).

In reconstructing the penthouse at the Rose, I have attached to the theater, at a point immediately above the gates, a bay window-like structure the same width as the gates. It projects forward over the gates and has centered in it a hinged sash about three feet wide and five feet six inches high.

MY LORDS' ROOMS

An entry in the *Diary* (Foakes and Rickert, p. 13) "pd for sellinges my lords Rome" may be interpreted as "paid for the ceilings in my lords' rooms," indicating that there were two or more rooms for my lords—unless one wishes to argue that Henslowe was paying for several ceilings in a single room. Certainly the term "sellinges" is not a gerund but a substantative with a plural ending, referring to the ceilings prepared for the work of the plasterer mentioned in the preceding entry: "paid for wages to the plasterer."

In chapter 8, in my discussion of the facade of the stage I have argued that "my lords Rome" was located on the same level as "the Rome over the tyerhowsse." Now the possibility that the gallery at the Rose and "my lords Rome" were the same place may be set aside for a more plausible arrangement.[5] The use made of the gallery in presenting plays was so extensive (Appendix C, "The Stairs," "The Gallery," "The Penthouse and the Window") that it is unlikely that it was used with any degree of regularity as a place for spectators—especially the nobility. Moreover, the gallery was awkwardly placed for spectators, offering in most cases little more than a view of the backs of the actors.

Several episodes in plays given at the Rose required a playing area above the stage in one of the walls that flanked it, from which place actors could watch others playing inside a discovery space or, what is more likely, before one. In *The Spanish Tragedy* (a-3) (4.3) it seems likely that a place above and at the side of the stage was used by the royal party to watch Hieronimo's play in which he "discovers" the body of Horatio (3045): "*He Shewes his dead sonne.*" At the same time, Revenge and the ghost of Andrea would have been, of necessity, placed in a similar opening on the opposite side of the stage if they were expected to see the discovery of Horatio's body. In another episode from the same play (2.2) Pedringano helps Lorenzo and Balthazar spy on Horatio and Bel-imperia (756): "*Pedringano sheweth all to the Prince, and Lorenzo, placing them in secret.*" A stage direction (769) "*Balthazar above*" locates him at the window, in the gallery, or in a room at one side of the stage. In any case then, Revenge and Andrea had to be above and at one side of the stage in order to view this action, to see the spies and their victims at the same time.

Juno and Iris are apparently placed above and at one side of the stage to watch the flaming mating scene between Jupiter and Semele in *The Silver Age* (b-2) (I4–K1): "*Juno and Iris plac'd in a cloud above"* (plate 22). It does not appear likely that Juno and Iris were in the window: they would have been blocked from the view of the audience and they could not have watched the action when Jupiter descended in the lift from the heavens.

In another Heywood play, *The Brazen Age* (b-2) (I3), "*All the Gods appeare above, and laugh, Jupiter, Juno, Phoebus, Mercury, Neptune,*" when Vulcan traps Mars and Venus in his net. And "*David sits above viewing*" Bathsheba as she is discovered "*with her maid bathing over a spring,*" at the beginning of *David and Bathsheba* (b-9). It is perhaps significant that only gods, or ghosts, or royal persons seem to use the places above and at the sides of the stage, which were normally employed as theater boxes for "my lords."

Two such theater boxes, or lords' rooms, are shown in my model (plate 1) placed directly above the doors on "one side" and "the other side" of the stage in the walls that flanked the stage. Spectators who used the boxes were "over the stage i' the Lords roome" (as Jonson says in 1599), and these boxes contained the best seats in the house from which to see and hear the plays. I show these boxes in my model and floor plan of the Rose (plates 1 and 15) as nine feet six inches deep and extending back along each side of the stage for twenty-two feet nine inches to join at right angles with the gallery in the wall at the rear of the stage. Before each of these boxes I have placed a wall three feet six inches high, similar to the one before the gallery. Although the two rooms may have been divided into several smaller rooms by partitions, I do not attempt to show such divisions. The posts before the boxes and the gallery were suggested by the vignette of the *Theatrum* on the 1616 title page of Jonson's *Workes* (plate 10).

THE HEAVENS

One suspects that Thomas Heywood was providing his readers with an idealized version of the "heavens" at the Rose, for which he wrote many of his early plays, when he describes "the covering of the stage, which wee call the heavens," in a theater supposedly built by Julius Caesar: "In that little compasse were comprehended the perfect modell of the firmament, the whole frame of the heavens, with all grounds of astronomicall conjecture."[6] "That little compasse" at the Rose was the underside of the penthouse shed, a platform supporting the hut and extending forward, like the hut, to the middle of the stage. However, only one reference can be found in the plays of the Rose suggesting that the underside of the penthouse shed may have been decorated to represent "the whole frame of the heavens." The reference is contained, appropriately enough, in Heywood's *The Brazen Age* (b-2) (L3). "*From the heavens discends a hand in a cloud, that from the place where Hercules was burnt, brings up a starre, and fixeth it in the firmament.*"

Of more interest than Heywood's comments upon the design and decoration of the heavens is his observation that it was the place "where upon any occasion their gods descended." The first suggestion that the heavens at the Rose were used by gods is found in a stage direction and confirmed by the dialogue in *A Looking Glass for London* (b-6) (1636–38), produced as an old play beginning 8 March 1592:

> *A hand from out a cloud, threatneth a burning sword.*
> K. *Cili.* Behold dread Prince, a burning sword from heaven,
> Which by a threatning arme is brandished.

This reference suggests that by March 1592 the Rose was provided with a heaven and a trap door or slot in the floor of heaven through which an object, "*a hand from out a cloud*," could be introduced into the action of the play. If the penthouse shed was completed by this time, all that was needed for intruding gods into the little world that was the stage of the Rose was the machinery, a hoisting device and a seat of some kind, and the "hut" to house the equipment.[7]

The first suggestion of the use of the lift at the Rose is found in *Alphonsus of Aragon* (b-6) which was given as an old play on 14 August 1594, and which contains the stage direction (Ind. 1–2): "*After you have sounded thrise, let Venus be let downe from the top of the Stage.*" The play ends (2109–10) with another stage direction: "*Exit Venus. Or if you can conveniently, let a chaire come downe from the top of the stage, and draw her up.*" These directions suggest that the lift was probably used to lower an actor onto the stage but that it was difficult to raise the actor from the floor of the main stage to the heavens. Moreover, the directions anticipate a problem in connection with the use of the lift that was never completely solved at the

Rose; although machinery of some kind, possibly a windlass, was later installed in the heavens, it was never used extensively to raise an actor all the way from the main stage to the heavens.

Faustus (b-5), given at the Rose for the first time as an old play on 2 October 1594, calls for the lift (5.2.2006) in a stage direction which reads: "*Musicke while the Throne descends.*" Here, no one is raised or lowered from the heavens, although we may believe that the throne, which was briefly lowered to give Faustus a glimpse of the heaven he had lost, was elaborately decorated and a rather heavy stage property. In this instance, in which the throne is lowered a short distance from the heavens and apparently raised again, one sees for the first time a practice which was to be repeated.

The lift was first used at the Rose both to lower actors onto the stage and to raise them from it in Heywood's *The Golden Age* (b-2) given at the Rose as a new play on 5 March 1595.[8] Near the end of the play (K2v) is the stage direction: "*Sound a dumbe shew. . . . Jupiter drawes heaven; at which Iris descends and presents him with his Eagle, Crowne and Scepter, and his thunder-bolt. Jupiter first ascends upon the Eagle, and after him Ganimead.*" Following the initial performance of *The Golden Age* the lift was overhauled, presumably in anticipation of Heywood's *The Silver Age* (b-2), a sequel to *The Golden Age*. The *Diary* (Foakes and Rickert, p. 7) shows that Henslowe made extensive alterations and repairs during Lent in 1595, at a total cost of £108.19. Immediately below this list of repairs he makes the following note: "Itm pd for carpenters worke & mackinge the throne In the hevenes the 4 of June 1595" the sum of £7.2.

The throne in the heavens was probably ready for use on 2 May 1595, for a second performance of *The Golden Age*. Certainly the work was completed by 7 May 1595, when *The Silver Age* (b-2) was presented as a new play. It called for the lift to be used at least seven times and possibly nine or more times.[9]

The use of the lift declines markedly in *The Brazen Age* (b-2) presented for the first time on 23 May 1595, as a sequel to *The Silver Age*. The lift is required only twice: "*Medea . . . hangs above in the Aire*" (G2v), and a hand "*descends*" from the heavens in a cloud, to the place where Hercules was burnt, "*brings up a starre, and fixeth it in the firmament*" (L3). Heywood wrote one more play for the Rose, *Jupiter and Io* (b-8), which may have required the use of the lift

(p. 158): "*A noise of thunder. Enter Jupiter in his glory, his Trisull in his hand burning; at sight of whom they stand afrighted.*" If the lift was actually used and Jupiter descended in this play given first on 7 April 1597, it is the last extant play written for the Rose that calls for the lift to be used to intrude gods into the world. It seems more likely, however, that the vogue ended with *The Brazen Age* (b-2) in May 1595.

Perhaps the lift may have been used in *Englishmen for My Money* (a-2), a comedy presented in 1598, containing an incident in which an unwelcome suitor is drawn up from the street in a basket and left hanging in front of a house for more than 400 lines (1706–2143). The scene in *David and Bathsheba* (b-9) (1536–645), in which Absalom "hangs by the haire," indicates that some kind of device was worked out, possibly involving the use of the lift. The *Diary* (Foakes and Rickert, p. 217) contains an entry made between 3 and 11 October 1602, showing that Henslowe paid fourteen pence "for poleyes & worckmanshipp for to hange absolome." If the lift was employed, the hanging of Absalom is the last record we have of its use in staging plays at the Rose.

In tracing the development and use of the lift one finds that it was apparently limited from the beginning by the fact that it was difficult to raise actors all the way from the stage floor to the heavens. In only two plays, *The Golden Age* and *The Silver Age*, do stage directions call unmistakably for actors to be raised all the way from the stage floor to the heavens. On the other hand, directions appear as early as 1594 for actors to be let down from the heavens and continue as late as October 1602, to call for the suspension of actors above the main stage. One surmises that Henslowe's experience with the lift in *The Golden Age* and, particularly, in *The Silver Age* was such that, regardless of their theatrical effectiveness, episodes calling for the use of the lift to raise actors from the stage to the heavens no longer found their way into new plays written after *The Silver Age* was produced in 1595. Apparently the way to heaven was difficult, even at the Rose.

10

Synchronous and Successive Staging

THUS FAR I have been concerned with the reconstruction of the stage in Henslowe's Rose theater. My conclusions about that stage have been brought together, for purposes of illustration, in a model built by my colleague Mr. William R. Duffy (plate 1). I should like to turn now to a consideration of the way the stage of the Rose was used in presenting plays. First, however, we ought to look briefly at two of the underlying principles of Shakespearean staging. E. K. Chambers employs the terms "synchronous" as descriptive of staging in the private theaters and "successive" as descriptive of staging in the public theaters (*ES* 3:88). Synchronous staging may be illustrated by the well-known plan for *The Castle of Perseverence* as shown, for instance, in Allardyce Nicoll's *Development of the Theater* (p. 72). About the castle are five seats or scaffolds: God's to the east, Belial's to the north, the World's to the west, Caro's to the south, and Covetousness's to the northeast. Mankind's bed is located beneath the castle. Each of these places remains unchanged throughout the play as the actor representing Mankind moves from one place to another during the course of the play. Two characteristics of this kind of staging are immediately apparent: 1) stage properties remain in view throughout the play regardless of their appropriateness, and 2) space is ordered and foreshortened, so that the distance between two places—God's throne and Belial's seat— is reduced to a few steps on stage.

Synchronous staging, Chambers believes, "proved inadequate to the needs of romanticism, as popular audiences understood it. . . . it gave way, about the time of the building of the permanent the- atres, to the alternative system, by which different localities were represented, not synchronously but successively, and each in its turn had full occupation of the whole field of the stage" (*ES* 3:88). Successive staging may be illustrated by several scenes in *I Henry VI* (b-8). The play opens with the entrance of the funeral procession of Henry V in Westminster Abbey. After the actors in this scene leave the stage, another group comes onto the stage for a new scene (1.2) which is located by one of the speakers who says (200), "At pleasure here we lye, neere Orleance." The location changes when the stage is cleared and an actor comes on (1.3) and announces, "I am come to survey the Tower this day. . . . Open the gates. 'tis Gloster that calls." Later in the play the same opening that represents the gates to the Tower of London apparently becomes "the Citie Gates, the Gates of Roan" (3.2.1424), and still later another entrance to a stronghold when Talbot commands (4.2.1950–51): "Go to the Gates of Burdeaux, Trumpeter,/ Summon their Generall unto the Wall." Chambers insists that one characteristic of successive staging was the removal of properties inappropriate to scenes that followed. The full occupation of the whole stage by a particular scene was not, he thinks (*ES* 3:89), "qualified by the presence in any scene of a property inappropriate to that scene."

Reynolds questions Chambers's idea that synchronous staging was used in private theaters and at court but never in the public theaters (*Red Bull*, p. 1): "How such a distinction could possibly exist when numerous plays were given interchangeably at these producing centers has not been made clear. Certainly such a divergence of practice seems highly improbable." Chambers recognizes that "there are, however, certain scenes in which one *domus* will not suffice, and two or possibly even three must be represented" (*ES* 3:98). "I think," he continues, "it must be taken that the background of a public stage could stand at need, nor merely for a single *domus*, but for a 'city'" (*ES* 3:100). In short, Chambers and Reynolds both recognize that the principle underlying the presentation of Shakespearean plays involves a fusion of synchronous and successive staging practices. Reynolds and Chambers disagree mainly about the use of stage properties. Chambers does not believe that the "audience had to watch a coronation through a fringe of trees or to pretend unconsciousness while the strayed lovers in a forest dodged each other round the corners of a derelict 'state'" (*ES* 3:89). Reynolds cites the passage from Chambers about the "derelict 'state'" in observing (*Red Bull*, p. 57) "that no such chair with a dais could be quickly put in place or removed. When the throne recurs in two or more scenes in the same play, it seems likely it remained wherever it was, at least as long as there was use for it; and—if not too much in the way—perhaps longer."

Both authorities reach their conclusions about the principles of Shakespearean staging by attempting finally to reconcile the practices found in the plays with the De Witt sketch of the Swan. Chambers says (*ES* 3:101):

Working then from the Swan stage, and only departing in any essential from De Witt's drawing by what appears to be, at any rate for theatres other than the Swan, the inevitable addition of a back curtain, we find no insuperable difficulty in accounting for the setting of all the types of scenes recognizable in sixteenth-century plays. The great majority of them, both out-of-door scenes and hall scenes, were acted on the open stage, under the heavens, with no more properties and practicable terrains than could reasonably be carried on by actors, lowered from the heavens, raised by traps, or thrust on by frames and wheels.

Reynolds observes (*Red Bull*, pp. 131–32):

The hard fact remains that the Swan picture permits no permanently curtained rear stage at all without structural rearrangement. . . . A possible reconciliation is suggested by various points already presented in earlier chapters, but not so far brought together in this connection. To state the idea as quickly and briefly as possible, it is this: instead of a permanently placed rear stage, a structural part of the theater, was there perhaps a curtained framework easily removable, and so not used in all plays and, as it happened, not present on the Swan stage at the time of De Witt's visit? Such a framework is at least a possible way to provide a discoverable space on the Swan stage with no fundamental change in construction.

Reynolds and Chambers have been misled, I believe, in their conclusions about the principles underlying stagecraft in Shakespearean England by these attempts to reconcile the practices found in the plays with the De Witt sketch of the Swan theater. The simple fact, as Beckerman has pointed out in his *Shakespeare at the Globe* (p. 100), is that plays written for the first Globe could not have been presented on a stage like the one shown in the sketch of the Swan unless changes were made to that stage. Certainly the plays of the Rose theater could not have been given on a stage like the one shown in the De Witt sketch without altering it. And I have found nothing in the plays of the Rose or in the Henslowe records to suggest that the stage of the Rose theater was provided with "a curtained framework easily removable . . . to provide a discoverable space" as Reynolds posits for the Red Bull (p. 132).

Insofar as staging at the Rose is concerned, we can reconcile the differences between Chambers and Reynolds. The practices followed in presenting plays in Henslowe's theater as we have described it would have involved the principles both of synchronous and successive staging, resulting in a fusion of medieval stagecraft with a particularly Elizabethan adaptation of the Vitruvian stage.

11

Medieval and Classical Staging Practices

IN RECONSTRUCTING the stage of the Rose, I have regularly referred to a number of staging practices that involved the use of the several parts of the stage including the trap, the gates, the openings in the walls about the stage, the penthouse, the gallery, and the lift. My aim has been to show that those features were present and arranged much as I have reconstructed them in the model (plate 1). It may be enlightening, therefore, to come at the problem from another direction, to show how the stage was used in presenting plays and to point out that it could have accommodated all the plays known to have been given there.

The practices followed in staging plays at the Rose do not seem to differ greatly from those followed in other out-of-doors public playhouses in use while Shakespeare was living. They were basically medieval practices, developing mainly out of the stagecraft of Greece and Rome. As Dr. Wickham observes, "The mediaeval theatre grew up under the shadow of its Greek and Roman forbears and it was to this past that it turned for enlightenment and instruction with ever increasing vigour from the twelfth century to the sixteenth" (*EES* 1:309).

Elements of medieval stagecraft (including its classical antecedents) are evident in a number of the practices followed in presenting plays of the Rose. Many of these, however, make very little demand upon the stage and it is this group that will be discussed first. Two openings are required when two processions enter and meet on stage. Otherwise, most of the seventeen practices described in this chapter require no more than an opening through which an actor or a group of actors can come onto the stage and leave it. I have drawn examples of these practices from both a-list and b-list plays. My purpose is to show that these practices are not restricted to the plays in either list and, incidentally, to document the fact that there is no measurable difference in the kind or clarity of the evidence provided by the plays in the a- or the b-lists. By extension, this suggests that the practices were widespread in the Elizabethan theater.

PROLOGUE, PRESENTER, OR CHORUS

Plays of the Rose frequently begin with a prologue, a presenter, or a chorus. Their function varies from play to play. In *Sir John Oldcastle* (a-1), for example, the prologue is used to explain that the subject of the play, Lord Cobham, is treated sympathetically. In Heywood's *Ages* (b-2 plays), Homer is used as a chorus to provide unity for the trilogy and to effect transitions within the series of episodes that begins with the struggle between Saturn and Jupiter and continues through the adventures of Hercules. In the *Looking Glass for London* (b-6), Oseas the prophet is brought in and seated on a throne over the stage to comment upon the various moralizing episodes. Skelton directs the rehersal, serves as prologue, introduces the dumb shows, takes the role of Friar Tuck in two a-2 plays, *The Downfall of Robert* and *The Death of Robert*. And in the second play he engages in conversation with a chorus to provide transition from the Robin Hood story to the Matilda episode.

CHORUS OR EPILOGUE TO END THE PLAY

The chorus that speaks at the end of *Faustus* is perhaps the best-known example of the use of a chorus or an epilogue to end one of the plays of the Rose. Homer appears and speaks at the end of each of Heywood's *Ages*, all plays in the b-list. *Fortunatus*, still another b-play, has an epilogue for the performance at court but apparently ended without one when it was presented at the Rose. *The Downfall of Robert* and its sequel, *The Death of Robert*, both end with choruslike passages. In the first of these two a-plays Skelton continues the role of the chorus and announces the matter to be treated in *The Death*. And in the second play, a four-line *"Epilogus"* is appended. Finally, *Sir John Oldcastle* (a-1) is an example of a play that begins with a prologue but does not end with an epilogue or chorus.

REPORTS BY MESSENGERS

Reports are often made by messengers for the purpose of providing background information needed to move the plot forward; such reports frequently enrich the drama by making indirect appeals to the audience to use its imagination. A good example of the several purposes a messenger's report may serve is found at the beginning of *I Henry VI* (b-8) when the Third Messenger appears to the lords attending the funeral of Henry V (1.1.120–52):

> *Win*. What? wherein Talbot overcame, is't so?
> 3. *Mes*. O no: wherein Lord Talbot was O'rethrowne:
> The circumstance Ile tell you more at large.
> The tenth of August last, this dreadfull Lord,
> Retyring from the Siege of Orleance . . .

The next thirty lines provide exposition necessary for the plot: news of Talbot's defeat. They also enrich the play, appealing to the audience's imagination to see and to be caught up in the story in which "valiant Talbot, above humane thought,/ Enacted wonders with his Sword and Lance." Another effective use of reports ends the first act of *II Tamburlaine* (b-6) (G5–G6v), with Techelles and Usumcasane reviewing their triumphs for Tamburlaine. The plot is moved forward in *The Shoemakers' Holiday* (a-2) (2.4) and the audience is given an account of an English victory when Dodger reports to Lincoln about the battle in France that Rowland Lacy avoided.

THE PLAY WITHIN THE PLAY

The use of the play-within-the-play is not one of the more common practices in plays of the Rose. The best known is probably Hieronimo's in *The Spanish Tragedy* (a-3) (4.4.2944–3045). *The Downfall of Robert* (a-2) begins as a play in rehearsal, and *John a Kent* (b-7) includes a play that takes up most of a scene (4.2.1247–392).

DUMB SHOWS

Dumb shows are employed in several plays of the Rose apparently for purposes of exposition and to provide transition from one episode or one section of a play to another. A clear explanation of

the use of these shows is found in *The Four Prentices of London* (b-8)
when a presenter enters and speaks (B4v–C1):

> Thus have you seene these brothers shipt to Sea
>
> . . . .
>
> Now to avoide all dilatory newes,
> Which might with-hold you from the Stories pith,
> And substance of the matter wee entend:
> I must entreat your patience to forbeare,
> Whilst we do feast your eye, and starve your eare.
> For in dumbe shews, which were they writ at large,
> Would aske a long and tedious circumstance:
> Their infant fortunes I will soone expresse.
>
> . . . .
>
> We will make bold to explane it in dumb Showe:
> For from their fortunes all our Scene must grow.

Four episodes follow in pantomime, each devoted to the fortune of
one of the four prentices. At the end of each episode the presenter
explains what is meant by the action in the episode. At the end of
the fourth episode the play picks up one of the brothers, Guy, and
the story is continued through dialogue and stage movement combined. *Captain Stukley* (a-3) uses a chorus and a dumb show to knit
together that portion of Stukley's life which might be called "Com-
icke historie" with his unfortunate end (I4v–K1). Another play in
the a-list, *The Downfall of Robert*, begins as a rehearsal for a play with
the director ordering the cast to

> Goe in, and bring your dumbe scene on the stage,
> And I, as Prologue, purpose to expresse
> The ground whereon our historie is laied.

The director has his cast run through the dumb show twice.

> Sir John, once more bid your dumbe shewes come in:
> That as they passe I may explane them all.

MUSIC

Vocal and instrumental music is used regularly in the plays of the
Rose. Sometimes music appears to be intruded with no more

reason than is found in modern musical comedies. During a scene in
Patient Grissil (a-1), for example, a song is introduced with the
following dialogue (1.2.89):

> *Jan*. Let not thy tongue goe so: sit downe to worke
> And that our labour may not seeme to long,
> Weele cunningly beguile it with a song.
> *Bab*. Doe master for thats honest cousonage.

The lyrics of the song, except for the chorus, are given and after the
song is ended an actor enters and the plot of the play is moved
forward. A stage direction is found in the introduction to *Alphonsus
of Aragon* (b-6) (44–47) calling for the entrance of the muses *"playing
all upon sundrie Instruments."* The play ends with the direction
"Exeunt omnes, playing on their Instruments." After the speech of the
Prologus, *David and Bathsheba* (b-9) (24–26): *"He drawes a curtaine,
and discovers Bethsabe with her maid bathing over a spring: she sings, and
David sits above vewing her."*

DANCE

Like music, dance is often intruded into the action in the plays of
the Rose, primarily, I think, to enrich the drama. Mephistopheles
offers an explanation for the use of dance and other enriching
elements in *Faustus* (b-5) (2.1.470–77):

> *Meph*. I'le fetch him somewhat to delight his mind.
> *Exit*.
> *Enter Devils, giving Crownes and rich apparell to Faustus: they
> dance, and then depart. Enter Mephostophilis.*
> *Faust*. What meanes this shew? speak Mephostophilis.
> *Meph*. Nothing *Faustus* but to delight thy mind,
> And let thee see what Magicke can performe.

Heywood builds much of the first two scenes of *A Woman Killed
with Kindness* (a-2) (A4–B2v) around allusions to dances and dancing; and he ends the second scene with a stage direction which reads
(B2v): *"They dance, Nick dancing, speaks stately and scurvily, the rest after
the Country fashion."* Dance is worked into the play in *David and
Bathsheba* (b-9) in the following episode (781–87):

Abs. Ammon, where be thy shearers and thy men,
That we may powre in plenty of thy vines,
And eat thy goats milke, and rejoice with thee.
Am. Here commeth Ammons shearers and his men,
    Absolon sit and rejoice with me.
Here enter a company of sheepheards, and daunce and sing.

ELABORATE COSTUMES

Henslowe's *Diary* may show something of the importance of elaborate costumes in staging plays at the Rose. He records payments totaling £6 to Thomas Heywood for the play *A Woman Killed with Kindness* (Foakes and Rickert, p. 224). A few entries earlier (p. 223) Henslowe paid out for the company £6.13 for "A womones gowne of black velluett for the playe of A womon kylld wth kyndnes." It will be recalled that the devils entered "*giving Crownes and rich apparell to Faustus*" (470–71) "to delight his minde" during the business of signing over his soul. The importance of costume is also suggested in another b-play, *I Tamburlaine* (A6–A6v). Tamburlaine enters with his followers and soldiers laden with treasure. During the scene, the dialogue suggests that he casts aside some of his garments with the comment:

Lie here ye weedes that I disdaine to weare,
This compleat armor, and this curtle axe,
Are adjuncts more beseeming Tamburlaine.

Peele's *Edward I* (b-9) is linked to production at the Rose in part by an item in Henslowe's *Diary*, in the inventory for 10 March 1598, "i longe-shanckes sewte" which I believe was the king's "sute of Glasse" (Foakes and Rickert, p. 317). A stage direction in the play (C2) reads: "*Enter the nine Lordes of Scotland, with their nine Pages: Gloster, Sussex, king Edward in his sute of Glasse, Queene Elinor, Queene Mother, the King and Queene under a Canopie.*"

FIREWORKS

Plays can be found in both lists calling for the use of fireworks. *Captain Stukley* (a-3) contains what may be described as a long dumb show before the battle of Alcazar. A stage direction in that dumb show reads (K1): "*Thunder-clap the sky is one fire and the blazing star appears which they prognosticating to be fortunat departed very joyfull.*" A stage direction in *Friar Bacon* (b-4) (1198–99) indicates the use of fireworks: "*Heere Bungay conjures and the tree appeares with the dragon shooting fire.*" And "*lightning flasheth forth*" in the episode in which the brazen head is destroyed (1635). A stage direction in *Jupiter and Io* (b-8) (p. 158) also calls for thunder and fireworks: "*A noise of thunder. Enter Jupiter in his glory, his Trisull in his hand burning; at sight of whom they stand afrighted.*"

MAGIC AND THE SUPERNATURAL

Dunston, one of the characters in *A Knack to Know a Knave* (a-4), is a magician capable of calling up a devil to carry out his commands (1582–83): "*Asmoroth ascende, veni Asmoroth, Asmoro[t]h veni. En[t]er the Devill.*" Three b-plays take their titles from leading characters who are magicians: *Friar Bacon*, *Faustus*, and *John a Kent*. Bacon and Faustus both have servants, Miles and Wagner, who dabble in magic. Bacon and Kent both have rival magicians, Bungay and John a Cumber. Devils appear regularly in both *Bacon* and *Faustus*, performing whatever tasks the magicians assign them. The Ghost of Andrea appears with Revenge to overlook and comment upon the action in *The Spanish Tragedy* (a-3). Medea calls up Calchas and sends him back to hell to do her bidding in *Alphonsus of Aragon* (b-6) (939–70). And in *The Brazen Age* (b-2), "*Medea with strange fiery-workes, hangs above in the Aire in the strange habite of a Conjuresse*" assisting Jason in taking the golden fleece (G2v).

HORROR

Horror was a staple in the plays of the Rose. *Titus Andronicus* (a-4) may be mentioned for its many gory and sensational episodes including cannibalism (Tamora is served a pie in which her sons are baked [K2v]). Scene 5 of Marlowe's *Massacre at Paris* (b-3) (322–543) is just what the title implies, a massacre. The business of bringing a human head on stage, as a stage direction indicates in *Edward I* (b-9) (H4v), "*Lluellens head on a speare,*" is rather tame when compared to such episodes in *The Spanish Tragedy* (a-3) as the murder of Horatio (909–23) and Hieronimo's play-within-the-play (2956–3053).

PROCESSIONS TO BEGIN SCENES

If a procession may be defined as the entrance of five or more people onto the stage in some kind of order at the same time, many scenes in plays of the Rose begin with processions. *Patient Grissil* (a-1) begins (1.1): *"Enter the Marquesse, Pavia, Mario, Lepido, and huntsmen: all like Hunters. A noyse of hornes within."* *Friar Bacon* (b-4) also begins with a procession: *"Enter, Edward the first malcontented with Lacy earle of Lincolne, John Warren earle of Sussex, and Ermsbie gentlemen: Raph Simnell the kings foole"* (1.1).

PROCESSIONS MEETING PROCESSIONS

A stage direction in *Titus Andronicus* (a-4) (C1v) reads:

Enter the Emperour, Tamora and her two sonnes, with the Moore at one doore.	*Enter at the other doore Bascianus and Lavinia, with others*

A procession meets a procession also in *John a Kent* (b-7) (137–40): *"Enter at one doore Ranulphe Earle of Chester, Oswen his son[n] young Amery Lord Mortaigue, with them the Countesse, her daught[er] Marian, and fayre Sidanen. At another doore enter the Earles Pembrooke. Moorton and their trayne."*

PROCESSIONS PASSING OVER THE STAGE

Sometimes reference is made in the dialogue to processions that pass across the stage. In other instances the directions themselves use the phrase *"pass over the stage,"* or *"passe by,"* or some similar variation; and in still other instances processions just march across the stage. In *The Spanish Tragedy* (a-2) a stage direction reads (210–11): *"The Armie enters, Balthazar between Lorenzo and Horatio captive."* Another stage direction appears at line 213: *"They enter and passe by."* The king orders (224): "Goe let them march once more about these walles," and a stage direction indicates (229) that they

"*Enter againe.*" The dialogue and a stage direction indicate that a procession enters and marches across the stage in *The Four Prentices of London* (b-8). Bella Franca concludes a speech saying (B4v):

> Toward sea they are gone, and unto sea must I
> A Virgines unexpected fate to try.   *Exit.*
> *Enter marching Robert of Normandy, the Captaine the*
> *foure brethren, Drumme, and Souldiers. Enter the Pre-*
> *senter.*
> *Pre.* Thus have you seen these brothers shipt to Sea,
> Bound on their voiage to the holy Land.

PROCESSIONS TO END SCENES

The extant plots of plays of the Rose, such as *Frederick and Basilea* (a-1), indicate that care was taken to get actors onto the stage on time. The same plots show little concern about getting actors off the stage, other than to give the stage direction "*exeunt*," which ends most scenes. Apparently some effort was made to get actors onto the stage but, once there, they were expected to find their way off at the proper time. Frequently dialogue near the end of scenes in plays of the Rose suggests that actors were expected to leave in a fixed order of some kind when royalty and military persons were portrayed. And when five or more persons were present at the end of a scene, enough for a procession, it seems likely that a procession was formed to leave the stage and end the scene. In *The Downfall of Robert* (a-2) much of the final scene of the play is taken up with arranging people on the stage to welcome the king and presenting them to him (2696–776):

> *Rob.* . . . . The trumpet, sounds, the king is now at hand:
> Lords, yeomen, maids, in decent order stand.
> *The trumphets sound, the while Robin places them.*

Presumably the group that was placed "in decent order" also left the stage in "decent order" at the end of the scene. The dialogue suggests as much (2777–81):

> *Rob.* Now please my king to enter Robins bower,
> And take such homely welcome as he findes

It shall be reckened as my happiness.
Kin. With all my heart; then as combined friends
Goe we togither, here all quarrelles ends.

Exeunt.

A clear indication that processions were often formed and that actors left the stage in order at the end of scenes is found in *Friar Bacon* (b-4). Ralph Simnell, the king's fool, has been disguised as Prince Edward; one of the prince's retainers asks that the jest be carried out (939–44):

> *Warren.* . . . I must desire you to imagine him all
> this forenoon the Prince of Wales.
> *Mason.* I will sir.
> *Raphe.* And upon that I will lead the way, onely
> I will have Miles go before me, because I have
> heard Henrie say, that wisdome must go before
> majestie.   ***Exeunt omnes.***

The point here is that order is observed, that royalty is expected to leave the stage first. A joke hinges on the fact that Miles, Bacon's stupid servant, has no more wisdom than Ralph has majesty.

THE NARRATIVE ORDERING OF TIME

Time is regularly compressed in plays of the Rose, whose authors are often found doing precisely the thing that Shakespeare speaks of in the prologue to *Henry V*: "Jumping o'er times,/ Turning the accomplishment of many years/ Into an hourglass." An example may be found in Munday's *The Death of Robert* (a-2). The friar speaks of Robin as dead (861), and Chester enters and asks that the play continue (864). The friar then compresses the action of many years into a few lines (904–10):

> You must suppose king Richard now is deade,
> And John (resistlesse) is faire Englands Lord.

Later in the play Fitzwater addresses Matilda and informs her that "five sad winters have their full course runne,/ Since thou didst bury noble *Huntington*" (2175–76). In the play Huntington's body was taken from the stage to be buried at Wakefield only about 1300 lines earlier. Perhaps the most dramatic, and certainly one of the more familiar, scenes in which time is compressed on the Shakespearean stage is found in *Faustus* (b-5) (5.2.1894–2092). In less than two hundred lines Marlowe recounts the last night of the magician's life, and in less than fifty lines the last hour rushes by: "*The Clock strikes eleven*" (2035); at line 2065 "*The Watch strikes*," and Faustus exclaims "O halfe the houre is past"; "*The clocke strikes twelve* (2083); "*Thunder, and enter the devils*" (2088); and Faustus cries in desperation, "I'le burne my bookes; oh *Mephostophilis*." "*Exeunt*" (2092).

THE NARRATIVE ORDERING OF SPACE

Sometimes in the plays of the Rose "space assumes whatever dimension the narrative requires" as Beckerman says is the case in plays of the Globe (p. 160). *Sir John Oldcastle* (a-1) contains an excellent example of the practice (2.1.515–652): a summoner enters with the intention of serving a process (522). "Well, this is my Lord Cobhams house, if I can devise to speak with him, if not, Ile clap my citation upon's doore." During the scene a constable enters looking for a robber and gets permission to search the alehouse in "Lord Cobhams libertie" (629). The constable then calls "Ho, who's within there?" The aleman comes on stage (634) and in turn calls, "Dorothy, you must come down to M. Constable" (651). And "*she enters*" (652). The door to Lord Cobham's house and the door to the alehouse in his "libertie" are both on stage and actors come from both during the same scene. Space is ordered for narrative purposes in two scenes in *Friar Bacon* (b-4) involving the use of the "glasse prospective." With this device in Bacon's study in Oxford, the audience and King Edward see Lacie pay court to Margaret at Fresingfield (5.682–822). And later (12.1808–69) this device enables the audience to watch with the sons of Lambert and Serlby as the young men's fathers kill each other in a duel also near Fresingfield. One of the clearest examples of the narrative ordering of space is found in *George a Green* (b-3). Jenkin meets the shoemaker of Wakefield who is "*sitting upon the stage at worke*," at the beginning of the scene (11.971). The shoemaker strikes Jenkin because he will not take his staff from his shoulder. The dialogue that follows

(1002–12) shows the practice of ordering space to tell a story on stage:

> *Jenkin.* . . . It is but the part of a clapperdudgeon
> To strike a man in the streete.
> But darest thou walke to the townes end with me?
> *Shoomaker.* I that I dare do: but stay till I lay
> in my Tooles, an I will goe with thee to the
> townes end Presently.
> *Jenkin.* I would I knew how to be rid of this fellow.
> *Shoom.* Come sir, wil you go to the townes end now sir?
> *Jenkin.* I sir, come.
> Now we are at the townes end, what say you now?
> *Shoomaker.* Marry come, let us even have a bout.

The end of town is clearly on stage because the two men remain on stage while Jenkin talks and bribes his way out of "a bout" (1029). They leave the stage together to go to the alehouse (1035).

12

Medieval Stagecraft and the Vitruvian Facade

THE STAGING practices discussed in this chapter and in those that follow develop from the fusion of medieval stagecraft (including its classical antecedents) with an Elizabethan adaptation of the Vitruvian stage. It is the thrust of this chapter and those that follow to show how those practices were worked out on a Vitruvian stage that was arranged and equipped much as I have reconstructed it (plate 1).

I hold that the gates, the penthouse above the gates, and the gallery at each side of the penthouse may be equated in play after play of the Rose with the mansions of medieval staging. I try to show that the stage properties were emblems, modified medieval mansions, lowered from the heavens, pushed up through the trap, thrust out through the discovery spaces, and sometimes carried or drawn onto the stage by actors. Together with the dialogue, these emblems or modified medieval mansions were used to indicate change in place, in time, and in the action, as well as to add visual enjoyment.

ENTER AND KNOCK

The opening scene of *The Downfall of Robert* (a-2) begins with the stage direction *"Enter sir John Eltam, and knocke at Skeltons doore."* The importance of this kind of stage direction, which occurs regularly in all the plays of the Rose, is that it sets the scene in a hall before a door to Skelton's room or else in the street before his house. In this instance the action probably takes place in a hall, since a few lines later (1.26): *"At every doore all the Players runne out."* We know in this instance, also, that the door on which Eltam knocks is a real door, one provided with a shutter capable of being opened and closed because a stage direction indicates that Skelton *"Opens the doore."* One of the characteristics of the enter-and-knock movement is that the opening through which the actor enters is never designated as leading to any specific place. On the other hand, the door at which the actor knocks is designated as, for example, "Skelton's doore." A similar incident is found in *George a Green* (b-3) beginning with a stage direction (612): *"Enter George a Greens boy Wily."* He speaks (616–19):

> Here dwels a churle that keepes away his love,
> I know the worst and if I be espied,
> Tis but a beating, and if I by this meanes
> Can get faire Bettris forth her fathers dore.

Two lines later (622) *"He knocks at the doore,"* and Grime enters. In *John a Kent* (b-7) the magician enters (856) and tries to get into a castle which has been taken by his rival John a Cumber (894). According to a stage direction *"he tryes the doore"* and says "The gate is fast my Lordes, bound with such charmes,/ as very easily will not be undoone." A significant point that may be made about this episode from *John a Kent* is that the *"doore"* and the *"gate"* are used to designate the same place on the stage.

BESIEGING EPISODES

A staging practice quite similar to the practice of enter-and-knock is the besieging episode and its variations. In its most common form, the episode begins with the entrance of a military force before the gates of a stronghold and the appearance of defenders on the walls who talk to the besiegers. A few examples from plays in each list will suggest how common besieging episodes are in plays of the Rose.

Death of Robert (a-2) (1566–71):

> *Enter Bruse, Richmond, Souldiers.*
> *Rich.* The Castle Gates are shut What ho; what ho;
> You that are servants to the Lady Bruse,
> Arise, make entrance for your Lord and friends.
> *Enter, or above, Hugh, Winchester.*
> *Hu.* We will make issue ere yee enter here.

Captain Stukley (a-3) (E3):

Enter Stukly Lieftenant: Auncient Drum and Soldiers, a noies within of driving beasts.
stuk. Are the gates shut alreadie? open how.
herb. Who knocks so boldly?
stuk. Ha? who's that above?
her. Herbart the Governor, who is that below?
Stuk. Stuley the captaine, knocks to be let in
herb. Stukley the captaine comes not in tonight.

Brazen Age (b-2) (F1–F2):
Hercules and "all the Argonauts" appear before the gates of Troy and the Trojans flee into the city to escape the "Sea-Monster," which Hercules destroys. When the Trojans watching from the walls refuse to admit the Argonauts, Hercules threatens: "Laomedon, Il'e toss thee from thy walles,/ Batter thy gates to shivers with my Club."

George a Green (b-3):
King James enters with soldiers at the beginning of the scene (273) and meets Jane a Barley's son. The king asks who is with the boy's mother and the boy replies:

> None but herself and houshold servants, sir:
> If you would speake with her, knocke at this gate.
> *James*. Johnie, knocke at that gate.
> *Enter Jane a Barley upon the walles.*

Jane refuses to admit the king.

THE USE OF SYMMETRY IN STAGING

Beckerman says that "the simplest order in art is symmetrical balance" (p. 165). He continues, "It is this type of composition which one observes in the Globe plays from time to time." The use of symmetry is clearly evident in many plays of the Rose, especially at the beginning of scenes (Appendix C, "*'One Side'* and *'the Other Side*,'" also "*'One Doore'* and *'the Other Doore'*"). Directions calling for actors to come onto the stage on *"one side"* and on *"the other side"* and,

I believe, to enter at *"one doore"* and *"the other doore"* are frequently developed into more complex stage pictures. *Look about You* (a-4), for instance, begins a scene (2.76–81) with the following direction: *"Sound Trumpets, enter with a Harrald on the one side, Henry the second Crowned, after him Lancaster, Chester, Sir Richard Faukenbridge: on the other part, K. Henry the Sonne crowned, Herrald after him: after him Prince John, Leyster, being set, enters fantasticall Robert of Gloster in a gowne girt: walkes up and downe."* *The Four Prentices of London* (b-8) contains several stage directions clearly employing symmetry, for instance: *"Enter at one dore Robert and Charles, they meete Eustace with his Trophee: Enter at another dore Godfrey Tancred, they meet Guy with his Trophee"* (I3).

In two of the plays of the Rose attributed to Shakespeare, symmetry is used to develop a rather unusual kind of besieging episode. The episode is important in studying the stage because it involves the use of the gates on stage with the openings that flanked them. The first episode is found at the beginning of *Titus Andronicus* (a-4) (1.1.A3): *"Enter the Tribunes and Senatours aloft: And then enter Saturninus and his followers at one dore, and Bassianus and his followers, with Drums and Trumpets."* (In the Folio of 1623, this stage direction reads *". . . at one doore, and . . . at the other, with Drum & Colours."*) Saturninus and Bassianus are rivals seeking admission at "the gates" to the *"Senate house."* A similar besieging episode employing symmetry in its development is found in *I Henry VI* (b-8). It appears likely that the confrontation of Gloucester and the Bishop of Winchester's forces at the gates to the Tower of London (1.1) involves the use of entrances from the opposite sides of the stage, although the stage directions are not specific. Certainly Shakespeare used the episode in more than one play. The whole of one scene in *King John* (2.1.291–919) involves rival armies before the gates of Angiers, with citizens appearing on the walls, and one of the stage directions indicates clearly that the rival armies come on stage at the same time from different places: *"Enter the two Kings with their powers, at severall doores."*

KNOCK AND ENTER

A less frequent practice than enter and knock is the one in which an actor *"knocks within,"* and a person on stage opens a door and admits the one who knocked. In *The Spanish Tragedy* (a-2), the episode with the painter begins with a stage direction (2137): *"One knockes within at the doore."* Hieronimo directs Pedro to "See who knocke[s] there." And Pedro responds, "It is a painter sir." Hieronimo orders Pedro to "bid him come in, and paint some comfort." Another example of the practice of knock and enter may be found in *The Golden Age* (b-2) in the scene in which Danaë is met inside the fort of brass (H1). A stage direction reads *"The 'larme bell rings,"* and one of the beldams guarding Danaë says: "It should be K. *Acrisius* by the sound of the clapper." Another beldam responds: "Then clap close to the gate and let him in." This speech is followed (H1v) by a stage direction *"Enter Acrisius,"* who speaks to his daughter a few lines later: "See! Danaë is descended. Fair daughter/ How do you brook this place?" Clearly the scene takes place inside the fort of brass because Danaë responds: "Like a prison: What is it else?"

13

The Use of Properties for Special Effects

THE PROPERTIES in Henslowe's inventories of the Admiral's goods in 1598 have provided explanations and insights for almost every study of Shakespearean staging practices since Malone printed the lists in 1790. Something of their value in establishing a repertory of extant plays of the Rose may be evident in Appendix A; the assistance provided by these items in identifying Heywood's *Ages* as plays associated with the Rose can be cited as an instance of their value to the present work.

The importance of the list of large properties to a study of the staging of plays at the Rose is obvious. Some of the items in "The Enventary tacken of all the properties for my Lord Admeralles men, the 10 of March 1598" are clearly identifiable in extant plays. For example, the "i cauderm for the Jewe" can be found in the 1633 quarto of Marlowe's *Jew of Malta* (b-5) where a stage direction calls for "*A Caldron discovered*" (K2). If this particular item does nothing else, it establishes the fact that the stage direction "*A Caldron discovered*" is theatrical rather than fictive. This list of large properties found in Greg (3:116–18) and Foakes and Rickert (pp. 319–21) provides external evidence for the existence of stage properties in the plays that might otherwise be ignored. One might, for instance, be inclined to dismiss as mere dialogue Venus's invitation to Adonis in *The Brazen Age* (b-2) (C3), "Come, let us tumble on this violet banke," except for the presence in the inventories of "ii mose banckes" (Foakes and Rickert, p. 320). Rose's pretty speech in *The Shoemakers' Holiday* (a-2) (1.2.1–2), "Here sit thou downe upon this flowry banke,/ And make a garland for thy *Lacies* head," would have been just that, a pretty speech, rather than a possible allusion to a stage property in a pretty speech. And the stage direction in *The Downfall of Robert* (a-2) (1490–91), "*Robin Hoode sleepes on a greene banke, and Marian strewing flowers on him,"* would probably have been set aside as "dramatic" rather than "theatrical," had the "ii mose banckes" never been recorded as stage properties in the possession of the Admiral's men in 1598. The presence of the "ii mose banckes" illustrates why care must be taken in following Bernard Beckerman's admonition that "only when use is clearly demonstrable in action or stage direction can we assume that a property is introduced" (p. 74). Beckerman, of course, is correct in trying "to guard against seeing a stage property where none exists." However, only one of the references to "bankes" in the plays of the Rose is so "clearly demonstrable in action or stage direction" that we can assume that a property was introduced: in *The Downfall of Robert* (a-2) (1490–91) *"Curtaines open, Robin Hoode sleepes on a greene banke."* Nevertheless, the presence of the "ii mose banckes" in the inventory and the stage direction in *The Downfall* require, at least, that references to "bancks" in the dialogue be recorded as suggesting the presence and use of a stage property. While we cannot be certain that a stage property was present and used in *The Shoemakers' Holiday* (a-2), when an actor says "Here sit thou downe upon this flowry banke" (1.2.1), we cannot be certain that it was not there.

Bernard Beckerman's conclusion (p. 74) that "larger properties which require placement or setting were charily employed" in Shakespeare's playhouse applies also to Henslowe's playhouse. Not only were they "charily employed" at the Rose, the manner in which they were introduced into the action is in most cases undesignated or unclear. Two hundred nineteen references in plays of the Rose either indicate or suggest the presence of properties; in 140 of these references we have no way of being certain just how those properties were introduced into the action. I believe, however, that some conclusions may be drawn about the way they were handled by considering first the seventy–nine references which indicate clearly the presence of stage properties and designate precisely the manner in which they were put onto the stage (Appendix B).

The seventy-nine references are to all kinds of stage properties, as we shall see. They are put onto the stage and taken from it in at least four ways. They are pushed up through the trap and onto the stage in four instances, and taken from the stage through the trap on two or three occasions. Stage properties are discovered, that is introduced into the action by drawing a curtain or opening a door or a shutter to reveal them, in ten instances; and on two occasions beds are taken from the stage, separated from the playing on the stage, by closing curtains. Properties were lowered from the heavens (or some place above the stage) in nine episodes. In four of these the properties were taken from the stage the same way in which they were introduced, and it may be inferred that the properties were so removed in all the episodes. Properties are brought onto the stage, that is, carried, thrust through an opening, or drawn out, in fifty-six episodes, and it may be inferred that most of them were removed from the stage the same way they were brought on.

The seventy-nine references to properties in this group have one thing in common: the dialogue and stage directions are concerned with the introduction of properties into the action to create a spectacular effect. There was something spectacular about the monsters that emerged from the trapdoor to do battle with Hercules in *The Brazen Age* (b-2) (B3 and H4), as there was something spectacular about the creatures discovered to Jason in the same play (G2–G2v) when he won the golden fleece. The throne that descended in *Faustus* (b-5) to give the magician a view of the heaven he has lost was no ordinary seat for an ordinary king (2006–14); nor was the cloud in which Jupiter *"ascends"* in *The Silver Age* (b-2) (K1) an ordinary cloud. Likewise, most of the litters, chairs, coffins, chariots, cages, and similar miscellaneous properties were carefully introduced into the action to create a special effect. Consequently, the stage directions and dialogue usually show how these properties were brought onto the stage and often how they were taken away.

Certainly, as Chambers suggests (*ES* 3:89), a trap was employed in *A Looking Glass for London* (b-6) (517–25) when *"the Magi with their rods beate the ground, and from under the same riseth a brave Arbour."* In *The Brazen Age* (b-2) stage properties representing monsters seem to have been pushed up through the trapdoor onto the stage. A stage direction and the dialogue indicate that Hercules beats a Fury *"downe to hell from whence it came,"* and *"When the Fury sinkes, a Buls head appeares"* (B3). Later in the same play (H4v), *"Gallus sinkes, and in his place riseth a Cocke and crowes."* The Silver Age (b-2) contains an episode in which the dialogue indicates that a chariot is taken from the stage through a trapdoor.

Stage properties are discovered, that is, introduced into the action by drawing a curtain or opening a door to reveal them, in at least ten instances. Four of these discoveries are made in two a-plays, *The Downfall of Robert* and *The Death of Robert*. In the first of these plays, a bench is discovered, or perhaps two chairs, *"within the curteines,"* which are opened and *"againe shut"* (52–56). A portion of this business is repeated (84–85): *"They infolde each other, and sit downe within the curteines."* Later in *The Downfall* (1490–91) a stage direction indicates that *"Curtaines open, Robin Hoode sleepes on a greene banke, and Marian strewing flowers on him."* The dialogue and a stage direction indicate that a throne is discovered in *The Death of Robert* (923–61), unless it can be established that the throne was provided with a curtain:

> *Fri.* . . . draw but that vaile,
> And there king John sits sleeping in his chaire.
> *Drawe the curten, the king sits sleeping, his sworde by his side.*

The dialogue and stage directions in the same play indicate that properties representing the bodies of a woman and her son are displayed, that is, discovered, by an actor standing on the walls of "Windsor castle" and opening a shutter of some kind (2702–80).

Old Hieronimo *"knocks up the curtaine"* (presumably installs one in an opening in the wall at the rear of the stage), according to a stage direction in *The Spanish Tragedy*, 1602 (a-3) (2909), and at a later place apparently opens it to discover the body of his son Horatio (3045): *"He Shewes his dead sonne."* Another very well known discovery episode in the plays of the Rose is indicated by a stage direction in *The Jew of Malta* (b-5): *"A charge, the cable cut, A Caldron discovered"* (K2). With these two episodes may be included one from *Faustus* (b-5): *"Hell is discovered,"* which may have made use of the "i Hell mought" listed in the inventory of the Admiral's properties by Henslowe in 1598.

Beds are discovered in episodes in *II Tamburlaine* (b-6) and in *Edward I* (b-9). Tamburlaine's wife dies in a scene (H2–H4v) which begins with a stage direction: *"The Arras is drawne, and zenocrate lies in her bed of state."* The scene ends with another stage direction: *"The Arras is drawne."* A stage direction in *Edward I* (F1) indicates that *"the Queenes Tent opens, shee is discovered in her bed."* Later (F2) a stage direction indicates that "*They close the Tent*"; and the dialogue continues on stage until another stage direction (F2v) reads "*The Queens Tent opens*," and presumably she is again discovered in her bed. "*The Nurse closeth the Tent*" (F4) and the action continues into a new episode in which a stage direction calls for "*The Novice and his company to give the Queene Musick at her Tent*" (F4v).

The dialogue and stage directions in *The Brazen Age* indicate that "the gates" are opened (G2–G2v) to discover the golden fleece and its terrible guards:

> *Jason.* . . . . to these dangers singly, I oppose
> My person as thou seest, when setst thou ope
> The gates of hell to let thy devils out?
> Glad would I wrastle with thy fiery Buls.
> . . . .
> *Oetes.* Discover them.
> *Two fiery Buls are discovered, the Fleece hanging over them,*
> *and the Dragon sleeping beneath them: Medea with strange*
> *fiery-workes, hangs above in the Aire in the strange habite of*
> *a Conjuresse.*

Henslowe's inventory of the Admiral's properties includes "i gowlden fleece" and "i baye tree" on which the Golden Fleece traditionally hung. These items are listed together on the same line (Foakes and Rickert, p. 319).

Among the properties lowered from the heavens or a place above the stage at the Rose is the throne in *Faustus* (b-5), which is to give the magician a view of what he has lost and then presumably be drawn back up into the heavens (2006–14).

> *Musicke while the Throne descends.*
> *Good.* O thou hast lost celestiall happiness,
> Pleasures unspeakeable, blisse without end.

A similar instance in which a stage property, this time a basket, is lowered from above may be found in *Englishmen for My Money* (a-2). One cannot be sure, however, whether the lift was used for this business because a pulley properly placed in the gallery would have served. Although the stage directions are few, the dialogue indicates quite clearly what happens. Three sisters decide to play a trick on an unwanted suitor by drawing him up in a basket and leaving him suspended over the stage until he is discovered by their father and lowered to the stage (1752–2143):

> *Laur.* . . . into that Basket, and I will draw you up.
> . . . .
> Sisters, the Woodcock's caught the Foole is cag'd.
> . . . .
> *Vand.* . . . ich mout neit cal: vor de Wenshes wil
> cut de rope and breake my necke.
> . . . .
> *Anth.* . . . Out alas, what's yonder?
> *Pisa.* Where
> *Fris.* Hoyda, hoyda, a Basket: it turnes, hoe.
> . . . .
> *Pisa.* . . . Let him downe.
> What with a Cushion too? why you provided
> To lead your life as did Diogines;
> And for a Tubb, to creep into a Basket.
> . . . .
> *Frisc. M. Mendall*, you are welcome out of the Basket.

In *The Golden Age* (b-2) (K2v) a stage direction indicates that a property representing an eagle is lowered to the stage, then raised and again lowered and raised:

Iris descends and presents him [Jupiter] with his Eagle . . . Jupiter first ascends upon the Eagle, and after him Ganimed.

A stage property representing a cloud is lowered to the stage in *The Silver Age* (b-2) (C3): *"Jupiter discends in a cloude."* Presumably a chair of some kind is lowered to the stage in the same play where a stage direction calls for Juno and Iris to *"descend from the heavens"* (F1). And at another place in *The Silver Age* (F1v) a stage direction indicates that a property representing a rainbow is lowered: *"Jupiter appeares in his glory under a Rainebow, to whom they all kneele."* The cloud employed earlier in this play is used again: *"Jupiter descends in his majesty"* (I4v) and *"ascends in his cloud"* (K1). The play ends with a stage direction indicating the use of a property of some kind when *"Jupiter, the Gods and Planets ascend to heaven"* (L1).

A property containing *"a hand in a cloud"* is lowered to the stage at the conclusion of *The Brazen Age* (b-2) (L3): *"from the heavens discends a hand in a cloud, that from the place where Hercules was burnt, brings up a starre, and fixeth it in the firmament."*

Frequently properties are brought onto the stage by the actors. Banquets, for instance, are brought on according to the stage directions in *The Spanish Tragedy*, 1602 (a-2) (521), *"Enter the banquet"*; in *Titus Andronicus* (a-4) (K2), *"Enter Titus like a Cooke, placing the dishes"*; and in another a-play, *Patient Grissil: "Enter Gwenthyan and Rice, she meanely, he like a Cooke. . . . a Table is set with meate"* (4.3.1–12). *The Battle of Alcazar*, plot (b-4) (90–93) directs: *"Enter a banquett brought in by mr. Hunt & w. Cartwright,"* and a stage direction in *The Silver Age* (b-2) (C4) reads: *"A banquet brought in."* In *David and Bathsheba* (b-9) (724–40) David orders his servants to "fetch me to eat, and give me Wine to drink" and a stage direction indicates that *"they bring in water, wine, and oyle, Musike, and a banquet."*

Canopies are brought onto the stage in *Alphonsus of Aragon* (b-6) with a stage direction calling for Alphonsus to enter *"with a Canapie carried over him by three Lords"* (1582–83), and in *Edward I* (b-9) with a stage direction reading (C2) *"Enter . . . the King and Queene under a Canopie."*

Litters and chairs are brought onto the stage with actors in them in four plays of the Rose. In *Englishmen for My Money* (a-2) (2434), Harvey enters, *"brought in a Chaire."* Abdilmelec enters *"in his chaire"* in *The Battle of Alcazar* (b-4) (1302). Mortimer is *"brought in a Chayre"* in *I Henry VI* (b-8), according to a stage direction (2.5.1069). In *Edward I* (b-9), Longshanks's Ancient is brought onto the stage *"borne in a Chaire"* (A2v), and later in the same play (D3), a stage direction indicates that two actors are brought onto the stage in a litter: *"The Trumpets sound, Queene Elinor in her litter borne by foure Negro Mores . . . one having set a Ladder to the side of the Litter, she discended, and her daughter followeth."*

Coffins, biers, and hearses are also carried onto the stage in several plays of the Rose. *Titus Andronicus* (a-4) contains a stage direction reading, in part, (A4): *"Enter . . . two men bearing a Coffin covered with black."* *"A Beere is brought in,"* Robin Hood sits down on it, dies, and is borne on it from the stage in *The Death of Robert* (a-2) (754–859). And in the same play (2908–13) a stage direction indicates that Matilda's body is brought onto the stage *"borne with Nuns"* and *"The Queene following the Biere."* Later the "Biere" is referred to as "Matildaes herse" (3045). A stage direction in *II Tamburlaine* (b-6) (H6) indicates that a procession enters with *"foure bearing the hearse of Zenocrate,"* which seems to be her coffin or bier, provided with a framework supporting a rich cloth—probably black or purple. Later in the same play (L7v), the dying Tamburlaine asks that his followers:

> Now fetch the hearse of faire Zenocrate,
> Let it be plac'd by this my fatall chaire,
> And serve as parcell of my funerall.
> . . . .
> *They bring in the hearse.*

Following the stage direction with which *I Henry VI* (b-8) begins, *"Enter the Funerall of King Henry the Fift,"* the dialogue indicates that the body is borne in a "Woodden Coffin" (1.1.27).

Chariots are drawn onto the stage, apparently by actors, according to stage directions in two b-plays. In *II Tamburlaine* (b-6) (K4), Marlowe's superwarrior is *"drawne in his chariot by Trebizon and Soria,"* a pair of captive kings, *"with bittes in their mouthes."* And in *The Silver Age* (b-2) (G3v) a stage direction calls for Pluto to enter in *"his Chariot drawne in by Divels."* A stage direction in *Captain Stukley* (a-3) (K1v) calls for two actors to be drawn in a chariot capable of carrying both of them: *"Enter muly mahamet with Calipolis drawne in their chariot."* The same business is called for in *The Battle of Alcazar*, plot (b-4) which directs (16): *"Enter in a Charriott Muly Mahamett & Calipolis."* It is not clear if two actors or only one is in the chariot mentioned in a stage direction in *The Battle of Alcazar* (b-4) (212): *"Enter the Moore in his Chariot, attended with his sonne."* In *Jupiter and Io* (b-8), Jupiter mentions a chariot but one cannot be sure it was brought onto the stage (161):

> *Jup.* Sweet Juno will you once more mount your Chariot,
> And keep your state above; My designes ended,
> I will not long be from you.

It may be appropriate to note here that a stage direction in *Edward I* (b-9) (H4v) indicates that an actor is drawn across the stage on a kind of frame or sledge like those on which traitors used to be drawn through the streets to execution: *"Enter David drawne on a hurdle with Mortimor and officers."* And *I Tamburlaine* contains an episode in which Bajazeth is drawn across the stage *"in his cage"* (D5). This property is brought onto the stage in several episodes in the course of the play until the Turk *"braines himself against the cage"* (E8v) and his wife also (F1) *"runs against the cage & brains herselfe."*

Thus far, I have discussed references to stage properties which were introduced into the action during the course of a scene to create rather spectacular effects. In general, the dialogue and stage directions indicate clearly the several ways in which the properties in the present group were introduced into the action. Twenty of the references indicate, or at least strongly suggest, that most of the properties in the group of seventy-nine were at times also taken from the stage in much the same way that they were introduced.

Certainly the trap was used to take away properties from the stage in *The Brazen Age* (b-2) when Hercules beats a Fury *"downe to hell, from whence it came,"* and *"When the Fury sinkes, a Buls head appeares"* (B3). And apparently the Bull's head sinks back through the trap when Hercules *"tugs with the Bull, and pluckes off one of his horns. Enter from the same place Achelous with his fore-head bloudy."* On one occasion, at least, the trapdoor seems to have been used for the removal of a property from the stage, even though the property, Pluto's wagon in *The Silver Age* (b-2), was drawn onto the stage by actors. At three points Pluto's speech suggests that he intends to leave the stage through the trapdoor (G4–G4v):

> Wee'l cleave the earth, and sinke again to hell.
> . . . .
>   Il'e hide this beauty
> From Gods and mortals, till I sinke to hell.
> . . . .
> Cleave earth, and when I stampe upon thy breast
> Sinke me, my brasse-shot wagon, and myselfe,
> My Coach-steeds, and their traces altogether
> Ore head and eares in Styx.

A number of the episodes in which properties were discovered in plays of the Rose end, as we have seen, with the closing of a curtain.

This occurs in *The Downfall of Robert* (a-2) (52–56), *II Tamburlaine* (b-6) (H2–H4v), and twice in *Edward I* (b-9) (F1).

The dialogue in *Englishmen for My Money* (a-2) shows that the basket in which Vandalle is suspended over the stage (1752–2143) is lowered to the stage to end the episode; we do not know, however, whether it was taken from the stage after it was lowered; possibly it was pulled up into the heavens if the machinery there was used. We do know that the cloud in which Jupiter descends in *The Silver Age* (b-2) (I4–K1) is drawn back into the heavens because Jupiter "*Speakes as he ascends in his cloud.*" And at the end of *The Golden Age* (b-2), when Jupiter's Eagle is lowered from the heavens, "*Jupiter first ascends upon the Eagle, and after him Ganimed*" (K2v).

Properties brought onto the stage are sometimes taken from the stage at the end of the episode. The bier that is brought onto the stage for Robin Hood in *The Death of Robert* (a-2) is carried off at the end of the episode according to the dialogue (839–59):

> *King.* . . . See you the bodie unto Wakefield borne
> . . . .
> *Song.* . . . Thus cast yee flowers and sing,
> And on to Wakefield take your way.   *Exeunt.*

In the same play, the bier (or hearse) on which Matilda's body is carried onto the stage is carried off the stage (3041–48). In *The Golden Age* (b-2) an episode begins with "*the foure old Beldams, drawing out Dana's bed: she in it*" (I1v), and ends with another stage direction (I2v), "*The bed is drawne in.*" *Edward I* (b-9) has an episode which begins with a stage direction (H4v): "*Enter David drawne on a hurdle*" on his way to be hanged. The episode ends with another stage direction "*Exeunt omnes*" (I1).

14

The Use of Bushes, Trees, Arbours, Bankes

THE SEVENTY-NINE references to properties introduced to create special effects may give some clues to the way properties were handled in the 140 references in which the dialogue and stage directions are unclear. The first and the most important properties in this larger group are features of the landscape: bushes, trees, "arbours," "bankes," and rocks. Fourteen references in the dialogue and stage directions indicate, and sixteen others suggest, that these objects were represented on stage by properties. Only in three instances, however, is it clearly designated just how properties in this group were put onto the stage: two trees were brought on and planted in *Fortunatus* (b-1) (1.3.1–19), a structural arbor was thrust up through a trapdoor in *A Looking Glass for London* (b-6) (517–25), and a *"greene banke"* was discovered by opening a curtain in *The Downfall of Robert* (a-2) (1490–91).

Bushes may have been present and used in four episodes found in three b-plays of the Rose. In two of the episodes the dialogue suggests that greenery is picked from bushes; the dialogue and stage directions indicate that a vine is "swallowed by a Serpent" in an episode that invites speculation, and one episode appears to involve the use of fictive bushes.

The strongest indication of the presence of bushes on the stage in Henslowe's playhouse is in the Temple Garden scene in *I Henry VI* (b-8), in which the dialogue calls for the followers of York and Somerset to break roses from two bushes (2.4.956–62):

> *York.* . . . Let him that is a true-borne Gentleman,
> . . . .
> From off this Bryer pluck a white Rose with me.
> *Som.* Let him that is no Coward, nor no Flatterer,

> But dare maintaine the partie of the truth,
> Pluck a red Rose from off this Thorne with me.

A Knack to Know an Honest Man (b-3) (372–75) contains a similar but much less dramatic episode in which the dialogue suggests that an actor plucks a sprig from a bush on stage:

> Now Fortunio let us see what beautie is,
> Seest thou not this sprig, is not fresh and greene,
> Now looke againe, a little violence makes it deform'd:
> Why such is beautie sir.

There is no reason, of course, why rosebushes or shrubbery could not have been placed on the stage and used in presenting these episodes. The action clearly demands that roses be picked in the Temple Garden scene, even though the actors may have reached the bushes by walking offstage and coming back with their roses. There simply is not much evidence to indicate that the bushes were actually present or to show how they were placed on the stage.

The dialogue and a stage direction indicate that Jonas sits down in the pleasant shade of "a spreading vine" in *A Looking Glass for London* (b-6) (2173–90) and calls the audience to

> behold the gladsome vine
> That did defend me from the sunny heate,
> Is withered quite, and swallowed by a Serpent.
> *A Serpent devoureth the vine.*

The stunt could have been staged with the serpent appearing in almost any opening on stage or in a trapdoor and "devouring" the vine which would have been pulled by a string into his mouth.

The dialogue in *A Knack to Know an Honest Man* (b-3) suggests that three men who hide in "these thickets" (20–61) may conceal themselves behind bushes on stage to witness a fight. It is quite possible, however, that the thickets were fictive rather than theatrical and that the actors merely moved offstage, creating the impression that they watched the fight from "these thickets." *Sir John Oldcastle* (a-1) contains an episode that illustrates the use of dialogue in the plays of the Rose to create the illusion of properties that cannot possibly be present on stage (412–32):

Enter the Lord Powes disguised, and shrowde himselfe.
Cobham What fellow's yonder comes along the grove?
Few passengers there be that know this way:
Methinkes he stops as though he stayd for me,
And meant to shrow himselfe amongst the bushes.
. . . .
Ile stay his comming, be he but one man,
What soere he be: *The Lord Powis comes on.*
I have beene well acquainted with that face.
Powis. Well met my honorable lord and friend
. . . .
Cobham My honorable lord, and worthy friend,
What makes your lordship thus alone in Kent,
And thus disguised in this strange attire?

If this scene is to be effective, Lord Powes must "*Enter,*" show himself to the audience, and then "*shrowde himselfe*," that is, conceal himself from the audience by leaving the stage. Thus Lord Cobham can describe Powes as being in the grove, and acting as though he "meant to shrow himselfe amongst the bushes."

Trees may have been brought onto the stage of the Rose through a trapdoor as a kind of stunt. They appear to have been carried on by actors in a b-play, *Fortunatus,* and to have been placed on stage near a property representing a rock in *The Brazen Age.* And though several property trees are listed in Henslowe's inventory in 1598, it seems possible that in a number of episodes posts on stage and perhaps the columns supporting the heavens may also have been designated as trees. Beckerman clearly supports the theory that parts of the stage were used to represent trees when he observes that it is "difficult to distinguish when prop trees are used and when stage posts" were employed in plays at the first Globe (p. 81). In a number of instances, even when references are made to single trees, I believe that the trees are fictive—designated by the dialogue as present in a place just beyond the view of the audience. We cannot, however, lightly dismiss an allusion to a tree as merely fictive. The evidence we have for the presence and use of prop trees is clear, and the suggestion is strong that posts and columns of the stage may have represented trees.

E. K. Chambers is "inclined to think that, at need, trees ascended and descended through traps" (*ES* 3:89). He is probably right in explaining Bungay's trick in the magic contest in *Friar Bacon* (b-4) (1197–280) as involving the use of the trap. Certainly a trap was employed, as Chambers suggests, in *A Looking Glass for London* (b-6) (517–25) when "*The Magi with their rods beate the ground, and from under the same riseth a brave Arbour.*"

A trap may possibly have been used in presenting the stunt in *A Looking Glass* in which "*A Serpent devoureth the vine*" (2171–90). Aside from these instances, however, Reynolds seems to be correct when he says (p. 71), "Chambers's idea . . . that the trees when incongruous to a scene could have been got out of the way by means of trapdoors, is not confirmed by the plays." Reynolds was speaking of plays that he identifies with the Red Bull (pp. 4–29), but many of them may also be identified with the Rose theater. In any case, the plays given at the Rose simply do not indicate that they regularly employed property trees which were, at need, put onto the stage and taken away through a trap in the floor of the stage.

Although, as Beckerman observes, it is not always very clear whether in a given episode prop trees or stage posts were employed in plays of the first Globe (p. 81), it is relatively easy to identify several prop trees in Henslowe's inventory as having appeared in particular plays of the Rose. The inventory (Foakes and Rickert, pp. 319–20) lists "i baye tree," "i tree of gowlden apelles," and "Tantelouse tre." The "baye tree" appears on the same line (63) in the inventory as the "i gowlden flece" and may be associated with that property which is "*discovered*" in *The Brazen Age* (b-2) (G2v). Foakes and Rickert (p. 320, n. 9) point to a possible connection of the "tree of gowlden apelles" with *Fortunatus* (b-1). This property may, of course, also be connected with *Friar Bacon* (b-4), which was the first play given at the Rose and which was still in the Admiral's hands in 1602 (Foakes and Rickert, p. 207). The tree raised by Bungay in *Friar Bacon* is clearly identified and described (1192–212):

> *Bung.* [I will] Shew thee the tree leavd with refined gold,
> Whereon the fearefull dragon held his seate,
> That watcht the garden cald Hesperides,
> Subdued and wonne by conquering Hercules.

. . . .
Vandermast. Joves bastard sonne thou libian Hercules
Pull off the springs from off the Hesperian tree,
As once thou didst to win the golden fruit.

Foakes and Rickert do not mention any possible identification of "Tantelouse tre" with extant plays, and I cannot place it as a property that may be connected with an extant play of the Rose.

Dekker's *Fortunatus* (b-1) contains references to three trees, and here one is able to distinguish in some instances between prop trees and the use of stage posts as trees. The play begins with Fortunatus sitting down on stage to sleep under a tree (1.1.60–64):

Fortunat. . . . . haile Signior tree, by your leave ile sleep under your leaves,
I pray bow to me, and Ile bend to you, for your backe and my browes
must, have a game or two at Noddie erre I wake againe: downe great heart,
downe. Hey, ho, well, well.
He lyes downe and sleeps.

Nothing appears in the dialogue or in stage directions to designate the manner in which this "tree" was brought onto the stage. It does not figure in the action beyond serving as a place against which Fortunatus leans and under which he lies to sleep. The leaves and branches of the tree need not be visible to the audience and the tree is not mentioned or used again. All that is needed to represent a tree is an upright resembling the trunk of a tree; a stage post, like those mentioned in the contract for the Fortune (Foakes and Rickert, pp. 306–10), or a column supporting the heavens would have served admirably.

The second and third trees mentioned in *Fortunatus* (1.3.1–20) are clearly prop trees. A stage direction indicates that actors "*bring out a faire tree of Gold with apples on it*," as well as "*a tree with greene and withered leaves mingled together, and little fruit on it*." Another stage direction reads: "*The song: whilst he sings, the rest set the trees into the earth*." Later (4.1) the trees are climbed (at least the tree planted by Vice) and fruit picked and eaten: "*Climes up*" and "*Eates one*" and "*Exit. He leapes downe*." Although the Vice and Vertue scenes in this play may have been additions for court representation, as Greg suggested (2:179), the principles involved in the use of prop trees applied also to the public playhouses. The author of *John a Kent* (b-7) was apparently thinking of a prop tree from which a man could descend onto the stage when he included the following stage direction (836): "*The fourth out of a tree, if possible it may be.*" If the author had envisioned the use of a column or a stage post for this business, it does not seem likely that he would have added the phrase "*if possible it may be.*" Rather, it seems that he is suggesting the use of a prop tree but admitting it might not be worth the trouble. Another property tree that may be identified with the public stage is the one in *The Brazen Age* (b-2): "*Enter Hercules from a rocke above, tearing down trees*" (L2). And it may be assumed that the same prop trees figure in the stage direction a few lines later (L2v) "*All the Princes breake downe the trees, and make a fire, in which Hercules placeth himselfe.*"

Prop trees or stage posts may have been used in a number of episodes in plays of the Rose in which the dialogue and often stage directions as well indicate the presence and use of a tree. In *The Battle of Alcazar* (b-4) (1268–86) crowns are hung "*upon a tree*" and "*One fals*" and "*The other fals.*" A stage direction indicates that "*Sacrepant hangs up the Roundelays on the trees, and then goes out,*" in *Orlando Furioso* (b-3) (572–73). "*Absalon hangs by the haire*" (1536) until he dies and Joab orders his soldiers to "*take the Traitor downe*" (1635) in Peele's *David and Bathsheba* (b-9). According to stage directions and the dialogue in *The Massacre at Paris* (b-3) (578–604) "*the Admirals body*" is hanged "heere upon this tree," and later they "*carry away the dead body.*" In *Titus Andronicus* (a-4) Aaron is apparently forced to mount a ladder to be hanged "on this tree" (I1) and then ordered down (I2v):

> Bring down the Divell for he must not die
> So sweet a death as hanging presently.

Warman seeks a "winter-bitten bared bough" on which to hang himself in *The Downfall of Robert* (a-2) and finds one (2374): "O here is one: thrice blessed be this tree." Much enters and offers to help Warman end his life (2435–37):

He takes the rope, and offers to clime.
Fitz. Downe sirra, downe: whether a knaves name clime you?

The dialogue and stage direction indicate that Much starts to climb a tree, but one cannot be sure from this evidence that the tree is on stage.

The use of a column supporting the heavens (or a post onstage) to represent a tree is strongly suggested by the dialogue and the apparent movement of the actors about the stage in consecutive scenes in *The Two Angry Women* (a-2) (1923–2021 and 2022–265). Both scenes take place "in the Cunny borough" or "at the cunnie berrie" as actors stumble around hunting for each other. Some have lights and others do not, as one actor observes that "It is so darke, I scarce can see my hand." The action begins with the entrance of Mall who says (1927):

Well here Ile set me downe under this tree
. . . .
But soft, a light, whose that? soule my mother,
Nay then all hid, I faith she shall not see me,
Ile play bo peepe with her behind this tree.

. . . .
Mis Bar. Mistress, Ile make ye wearie ere I have done.
Mal. Faith mother then Ile trie how you can runne,
Mis. Bar. Will ye?
Mal. Yes faith.   *Exeunt.*

. . . .
Mis Gou. Why tis so darke we shall not finde the way.
Fran. I pray God ye may not mother till it be day.
Coom. Sbloud take heed mistresse heres a tree.
. . . .
Nay, Ile grope sure, where are yee? *Hodge.* Heere.
Coom. A plague on this poast, I would the Carpenter had bin hanged that
set it up for me, where are ye now?
Hodge. Heere.   *Exit.*
Coom. Heere, o I come, a plague on it, I am in a pond mistres.
Hod. Ha, ha, I have led him into a pond, where art thou Dick?
Coomes. Up to the middle in a pond.
Hodg. Make a Boate of thy Buckler then, and swim out, are yee so hot with
a pox? . . . Ile be gone . . . *Exit.*
                              Enter Coomes.
Coom. Heeres so hoing with a plague, so hang and ye will for I have bin
almost drownd.

The movement of the actors in the scenes that have been traced here suggest that "this tree" about which Mall plays "bo peepe" with her mother (1950), and "this poast" (2250), into which Coomes runs, are both represented by columns that support the heavens—perhaps the same column. It should also be noted that the pond into which Dick Coomes stumbles is a fictive pond, one that is located offstage.

Still another instance in the plays of the Rose that suggests the use of a column to represent a tree is found in *John a Kent* (b-7) (1394–420):

> *Enter Shrimpe leading Oswen and Amery about the tree.*
> *Oswen.* were ever men thus led about a Tree?
> still circkling it, and never getting thence?
> . . . .
> *Amery.* . . . but we get no further
> then in a ring to daunce about this tree
> . . . .
> *Oswen* Lend us your ayde to rayse us to our feet
> that we may get from this accurssed tr[ee]
> > *they help th[em.]*

This incident is one that is involved in a contest between two magicians. Consequently, I am not sure that a prop tree or a column was actually required, although one is mentioned in a stage direction. A tree is mentioned in the dialogue at an earlier place in the same play (1131–34):

> How say ye Lordes? now credit John a Kent.
> See where they are, and at the selfe same tree,
> where he assured us all of them would be.

Again, it may be a prop tree, or a part of the stage, or a fictive tree.

Two a-plays and a b-play contain episodes which illustrate the difficulty of being sure whether a prop tree or a part of the stage was used to represent a tree, or whether the reference was to a fictive tree. Several references are made in *The Spanish Tragedy*, 1602 (a-3) (2063–245) to a tree that Hieronimo and his wife confuse with the arbor in which Horatio was hanged. They are both mad with grief, as is the painter, who is asked (2182): "canst paint me such a tree as this?" In *Edward I* (b-9) (H2) the Friar says:

I must hang up my weapon upon this tree, and come *per misericordian* to the mad Potter *Mortimor*, wring thy hands Friar, and sing a pittiful farewell to thy pikestaffe at parting.

The Friar having sung his farewell to his Pikestaffe, a takes his leave of Cambria, and exit the Friar.

The Downfall of Robert (a-2) includes an episode in which it seems that a tree to be used for hanging men may be located offstage, just out of sight of the audience (810–11):

> *Joh.* Yonders their mothers house, and here the tree,
> Whereon (poor men) they must forgoe their lives.

The men, Scarlet and Scathlock, are rescued (989–99), after apparently having been taken from the stage to be hanged. Scathlock ends a speech at 981, and though no stage direction shows that he or Scarlet leaves the stage, they are both required by a stage direction to enter with others at line 989: "*Enter little John, Much, Scarlet and Scathlock.*"

One can be confident that prop trees rather than stage posts were used in plays of the Rose when the trees were thrust up through the trap, taken away through the trap, as was possibly done in *Friar Bacon* (1190–1200), brought onto the stage, climbed, their fruit picked as in *Fortunatus* (1.1, 1.3, and 4.1), or torn down and stripped of leaves as in *The Brazen Age* (L2 and L2v). Of course one cannot always be certain that a prop tree was not used, just because a stage post could have served. However, I am inclined to believe that when a stage post or a fictive tree could have served it did indeed serve.

As we have seen, an arbor or bower is brought through the trapdoor in the floor of the stage in *A Looking Glass for London* (b-6) (517–25). It may also be used later in the same play (1511–16) when Alvida requests her ladies to "go sit you downe admist this bower" and a stage direction reads *"Enter the bowers."* The structure raised from beneath the stage in *Looking Glass* may also have been used in *The Spanish Tragedy*, which was presented at the Rose for the first time on 14 March 1592, just six days after Lodge's play was first presented at the Rose. Horatio is shown hanging in a latticework arbor on the title page of the 1615 quarto of *The Spanish Tragedy*, and the dialogue and stage directions in the play (2.4.862–942) are consistent with the use of a property like the one shown there.

References to an arbor in *The Golden Age* (b-2) (E2) seem to be fictive:

> *Jup.* . . . . behold a place
> Remote, an Arbor seated naturally,
> Trim'd by the hand of nature for a bower,
> Skreen'd by the shadowy leaves from the Suns eye.
> Sweet will you sit, or on the verdure lye?

Likewise, the reference to the "Arbour" prepared in *The Brazen Age* (b-2) for Venus's assignation with Mars seems to be fictive rather than a reference to a structural stage property. Since the lovers are caught in Vulcan's "net of wire" in this episode (I2–I3), it would not be practical to have them trapped within a small structure where they would be more or less concealed from the gods who appear above the stage and laugh at their discomfort.

A third reference to an arbor is found in *The Blind Beggar of Alexandria* (b-3). Irus directs Samathis to prepare a banquet in an "arbour" (275), and the banquet is later brought onto the stage. There is no indication, however, that a structural stage property was employed as the place in which the banquet was served (542–646). While the "arbours" in the two *Ages* plays and *The Blind Beggar* are almost certainly fictive, the presence and use of the structural arbor in *A Looking Glass* and probably in *The Spanish Tragedy* suggest that all references to arbors and bowers should be considered with care; surely the possibility of the use of a stage property should be noted before we set the references aside.

I have discussed (in chapter 13) "bankes," stage properties apparently constructed to resemble "a raised shelf or ridge of ground," two of which are included in Henslowe's inventory of 1598 as "ii mose banckes." I have further pointed out that we cannot set aside several references in plays of the Rose to "bankes" which may seem to be fictive. The two references to rocks in *The Brazen Age* (b-2) (E4v–F1v and L2–L2v) are quite similar to references to "bankes" and "arbours"; the textual evidence for their presence and use is not convincing; yet the presence of "i rocke" with other large stage properties in the Admiral's inventories indicates that such properties were actually used.

15

The Use of Tents, Beds, Thrones

TENTS, pavilions, beds, and thrones all require the use of curtains and, I believe, a recessed area, or discovery space. Beds and thrones are also presented by the opening of tents in two b-plays. It may be practical, therefore, to consider these kinds of properties as a group because of their apparent relation in the presentation of plays at the Rose.

References to tents in five plays of the Rose show clearly that the stage represents an area before a tent, and it is possible that the directions in a sixth, *I Troilus and Cressida*, plot (a-1) (36–40) have the same significance:

> Enter Diomede to Achillis [tent]
> to them menalay, to them Ulisses
> to them achillis in his Tent to
> them Ajax wth patroclus on his
> back.   exeunt

In three of the plays the inside of the tent is clearly separated from action onstage by a curtain that is opened or closed. Remilia enters a tent in *Looking Glass for London* (b-6) and orders "these Curtaines" closed. Later Rasni goes to "Remelias royall Tent" and "*He drawes the Curtaines and findes her stroken with Thunder, blacke*" (552–53). In *Edward I* (b-9) (F1) the King "*goes into the Queens Chamber, the Queenes Tent opens.*" At the end of this episode (F2), the king remains onstage engaged in conversation with his retainers and according to a stage direction, "*They close the Tent.*" Stage directions in *David and Bathsheba* (b-9) indicate that David "*goes to his pavillion, and sits close a while*" (1911). At a later place (1929): "*He lookes forth, and at the end sits close againe.*" Still later, at line 1935, Joab "*unfolds the pavillion.*"

The tent is apparently represented by an opening in the wall of the stage in *II Tamburlaine* (b-6) (I6v), since a direction indicates that

an actor can be seen sitting in that opening. The direction, however, does not mention a curtain:

> *Alarme: Amyras and Celebinus issues from the tent*
> *where Caliphas sits asleep*

Actors go into the tent and come out of it onto the stage a number of
times during the episode which follows and it ends with the stage
direction (I8v): *"He goes in and brings him out."*

In one other play, *The Four Prentices of London* (b-8), an actor is
called onto the stage from a tent, but it is not clear from the dialogue
and stage directions that the opening through which the actor
comes onto the stage is the entrance to the tent (L2–L2v):

Eust. The poore boy [that is, "the French Lady"] brother, stayes within my
Tent.

. . . .

You have pardoned him?
Gu. I have.   *Eust*. Then *Jacke* appeare:
                                                 Enter the French Lady.

I have found nothing in the plays of the Rose to indicate that tents
were properties brought onto the stage and set up as in *Richard III*
(5.3.3433): "Here pitch our Tent, even here in Bosworth field."
"The secound parte of the Seven Deadlie sinnes" begins with a
direction *"A tent being plast one the stage for Henry the sixt he in it A sleep
to him the Leutenāt."* This fragment is sometimes assigned to the Rose
(Greg 3:129), but I have not included it with the plays of the Rose
because Chambers believes that it may "be assigned to a revival by
the Admiral's or Strange's men about 1590" (*ES* 3:497), before they
began playing at the Rose in 1592.

Regardless of whether tents were properties that were brought
onto the stage and set up, or whether they were represented by
curtains placed in an opening in the wall of the stage, they required
the use of an opening leading to places behind the stage when actors
appearing in beds or on thrones and seats were to be *"discovered"* as
the queen is in *Edward I* (b-9) when *"The Queens Tent opens, shee is
discovered in her bed"* (F1).

Beds were used in twelve different episodes in seven plays of the

Rose. It is difficult to come to a conclusion about the way they were introduced into the action because it seems in at least two instances that they were brought into the gallery rather than onto the stage. Moreover, while beds were sometimes *"discovered"* by drawing aside a curtain or arras before an opening, it seems that the beds themselves were on occasion fitted with curtains which were drawn aside to discover actors in the bed. In three episodes in the plays the dialogue and stage directions do not indicate clearly just how the beds were put onto the stage or taken from it; in two instances they are discovered and later separated from the action on the stage by a curtain that was closed; in one instance in each of the seven plays they seem to have been brought onto the stage, thrust out through an opening or drawn out by property men; and in two of those seven episodes they were taken from the stage the same way that they were brought onto the stage.

In Heywood's *Golden Age* (b-2) a stage direction reads *"Enter the foure old Beldams, drawing out Dana's bed: she in it. They place foure tapers at the foure corners"* (I1v). The bed seems to have been brought into the gallery because Jupiter enters after the beldams leave the stage and says (I2):

> Yon is the doore, that in forbidding me
> She bad me enter. . . . This purchase I must win
> Heavens gates stand ope, and Jupiter will in.

Jupiter's speech is meaningless if Danaë's bed is on the stage. As I reconstruct the movement, he leaves the stage and goes up to the gallery where the action continues:

Danae?   *He lyes upon her bed.*
Dan. Who's that?   *Jup.* 'Tis I, K. Jupiter.
. . . .
Dan. . . . I'le dive into my bed.
. . . .
Jup. . . . I would dive after.   *Jupiter puts out the lights*
                                          and makes unready.
Dan. Good my Lord forbeare
What do you meane? (oh heaven) is no man neere,
If you needs, for modesties chast law,
Before you come to bed, the curtaines draw.

. . . .
The bed is drawne in, and enter the Clowne new wak't.

It would have been prudent for Jupiter to have drawn the curtains on the bed, as Danaë requested, to prevent the beldams from discovering him when the bed is *"drawne in"* (I2v).

The other episode in which a bed is brought into the gallery is in *The Massacre at Paris* (b-3). This occurs when the Guise directs one of his men, Gonzago, to go to the admiral's house to murder him (337–78):

> *Exit Gonzago and others with him.*
>
> . . . .
> *Retes.* But look my Lord, ther's some in the
> Admirals house.
> > *Enter into the Admirals house,*
> > *and he in his bed.*
>
> . . . .
> *Gonza.* [*Enters above*] Where is the Admirall?
> *Admi.* O let me pray before I dye.
>
> . . . .
> *Guise,* [*below*] *Gonzago,* what is he dead?
> *Gonza.* I my Lord.
> *Guise.* Then throw him down.
> *Anjoy.* Now cosin view him well, it may be it is
> some other, and he escapte.
> *Guise.* Cosin tis he, I know him by his look.

The fact that curtains were attached to the bed in *The Golden Age* and that they were closed before the bed was *"drawne in"* (I2v) suggests that it may be difficult to determine in other plays of the Rose when a bed containing an actor is discovered and when an actor is discovered by drawing a curtain on a bed. A case in point is *The Battle of Alcazar* (b-4), in which a bed is used in the two dumb shows at the beginning of the play (25–39):

Enter Muly Mahamet and his sonne, and his two young brethren, the Moore sheweth them the bed, and then takes his leave of them, and they betake them to their rest.

. . . .
Enter the Moore and two murdrers bring in his uncle Abdelmunen, then they draw

the curtains and smoother the yong princes in the bed. Which done, in sight of the unkle they strangle him in his chaire, and then go forth.

In three of the episodes the references to beds do not indicate how they were put onto the stage. For example, we cannot know from the stage directions in *The Battle of Alcazar* just how the bed was introduced into the action or how it was taken from the stage. It could have been, if the stage directions are taken literally, *"discovered,"* or it could have been thrust onto the stage through an opening and the princes discovered in the bed when *"they draw the curtains and smoother"* them.

In *Edward I* (b-9) a stage direction indicates that the *"Bishop Speaks to her in her bed"* (G3). And in the last scene in the same play a stage direction reads (I1): *"Elinor in child-bed, with her daughter Jone, and other Ladyes."* While the dialogue and subsequent action makes it clear that Joan and the other ladies are in attendance, rather than in the bed, there is no indication about the manner in which the bed was put onto the stage.

In two episodes the stage directions show clearly that a curtain is drawn before an opening and a bed discovered with a person in it. *"The Arras is drawne, and zenocrate lies in her bed of state,"* in *II Tamburlaine* (b-6) (H2). And in *Edward I* (F1) the King *"goes into the Queenes Chamber, the Queenes Tent opens, shee is discovered in her bed."*

Actors are apparently brought onto the stage in beds in seven episodes in seven different plays of the Rose. The clearest indication of this practice is found in *The Silver Age* (b-2) where a direction reads (I4v): *"Enter Semele drawne out in her bed."* In another of Heywood's plays, *A Woman Killed with Kindness* (a-2), a stage direction reads (H2v): *"Enters Mistris Frankeford in her bed."* And in still another, *The Golden Age* (b-2), Heywood includes a direction reading (C2): *"Enter Sibilla lying in child-bed."* And I have already cited the stage direction in *The Golden Age* (I1v): *"Enter the foure old Beldams, drawing out Dana's bed: she in it."* Likewise, I have cited a direction in *The Massacre at Paris* which appears, as does the episode with *"Dana's bed,"* to indicate that a bed is brought into the gallery. Also earlier in the Marlowe play a stage direction indicates (300): *"Enter the Admirall in his bed."* Finally, there is movement in *Edward I* which indicates that a bed is brought out. The queen's tent is closed with a stage direction (F2) and the king and members of his party remain on stage and talk. During the conversation, gifts are presented to the king for his newborn son (F2v–F3):

Long. We thanke them all and wil present our Queene with these curtesies and presents bestowed on her young Son . . . .   *Exite. 4. Barons*
The Queens Tent opens, the King his brother the Earle of Gloster enter.
Elinor. Who talketh there?
Longsh. A friend Madam.
Jone. Madam, it is the King.
Elinor. Welcome my Lord: ho ho, what have wee there?

It may be inferred from this episode that the queen's tent had been set up on the stage and her curtained bed discovered by unfolding a part of the tent. She was then discovered in her childbed when curtains attached to the bed were drawn aside. Or else it may be inferred that curtains were drawn aside before an opening on stage that represented her tent and she was brought out onto the stage in the bed with her newborn child. The tent has been opened and the queen cannot see her visitors because she asks, "Who talketh there?" She does see her visitors and the gifts when she says, "Ho ho, what have wee there?"

It is evident from the twelve episodes in the plays of the Rose that the directions and the dialogue are not consistent in what they have to say about the way beds were put onto the stage and taken from it. It is significant, I believe, that the amount and kind of information provided about the way beds were handled varies from scene to scene within the same play. In *Edward I* (b-9) a bed is discovered and taken from the scene by closing a curtain (F1v–F2); in an incident that follows a bed is brought onto the stage and separated by a curtain from the stage to end an episode (F2–F2v). And in two more episodes in the same play no indication is given of the way the beds were put onto the stage or taken from it. Beds are handled differently in two episodes in *The Golden Age* (b-2) (C2 and I1v–I2v). In the first the bed is brought onto the stage with an actor in it, but there is no indication of how it is taken off; in the other the bed is apparently drawn into the gallery, and at the end of the episode curtains are closed on it and it is then drawn from the gallery. In Marlowe's *Massacre at Paris* (b-3) stage directions twice call for an actor to "*Enter . . . in his bed*" (300 and 355–56), once on the main stage and once, I have argued, in the gallery. In neither instance are provisions made for taking the bed from the stage at the end of the episode. The same author in his *II Tamburlaine* (b-6) begins an episode by discovering a bed with a stage direction "*The Arras is drawne*" (H2) and ends the episode, separating the bed from the stage, by using the same direction (H4v): "*The Arras is drawne.*"

The information provided by stage directions and the dialogue about the use of beds in plays of the Rose may be taken, I believe, as embellishment upon a conventional practice that was followed in putting beds onto the stage and taking them off. The several seeming inconsistencies can all be explained if we begin with the assumption that beds were regularly thrust or drawn onto the stage through an opening at the beginning of an episode, then withdrawn at the end of that episode. Thus beds could have been drawn into the gallery and removed from that place, as I suggest they were in *The Golden Age* (I1v–I2v) and *The Massacre at Paris* (355–56). Some beds may have been provided with curtains which were opened to discover actors in bed—after the bed was thrust upon the stage; this seems to be the case in *The Battle of Alcazar* (25–39), when the young princes are discovered and smothered in bed. In some instances the opening through which the beds were thrust onto the stage were themselves provided with curtains; as the stage directions indicate, these curtains were opened in *II Tamburlaine* (H2) to discover a bed, which, I suggest, was then thrust onto the stage. At the end of the episode the bed was drawn back through the opening and the curtains were then closed (H4v). It is possible that a tent was placed on stage and opened to discover a bed and closed to remove the bed from the action on stage, as may have happened in *Edward I* (F1v–F2). If this was the case, then the tent had to be placed before an opening in the wall (or over a trapdoor) and the bed introduced through the opening (or the trap).

Beds are likely to be assigned to discovery spaces because they are frequently associated with curtains, sometimes attached to the bed and often present in the opening through which they are brought onto the stage. In fact, I know of no instance in plays of the Rose in which a door is opened and a bed brought through it onto the stage. Even though beds are associated with curtains, we must

not make the mistake of assuming that episodes involving the use of
beds were played within a recessed area as might be inferred from
the stage directions in *II Tamburlaine* (H2–H4v):

*The Arras is drawne, and zenocrate lies in her bed of state, Tamburlaine sitting by
her: three Physitians about her bed, tempering potions.*
Theridimas, Techelles, Usumcasane, and the three sonnes.

Too many people are involved in this scene for it to be confined to a
recessed area behind a curtain line. It must for theatrical reasons
spill out onto the stage. The actors' difficulties in being seen and
heard in beds are obvious, and there is no reason to believe that the
actors would have increased those difficulties by remaining within a
recessed area. At least two instances are found in plays of the Rose
when motivation was provided by the playwright to overcome the
problems of being seen and heard in bed. In *A Woman Killed with
Kindness* (a-2), Anne asks to be raised in her bed as she lies dying
(H3): "Raise me a little higher in my bed." She makes no attempt
even to justify or explain her request, as Queen Elinor does before
she dies in *Edward I* (b-9) (I1):

> And raise me gentle Ladyes in my bed,
> That while this faultring engine of my speach.
> I leane to utter my concealed guilt,
> I may respect and so repent my sinnes.

Both requests are motivated by considerations of stagecraft: actors
must be seen and heard. For that reason as much as any, beds had to
be thrust out onto the stage.

Richard Hosley examines 152 extant plays written for Shakespeare's company, and finds 21 plays (excluding *Othello*) that require the staging of a bed or beds in a total of 23 instances. In
"The Staging of Desdemona's Bed" (*SQ* 14:57–65), he proposes

the theory that Desdemona's bed, in productions of *Othello* by the King's
Men, was presented to the view of the audience not by being discovered
but by being brought on stage through a tiring-house door: the bed with
Desdemona lying in it, is "thrust out" of the tiring-house by stage-keepers
or attendant players; the bed-curtains are manipulated as called for by the
dialogue; and when Lodovico says "Let it be hid" the bed, on which are

now lying the bodies of Desdemona, Emilia, and Othello, is "drawn in" to the tiring-house through one of its doors.

Thrones are present and used, according to the stage directions and dialogue, in twenty-three episodes in plays given at the Rose. They are strongly suggested by the dialogue in five other episodes; and though no attempt is made to tabulate the instances in which kings are present on stage and thrones are not mentioned, it may be inferred from the large number of such instances that chairs of state were present and used on more occasions than the twenty-eight that have been recorded here.

The stage directions and dialogue do not designate the way in which thrones are regularly put onto the stage and taken from it. In *Faustus* (b-5) *"the Throne descends"* (2006) to give the Magician a glimpse of the glory that he has lost. In *A Looking Glass for London* (b-6) a stage direction reads *"Enters brought in by an Angell Oseas the Prophet, and set downe over the Stage in a Throne"* (159–60). The "List of Irregular, Doubtful, and Variant Readings" in the Malone Society Reprint of the play notes that the third and fourth quartos print "set" as "let" and that Dyce emends "set" to "let" in his edition. Dyce's emendation, however, is classified by Greg, who supervised the Malone Society Reprint, with the "readings or conjectures of modern editors and critics which are definitely to be rejected" (*MSR*, p. xii).

Reynolds, who discusses the problems of staging thrones at length (*Red Bull*, pp. 53–65), concludes: "It was stored, I am still inclined to believe, because of Henslowe and Jonson, in the 'hut' above and manipulated from there." Henslowe records (Foakes and Rickert, p. 7) the payment of £7.2 on 4 June 1595 "for carpenters worke & mackinge the throne In the hevens." Elsewhere (chapter 9 and Appendix A) I argue that the work on the throne in the heavens was connected with the production of Heywood's *Ages*, especially *The Silver Age*. Jonson's complaint in the prologue to *Every Man in His Humor*, about the "creaking throne [which] comes downe, the boys to please," was included with his complaint about sensationalism and its inept devices such as the "nimble squib," the "rolled bullet," and the "tempestuous drum." It is quite possible that the creaking throne about which Jonson complains was the one made for Henslowe and which, disguised as an "eagle," "cloud," and "rainbow" in Heywood's *Ages*, came down "the boys to please" at the Rose theater. In his discussion of staging practices at the Red Bull Reynolds concedes, however, that when the throne consisted of "a movable chair on a dais, or of several chairs, certainly one cannot imagine it lowered from the 'heavens' with either safety or solemnity" (p. 54).

In at least four plays of the Rose there is need for more than one throne in a given episode. Zabina and Zenocrate are both placed in thrones in *I Tamburlaine* (b-6) (C8v–D1), and King Henry II and his son are both seated in elevated thrones in *Look about You* (a-4) (76–95). An episode in *Alphonsus of Aragon* (b-6) (774–847) indicates that three of Alphonsus's followers are seated in thrones and crowned by their leader. A stage direction in *Edward I* (b-9) (A3v) indicates that "*the Queene Mother being set on the one side, and Queene Elinor on the other, the king sitteth in the middest mounted highest, and at his feete the Ensigne underneath him.*"

Reynolds thinks that when the throne "consisted of a seat shaded by a canopy and fastened on a dais . . . it would have been easier to lower it from the heavens than shove it through the doors" (*Red Bull*, p. 54). His argument here relies heavily upon his thesis that the throne was placed near the front of the stage when it was used (p. 64): "Since the most conspicuous place is surely the front of the stage . . . that is where the state must stand." But the most conspicuous place on a stage provided with a rear wall is not, of course, the front of the stage; it is "upstage center," that is, as close to the wall at the rear of the stage as possible and in the center with reference to the sides of the stage. The farther forward the throne is placed on a platform stage in a circular theater building, the more difficult it is for all the spectators in a full house to see and hear the actor playing the king. And it would be especially difficult if the high-backed chair of state were covered with a canopy, as Reynolds believes it was.

Reynolds stresses the point that it would be awkward to handle "a raised chair, especially when surmounted by a canopy, in the restricted height of the rear stage as it is usually imagined" (p. 57). Unquestionably many of the thrones used in plays at the Rose were elevated. In *The Spanish Tragedy* (a-3) the Viceroy "*Falles to the ground"* from a "Regall throne . . . higher than my fortunes reach" (312–16). Twice Marlowe has his heroes ascend their thrones by using their defeated opponents as footstools. In *I Tamburlaine* (b-6) Bajazeth is made to serve as a "foot-stoole" and *"He gets up upon him to his chaire"* (D5–D5v). In *Faustus* (b-5) the Pope *"ascends"* to "Saint Peters Chaire" by stepping on the back of Saxon Bruno. References to an elevated throne are made twice in *The Golden Age* (b-2). Titan addresses Saturn (B2): "Descend proud upstart, trickt up in stoln weeds/ Deckt in usurped state." And Diana commands (D4v), "Come Fawns, and Nymphs, and Satyres, girt us round/ Whilst we ascend our state." In *The Downfall of Robert* (a-2) (44–45) *"Ely ascends the chair,"* and then repeats the action (71) as the prologue explains it. The throne on which John sits in *The Death of Robert* (a-2) (923–61) must be elevated because in one place the queen *"ascends"* the throne to look at the sleeping king and then *"descēdeth"* (959–61). A stage direction in *Fortunatus* (b-1) reads *"Fortune takes her Chaire, the Kings lying at her feete, she treading on them as shee goes up."* At line 140, *"She comes downe."* In *David and Bathsheba* (b-9), David is asked why he does not "mount his throne" (872).

Although many thrones were elevated, I find nothing to show conclusively that they were provided with a canopy. Nor is there any reason to believe that they were difficult to move about. Even so, the thrones that were regularly employed at the Rose were presumably somewhat different from the "royall chariot or estate" mentioned in *II Tamburlaine* (b-6); Amyras mounts this one (L7), which was earlier pulled onto the stage and taken from it by Tamburlaine's "pampered Jades of Asia," a pair of captive kings. King Henry IV is seated on his throne in *The Famous Victories* (b-3) when he asks his retainers to "Remove my chaire a little back, and set me right" (C4). The dialogue and stage directions in related episodes indicate that a throne or "State" was put onto the stage in *Faustus* (b-5). In the first episode (1184–86) Martio orders

> Good *Fredericke* see the roomes be voyded straight,
> His Majesty is comming to the Hall;
> Go backe, and see the State in readiness.

The Emperor enters in a procession following a *"Senit"* (1235), and presumably seats himself in his throne to see Faustus present

"Great Alexander and his beauteous Paramour." Reynolds's theory that thrones were regularly stored in the heavens and manipulated from there cannot be accepted as an explanation for the way thrones were put onto the stage and taken from it at the Rose theater.

The association of thrones with curtains or with royal persons seated within curtains is persistent in plays of the Rose. But only in *The Death of Robert* (a-2) (923–25) is it suggested that a throne is provided with a curtain: *"Drawe the curten, the king sits sleeping."* The direction could also suggest that the curtain is located before a discovery space, a recessed place, and the throne is *"discovered"* with the king asleep in it. I have interpreted this episode as a "discovery," the only clearly indicated discovery of a throne in the Rose's plays.

The use of thrones or seats of state is suggested by the discovery of royal persons in seats behind curtains in three episodes that ought to be considered here. In a b-play, *II Tamburlaine*, *"Amyras and Celebinus issues from the tent where Caliphas sits asleep"* (I6v). Caliphas is later called from the tent and comes onto the stage. The seat on which the son of the "Mightie Monarque" sits does not figure prominently in this episode, although Tamburlaine is twice concerned about having Zenocrate in a chair of state (C8v–D1 and G3). And he insists that Amyras "mount my royall chariot of estate,/ That I may see thee crown'd before I die." It seems possible that Caliphas has a formal seat of some kind and that he is pulled from it when Tamburlaine *"goes in and brings him out [of the tent]"* and then kills him for cowardice (I8v).

Seats of state may have been located behind curtains in *Edward I* (b-9) and in *David and Bathsheba* (b-9), but in only one is a throne mentioned. Their presence and use is, however, strongly implied by the fact that in both plays both rulers earlier appeared on elevated thrones. Both plays were written by George Peele, and in both, the rulers are depicted as coming from or going into their pavilions. In *Edward I* a party goes to *"the Kings Pavillion: the King sits in his Tent with his Pages about him"* (G3), he comes out and goes with the party to speak with the queen *"in her bed."* In *David and Bathsheba*, the ruler *"goes to his pavillion and sits close awhile"* (1911). *"He lookes forth, and at the end sits close againe"* (1929). Joab enters and *"unfolds the pavillion"* (1935). The general then lectures his ruler who sits mourning for Absalom (1948–88):

Is Israels throne a Serpent in thine eyes,
And he that set thee there, so farre from thankes,
That thou must curse his servant for his sake?
. . . .
Advance thee from thy melancholy denne,
And decke thy bodie with thy blisfull robes,
Or by the Lord that swaies the heaven, I sweare,
Ile lead thine armies to another King,
Shall cheere them for their princely chivalrie,
And not sit daunted, frowning in the darke,
. . . .
Abisay. Come brother, let him sit there till he sincke,
Some other shall advance the name of Joab.
                    Offers to goe out.
. . . .
                                        He riseth up
. . . .
David. . . . Courage brave captaines, Joabs tale hath stird,
And made the suit of Israel preferd.

The dialogue and stage directions in this episode indicate that for
the purposes of the play the throne was placed in a recessed area and
that it was difficult to see the actor seated on the throne. At least the
place in which David is seated is referred to as a "melancholy denne"
(1967) and the ruler is described as sitting "daunted, frowning in the
dark" (1972).

Richard Hosley provides an explanation for discoveries such as
these in his article "The Discovery-Space in Shakespeare's Globe."
He explains (*SS* 12:44–45) that in plays there,

discoveries are essentially "shows," or disclosures, of a player or object
invested with some special interest or significance. (Alternatively they
might be described as *tableaux vivants* and still lifes.) Furniture is involved only in so far as the discovered player requires something to sit or
lie upon so that he may be shown effectively . . . . Unless a 'show'
is to be presented, necessary furniture is always carried on stage.

Bernard Beckerman is conscious of the close association of the use
of thrones and curtains at the first Globe (p. 78). He observes
that "though a curtain could be utilized to reveal the state in

these cases, I incline to the theory that the state was brought or thrust out."

Hosley and Beckerman are probably correct in their opposition to the theory that thrones were regularly discovered in plays given at the Globe and that scenes were acted in a recessed area behind a curtain line. Except for the episode in *David and Bathsheba* (b-9) (1911–2011), in which David deliberately goes into a recessed area to mourn for Absalom, thrones are regularly put onto the stage in plays of the Rose. It is significant that the throne is placed so that David can withdraw and then look out, withdraw again, and finally come forth and deliver a speech of affirmation at the end of the play. There is no question but that David's throne was placed behind curtains at the rear of the stage so that with a step or two he could be in a theatrically effective position onstage. I propose the theory that thrones, like beds, were regularly thrust through an opening provided with curtains and located in the wall at the rear of the stage, an opening not far from the center of the stage with reference to the two sides. Such a theory provides an explanation for the frequent association of thrones with curtains. The distance would never have been great: three or four feet forward and the throne would have been visible to all; three or four feet back and it could have been concealed by a curtain. Thus I would explain the "discovery" episode in *The Death of Robert* (a-2) (923–61), which begins

> *Fri.* . . . draw but that vaile,
> And there king John sits sleeping in his chaire.
> *Draw the curten, the king sits sleeping, his sworde by his side.*

If I am correct, the dialogue and stage directions here call for the curtain to be opened and a stagehand or two to shove the throne forward onto the stage. At the end of the long episode, it was drawn back. Thus I account for the twenty-one instances in which thrones were clearly present and used in plays of the Rose, regularly without any indication in the dialogue or stage directions as to how they were put there or how they were taken away. I suspect that the practice of thrusting thrones out and withdrawing them was so pervasive that in many instances they were used without allusions to their use surviving in the dialogue or stage directions.

The episode in *The Famous Victories* (b-3) (C3v–D1) in which Prince Hal takes his sleeping father's crown may well provide the clearest illustration of the way in which thrones were put onto the stage and taken off in plays of the Rose. The episode begins with a stage direction which makes no mention of a throne. Its presence and use must be inferred from the dialogue and action that follow. The king asks his retainers to

> Draw the Curtaines and depart my chamber a while,
> And cause some Musicke to rocke me asleepe.
> *He sleepeth.*   *Exeunt Lords.*
> *Enter the Prince.*

The dialogue at a later place will indicate that the prince takes the crown from his sleeping father and leaves the stage. Henry's retainers return:

> *Enter Lord of Exeter and Oxford*
> . . . .
> *Hen.4.* . . . . But good my Lords take off my Crowne,
> Remove my chaire a little backe, and set me right.
> *Ambo.* And please your grace, the crown is takē away.

After the prince is discovered with the crown, explains his action, and is forgiven, the episode ends with a speech by the king:

> Draw the Curtaines, depart my Chamber,
> And cause some Musicke to rocke me asleepe.
> *Exeunt Omnes.*
> *The King dieth.*

The king's request to his retainers to "Draw the Curtaines" at the beginning of the episode must refer to the curtains through which he is brought onto the stage. His request to "Remove my chaire a little backe, and set me right," indicates that he is in a chair or throne, and that it is capable of being moved by his retainers. His request at the end of the episode to his retainers to "Draw the Curtaines" motivates the business of closing the curtains after the king is removed from the stage in his throne. He must be taken from the stage because the episode that follows begins with a reference to his death.

16

The Use of Chairs and Tables

SEATS of all kinds except thrones—that is, stools, benches, and chairs—may be considered together with "the bench," "the barre," and tables, as well as properties used in staging eighteen banquets at the Rose. In twelve episodes there is evidence in the plays that banquets are brought onto the stage, but in only two episodes is explicit provision made for removing them. Nevertheless there is no reason not to believe that all eighteen of the banquets were brought onto the stage at the beginning of the episode and taken away at the end of it.

It is not clear just how tables and seats are handled in staging banquets. Beckerman notes that "it was customary in Elizabethan life for banquet tables to be portable"; and he observes that in plays given at the first Globe "the evidence concerning the table as stage property shows that the introduction of banquet tables does not depend upon an enclosure" (p. 76). Nothing in the plays of the Rose even suggests that tables were set up or discovered in a recessed area.

Neither tables nor seats are mentioned in the stage directions for the two episodes in which banquets are brought onto the stage and then removed. In *Friar Bacon* (b-4) (1325–63) Miles enters "*with a cloth and trenchers and salt*" and speaks of covering the table "with trenchers salt and cloth." He later enters with "*a mess of pottage and broth*" (1339) and presumably clears away the banquet at Bacon's command, "Miles take away, and let it be thy dinner" (1363). A stage direction with dialogue in *A Woman Killed with Kindness* (a-2) shows servants passing across the stage after having cleared a banquet table (D2v–D3):

Enter 3. or 4. Servingmen, one with a Voyder and a Woodden knife, to take away all, another the salt and bread; another the Table-cloth and Napkins, another the carpet. Jenkin with two lights after them.

Jenk. So, march in order and retyre in battle ray, my maister and the guests have supt already, als taken away, here now spred for the servingmen in the hal, Butler it belongs to your office.

Stage directions and the dialogue in *Patient Grissil* (a-1) indicate that a table is laid, food set out, and stools brought on stage to seat "*a company of beggers*." It is not clear how many beggars are involved or whether they all sit to eat because "*A drunken feast*" ends the episode (4.3.1–47).

A courtly king, Rasini, directs his lady to seat herself in the "royall throne" and bids his lords to seat themselves "at feast" in *A Looking Glass for London* (b-6) (1847–57). In *George a Green* (b-3) (1179–340), the Pinner orders "a stand of Ale . . . set in the Market place" and some are seated "at the boord." A table is mentioned twice in the stage directions during a banquet in *King Leir* (b-6) (2091–355), although the manner in which the table is brought onto the stage is not indicated. Reference is made in the dialogue in *The Golden Age* (b-2) (C4v–D1v) to the "boord" and to "the table," but nothing appears in the dialogue or stage directions to show how the table was put on the stage. Eleven persons, the largest number known to have been present at a banquet in a play of the Rose, are seated on stools in *The Silver Age* (b-2) (H2–H3). Although there is no indication how the stools are brought onto the stage, the banquet ends in "*A confused fray with stooles, cups & bowles*."

Normally banquets are rather intimate affairs with only two persons (in the case of four banquets), four persons (four banquets), five persons (two banquets), or six persons (three banquets) at the table. Occasionally more attend; Titus serves Tamora's sons "baked in this Pie" to seven guests, and nine are present at a feast in *The Brazen Age* (b-2) (E1v–E3v). The dialogue usually indicates that the guests are seated; twice it is apparent that stools are used. Otherwise little appears in the references to these episodes to show the manner in which they were staged.

The way in which tables, stools, benches, and chairs are introduced into the action is designated by directions or the dialogue in only nine instances aside from the times they are used in the staging of banquets. The presence and use of various kinds of seats and tables is clearly indicated in nineteen other episodes, but there is nothing in the dialogue or stage directions to show how they were introduced into the action. Finally there are thirty-three episodes in which the presence and use of various kinds of seats and tables are suggested, but we simply cannot tell from the references to them if they were actually present and used.

Let us look at the nine instances in which the stage directions and dialogue show how seats and tables are introduced into the action. A stage direction in *The Downfall of Robert* (a-2) requires the discovery of a seat large enough for Robert and Marian to sit down in together behind curtains (52–53): *"they infolde each other, and sit downe within the curteines."* In *Captain Stukley* (a-3) Tom directs his servant to "bring the chaire and let my father sit" (B2). And Hieronimo directs Balthazar to "Bring a chaire and a cushion for the King" at the beginning of the play-within-the-play in *The Spanish Tragedy* (a-3). A stage direction indicates (2927): *"Enter Balthazar with a chaire."* Tables and seats are brought onto the stage for a backgammon game in *Two Angry Women* (a-2) (68–141), although the seats are not mentioned. In Heywood's *Woman Killed with Kindness* (a-2) (D4v), tables and stools are brought in for four people to play at cards. And in the same author's *Four Prentices of London* (b-8) (F2), a stage direction for a council meeting mentions tables and *"Formes,"* a kind of "long seat without a back": *"Enter the old Soldan, the yong Sophie, Tables and Formes, and Moretes, Turnus, with drumme and Souldiers."* Except for this last instance—the accidental reference to the routine introduction of properties—the several references to the way in which tables and seats are put onto the stage are all concerned with creating a special effect, or with the introduction of an unusual property like the *"Tables"* in the *Two Angry Women*, that is, "each of the two folding leaves of a backgammon board."

References in dialogue or stage directions indicate the presence and use of seats and tables of various kinds in nineteen episodes in plays of the Rose. In two of these episodes tables are required, and at one of the tables seats must be provided for three men. However, in none of the episodes is it shown just how the properties were put onto the stage or taken from it; and only rarely are we shown anything about their characteristics. *Captain Stukley* (a-3) contains a stage direction indicating that *"Bags are set one the Table"* (I2v). *Sir John Oldcastle* (a-1) requires a table for seating three men (2086–88):

Enter Cambridge, Scroope, and Gray, as in a Chamber, and set downe at a table, consulting about their treason: King Harry and Suffolke listning at the doore.

A stage direction in *The Battle of Alcazar* (b-4) (38–39) indicates that *"They strangle him in his chair, and then goe forth."* And in *George a Green* (b-3) a direction reads, *"Enter a Shoomaker sitting upon the stage at work"* (970–71); he had his tools with him and presumably was seated on a bench or stool of some kind. Three people sit down on a bench of some kind in *Titus Andronicus* (a-4) (F4v–G1) while Lavinia *"takes the staffe in her mouth, and guides it with her stumps and writes."* The Doctor is seated in his study, possibly discovered, in *Faustus* (b-5) (28–29): *"And this the man that in his study sits./ Faustus in his study."* The dialogue in *A Knack to Know an Honest Man* (b-3) indicates that a mother sits down with her daughter at her feet (662–77): *"Sem. . . . Yonder sits chastitie at beauties feete."* The dialogue and stage directions indicate that at least six people are seated during a play-within-a-play in *John a Kent* (b-7) (1187–392). The Maris of London is bound in a chair and killed by having a serpent applied to her breast in *Edward I* (b-9) (H1); no provision is made in the dialogue or stage directions for removing the body from the stage at the end of the episode. The dialogue in *Jupiter and Io* (b-8) (171–74) indicates that Mercury sits by Argus and tells him stories to charm him to sleep. In *The Downfall of Robert* (a-2) a stage direction indicates that Robert *"Flings away his napkin, hat, and sitteth downe"* (172). Later the dialogue and stage directions in the same play (303–20) indicate that at least five persons are seated for a kind of play-within-a-play. Still later (1629–30) a stage direction reads: *"Enter John crowned, Queene Elianor, Chester, Salsbury, Lord Prior, sit downe all. Warman stands."* In *The Death of Robert* (a-2) (1313), *"Matilda faints, and sits downe."* Seats for seven persons, on a level or levels below two elevated thrones, are indicated by the dialogue and stage directions at the beginning of *Look about You* (a-4) (76–95). The play ends with an episode demanding seats for about twelve on three or four levels below an elevated throne (2821–92). In addition, *Look about You* contains a stage direction in which an actor *"drinkes and falls over the stoole"* (1503). The dialogue in *Sir John Oldcastle* (a-1) seems to indicate that seats were used in the "Alehouse" in Lord Cobham's Liberty (694–710):

Doll to the Priest I pray thee sweetheart be quiet,
I was but sitting to drinke a pot of ale with him.

Typical of the thirty-three references which suggest but do not indicate the presence and use of several kinds of seats and tables are the stage directions and dialogue concerning "the bench" and "the barre." It is uncertain whether the two allusions made to "the bench" in *George a Green* (b-3) (98–107) refer to a stage property. The same problem occurs in *The Famous Victories* (b-3) with reference to "the chaire" occupied by the Lord Chief Justice and "the barre," the barrier or wooden rail at which prisoners are stationed before him for trial (B2–B2v). Again, in *Sir John Oldcastle* (a-1) "the bench" is mentioned twice, as is "the barre" in a courtroom episode, but it is not clear whether these properties were actually present and used (2541–642).

I am inclined to the theory that many of the thirty-three references that suggest the use of properties like "the bench," and "the barre," are references to concrete, functional objects involved in the presentation of the play. Though it is fruitless to insist upon the actual presence and use of any particular kind of seat or table in a specific episode, I will insist on the possibility—indeed, the probability—that many such references are to properties that were present and used.

On the basis of what we know about the properties in Henslowe's inventories (Foakes and Rickert, pp. 316–25) and the way they were used in extant plays of the Rose, we can make the following generalizations about the use of various kinds of seats, tables, and related properties: 1) Like the throne in *Faustus* (b-6) (2006–14) they could have been lowered from the heavens. 2) They could have been *"set downe over the Stage,"* presumably in the penthouse or gallery, as was a throne for Oseas in *A Looking Glass for London* (b-6) (159–60). 3) They could have been pushed up through the trapdoor like the "brave Arbour" for "faire Remilia" in the *Looking Glass* (517–25). 4) Certainly they could have been "discovered" as in *The Death of Robert* (a-2) where a stage direction reads (925): *Drawe the curten, the king sits sleeping, his sword by his side."* 5) They could have been brought onto the stage, with or without specific reference to them in stage directions as in the several banquet episodes. 6) Finally, we can never assume that seats and chairs (or any other properties at the Rose) were always present merely because they were mentioned, or that they were absent simply because they were not mentioned, or that they were consistently introduced into the action the same way.

17

Some Utilitarian Practices

REGARDLESS of where they may have originated, sixteen of the practices followed in presenting plays at the Rose appear to be more frequently associated with Shakespearean stagecraft than with its medieval antecedents. I suspect these practices result from the imaginative handling of staging problems arising from the adaptation of medieval stagecraft to the distinctive Elizabethan concept of the Vitruvian stage. That concept, Dr. Frances Yates argues in her *Theatre of the World*, found its way into England through John Dee's preface to Henry Billingsley's English translation of Euclid in 1570. Dr. Yates says that "judging by the Preface, what interested Dee in architectural theory was the basic theory of proportion in its mathematical and symbolic aspects" (p. 36). And she suggests that "the influences of Dee's Vitruvianism should be sought . . . among the class of people to whom Dee addressed his Preface, the middle-to-artisan class." She points to James Burbage, who built the Theatre in Shoreditch in 1576, as the kind of man Dee was addressing (p. 40).

Dr. Yates observes that the public theaters of Shakespearean London, which she believes to have retained the general plan of Burbage's Theatre, did not use the perspective scenes mentioned by Vitruvius, developed by Serlio in Italy and introduced into England by Inigo Jones in the Stuart Masques. Dr. Yates notes that paradoxically "it was actually the non-classical aspect of this theatre [the Burbage type theater], its flexible mode of indicating change of scene, which preserved it from the suffocation of the perspective scenes which destroyed the true characteristics of the ancient theatre" (p. 125).

In any case, the sixteen staging practices of the Rose that remain to be discussed are primarily utilitarian. And yet they can be much more than just utilitarian. These practices, together with the practices employed in handling stage properties as emblems, or modified medieval mansions, are poetic and theatrical devices for effecting, even transcending, reality. They are direct and indirect appeals to the imagination of the audience. Shakespeare deliberately points to these devices in his Prologue to *Henry V* where the chorus asks the audience to

> Piece out our imperfections with your thoughts.
> Into a thousand parts divide one man,
> And make imaginary puissance
> Think when we talk of horses that you see them
> Printing their proud hoofs i' the receiving earth.

I shall begin with those of the sixteen practices that appear to be primarily utilitarian and proceed to those that are both utilitarian and imaginative—those that make direct and indirect appeals to the audience to use its imagination.

SITTING OR LYING DOWN UPON THE STAGE

Sometimes actors sit or lie down upon the stage to rest or to sleep. During this interlude something happens that moves the play forward. *Sir John Oldcastle* (a-1) contains a good example (5.9.2374–76):

> *Enter sir John Old-castle, and his Lady disguisde.*
> *Oldca.* Come Madam, happily escapt, here let us sit,
> This place is farre remote from any path,
> And here awhile our weary limbs may rest.

They both fall asleep and are apprehended near the body of a murdered man (2473–75), hidden during an earlier scene (2312–20). Similarly, *Fortunatus* (b-1) begins with an actor lying down on the stage to sleep while a dumb show is presented (1.1.64): "*He lyes downe and sleeps: Enter a Carter, a Tailor,*" and the dumb show begins. Urias lies down on stage in *David and Bathsheba* (b-9) until David calls for wine and asks him to "pledge the King." Stage directions supplement the dialogue to make clear what happens (500–501): "This ground before the king my masters dores, *He lies downe.* Shall be my couch." And in response to David's command (512), "Arise Urias, come and pledge the King. *He riseth.*"

CLEARING THE STAGE OF PROPERTIES

The extant plots of plays of the Rose indicate that care was taken in getting actors onto the stage in the proper order with the necessary properties. Greg's conjectural reconstruction of a portion of *The Battle of Alcazar*, plot (b-4) shows something of this concern:

E[n]ter the Presenter: to him
    2 domb shew
En[te]r above Nemesis, Tho: Dro[m] to
them 3. ghosts w. kendall Dab. [& Harry:]
[t]o them [l]ying behind the curt[a]ines 3.
Furies: Parsons: Georg & Ro: T[ail]or
one wth a whipp: a nother wth a [b]lody
tor[ch]: & the 3d wth a Chop[ping] Kni[fe]: exeunt

The single word *"exeunt"* suggests that other arrangements were necessary for getting properties off the stage at the end of an episode or a scene. Frequently cues are found in the dialogue to prompt the actors in clearing properties from the stage. In *The Shoemakers' Holiday* (a-2) (4.1.66–68) Firke complains that it is time for breakfast and Hodge agrees.

Hodge. Ist so? why then leave worke Raph, to breakfast, boy looke to the tooles, Come Raph, Come Firke.   *Exeunt.*

In *The Brazen Age* (b-2) (K3v) properties representing the labors of Hercules are brought on stage according to a stage direction and provision is made in the dialogue (L3–L3v) to remove them from the stage:

Jas. . . . Princes your hands, take up these monuments
Of his twelve labours in a marble Temple
(We will erect and dedicate to him)
Reserve them to his lasting memory.

REMOVAL OF BODIES FROM THE STAGE

After Warman is murdered in *The Death of Robert* (a-2), Robin Hood asks one of the actors to help him take the body from the stage. The business is strongly motivated (231–35):

Rob. Well, I am sorie; but must not be sad
Because the King is comming to my bower.
Help mee, I pray thee, to remooue his bodie,
Least he should come and see him murdered.
Sometime anone he shall be buried.   *Exit*.

The practice of having bodies removed from the stage so that action can continue in a new fictional place is shown clearly in *The Massacre at Paris* (b-3). The Guise murders the pedants (533–35):

Come sirs, Ile whip you to death with my punniards
point.   *he kils them*.
An. Away with them both.   *Exit Anjoy*.

It is theatrically neat for Anjoy to direct that the bodies of the two pedants be taken away and that he assist because the action clears the stage for the next scene in which he is the principal speaker.

COUPLETS TO END SCENES

The plays of the Rose frequently employ couplets to end scenes as in *Patient Grissil* (a-1) (1.1.77–78):

But if sweet peace succeede this amorous strife,
Ile say my wit was best to choose a wife.   *Exeunt*.

A couplet ends scene 5 of *King Leir* (b-6) (466–67):

Camb. Then let us haste, all danger to prevent
For feare delayes do alter his intent.   *Exeunt*.

And in Shakespeare's *I Henry VI*, (b-8) the scene in the Temple Garden (2.4.1066–67) ends with the following couplet:

Come, let us foure to Dinner: I dare say,
This Quarrell will drinke Blood another day.
                                    Exeunt.

ENTERING IN THE MIDST OF CONVERSATION

Beckerman says (p. 178) that "the most frequent type of entrance [in the Shakespearean Globe plays] is that of the mid-speech," which accounts for over forty percent of the scene beginnings. This type of entrance is also used frequently in the plays of the Rose. In *Sir John Oldcastle* (a-1), for instance, Sir John of Wrootham and Doll enter with Doll speaking (3.3): "By my troth, thou art as jealous a man as lives." Obviously Doll is responding to something that Sir John has said. A mid-speech entrance is found in *King Leir* (b-6) where a stage direction reads (4.341–42): "*Enter the Gallian King with Mumford, and three Nobles more.*" The King speaks (343–44): "Disswade me not, my Lords, I am resolv'd,/ This next fayre wynd to sayle for Brittany." Here it would appear that a conversation has been going on as the group enters.

DIRECT APPEALS TO USE IMAGINATION

The prologue to *Fortunatus* (b-1) contains one of the few direct appeals to the audience to use its imagination that we find in plays of the Rose: "Our muse intreats,/ Your thoughts to helpe poore Art. . . . Your gracious eye/ Gives life to *Fortunatus* historie." The similarity of this passage to the one in the prologue of *Henry V*, with its allusion to "this Wooden O," need not be stressed. Usually the appeals to the audiences at the Rose, and, I believe, at the Globe also, were indirect rather than direct. Another of the direct appeals is found in *The Death of Robert* (a-2). Friar Tuck engages the chorus in conversation about what is to happen in the remainder of the play: "You must suppose king Richard now is deade,/ And John (resistlesse) is faire Englands Lord" (903–04). A clearer and more direct appeal, however, is found in another a-play, *Captain Stukley* (a-3), in a speech by the chorus (L3):

> Thus of Alcazars battell in one day
> three kings at once did loose their haples lives.
> Your gentle favour must we needs entreat,
> For rude presenting such a royall sight,
> Which more imagination must supply:
> Then all our utmost strength can reach unto.

And finally a direct appeal is made to the audience to use its imagination in *The Four Prentices of London* (b-8) in which a presenter says (C1):

Imagine now yee see the aire made thicke
With stormy tempests, that disturbe the sea:
And the foure windes at warre among themselves:
And the weake barkes wherein the brothers saile,
Split on strange rockes, and they enforc't to swim:
To save their desperate lives.

ALLUSIONS AND REPORTS

In plays of the Rose, it frequently happens that allusions are made
to objects, and reports are made about action in progress that cannot
be seen by the audience. *Look about You* (a-4) opens with a stage
direction and dialogue that clearly illustrate this practice:

> *Enter Robert Hood a young Noble-man, a servant with him, with ryding
> wandes in theyr handes, as if they had beene new lighted.*
> Robert.
> Goe, walke the horses, wayte me on the hill,
> This is the Hermits Cell, goe out of sight:
> My busines with him must not be reveal'd,
> To any mortall creature but himselfe.
> *Serv.* Ile waite your honour in the crosse high-way. *Exit.*

The "crosse high-way" on the hill where the horses are to be walked
and the servant is to wait are out of sight of the audience, and in this
instance presumably out of sight of the "Hermits Cell." Another
clear example of an actor onstage reporting on action taking place
offstage is found in *I Henry VI* (b-8) (3.3.1614–24):

> *Drumme sounds afarre off.*
> *Pucell.* . . . . Hearke, by the sound of Drumme may you
> perceive Their Powers are marching unto Paris-ward.
> *Here sound an English March.*
> There goes the Talbot, with his Colours spred,
> And all the Troupes of English after him.
> *French March.*
> Now in the Rereward comes the Duke and his:
> Fortune in favor makes him lagge behinde.
> Summon a Parley, we will talke with him.
> *Trumpets sound a Parley.*

A rather well known instance in which actors onstage watch and discuss action occurring offstage is found in *A Woman Killed with Kindness* (a-2); it is the scene (B2v–B3) in which Sir Charles and Sir Francis watch and comment upon the performances of their hawks, which are high overhead and out of sight of the audience.

DIALOGUE TO INDICATE THE PLACE OF THE ACTION

Dialogue is used regularly to indicate the place in which the action is set in plays of the Rose. A good example of how this is done can be found in the opening scene of *Look about You* (a-4) (1–6) which we just examined:

> *Robert.*
> Goe, walke the horses, wayte me on the hill,
> This is the Hermits Cell, goe out of sight.

The author of *The Famous Victories* (b-3) (A2) uses the device of having one character ask about the location:

> But tell me sirs, whereabouts are we?
> *Tom.* My Lord, we are now about a mile off London.

In *I Henry VI* (b-8) an actor walks on stage (3.2.1424) and simply says to his fellow actors: "These are the Citie Gates, the Gates of Roan,/ Through which our Pollicy must make a breach."

LIGHTS TO INDICATE NIGHT AND DARKNESS

One of the better known practices at the Rose, where plays were presented during the daylight hours, was the use of lanterns, lamps, torches, candles, or any kind of lights to indicate that action in a scene occurred at night or in a dark place. Lights are called for in the dialogue and in the stage directions for a game of cards played in Frankford's house after supper in *A Woman Killed with Kindness* (a-2) (D4v). Jenkins directs one of his fellows to put "candles and candle sticks there," and a stage direction reads: *"They spread a Carpet, set downe lights and Cards."* The time and atmosphere for the brazen head scene in *Friar Bacon* (b-4) is suggested by the following stage direction (1561–63): *"Enter Frier Bacon drawing the courtaines with a white sticke, a booke in his hand, and a lampe lighted by him, and the brasen head and miles, whith weapons by him."*

THE ASIDE

Plays of the Rose call regularly for actors to say something that by convention is not supposed to be heard by others on stage. In *Sir John Oldcastle* (a-1), for example, Lord Cobham is invited by Cambridge, Scroope, Gray, and Chartres to join in the plot against the life of King Henry (3.1.1044–102); all five are on stage at the time Cobham responds (1102):

> *Cobb.* Notorious treason! yet I will conceale *aside*
> My secret thoughts, to sound the depth of it.
> My lord of Cambridge, I doe see your claime,
> And what good may redound unto the land,
> By prosecuting of this enterprise.

The first two lines of Cobham's response must not, for the purposes of the plot, be heard by the others on stage because they might suspect him of doing what he actually does later in the play—betraying them to the king. Seven asides are called for by stage directions in *The Jew of Malta* (b-5) for the scene between Barabas and Lodowick (D4–E1), an episode that requires about sixty-five lines (793–858) in the Tucker Brooke edition. Only two actors are on stage at the time and, while some of Barabas's insults might have been accepted by the love-smitten son of the governor, the threats to Lodowick's life were not intended for his ears. They were real and they were carried out through Barabas's machinations (F1v). Likewise, two exceptionally long asides designated in *The Four Prentices of London* (b-8) by stage directions as *"private to himselfe"* and as *"private"* are not supposed to be heard by the persons on stage when they are uttered (C2–C2v):

> *Guy.* Sweet Lady, all my powers I owe to you:
> For by your favour I ascend this height,
> Which seates me in the favor of a Prince.
> A Prince, that did he know me, in the stead *private to himselfe*.

Of doing me honour would cut off my head.
Hee did exile my father; cast me downe;
And spurd with envious hate, distrest us all.
Since fortune then, and the devouring Seas,
Have rob'd me of my brothers, and none left
Of all my fathers sonnes alive but I:
Take this advantage, and be secret, *Guy*.
Meete this occasion; and conclude with fate,
To raise againe thy fathers ruin'd state.
Lad. Fie niggard, can you spend such pretious breath,
Speake to yourselfe so many words apart;
And keepe their sound from my attentive eare,
Which save your words no musicke loves to heare?
Guy. What would you have me say?
Ladie. Would I might teach thee!
Oh that I had the guidance of thy tongue! *private*.
But what would that availe thee foolish Girle?
Small hope in those instructions I should finde,
To rule your tongue, if not to guide your minde.

Beckerman says (p. 162) that "the Globe players, in staging of asides, did not think in terms of creating an illusion of actuality but of relating the crucial elements of the narrative to each other." However, the following points ought to be kept in mind with reference to the staging of asides in plays of the Rose: 1) Asides may be traced to the playwright who includes them (but does not always mark them as "*aside*") for the purposes of plot or to show something in a character's mind. 2) Because no man deliberately lies to himself, the person who is speaking to himself when he delivers an aside may be depended upon as revealing the truth about his feelings. 3) The aside is supposed to be unheard by at least one person on stage at the time it is delivered. 4) Actually, the aside must be loud enough for the audience to hear it; consequently, reason dictates that it is also heard by the person who is not supposed to hear it. 5) The speaker, therefore, must in some way signal to the audience that what he is saying is an "*aside*," is "*private to himself*," as in the speech quoted from *The Four Prentices*. 6) The person who is not supposed to hear the remarks must indicate by his reaction that he does not hear. In the example cited from *The Four Prentices*, the French Lady complains (C2v):

> Fie niggard, can you spend such pretious breath,
> Speake to yourselfe so many words apart; *private*.
> And keepe their sound from my attentive eare,
> Which save your words no musicke loves to heare?

7) The final point to be made about the staging of asides in plays of the Rose is that the use of the term "aside" describes the manner in which these episodes were presented: the speaker simply turned aside from those who were not supposed to hear the remarks *"private to himselfe."* In this way he signaled to the audience the nature of his speech. Now Beckerman is correct in pointing out that the distance between the speaker and those who were not to hear was unimportant (p. 161). They could have been close enough to touch each other, as in the instance he cites from *Pericles* (1.1.81–90). The important thing was not the distance but the signal for the "aside," regardless of whether it was given by a movement on the stage, a gesture, by a special tone of the voice, or by all of these. Consider, for example, the way the playwright signals "asides" in the Lodowick-Barabas scene of *The Jew of Malta* (b-5) (D4–E1). As the scene begins, Barabas insults Lodowick: "The slave looks like a hogs cheek new sing'd." Although the insult is not marked as an aside, the dialogue that follows the insult indicates that Barabas had turned and walked away from Lodowick as he spoke.

> *Lod.* Whither walk'st thou Barabas?
> *Bar.* No further: 'tis a custome held with us
> That when we speake with Gentiles like to you,
> We turne into the Ayre to purge ourselves.

Barabas's reply, of course, permits him to turn away frequently during the remainder of the episode, "to purge" himself and at the same time deliver an insulting "aside." In the 1633 quarto, seven of Barabas's speeches that follow in this episode are marked as asides. One may conclude with Beckerman (p. 162) that there was no attempt in staging these incidents to create "an illusion of actuality," and that "what is true of the aside is equally true of observations, disguises, concealments, parleys, and other theatrical devices" in the plays of the Globe; and one may extend these conclusions generally to the plays of the Rose. What is more important, however, is that the actors and the playwrights were careful in staging these incidents to signal that they were engaged in a situation calling for the use of imagination.

THE SOLILOQUY

Regularly in plays of the Rose, an actor remains onstage at the end of a scene or comes onto the stage alone and speaks to himself, delivering a soliloquy. The episode must be clearly recognized for what it is—a theatrical device akin to the aside. As in the aside, the speaker is talking to himself and one may accept his words as a true indication of his feelings. *The Shoemakers' Holiday* (a-2) has Lacy explain his plans to disguise himself as a shoemaker and work with Simon Eyre in Tower Street in order to be near Rose (1.3.1–24). A long portion of Faustus's last night (5.2.2035–90) is a soliloquy, in which the author gives his audience a chance to look into the mind of the doomed man. And in *David and Bathsheba* (b-9) another doomed man, Achitophel, comes onto the stage alone and speaks to himself (1480–1504) before he leaves to take his own life.

OVERLOOKING-OVERHEARING EPISODES

Overlooking-overhearing episodes are of two kinds, with a number of variations between them. In the first kind, the audience is aware of the presence of the observers who are apparently concealed from those they watch. *Sir John Oldcastle* (a-1) contains an episode of this kind (2086–115):

Enter Cambridge, Scroope, and Gray, as in a chamber, and set downe at a table, consulting about their treason: King Harry and Suffolke listening at the doore.

Aside from this stage direction, the presence of the king and Suffolk is not indicated in any way while the conspirators talk (2089–113). Finally *"the King steps in to them with his Lordes"* (2114–15), and from his speech it is clear that he has heard everything the conspirators talked about. Presumably the king and Suffolk have been visible to the audience during part of the time the conspirators talked, while the remainder of the lords were hidden from the audience. And certainly, for the purposes of the plot, none of the conspirators are supposed to have been aware of the presence of the king and his retainers.

In the second kind of episode, the observers "stand close" or "stand aside" as in *Patient Grissil* (a-1) and comment upon the things they see and hear as they watch (3.2.1–64):

> *Enter Urcenze and Onophrio at severall doores, and Farnezie in the mid'st*
> Far. . . . . every man take his stand, for there comes a most rich purchase of mirth.

· ·

> *Enter Emulo with Julia.*
> Ono.   His arme in a scarfe? has he been fighting?
> Far.   Fighting? hang him coward.
> Urc.   Perhaps he does it to shew his scarfe.
> Far.   Peace, heere the asse comes, stand aside, and see him curuet.

As Julia and Emulo talk, the trio observing them comments upon the conversation of the pair until all three agree with Farnezie (60) to "step in."

The first kind of overhearing-overlooking episode is also found in *George a Green* (b-3). The Earl of Kendal enters with "a traine of men" and they decide to "stand in some corner for to heare,/ What braving tearmes the pinner will breathe,/ When he spies our horses in the corne" (451–53). The Earl and two men "meete" George and Jenkin as they go to take the horses to the pound (484). And when George strikes the earl (528) the rest of the party comes onto the stage (535): "*Enter all the ambush.*" An example of the second kind of episode is found in *King Leir* (b-6). The Gallian King and Mumford "stand close" (597) when Cordella enters and they listen and talk to each other as she talks to herself about her miseries. The king then goes to her and says (636–37): "Vouchsafe to me, who have o're-heard thy woes,/ To shew the cause of these thy sad laments." Sometimes, it appears, the two kinds of episodes may be used in the same play, as in *John a Kent* (b-7). In one instance (775–94) the observers agree not to disturb the person they are watching "but give him leave, till his owne leysure him." Finally the person who has been watched speaks to the observers. At a later place in the same play (1047–96) a stage direction in the margin reads "*En[ter] John a K[en]t listening.*" For the purposes of the plot Kent must not be seen, and he gives no indication of his presence until after the people he has been observing leave the stage. At that time he comments in a soliloquy upon what he has heard (1084–96).

INVISIBILITY

Sometime after 3 April 1598, Henslowe purchased "a robe for to goo invisible" along with "a gown for Nembia" at a total cost of £3.10. Several plays presented at the Rose before 1598 call for people to become invisible, but nothing in the dialogue or stage directions indicates that a costume was involved. Magicians figure in most of the incidents, placing charms on specific persons who immediately become invisible to everyone but the magician and the audience. In *A Knack to Know a Knave* (a-4), Dunston calls for Asmoroth to ascend and orders him to "follow me invisible" (1595) as they leave the stage together. In a subsequent scene Dunston calls, "Veni Asmoroth," and brings Alfrida and Ethenwald before the king (1716–20). A stage direction (1716), "*Here enter Alfrida disguised with the Devil*," indicates that the devil appears although no mention is made of him and Dunston quickly dismisses him (1725): "Asmoroth away." Presumably Asmoroth was invisible to every-one except the magician and, of course, the audience. In *Faustus* (b-5) Mephistopheles puts a charm on the scholar so he can "walke invisible to all" (but not to the audience) (3.2.1025–126) and upset the pope at Saint Peter's feast. And in still another play involving a magician, *John a Kent* (b-7), Shrimp is invisible (but not to the audience) as he romps around people and leads them on a "merrie walke" (4.1.1098–187).

DISGUISE

Actors are disguised for the purpose of plot in over half of the extant plays of the Rose. Rowland Lacy, for instance, disguises himself as a shoemaker in order to be near Rose Otley in *The Shoemakers' Holiday* (a-2) (1.3.1–24). Ralph Simnell dresses in Prince Edward's clothes and the Prince, Warren, and Ermsby disguise themselves in various ways in *Friar Bacon* (b-4): "*Enter Raphe Simnell in Edwardes apparrell, Edward, Warren, Ermsby disguised*" (5.513–14). Joan and four soldiers disguise themselves as French peasants in order to pass through the "Gates of Roan" in *I Henry VI* (b-8) (3.2.1422–23): *"Enter Pucell disguis'd, with foure Souldiors with Sacks upon their backs."*

BOY ACTORS IN WOMEN'S ROLES

Only two plays of the Rose seem to allude to the practice of using boys to represent women on stage; neither of them treats the subject with the boldness found in the epilogue to *As You Like It* in which the actor in the role of Rosalind declares:

If I were a Woman, I would kisse as many of you as had beards that pleas'd me, complexions that lik'd me, and breaths that I defi'de not: And I am sure, as many as have good beards, or good faces, or sweet breaths, will for my kind offer. when I made curt'sie, bid me farewell.

The actor in the role of Skelton in *The Downfall of Robert* (a-2) admonishes the players including "the boyes and Clowne" who run out to greet Sir John (29–32):

> Faith little Tracy you are somewhat forward:
> What, our Maid Marian leaping like a lad?
> If you remember, Robin is your love:
> Sir Thomas mantle yonder, not sir John.

The actor who plays the daughter of the French king assumes the disguise of a page to be with Guy (F1v) in *The Four Prentices of London* (b-8). When the page is presented as the daughter of the French king and Guy kisses her, Guy is teased by his brother in an episode that surely shares with the audience the irony of the situation: the fact that women's roles were played by boys. Part of the episode follows (L2v):

> *Eust*. Fie are you not ashamn'd to kisse a boy,
> and in your armes to graspe him with such joy?
> *Guy*. She is no boy, you do mistake her quite.
> *Eust*. A boy, a Page, a wagtaile by this light.
> What say you sister?
> *Bell*. Sure he told me so,
> For if he be a maide, I made him one.

Eust. Do not mistake the sex man, for he's none,
It is a rogue, a wag, his name is Jack,
A notable dissembling lad, a Crack.
Guy. Brother, 'tis you that are deciv'd in her,
Beshrew her, she hath beene my bedfellow
A year and more, yet I had not the grace.
Brothers receive a sister; reverent father
Accept a daughter, whilst I take a wife.
....
Fren.L. A wonderous change she that your Page hath beene
Is now at length transform'd to be your Queene.
Pardon me Guy, my love drew me along,
No shamelesse lust.

OFFSTAGE SOUNDS

The hunting scene in *Titus Andronicus* (2.2.D1) begins with a stage direction: "*Enter Titus Andronicus, and his three sonnes. making a noise with hounds & hornes.*" Here the noise may have been made offstage, but could have continued onstage after the party enters. However, in a direction that follows a few lines later, the noise must be offstage: "*Here a crie of Hounds, and windhornes in a peale: then enter Saturninus, Tamora, Bascianus, Lavinia, Chiron, Demetrius, and their Attendants.*" Sound here is used to provide background for the action set in the woods where hunting is taking place. A clock, apparently offstage, in *A Looking Glass for London* (b-6) "*Strikes 4 a clocke*" according to a stage direction (4.337), permitting a usurer to refuse to accept payment and "stand to the forfeyt of the recognisance." And a brawl offstage is represented in *I Henry VI* (b-8) (3.1.1281 and 1286) by stage directions reading: "*A noyse within, Downe with the Tawny-Coats,*" and "*A noyse againe, Stones, Stones.*"

18

Conclusion

I HAVE reconstructed the stage of the Rose (plates 1, 14, and 15) with the idea that it was an Elizabethan adaptation of the Vitruvian stage, an adaptation in which the perspective scenes developed in Italy by Serlio were not used. And I have proceeded on the assumption that the stage had the facilities and equipment necessary for the presentation of the forty-three plays extant in texts surely or probably given there. In the absence of specific measurements for the stage, I have constructed a Vitruvian plan for the Rose (plate 17), based on a scale that represents the inside diameter of the building as ninety-one feet. From this plan I have derived most of the horizontal measurements needed for the construction of a model and floor plans to illustrate my findings (Appendix D). The vertical measurements have been taken from the contract for the Fortune (Foakes and Rickert, pp. 306–10). I do not claim that the measurements used in reconstructing the stage are precise; they are suggestive and illustrative, nothing more.

I have been concerned mainly with the facilities of the stage and its equipment, such things as the openings in the walls, the doors, the windows, the lift, the curtains, and stage properties. And I have tried to find out how they were arranged and used. Relying in part upon the method suggested by Professor George F. Reynolds in his study of the Red Bull (p. 48), I have "blocked" the action in all the plays, that is, traced the movement of the actors about the stage, line by line, through the texts of the plays given at the Rose. I found from the patterns of movement in the plays, from the demands the plays made upon the stage, and from the other available evidence that the stage was a rectangular platform. It extended to the center of the theater building and was enclosed on three sides by walls in which there were five openings arranged much as I show them in plate 1.

Turning from the reconstructed stage to some forty-one staging practices commonly used in Elizabethan theaters and apparently required by the plays of the Rose, I have tried to show how this stage functioned in presenting the plays in the repertory.

I have found that the principal opening in the wall at the rear of the stage (the tiring-house wall incorporated into the frame of the playhouse) was the gates. This opening was used regularly to represent entrances to strongholds and other places requiring a door that could be opened and closed. Also in the wall at the rear of the stage were two discovery spaces provided with curtains, one on each side of the gates. These openings were used to represent passageways leading to other entrances to fortified places, or doors leading to other rooms inside a house, or entrances to such specific places as the court of guard in *I Henry VI* (b-8) (2.1), the Porters lodge in *The Golden Age* (b-2) (H3), the tent in *II Tamburlaine* (b-6) (I6v–I7), Jane's semsters shop in *Shoemakers' Holiday* (a-2) (3.4) or to Hodge's shop in the scene that follows (4.1) in the same play. More frequently, however, these discovery spaces—openings provided with curtains—were used as recessed places in which to store thrones, beds, tables, chairs, tombs, rocks, trees, arbors, and similar large stage properties which were "discovered," that is, thrust out upon the stage when they were needed and withdrawn and concealed behind the curtains when the actors no longer needed them.

The most significant point to be made about all the openings in the wall at the rear of the stage (the gates, the discovery spaces, the penthouse with its window, and the gallery) is that they were used to represent specific places, or entrances to specific places. The gates, for example, are used in *I Henry VI* (b-8) to represent "the Citie Gates, the Gates of Roan" (3.2). The curtained opening before a discovery space is used in *Friar Bacon* (b-4) (1561–694) to represent the entrance to Bacon's study, "my cell" (1573), which is clearly on the main stage and not in a recessed area behind the stage. The gallery is used regularly to designate the walls of some particular stronghold as in *II Tamburlaine* (b-6) (K6v): "*Enter the Governor of Babylon upon the walles, with others.*" The penthouse and the window frequently designate such a specific place as the room in which Bel-imperia is imprisoned in *The Spanish Tragedy* (1724–41).

The gates, the two discovery spaces, the gallery, and the penthouse with its window were used at the Rose in much the same way that *mansions* were used in medieval staging in such a play, for example, as *The Castle of Perseverance*. Like the *mansions*, the several openings in the wall at the rear of the stage of the Rose were fixed places for playing, places in and around which the action moved and developed.

An important distinction must be made, however, between the way the openings in the wall at the rear of the stage of the Rose were used and the way *mansions* were employed. The *mansions* represented one particular place throughout the play; for instance, the castle of perseverance remained just that throughout the play of *The Castle of Perseverance* and the "scaffolds" of God, Belial, the World, Caro, and Covetousness remained unchanged in their designations, as did the bed for "Mankynde" within the castle. On the other hand, quite frequently the Shakespearean "muse intreats, / Your thoughts to helpe poor Art," changing the designation of a particular opening several times in a single play to represent different places or entrances to different places. For instance, the gates are used in *I Henry VI* (b-8) not only to represent "the Gates of Roan," but the entrances to "the Tower" of London (1.3), to Orleans (2.1), and to Bordeaux (4.2). In the same play actors use the gallery to represent walls or turrets above Orelans (1.4, 1.6, 2.1), "Roan" (3.2), and Bordeaux (4.2). The structure which I have identified as the penthouse with the window represents in *Titus Andronicus* (a-4) "the Senate house," when Saturninus and Bassianus leave the stage through the gates and "goe up into the Senate house" (A4); and in the same play, the penthouse is used to represent Titus's study, from which he descends to meet Tamora and her sons (I3v).

Two discovery spaces appear to be used in continuous action in the "dumbe shewes" in the play-within-a-play at the beginning of *The Downfall of Robert* (a-2) to represent places in Skelton's house that are used, in turn, to represent the court of King Richard and the bower within which Robert and Marian are to seek refuge in Sherwood Forest (45): "*Ely ascends the chaire* [Richard's throne]," and a few lines later (52–53) Robert and Marian "*infolde each other, and sit downe within the curteins.*" Later in the play one of these discovery spaces is designated as the entrance to Ely's hiding place "in Kent, within a mile of Dover" (1104). Still later a throne in or before a discovery space is used to represent the court of King John (1631), following a scene in which a discovery space is used to represent Robert and Marian's bower in Sherwood Forest (1490–91). We cannot be sure which of these discovery spaces was used in presenting a particular scene; we can be certain, however, that both discovery spaces, like the other openings in the wall at the rear of the stage of the Rose, were frequently used in a single play to represent more than one place.

The *"one doore"* and *"the other doore"* at *"one side"* and *"the other side"* of the stage are used in the development of the action in more than three-fourths of the 689 scenes contained in the plays of the Rose. The action in this large group of scenes follows one of three basic patterns: 1) Two hundred thirty-seven scenes begin in *"one doore"* or *"the other doore"* (occasionally in both of them as at the beginning of *Titus Andronicus*) and move directly to the gates or to one of the discovery spaces in the back wall; apparently, as the scene is developed, the action flows in and out of any of the openings in the back wall, as the plot of the play may require; and finally when the scene reaches its climax, the action moves offstage— presumably through the door opposite the one in which the scene originated. 2) One hundred eighty-four scenes follow a pattern of action similar to the movement of processions. These scenes begin in a door at the side of the stage, flow onto the stage and are developed through dialogue and intruded episodes of one kind or another; then they move offstage through the door opposite the one used for the entrance. 3) One hundred nine scenes are involved in the presentation of stage battles. They follow one of two patterns of action, both of which employ the *"one doore"* and *"the other doore."* One pattern is processionlike, while the other is excursionlike with opposing forces rushing onto the stage from doors flanking the stage and then withdrawing through the same door.

The 388 processions in the plays and the processionlike movement in some 421 or more scenes encourage one to think of the scenes in plays of the Rose as representations of the parade of life. A significant point, I believe, about the use of the *"one doore"* and *"the other doore"* in the processionlike scenes is that these openings, like the trapdoor in the heavens and in the floor of the stage, lead to undesignated places or places whose location is indicated only in a vague way. Only on rare occasions do scenes in plays given at the

Rose begin with a stage direction calling for actors to enter from a specific place. And it is almost as rare for scenes to end with stage directions calling for actors to exit into a specific place. The most frequently used of all stage directions in plays of the Rose are those including the words *"Enter"* and *"Exit"* or *"Exeunt."* Almost every scene in every play begins with actors entering from some undesignated place and ends with actors leaving the stage for an unnamed destination. It seems probable that the absence of pictures of the stage showing these doors, except in two of the recently discovered Fludd drawings (plates 7 and 8), and the fact that these doors are not used to represent entrances from or exits to specific places has obscured knowledge of the presence of these most regularly used openings in the walls of the stage of the Rose. In a sense, the *"one doore"* and *"the other doore"* at the Rose are similar to the *parodoi* of the Greek theater, as the lift in the heavens and the trapdoor in the floor of the stage are similar to the *mechane* and "Charon's steps."

On the basis of what I have found out about the stage of the Rose and the way it was used, I have described Henslowe's playhouse and the practices followed there as a happy fusion of medieval stagecraft (including its classical antecedents) and Elizabethan Vitruvianism. The stagecraft at the Rose, however, transcended that of the theaters from which it developed; it became more flexible and more imaginative. Through the use of a few openings in a wall or walls and a few stage properties such as beds, chairs, tables, thrones, and tombs, the stage of the Rose became a little world. I am sure that it is significant that two well-known Shakespearean playhouses were designated as the Globe and Fortune—betokening, "this little world" and the capricious goddess who holds some sway within it. Be that as it may, the *"one doore"* and *"the other doore,"* the lift, and the trapdoor in the floor of the stage were simply entrances to and exits from a place representing the world. Through the door at *"one side"* or *"the other side"* of the stage entered men and women in the parade of life to act out their stories. In the processionlike scenes, the wall at the rear of the stage usually represented either explicitly or implicitly a particular place in the world such as a castle, a court, or a house, or a room inside a house, or a street, or a forest. The several openings in the wall were used in such scenes to represent entrances from and exits into the particular place. The wall at the rear of the stage was a multipurpose setting provided with openings capable of being changed at will, by the use of dialogue and stage properties, to lead to any specific place in the world.

If the stage of the Rose was generally similar to the stages in the permanent out-of-doors public playhouses in which Shakespeare's plays were given, what has been found out about the existence, location, and use of the several openings in the walls around the stage of the Rose may be applied generally to the Shakespearean stage and its practices. The scope, that is, the universality and moral relevance, of the plays of the Rose and the plays of Shakespeare has long been obscured by their association with the De Witt sketch of the Swan and theaters reconstructed upon the assumption that the sketch was typical of the stages in Shakespearean playhouses. The *"one doore"* and *"the other doore"* in walls at the side of the stage have been confused with entrances to particular places, even in reconstructions in which it is recognized that there were walls at the side of the stage.

With our loss of knowledge about the existence and the purpose of the *"one doore"* and *"the other doore,"* we have lost sight of the parade of life as an element in Shakespearean drama. As a result we may have lost something of the import of the words of Chaucer's Egeus when he observes in the Knight's Tale that

> This world nys but a thurghfare ful of wo,
> And we been pilgrymes, passunge to and fro.

In fact, Jaques's remarks

> All the world's a stage,
> And all the men and women merely players.
> They have their exits and their entrances.

may become as meaningless as they are to unsympathetic students forced to memorize the speech.

When we lose sight of the parade of life as an element in Shakespearean drama we also lose our understanding of the concept of the world as a stage and the stage as a world—the very name of Shakespeare's Globe loses its significance. And with it we lose more than our sense of the universality of the drama, we lose sight of its moral relevance. The trapdoors leading to heaven and hell become quaint vestigial elements, meaningless, unless they are understood as a part of the concept of the stage as a little world in which we see man tested by the forces above and below him. As Professor Thomas B. Stroup puts it in his *Microcosmos* (pp. 179–80), the Shakespearean play takes its shape "from the testing force of Providence. . . . As the protagonist moves in pageant and encompassing actions across the stage of the world he is proved, like Job or like Jonah, and in his proving he undergoes a testing. Often, and in the tragedies especially, this proving follows the pretty well-recognized pattern of Christian tests."

Restoration of the *"one doore"* and *"the other doore"* to the Rose, along with an understanding of the way they were used with the gates and the discovery spaces in the rear wall, provides the student and scholar with a stage on which he can actually trace the movement in the plays of Shakespeare and his contemporaries. This is a stage that permits us to reassign to the Shakespearean play its basically processional and ritualistic characteristics. It is a stage that endows those plays once more with a portion of their double heritage from the classical and the medieval theater. It is a stage that allows us to insist with vigor upon something of which we have always been aware: the universality and the moral relevance of Shakespearean drama.

Appendices

A

The Material Related to the Rose

THE PROBLEM of assembling and using the material containing evidence about the staging and the stage of the Rose theater involves four steps: 1) the material must be identified; 2) it must be obtained in reliable form—in pictures of independent authority, in authentic documents related to the theater, in accurate editions of the plays; 3) it must be evaluated and classified according to its reliability; and 4) it must be arranged in some convenient and logical order. These tasks have been simplified by Professor Reynolds's study of the Red Bull, and, of course, by the work done by W. W. Greg, E. K. Chambers, and others.

Reynolds says (*Red Bull*, p. 30) that the evidence about the Shakespearean stage is of three kinds: "contemporary pictures of the exteriors of the theater and especially of the interior; contemporary contracts, descriptions, and allusions outside the plays; and the evidence furnished by the plays themselves." This is a workable grouping, and I use it for the materials related to the Rose; for easy reference, however, these groups have been labeled: 1) Pictures of the Rose, 2) Documents of the Rose, and 3) Plays of the Rose.

PICTURES OF THE ROSE

Among the pictures which may show the exterior or the interior of Henslowe's theater are two maps, six engravings, two sketches, and six woodcuts. These pictures are described below.

Norden's Map of London, 1593 (plate 2)

I. A. Shapiro says (*SS* 1:27) "the first map to show any of the [Bankside] theatres is Pieter van den Keere's engraving of John Norden's map of London for the latter's *Speculum Britanniae Pars . . . Middlesex* (London, 1593)." The Rose, labeled "The playhowse," is located in this map precisely as it is described in the Henslowe-Cholmley partnership agreement of 10 January 1586/7. The copy that I use was provided by the Birmingham Reference Library.

Norden's Revised Map of London, 1600 (plate 3)

A revised version of Norden's map of 1593 was discovered in the Royal Library at Stockholm and brought to the attention of modern scholars by I. A. Shapiro in 1948 (*SS* 1:25–37). The revision was set in an engraved panorama of London bearing the title *Civitas Londini* and the date 1600. Shapiro says of the inset that "Norden has brought his map of 1593 . . . up to date by inserting the Swan Theatre built c. 1595, and the Globe, built in 1599." The Rose appears in this map in its known location, between the "Bearegard" and the recently erected Globe, although Henslowe's playhouse has this time been incorrectly labeled "The Stare." The copy that I use was provided by the Royal Library, Stockholm, Sweden.

Civitas Londini, 1600 (plate 4)

The engraved panorama, *Civitas Londini*, 1600, shows all four of the theaters on the Bankside as polygonal structures and locates them as they appear in the Norden map, which is set into the panorama. This engraving is contemporary with the Rose and contains a representation of that playhouse. The copy that I use was provided by the Royal Library, Stockholm, Sweden.

Hondius View of London, 1610 (plate 23)

Hondius's engraving is set into the map of Great Britain in John Speed's *Theatre of the Empire of Great Britain* published in 1611. The engraving is inscribed "Graven by I. Hondius . . . 1610," but according to Shapiro (*SS* 1:31–32), "It is probable that the inset view was merely engraved by Hondius from a drawing by another hand, possibly some years earlier in date. The representation of London north of the Thames appears to be based on Kip's 1604 engraving of the Triumphal Arch erected in Fenchurch Street for James I's entry into the city. Though there are some suggestions of indebtedness to *Civitas Londini* for the view of the south bank, this may be original." The possibility that the Hondius engraving was derived from a drawing made while the Rose was standing necessitates the inclusion of this engraving with pictures of the Rose; if the Rose was in existence when the original was drawn, it is the theater shown in the foreground and the Globe, lying farther south and east, has been sacrificed for the ornamental border around the inset. The copy that I use was provided by the British Museum.

Delaram's View of London [1615–24?] (plate 24)

Three Bankside theaters are shown beneath the legs of a horse bearing James I in an undated engraving by "Francisco Delarame." Shapiro is of the opinion that "the Delaram background may have been derived from the Hondius view (the converse is clearly impossible) or both may be derived from the same original, now lost" (SS 1:32–33). The circular theater in the foreground is possibly Henslowe's Rose. The copy that I use was provided by the Royal Library, Windsor Castle, Berkshire.

Holland's *Herwologia Anglica*, title page, 1620 (plate 25)

Two circular theaters are shown on the Bankside in this engraving which Shapiro says (SS 1:33) "may be derived from the same original" as the Hondius. Again, the relationship of this engraving to the Hondius view is the basis on which it has been included with the pictures showing what is possibly the Rose theater. The copy that I use was provided by the Birmingham Reference Library.

Bankside Section from Merian's View of London, 1638 (plate 26)

Shapiro is of the opinion that Merian's View is derived from *Civitas Londini*, 1600, and from Visscher's View (SS 1:31). Merian shows four polygonal theaters on the Bankside, an error for which Shapiro advances the theory that "Merian must have noticed that *Civitas Londini* and Norden's inset map both show four theatres on the Bankside and decided to repair Visscher's omission; not realizing that Visscher had misplaced his 'Globe,' Merian inserted the missing theatre in its correct relative position assuming Visscher's siting to be accurate. Unfortunately for Merian, the Rose Theatre had disappeared some thirty years before he made his engraving." The possibility that the Rose is represented as it was pictured in an earlier drawing necessitates the inclusion of the Merian View with pictures of the Rose. The copy I use was provided by the London Topographical Society.

Baker's *Chronicle*, title page, 1643 (plate 27)

J. Q. Adams reproduces in his *Shakespearean Playhouses*, facing p. 146, the inset from the title page of Sir Richard Baker's *Chronicle* and holds that the inset showing a polygonal theater and a circular theater is related to the Hondius view. The possibility, then, that the circular theater in the foreground may represent the Rose warrants the inclusion of the inset with pictures of the Rose. The copy that I use was provided by the British Museum.

Sketch on Henslowe Letter, 28 September 1593 (plate 28)

R. A. Foakes and R. T. Rickert (SS 13:111–12) call attention to a sketch "in a reddish-brown ink" on the third page of a letter written in Henslowe's hand to Edward Alleyn and dated 28 September 1593. Identified as Dulwich College MSS. I. 14 in G. F. Warner's *Catalogue*, the letter with the sketch was noted by Greg (3:39), who observed that "There are several pen and ink sketches on the outer leaf, one apparently for some scenery in perspective." Foakes and Rickert assert (*SS* 13:112) that "It seems likely . . . that the sketch reproduced is by Henslowe, although it is in a different ink from the letter and cannot be dated." It is possible that this sketch is related to the Rose. The copy that I use was provided by the Governors of Dulwich College.

Scene from *Titus Andronicus*, 1595 (plate 29)

Probably the best contemporary picture of a play in progress on the Elizabethan stage is a sketch generally attributed to Henry Peacham, 1595. Seven characters are shown in a stage picture illustrating one of the episodes at the beginning of the first scene in *Titus Andronicus*. Immediately below the sketch are forty lines of text drawn, mostly, from the play. J. Dover Wilson (*SS* 1:17–24) is "pretty confident that '1594' or '1595' is the correct translation" of the dated signature "Henricus Peacham" that appears on the page with the drawing. Wilson and, less confidently, E. K. Chambers (*Facts and Problems* 1:313) suggest that the text below the drawing is derived from the 1623 folio. John Munro argues (*TLS* [10 June 1949], p. 385) that "the words and the pictures match satisfactorily—in fact, that the artist added the lines from the play, or had them added, in order that his picture should be readily interpreted." He believes that the picture and the text below it were based on a version of the play antedating the appearance of Alarbus as a character in the drama. Alarbus is on stage in the Quarto of 1594: "*Exit Titus sonnes with Alarbus.*" Wilson contests Munro's theory (*TLS* [24 June 1949], p. 413), and Munro replies (1 July 1949, p. 429). If Munro is correct, the picture and the text are representative of a version of the play given before it was at the Rose where the *Diary* (Foakes and Rickert, p. 21) lists performances on 23 and 28 January, and 6 February 1594. The copy that I use was provided by the Courtault Institute of Art and is reproduced with the permission of Lord Bath.

Zenocrate from *Tamburlaine the Great*, 1597 (plate 30)

A woodcut of Zenocrate appears on the lower half of sig. F5 in the 1597 edition of *I* and *II Tamburlaine*. This edition is close enough to the time of the production of the plays at the Rose for the woodcut to be included with pictures related to the Rose theater. The copy I use was provided by the Henry E. Huntington Library.

Tamburlaine from *Tamburlaine the Great*, 1597 (plate 31)

The woodcut of Tamburlaine which appears on sig. F5v in the 1597 edition of *I* and *II Tamburlaine*, like that of Zenocrate, is close enough in date to the production of the plays at the Rose for it to be included with pictures of the Rose. The copy I use was provided by the Henry E. Huntington Library.

The Spanish Tragedy, title page, 1615 (plate 32)

The well-known woodcut of the murder of Horatio appears for the first time on the title pages of the two editions of *The Spanish Tragedy* printed in 1615. This picture seems to be rather close to a stage production, probably to the one at the Rose. However the cut showing the body of Horatio hanging in a structural arbor does not appear on the title page of either the undated quarto or the 1602 quarto, both of which seem to be representative of productions at the Rose, the former in 1592–93 and the latter in 1597.

A structural arbor was used in *A Looking Glass for London* (517–22) given at the Rose for the first time on 8 March 1592:

> *Rasni*. Maġi for love of Rasni by your Art,
> By Magicke frame an Arbour out of hand,
> For faire Remilia to desport her in.
> Meane-while, I will bethinke me on further pomp.
> *Exit*.
> *The Magi with their rods beate the ground, and*
> *from under the same riseth a brave Arbour*.

Clearly the "Arbour" is a structure of some kind "For faire Remilia to desport her in," although she never uses it. It is possible that the same stage property was used at the Rose just six days later for the first performance there of *The Spanish Tragedy*, 14 March 1592 (Foakes and Rickert, p. 17). The trellislike arbor shown in the woodcut on the title page of the 1615 edition satisfies the requirements for the action in the quarto of 1602 (2.4 and 5). The copy I use was provided by the University Library, Cambridge, England.

Four Prentices, title page, 1615 (plate 33)

The fact that this woodcut is much closer in time to a production of the play at the Red Bull than it is to a production of the play at the Rose must reduce the value of the evidence contained in the picture. The copy I use was provided by the Bodleian Library.

Faustus, title page, 1616 (plate 34)

The evidence this woodcut may offer about the stage and the staging practices of the Rose is of doubtful value. It may not depict the actual location of the scene, because it shows Mephistopheles rising from hell in response to Faustus's incantations (1.3), and indicates that the conjuring takes place inside a room. While nothing in the dialogue of this scene rules out the location of the action in a room, the dialogue elsewhere (1.1.172–74) indicates that the conjuring scene is to take place in a "bushy grove," which is also referred to as a "solitary Grove." The picture may well represent a production of *Faustus* at the Fortune, where it was apparently given in 1602, or at any one of a number of theaters, because it was a very popular play. At best, this woodcut only possibly represents a production of that play on the stage of Henslowe's theater. The copy I use was provided by the British Museum.

Friar Bacon, title page, 1630 (plate 35)

The woodcut on the title page of the second edition of *Friar Bacon*, printed in 1630 for Elizabeth Allde, is almost valueless as evidence on the stage and staging at the Rose. Greg points out in his introduction to *Friar Bacon* (*MSR* 1926, p. vi) that "the block was, indeed, cut, not for the play, but for the chapbook of 'The Famous Historie of Fryer Bacon' and appears in the earliest known edition, that of 1627. It evidently came into the hands of Elizabeth Allde through her being commissioned to print an edition of the chapbook for F. Grove in 1629." The copy I use was provided by the Bodleian Library.

DOCUMENTS OF THE ROSE

Most of the documents containing evidence about the stage of the Rose and the way it was used are found in W. W. Greg's edition of Henslowe's *Diary* and *Papers*, and in Greg's *Dramatic Documents from the Elizabethan Playhouses*, which includes the manuscript of "The Part of Orlando," and the "Plots" for *The Battle of Alcazar*, *Frederick and Basilea*, and *I Troilus and Cressida*. ("The Part of Orlando" and the Plots are discussed in the section that follows, "Repertory of Extant Plays of the Rose.") Both Greg's edition of the *Diary* and R. A. Foakes and R. T. Rickert's more recent edition, *Henslowe's Diary*, are used. Chambers (2:405–10) refers to a few additional documents in his brief account of the Rose and includes throughout his *Elizabethan Stage* matter of importance that may be related to the Rose. Generally, however, the documents of the Rose with which I am concerned are those edited by Greg and by Foakes and Rickert.

The scholarship which attests the importance of the Henslowe documents to a study of the Elizabethan stage, and that scholarship which links these documents to the Rose, need not be reviewed here in detail. Foakes and Rickert (p. xl) describe the *Diary* as "the primary source for the theatrical history of the Elizabethan age." Chambers (2:408) says of the *Diary* that "the assumption, in the absence of evidence to the contrary, that until he acquired a share in the Fortune Henslowe had no proprietary interest in any other theatre must explain the assignment to the Rose of all the playing recorded in the diary between 1592 and the autumn of 1600, with the exception of the few performances definitely stated to have been at Newington Butts."

PLAYS OF THE ROSE

Eighty-nine plays or fragments of plays have sometimes been identified with works produced at the Rose theater. Sixteen of these may be classified according to the scheme used by Reynolds (*Red Bull*, p. 5) as a-plays, "plays which we have good reason to believe were given" at the Rose "in the years we are concerned with, and whose texts may reasonably be taken as representing their performances there." Twenty-seven of the plays identified with the Rose may be classified as b-plays, "plays which were probably, but not surely," given at the Rose, as well as "plays surely given there but whose texts as we have them may not represent . . . performances" at the Rose. Forty-six of the plays sometimes identified with the Rose may be classified as c-plays, "plays only possibly connected" with the Rose and therefore "of little or no authority" as evidence about the stage of Henslowe's theater and its practices.

The plays in the a- and b-lists may be further divided into subgroups according to the degree of certainty with which their extant texts appear to be representative of production at the Rose. Two plots and two plays, *Frederick and Basilea*, plot; *I Troilus and Cressida*, plot; *Sir John Oldcastle*, and *Patient Grissil* were written for the Rose and are extant in a text related to the production of the play at that theater. These texts are designated as a-1 plays. The evidence in six texts designated as a-2 plays is just as reliable as that found in a-1 plays, although the stage historian might prefer under most conditions to work with prompt-books. Henslowe's *Diary* shows that these plays were written specifically for production on the stage of the Rose. All six were printed shortly afterwards from the author's manuscript or a nontheatrical copy close to that manuscript. The six are *Downfall of Robert*, *Englishmen for My Money*, *Death of Robert*, *Two Angry Women*, *Shoemakers' Holiday*, and *Woman Killed with Kindness*.

Several of the plays of the Rose appear in the *Diary* following Henslowe's notation "ne." Foakes and Rickert (p. xxx) suggest that "one possibility which covers all occurrences of 'ne' is that this refers to the licensing of a playbook for performance by the Master of the Revels. . . . A license was required for a new play, presumably for a revival, at least when substantial revision had been made of the play, and also, it is probable, in a variety of circumstances." If the editors of the Henslowe material are correct about the use of "ne," then one may begin with the assumption that a "ne" play was shaped, altered when necessary, for presentation on the stage of the Rose; such a play ought to speak with the same degree of authority about the physical characteristics and the practices of the stage of the Rose as a play written specifically for production at the Rose. The extant text of a "ne" play printed shortly after its presentation at the Rose and bearing marks of transmission through a playhouse may be considered as containing evidence of unquestionable reliability about the stage of the Rose. Three such texts are extant and have been designated for this study as a-3 plays: *The Spanish Tragedy*, 1602; *Captain Stukley;* and *A Humorous Day's Mirth*. Likewise, it may be held that two a-4 plays, *Titus Andronicus* and *A Knack to Know a Knave*, presented at the Rose as "ne" plays and printed shortly afterwards from the author's manuscript or a nontheatrical copy close to that manuscript, speak with unquestionable reliability about the stage of the Rose. With the two a-4 plays, I include *Look about You*, a play that has not been identified clearly with entries in the *Diary*. However, it is described on its title page in 1600 as having been *"lately played"* by the Admiral's men. Like the two other a-4 plays, it is extant in a text printed shortly after its production at the Rose from the author's manuscript or a nontheatrical copy close to that manuscript.

Thomas Dekker's *Fortunatus* illustrates one of the differences between plays in the a-list and the b-list; while it was unquestionably written for the Rose and apparently given there, it was printed from a text that Fredson Bowers believes to have been used for the performance of the play at court (1:108–09). I have designated it as a b-1 play to set it apart from other texts "probably" representative of production at the Rose because it is the only one of the several plays of the Rose given at court and extant in a text showing something of that performance. In Greg's opinion, "the alterations for court representation consisted, doubtless, of the addition to the Prologue and Epilogue for Court, and of the Virtue and Vice scenes . . . and such modifications as were necessary to make these fit into the general scheme."

I argue at length (pp. 199–214) that Thomas Heywood's *The Golden Age*, *The Silver Age*, and *The Brazen Age* were written for the Rose, where all three were presented as "ne" plays in 1595 and two were revived in 1598. Heywood's original manuscripts, or copies derived from them, fell into the hands of Nicholas Oakes. He printed them in 1611 and 1613, with addresses "To The Reader" affixed by the author. However, the extant texts of these plays are generally assigned to production at the Red Bull, and some authorities question the identification of *The Golden Age* with Henslowe's playhouse. I have designated the texts of the *Ages* trilogy as b-2 plays rather than include them with the a-plays.

Six texts of plays of the Rose that have been described as "bad quartos" have been designated as b-3 plays. Four of them were presented as "ne" plays: *Massacre at Paris*, *A Knack to Know an Honest Man*, *Famous Victories*, and *Blind Beggar of Alexandria*. Two, *Orlando Furioso* and *George a Green*, were presented without the "ne" notation and consequently are often referred to, with plays similarly entered in the *Diary*, as "old" plays. One of the six "bad quartos," *The Famous Victories of Henry V*, was "probably" given at the Rose, while the other five were "surely" presented there. All these pieces, which may be described as texts of plays surreptitiously obtained and seriously cropped, were printed at about the time the pieces with which they are identified in the *Diary* appear to have stopped playing at the Rose; and it may be assumed that the texts are probably representative of the production of the play at the Rose.

It should be added that from the point of view of the historian of the stage, "bad quarto" is not a pejorative term. Perhaps the best description of a "bad quarto" may be taken from the remarks of the editors of the First Folio of Shakespeare where they speak "To the great Variety of Readers" about "diverse stolen, and surreptitious copies [of Shakespeare's plays], maimed, and deformed by the frauds and stealths of injurious imposters, that exposed them"—that is, who published them as quartos. Kirschbaum says in his "Census of Bad Quartos" (*RES* 14 [1938]:20) that "the simplest way to describe a bad quarto is to state that it cannot possibly represent a written transcript of the author's text." He goes on to point out that "all hypotheses concerning these corrupt versions [of Elizabethan and Jacobean plays] imply, to a greater or less degree, a stage of memorial transmission." Certainly such transmission may destroy poetic ideas and meter. On the other hand, an eyewitness's account, or a shorthand report, or an actor's recapitulation of what happened on stage in presenting a play is evidence of some importance about the stage, and it is just as reliable as the witness (or the reporter, or the narrator) is perceptive and accurate.

The texts of two plays and fragments representative of the production of two others at the Rose have been designated as b-4 plays: *Friar Bacon*, *The Battle of Alcazar*, *The Battle of Alcazar*, plot, and *Orlando Furioso*, part. All have been clearly identified or else generally accepted as having been given at the Rose and printed shortly afterwards from copy bearing marks of transmission through a playhouse—presumably the Rose. However, the plays do not bear the notation of "ne" in the *Diary*, which omission is usually taken as showing that they were "old" plays—plays written for presentation at some theater other than the Rose and probably played at that theater before they were given at the Rose.

The texts of *The Jew of Malta*, and *Faustus* have been designated as b-5 plays. Both were presented at the Rose as "old" plays. Both were printed many years later from copy bearing marks of transmission through a playhouse—possibly more than one. Some of the marks of transmission of the texts through the playhouse are clearly identifiable in both plays with production at the Rose.

Four plays unquestionably presented at the Rose, *Looking Glass for London*, *King Leir*, *I* and *II Tamburlaine*, and one generally accepted as having been given there, *Alphonsus of Aragon*, have been designated as b-6 plays. They are extant only in a text printed from the author's manuscript, or a nontheatrical copy close to that manuscript, which was apparently intended for presentation at some theater other than the Rose. The two *Tamburlaine* plays were published in editions in 1593, before they were given at the Rose, and again in 1597, after they were played for Henslowe. Ellis-Fermor says in her edition of *Tamburlaine* (p. 282) that these editions are derived "independently of each other" from one printed in 1590. The remaining three texts were printed after the plays were presented at the Rose.

John a Kent has been designated as a b-7 play. While it was probably given at the Rose, it is extant only in the author's manuscript annotated for use as a prompt-book, perhaps for a performance at some other theater. The texts of three plays printed years after they were given at the Rose have been designated as b-8 plays. Shakespeare's *I Henry VI*, for example, is extant only in the Folio of 1623, although it bears marks of stage production that may have come from the Rose, where a "harey the vi" was given as a "ne" play in 1592. With *I Henry VI*, I have included *Four Prentices of London*, and *Jupiter and Io*, both of which were printed many years after they were at the Rose. Finally, I have designated the texts of two pieces given at the Rose as b-9 plays. One, *Edward I*, has been described by Kirschbaum (p. 30) as a "bad quarto." The other, *David and Bathsheba*, like *Edward I* is extant only in a text printed from copy derived from a playhouse where the piece was given before it was played at the Rose.

A list of the forty-three plays in the repertory of extant plays of the Rose follows; they are arranged within the several groups in the order in which they are first mentioned in Henslowe's *Diary*, and the number preceding the short title is the one assigned by Greg in his *Commentary* (2:148–235).

a-1 plays: 108 *Frederick and Basilea*, plot; 172 *I Troilus and Cressida*, plot; 185 *Sir John Oldcastle;* 187 *Patient Grissil*.

a-2 plays: 125 *Downfall of Robert;* 126 *Englishmen for My Money;* 127 *Death of Robert;* 136 *Two Angry Women;* 176 *Shoemakers' Holiday;* 278 *Woman Killed with Kindness*.

a-3 plays: 16 *Spanish Tragedy*, 1602; 96 *Captain Stukley;* 106 *Humorous Day's Mirth*.

a-4 plays: 23 *Knack to Know a Knave;* 37 *Titus Andronicus;* 179 *Look about You*.

b-1 plays: 189a *Fortunatus*.

b-2 plays: 70 *Golden Age;* 71 *Silver Age;* 72 *Brazen Age*.

b-3 plays: 3 *Orlando Furioso;* 26 *Massacre at Paris;* 29 *George a Green;* 58 *Knack to Know an Honest Man;* 82 *Famous Victories;* 88 *Blind Beggar of Alexandria*.

b-4 plays: 1 *Friar Bacon;* 2 *Battle of Alcazar;* *Battle of Alcazar*, plot; 3 *Orlando Furioso*, part.

b-5 plays: 7 *Jew of Malta;* 55 *Faustus*.

b-6 plays: 14 *Looking Glass for London;* 39 *King Leir;* 50 *Alphonsus of Aragon;* 52 *I Tamburlaine;* 64 *II Tamburlaine*.

b-7 plays: 62 *John a Kent*.

b-8 plays: 11 *I Henry VI;* 47 *Four Prentices of London;* 103 *Jupiter and Io*.

b-9 plays: 75 *Edward I;* 269a *David and Bathsheba*.

Forty-six plays classified as c-plays and excluded from further consideration are listed below. The number at the left of the short title is the one used by Greg in discussing the play with entries in the *Diary* that may be related to the piece (2: 148–235). The reference in parentheses at the right of the short title is to a discussion by Chambers or some other authority which may indicate why the play has not been included in the repertory. 4 *I Jeronimo* (ES 4:22); 6 *Alphonsus, Emperor of Germany* (ES 4:2); 13 *II Seven Deadly Sins*, plot (ES 3:496); 24 *The Comedy of Errors* (*Facts and Problems* 1:310); 24 *The Merry Wives of Windsor* (Greg 2:156); 30 *The Tragedy of King Richard the Third* (*Facts and Problems* 1:303); *The True Tragedy of Richard the Third* (Greg 2:158); 32 *Fair Em* (ES 4:11); 59 *Caesar and Pompey* (ES 3:259); 60 *The Virgin Martyr* (ES 3:298); 63 *Match Me in London* (ES 3:297–98); 65 *Edward the Fourth* (ES 4:10); 69 *The Wonder of a Kingdom* (ES 3:299); 78 *May Day* (ES 3:256); 79 *The Wonder of Woman, or Sophonisba* (ES 3:433); *A New Wonder, A Woman Never Vexed* (ES 3:474); 83 *The Valiant Welshman* (ES 4:51); 90 *I Tamar Cam*, plot (ES 4:47–48); 92 *The Iron Age* (ES 3:345); 95 *The Mayor of Quinborough* (ES 3:442); 103 *Apollo and Daphne*

(ES 3:346); *Amphrisa (ES* 3:346); *Deorum Judicium (ES* 3:346); *Misanthropes* *(ES* 3:346); 105 *The Birth of Merlin (ES* 3:474); 113 *Edmund Ironside (MSR,* 1927); 115 *Trial of Chivalry (ES* 4:50); 118 *Thierry and Theodoret (ES* 3: 230); 123 *Dido Queen of Carthage (ES* 3:426); 124 *The Sun's Darling (ES* 3:299); 138 *The Gentleman Usher (ES* 3:251); 153 *Monsieur D'Olive (ES* 3:251); 161 *The Thracian Wonder (ES* 4:49); 165 *All Fools (ES* 3:252); 166 *A Maidenhead Well Lost (ES* 3:347); 171 *Sir Clyomon and Clamydes (ES* 4:6); 190 *Two Lamentable Tragedies (ES* 3:518); 195 *The Whore of Babylon (ES* 3:296); 197 *Lust's Dominion* (Bowers's *Dekker* 4:117–28); 204 *Grim the Collier of Croydon (ES* 4:16); 206 *The Blind Beggar of Bethnal Green (ES* 3:285); 261 *Like Will to Like (ES* 3:317); 263 *The Tragedy of Hoffman (ES* 3:264); 264 *Nobody and Somebody (ES* 4:37); 265 *Royal King and Loyal Subject (ES* 3:341); 270 *Sir Thomas Wyat (ES* 3:294).

REPERTORY OF EXTANT PLAYS OF THE ROSE

Forty-three plays whose extant texts may be associated with production at the Rose theater are listed below with comment upon the stage and textual histories of each of the several pieces. The number used by Greg appears at the left of each entry and determines the order of the listing.

1 *Friar Bacon* (b-4)
    THE HONORABLE HISTORIES *of frier Bacon, and frier Bongay.* . . . *Made by Robert Greene . . . London, Printed for Edward White . . . 1594.* Edited by W. W. Greg. Malone Society Reprints. Oxford: University Press, 1926.
    There is no question about the identification of this play with a piece given at the Rose seven times by Strange's men between 19 February 1592 and 30 January 1593. It was performed twice, on 1 April and 5 April 1594, while the Queen's men and Sussex's men were acting together at the Rose (Greg 2:149). Jewkes (p. 122) finds that the text, printed in 1594 as played by "her Majesties servants," bears "marks of transmission through the playhouse."

2 *The Battle of Alcazar* (b-4)
    THE BATTELL OF ALCAZAR. . . . *plaid by the Lord high Admirall his servants.* . . . *Imprinted at London by Edward Allde for Richard Bankworth . . . 1594.* Edited by W. W. Greg and Frank Sidgwick. Malone Society Reprints. London: Chiswick Press, 1907.

The Battle of Alcazar, plot (b-4)

The Plott of the Battell of Alcazar. W. W. Greg's reproduction and transcript in *Dramatic Documents from the Elizabethan Playhouses*. Oxford: Clarendon Press [1931]. Greg (2:149) and Chambers (3:460) are in apparent agreement about the identification of this play and "plott" with the Rose. Chambers says, "From 21 Feb. 1592 to Jan. 1593 Strange's men played fourteen times for Henslowe *Muly Mollocco*, by which this play, in which Abdelmelec is also called Muly Mollocco, is probably meant." Chambers believes that "the 'plot' must belong to a later revival by the Admiral's datable, since both Alleyn and Shaw acted in it, either in December 1597 or in 1600-2." The Malone Society Reprint represents the play as it was published in 1594; this was about one year after the last recorded entry of its first run at the Rose. Jewkes (p. 127) finds "many evidences in the stage directions of notations characteristic of a prompter," while "evidences of the author's hand remain in certain longer and more descriptive directions."

3 *Orlando Furioso* (b-3)

THE HISTORIE OF Orlando Furioso. . . . *LONDON, Printed by John Danter for Cuthbert Burbie*. . . . *1594*. Edited by W. W. Greg and Robert B. McKerrow. Malone Society Reprints. Oxford: University Press, 1907.

Orlando Furioso, part (b-4)

Manuscript of the part of Orlando in Robert Greene's *Orlando Furioso*. W. W. Greg's reproduction and transcript in *Dramatic Documents from the Elizabethan Playhouses*. Oxford: Clarendon Press [1931].

The identification of *Orlando Furioso* with the Rose is uncontested. However, the play is represented only by a "part," with actor's cues, and by a rather seriously cropped edition printed in 1594 which Greg (2:150) believes represents the play as it was acted in the provinces. Chambers (3:329) says of the extant manuscript "part," "Doubtless it belonged to Alleyn." Greg (3:155) says: "The play, which was printed in quarto in 1594, appears to have originally belonged to the Queen's men, and probably passed to Lord Strange's company at the end of 1591. It was played by them at the Rose . . . and it is presumably to this revival that the present MS. [part] belongs." According to Greg (3:155), "the MS. and printed texts differ considerably . . . and the question of the relationship of the two is not very clear." The play is included among the "bad" quartos (Kirschbaum, *RES* 14:29).

7 *The Jew of Malta* (b-5)

The Famous TRAGEDY OF THE RICH JEW OF MALTA. . . . by Chris-topher Marlo. . . LONDON: Printed by I. B. for Nicholas Vavasour. . . . 1633.
Photocopy. Ann Arbor, Mich.: University Microfilms.

This play is linked directly to production at the Rose by the "i cauderm for the Jewe," which appears in Henslowe's inventory of the Admiral's properties for 10 March 1598 (Foakes and Rickert, p. 321). Greg (2:151) and Chambers (3:424–25) are in general agreement about its history and its identification with the Rose. Jewkes says (p. 302), "The indications point to a text which was probably altered from Marlowe's original, since his directions are normally long and descriptive. The state of the directions would probably be inadequate for a prompt-book, but there are certain traces of use in the playhouse."

11 *I Henry VI* (b-8)

The first Part of Henry the Sixt. In *Mr. WILLIAM SHAKESPEARES COMEDIES, HISTORIES, & TRAGEDIES.* From the Norton Facsimile of the First Folio of Shakespeare. Prepared by Charlton Hinman. New York: W. W. Norton, 1968.

The identification of the play in the 1623 folio with "harey the vi" given as a "ne" piece at the Rose has been accepted by Greg (2:152), Chambers (*Facts and Problems* 1:292), and others. Strange's men presented the play first on 3 March 1592 and repeated it for a total of sixteen performances continuing through 31 January 1593. Obviously it was popular and Henslowe's profits were great. This fact is cited to support the identifica-tion of Shakespeare's play with the Rose. The strongest evidence for identification of the play with the Henslowe playhouse is, however, an allusion in Nashe's *Pierce Penilesse*, entered in the *Stationers' Register* on 8 August 1592, attesting the popularity of a play in which "brave Talbot" is slain—the English hero who falls in *I Henry VI*. Nashe's allusion follows: "How it would have joyed brave Talbot (the terror of the French) to thinke that after he had lyne two hundred yeares in his Tombe, hee should triumphe againe on the Stage, and have his bones embalmed with the teares of ten thousand spectators at least (at severall times), who, in the Tragedian that represents his person, imagine they behold him fresh from bleeding." Peter Alexander and more recently Andrew Cairncross (Arden Edition, *The First Part of King Henry VI*, 1962, xxxi–xxxv) have contested the identification of *I Henry VI*, in the 1623 folio, with the play given at the Rose. The epilogue to *Henry V* mentions performances of "Henry the Sixt, in Infant Bands crown'd King," presumably years after the performances of "harey the vi" at the Rose. Jewkes believes (p. 155) that "the copy from which the printer worked must have had some connection, at some period, with performance."

14 *A Looking Glass for London* (b-6)

A Looking Glasse for LONDON AND England. Made by Thomas Lodge Gentlemen, and Robert Greene. . . . LONDON Printed by Thomas Creede . . . to be sold by William Barley. . . . 1594. Edited by W. W. Greg. Malone Society Reprints. Oxford: University Press, 1932.

Strange's men revived this play and presented it at the Rose four times between 8 March and 7 June 1592 (Greg 2:153). Neither Greg nor Chambers (3:328) contests the identification of this play with Henslowe's theater. The Malone Society Reprint used here is based on the earliest edition, entered in the *Stationers' Register* on 5 March 1594 and printed the same year. Jewkes finds "considerable evidence that the play was printed from copy close to the author's original" (p. 202).

16 *The Spanish Tragedy* (a-3)

THE Spanish Tragedie . . . Newly corrected, amended, and enlarged with new additions of the Painters part, and others, as it hath of late been divers times acted. . . . Imprinted at London by W. W. for T. Pavier. . . . 1602. Edited by W. W. Greg and Frederick S. Boas. Malone Society Reprints. Oxford: University Press, 1925.

The authorities agree upon the identification of this play as the one given by Strange's men sixteen times for Henslowe between 14 March 1592 and 22 January 1593. It was revived by the Admiral's men as "ne" and played thirteen times between 7 January 1597, and 11 October 1597. The performance on 11 October 1597 was given jointly by the Admiral's and Pembroke's men.

The complicated history of the four extant editions, which may represent production of *The Spanish Tragedy* at the Rose, is discussed in the Malone Society Reprints of the Undated (1592) Quarto and the 1602 Quarto "with additions." From these discussions it is apparent that: 1) the Undated Quarto "printed by Edward Allde, for Edward White" was published while Strange's men were playing the piece at the Rose in 1592; 2) the 1594 Quarto "reproduces the undated Quarto, without any change that is not attributable to the printer" (*MSR* 1948); 3) the 1599 Quarto, in turn, is a "reprint" of the Quarto of 1594; and 4) the 1602 edition is based on the 1599 Quarto "and was 'enlarged' by the insertion of five new passages."

The Malone Society Reprint of the 1602 Quarto is used as the best representative of production of *The Spanish Tragedy* at the Rose. It was selected partially on the basis of Greg's hypothesis (*MSR* 1925, pp. xviii–xix) that the five new passages, about 340 lines, in the edition of 1602 are those "which we may suppose justified the announcement of *Jeronimo* as a new play in 1597" rather than the "adicians" in 1601 and the "new adicyons for Jeronymo" in 1602 for which Jonson was paid a total of almost five pounds. The 1602 quarto may contain additions made at the Rose, and is derived from one which Jewkes believes (p. 124) "came through the playhouse."

23 *A Knack to Know a Knave* (a-4)

A most pleasant and merie new Comedie, Intituled, A Knacke to knowe a Knave . . . played by ED. ALLEN and his Companie. With KEMPS applauded Merrimentes. . . . Imprinted at London by Richard Jones. . . . 1594. Edited by Arthur Brown, G. R. Proudfoot and William A. Armstrong. Malone Society Reprints. Oxford: University Press, 1963.

None of the authorities has contested the identification of this play with a piece usually entered in the *Diary* as "the cnacke." It was played by Strange's men seven times between 10 June 1592 and 24 January 1593. The play was entered in the *Stationers' Register* on 7 January 1594, and printed the same year. According to Jewkes (p. 204) "An author's manuscript may have provided the copy for this play, or at least a transcript from the author's copy with no notations for performance."

26 *The Massacre at Paris* (b-3)

THE MASSACRE AT PARIS. . . . As it was plaide by the right honourable the Lord high Admirall his Servants. Written by Christopher Marlow. AT LONDON Printed by E. A. for Edward White. . . . [c. 1594]. Edited by W. W. Greg. Malone Society Reprints. Oxford: University Press, 1928.

No question exists about the identification of this play with a piece given by Strange's men for Henslowe as "ne" on 30 January 1593. It was played ten times again, between 19 June 1594 and 25 September 1594. It is also possible that this is the play for which Henslowe lent to Bird, on three occasions, a total of £2.12 to purchase properties for a revival in late 1598. The play was revived at the Fortune in 1601–02. Although the play was not entered in the *Stationers' Register* and the title page does not carry a date, it was published "*As it was plaide by the right honourable the Lord high Admirall his Servants.*" The Admiral became Earl of Nottingham in 1596; consequently most of the authorities are inclined to date the present text around 1594 (*MSR* 1928, p. vii). Only one play, *Look about You*, is printed after this date in which the Admiral's new title is not used. Greg says of the text (p. x) that "even among admittedly garbled versions it has an evil distinction, and must for shortness and fatuity be classed with such pieces as *The Famous Victories of Henry V* and *Orlando Furioso*." The play is listed by Kirschbaum with the "bad" quartos (*RES* 14:30).

29 *George a Green* (b-3)

A PLEASANT CONCEYTED COmedie of George a Greene, the Pinner of Wakefield. As it was sundry times acted by the servants of the right Honourable the Earle of Sussex. Imprinted at London by Simon Stafford, for Cuthbert Burby. . . . 1599. Edited by W. W. Greg and F. W. Clarke. Malone Society Reprints. Oxford: University Press, 1911.

None of the authorities has contested the identification of this play with a piece played for Henslowe five times by Sussex's men between 29 December 1593 and 22 January 1594. It was entered in the *Stationers' Register* on 1 April 1595 and printed in 1599. One has no way of knowing at the present time why the printing was delayed, or whether an earlier edition was printed. Jewkes finds this "another play somewhat removed from Greene's original in the course of transmission through the playhouse" (p. 122). Kirschbaum lists it as a "bad" quarto (*RES* 14:40–42).

37 *Titus Andronicus* (a-4)

THE MOST LAmentable Romaine Tragedie of Titus Andronicus. . . . LONDON, Printed by John Danter. . . to be sold by Edward White & Thomas Millington. . . . 1594. Edited by Joseph Quincy Adams. Folger Shakespeare Library Publications. New York and London: Charles Scribner's Sons, 1936.

None of the authorities contests the identification of *Titus* with a play performed by Sussex's men as "ne" on three occasions at the Rose, 23 and 28 January and 6 February 1594. The edition used here was entered in the *Stationers' Register* by John Danter on 6 February 1594, the day that the last performance of the play at the Rose is recorded in the *Diary*. Danter printed it in the same year. Chambers (2:130) explains the circumstances involved in the printing of *Titus* as follows: "Alarmed at the further inhibition of plays in February, they [Sussex's men] allowed the revised *Titus* and unrevised texts of *The Taming of a Shrew* and *The Contention* to get into the hands of the booksellers." Jewkes says the play seems to have had "quite a history of transmission" and points to the title page of the 1594 quarto which claims that it was acted by Pembroke's, Derby's, and Sussex's men before it was printed (p. 159). Jewkes goes on to say, however, that "the condition of the text of the Quarto suggests that the printer worked from a manuscript which had not been prepared for performance."

39 *King Leir* (b-6)

THE True Chronicle History of King Leir and his three daughters, Gonorill, Ragan, and Cordella. As it hath bene divers and sundry times lately acted. LONDON, Printed by Simon Stafford for John Wright. . . . 1605. Edited by W. W. Greg and R. Warwick Bond. Malone Society Reprints. Oxford: University Press, 1907.

Leir was given at the Rose on 6 and 8 April 1594 by the Queen's and Sussex's men. The play was entered in the *Stationers' Register* on 14 May 1594, but no copy of this edition is known—if it, indeed, was printed at that time. It was printed in 1605 after again having been entered in the *Stationers' Register* on 8 May of that year. Chambers (4:25) says of the text of the extant edition:

The authorship is quite obscure. . . . The publishing history is also difficult. . . . The play was clearly regarded as distinct from that of Shakespeare, which was entered to N. Butter and J. Busby on 22 Nov. 1607, and it, though based on its predecessor, is far more than a revision of it. It seems a little improbable that Leire should have been revived as late as 1605, and the 'Tragecall' and 'lately acted' of the title page, taken by themselves, would point to an attempt by Stafford to palm off the old play as Shakespeare's. But although 1605 is not an impossible date for Shakespeare's production, 1606 is on other grounds more probable.

Jewkes (p. 202) finds no clear evidence of preparation by a stage reviser or prompter and concludes, "It seems probable that an author's manuscript or a non-theatrical transcript formed the copy for the play."

47 *The Four Prentices of London* (b-8)

THE Foure Prentises of London. . . . Acted, at the Red Bull. . . . Written by Thomas Heywood. . . . Printed at London for J. W. 1615. Photocopy. Ann Arbor, Mich.: University Microfilms.

Chambers (3:340) reviews the problems related to the identification of this play with at least three pieces mentioned in the *Diary*, but does not contest its identification as a play of the Rose. His suggestion that it may have been the *Jerusalem* given by Strange's men on 22 March and 25 April 1592 seems less plausible than Greg's identification (2:166) of the play as the *Godfrey of Bulloigne* given twelve times by the Admiral's men betweeen 19 July 1594 and 16 September 1595. Greg (2:230) suggests that the "iiii lances for the comody of Thomas Hewedes & Mr. Smythes" on 3 September 1602 may indicate a revival of this play by Worcester's men at the Rose. This suggestion strengthens the probability that the play was originally given at the Rose, even though it was printed in 1615 as "acted, at the Red Bull." Jewkes finds (p. 130) that "the evidence is of a manuscript which had done duty in the playhouse, and was probably glanced over by Heywood before being printed."

50 *Alphonsus of Aragon* (b-6)

THE COMICALL HISTORIE OF *Alphonsus, King of Aragon. . . . Made by R. G. . . . Printed by Thomas Creede. 1599.* Edited by W. W. Greg. Malone Society Reprints. Oxford: University Press, 1926.

Neither Chambers (3:327) nor Greg (2:167) seriously contests the identification of this play with a piece revived for Henslowe at the Rose and played there eight times between 14 August 1594 and 5 February 1595. The identification is based largely on the fact that Mahomet speaks out of a brazen head (4.1) and that the Admiral's inventories list an "owld Mahemetes head" in 1598. The extant text seems to have been printed from one close to the author's manuscript. Jewkes (pp. 119-20) cites Greg's conclusion that there is no evidence of the text having done duty in the playhouse, and notes that Chambers and Van Dam had similar opinions.

52 *I Tamburlaine* (b-6)

Tamburlaine the Great. . . . As it was acted: by the right Honorable, the Lord Admyrall his Servantes. . . . Printed at London by Richard Johnes. . . 1597. Photocopy. Ann Arbor, Mich.: University Microfilms.

The identification of this play with one given at the Rose by the Admiral's men is uncontested by Greg (2:167) and Chambers (3:421). It ran fifteen times between 28 August 1594 and 12 November 1595. The "2 pt. of tamberlen" ran seven times between December 1594 and November 1595. The Admiral's inventories (Greg 3:116-20) list items that have been identified as Tamburlaine's cage, bridle, coat, and breeches. Ellis-Fermor says in her edition of the play (p. 282) that "the text of 1590 is the *editio princeps* from which are derived, independently of each other, 1593 and 1597. The 1605/6 is derived from 1597." Richard Jones notes in his remarks "To the Gentlemen Readers and others," in the 1590 edition, "I have (purposely) omitted and left out som fond and frivolous jestures, digressing (and in my poore opinion) far unmeet for the matter, which I thought, might seeme more tedious unto the wise." These remarks also appear in the 1597 edition. Jewkes says (p. 114), "There is nothing to prove connection of the copy with actual performance." He is speaking here of the texts of both *I* and *II Tamburlaine*.

55 *Faustus* (b-5)

The Tragicall History of the Life and Death of Doctor Faustus. Written by Ch. Mar. . . . LONDON, Printed for John Wright. . . . 1616. Edited by W. W.

Greg in *Marlowe's Doctor Faustus 1604–1616: Parallel Texts*. Oxford: Clarendon Press, 1950.

Faustus may be identified with the "ffostose" performed at the Rose by the Admiral's men and the Admiral's and Pembroke's men twenty-five times between 30 September 1594 and October 1597. The play was entered in the *Stationers' Register* on 7 January 1601 by Thomas Bushell; and the earliest extant edition, in the long and complicated textual history of this piece, was printed by "*V. S. for Thomas Bushell*" in 1604. Greg argues that the 1616 edition of *Faustus* is more nearly representative of the original version of the play than the earlier 1604 edition. "It is . . . with some confidence that I advance the conclusion that none of the passages peculiar to B [that is, the 1616 edition] represent the additions paid for by Henslowe in 1602, and that structurally at any rate the B-text preserves the more original, and the A-text [1604 edition] a maimed and debased, version of the play" (*Parallel Texts*, p. 29). Greg also points out (*Parallel Texts*, p. 33) that "the A-text calls, it seems, for nothing beyond a bare stage" while the B-text calls for many theatrical effects including, for example, "the hovering dragon" which is listed among the properties belonging to the Admiral's men. Jewkes says (p. 116), "Much confusion and mutilation are evident in the treatment the texts [1604 and the 1616 editions] received during the course of their transmission through the theater." Clearly, the text of the 1616 quarto bears marks of production at the Rose between 1594 and 1597.

58 *A Knack to Know an Honest Man* (b-3)

A PLEASANT CONCEITED COMEdie, called, A knacke to know an honest Man. . . . LONDON, Printed for Cuthbert Burby. . . . 1596. Edited by W. W. Greg and H. DeVocht. Malone Society Reprints. Oxford: University Press, 1910.

This play was produced at the Rose as "ne" on 22 October 1594 and given twenty-one times through 3 November 1596. The play was entered in the *Stationers' Register* by Cuthbert Burby on 26 November 1595, while it was still in production at the Rose. It was printed for Burby in 1596, but one has no way of knowing whether the publication was held up until the run of the play was completed. Chambers believes (4:24) that "the text is confused and probably surreptitious." Kirschbaum classifies the text with the "bad" quartos (*RES* 14:32).

62 *John a Kent* (b-7)

Manuscript of *The Book of John a Kent & John a Cumber* signed by "Anthony Mundy." Edited by W. W. Greg and Muriel St. Clare Byrne.

Malone Society Reprints. Oxford: University Press, 1923.

The Admiral's men presented "the wiseman of weschester" as a "ne" play at the Rose on 2 December 1594 where it continued for thirty-two performances through 18 July 1597. And the Admiral's inventories for March 1598 list "Kentes woden leage" among the properties (Foakes and Rickert, p. 320). Although the extant manuscript does not show that John a Kent, the wise magician from Weschester, had a wooden leg or needed one, several portions of the manuscript are missing. Or the wooden leg may have been required as a result of some tradition about the man of which we are now ignorant. In any case, Chambers (*ES* 3:446) does not contest Fleay and Greg's identifications (2:172) of the extant manuscript of *John a Kent* with the *Wise Man* and the Rose theater, other than to point out "if the identification is correct, it is not easy to see how the MS. can be earlier than 1594." Muriel St. Clare Byrne concludes that "it is by no means impossible that the *Wise Man* may have been a revision of *John a Kent*. . . but there is no secure basis for speculation" (*MSR*, p. x). Greg in 1942 (*Shakespeare First Folio*, p. 162) points out that the manuscript was annotated for use as a prompt-book by the same "book-keeper" as *Sir Thomas More*. I. A. Shapiro (*SS* 8:102) argues that the date below Munday's signature at the end of the manuscript should read "Decembris 1590" rather than "1595" or "1596" as it has been widely interpreted. If Shapiro is correct, the play could have been acted at another theater before it was presented at the Rose. Even so, the possibility remains that the extant manuscript with its annotations was the prompt-book for the play as it was given at the Rose, where we know from the *Diary* that Munday was regularly employed as a playwright until playing stopped at that theater.

64 *II Tamburlaine* (b-6)
    THE SECOND PART OF The bloody conquests of mighty Tamburlaine.
    See above, 52.

70 *The Golden Age* (b-2)
    THE GOLDEN AGE. . . . As it hath beene sundry times acted at the Red Bull, by the Queenes Majesties Servants. Written by Thomas Heywood. . . . LONDON, Printed for William Barrenger. . . 1611. Photocopy of Huntington Library copy. Ann Arbor, Mich.: University Microfilms.

71. *The Silver Age* (b-2)
    THE SILVER AGE. . . . Written by Thomas Heywood. . . . LONDON, Printed by Nicholas Okes, and are to be sold by Benjamin Lightfoote. . . . 1613. Photocopy of STC 13365. Ann Arbor, Mich.: University Microfilms.

72 *The Brazen Age* (b-2)

THE BRAZEN AGE. . . . Written by Thomas Heywood. LONDON, Printed by Nicholas Okes, for Samuel Rand. . . . 1613. Photocopy of Huntington Library copy. Ann Arbor, Mich.: University Microfilms.

Wilfred Jewkes begins his discussion of the texts of *The Golden Age*, *The Silver Age*, and *The Brazen Age* (p. 135) with the statement that "these plays bear considerable resemblance to each other, and were planned together, printed by Nicholas Oakes, and acted by the Queen's company between 1609 and 1613, so that they can be easily considered together." Jewkes's statement is probably correct, although the only evidence that the trilogy was acted by the Queen's men is found on the title page of *The Golden Age*, describing that particular play printed in 1611 as "*acted at the Red Bull, by the Queenes Majesties Servants.*" Also, Jewkes seems to be correct when he says in his discussion of the texts (p. 136) that "the impression these three plays leave is that of being printed from copy which had seen use in the playhouse, but from which most traces of such use must have been erased." And despite his impression about these plays, he correctly classifies the extant texts with those "probably printed from copy close to the author's original manuscript, with no signs of alteration" (p. 345). He is mistaken, however, when he identifies the company originally acting the *Ages* plays as the Queen's company.

The *Ages*, as Reynolds has said (*Red Bull*, p. 9), "demand some of the most spectacular staging ever suggested for the Elizabethan public stage." And now that Jewkes has established that the extant texts were printed from copy close to the author's original, it is of some import to this study of the Rose stage and its practices that the first three of Heywood's *Ages* be clearly identified as plays written specifically for the Rose theater.

Henslowe's *Diary* and the plays themselves show that *The Golden Age*, *The Silver Age*, and *The Brazen Age* were written for the Rose and presented there by the Admiral's men for the first time in 1595. And there is little in the history of the plays up to the time they were printed (1611 and 1613) to support the general assumption that they were revised for production in other theaters after the trilogy was broken up at the Rose late in 1595 or early in 1596. Unfortunately, George F. Reynolds's assignment of the first three *Ages* to the repertory of the Red Bull (p. 9) has created the impression that the plays were written for the Red Bull or else were revised for production on the stage of that theater. This impression has become so pervasive that F. S. Boas, for example, says in his *Thomas Heywood* (London: Williams and Norgate, 1950), p. 83, "it seems . . . that F. G. Fleay was partly right in his view that the *Ages* were revised versions of plays acted by the Lord Admiral's men."

Actually, the extant version of the *Ages* trilogy has been linked directly to production at the Rose by properties and costumes listed in Henslowe's inventories of 10 and 13 March 1598 (Foakes and Rickert, pp. 316–23). Frederick Gard Fleay in his *Biographical Chronicle of the English Drama: 1559–1642* (London, 1891) (1:283–84) cites several items in the inventories to identify *The Golden Age* as "seleo & olempo," a "ne," play given at the Rose on 5 March 1595. And Fleay identifies *The Silver Age* and *The Brazen Age* as "ne" plays given at the Rose on 7 and 23 May 1595 as *I* and *II Hercules*. Greg, in 1908, supports Fleay's identification of *The Silver* and *Brazen Ages* but hesitates over the identification of *The Golden Age* with "seleo & olempo" (2:175). In 1915, John S. P. Tatlock asserts that "what evidence there is points to 1594–6 as the date of the five plays [the *Ages*] which were perhaps Heywood's earliest works" (*PMLA* 30:718).

The identification of the *Ages* with the Rose seems to have been accepted generally until Chambers published his *Elizabethan Stage* in 1923. Chambers is skeptical and often impatient of the "ingenious attempts" of Fleay and Greg to identify plays in the *Diary*. He considers the identification of *The Golden Age* with "seleo & olempo" as "hazardous," but concedes to the identification of *The Silver Age* and *The Brazen Age* as the two Hercules plays: "It may be so" (2:145, 3:344–45). Elsewhere Chambers is almost splenetic when he discusses some of the identifications by Fleay.

Since the publication of Chambers's work there have not been many attempts to identify the *Ages* with items in Henslowe's inventories of 1598. The most significant, perhaps, was made in 1946 by Allan Holaday (*JEGP* 45:438), who lists the costumes and properties noted in Henslowe's inventories by Fleay, Greg, and Tatlock to show that Heywood used the 1595 Hercules plays of the Rose "when he prepared the *Silver* and *Brazen Ages*" for publication. Generally, Fleay has been ignored, Chambers followed, and as a result conclusions have been drawn incorrectly about Heywood's work by those who assume that the *Ages* were written for the Red Bull or that they are extant only in versions representing production at that theater.

Chambers's authority, however, can hardly brush aside the fact that twenty-five items (properties and costumes) in Henslowe's inventories of 1598 are called for by the dialogue and stage directions in Heywood's first three *Ages*. Regularly, those who oppose the identification of the *Ages* with the Rose ignore the dialogue and stage directions that tie the extant plays to items in Henslowe's inventories. And what is more remarkable, those who support the identification do not point out that the dialogue and stage directions call for many items in the inventories that cannot possibly have been used in any known plays except Heywood's trilogy. Only Holaday points to some of the dialogue and stage directions to link a few of the items in the inventories to the plays, adding several items to the lists made by Fleay, Greg, and Tatlock including "i rocke," "i Hell moght," "i baye tree," "the clothe of the Sone & Mone," "i eleme bowle," "i lyon," and "ii lyon heades" (p. 438). I shall undertake here to list all of the costumes and properties in the inventories (Foakes and Rickert, pp. 316–23), that have been identified with the *Ages*, adding some items that appear to have gone unnoticed. And I shall cite the dialogue and stage directions that link the items in the inventories to the extant Heywood plays.

i senetores gowne, i hoode, and 5 senetores capes (p. 317, line 16)

As far as I know, the items above have not been identified with the *Ages* or with any of the plays in the repertory of the Rose. Although these costumes could have been used by the "*Senatours aloft*" in the opening scene of *Titus Andronicus*, I suggest that "senetores" is Henslowe's spelling for "centaurs." Listed with "Clownes Sewtes and Hermetes Sewtes, with divers other sewtes," the items seem to refer to the garb worn by the six centaurs with whom Hercules battles in *The Silver Age* (H2–H3v): "*Nessus, Euritus, Chiron, Cillarus, Antimachus, Hippasus.*" The "gowne" and "hoode" ought to have been worn by the leader of the centaurs, Nessus, and the capes by his five followers. Nessus escapes in the battle and reappears in *The Brazen Age* (B4–C2), finally to be slain by Hercules. It is fit that Nessus be better garbed than his followers who fight briefly and are slain.

i sewtte for Nepton (p. 317, line 17); *Nepun forcke & garland* (p. 319, line 68)

"*A flourish. Enter Jupiter, Juno, the Lords of Creet, Melliseus, Archas, Neptune, and Pluto*" (*Golden Age*, G3v). "*Sound. Neptune drawes the Sea, is mounted upon a sea-horse, A Roabe and Trident, with a crowne are given him by the Fates*" (*Golden Age*, K2v). "*All the Gods appeare above, and laugh, Jupiter, Juno, Phoebus, Mercury, Neptune*" (*Brazen Age*, I3).

Hercolles lymes (p. 318, line 25)

Ernest Schanzer points out (*RES* 11:19–20) that, "lymes" here almost certainly has the meaning of *limb:* "The pieces of a suit of armour," although the earliest instance of this usage is found in Davenant's *Gondibert*, 1651 (p. 19, n. 3). Hercules appears as an armed champion, if one may believe the dialogue in *The Silver Age* (B2), when he triumphs over Achelous for the hand of Deianeria: "*Oen.* Brothers, conduct these Champions to the lists. . . . Stand fourth you warlike Champions, and expresse/ Your loves to Deianeria, in your valours." Listed in the inventory with "sewtes," "Hercolles lymes" could surely not be identified as dismembered portions of the hero's body. He is invincible and must take his own life when it becomes unbearable: "Record this/ Though by the Gods and Fates we are orethrowne,/ Alcides dies by no hand but his owne" (*Brazen Age*, L3).

i rocke (p. 319, line 56)

The "i rocke" is listed with large stage properties and on the same line with such items as "i cage, i tomb, i Hell mought." A stage-property "rocke" is used twice in *The Brazen Age*. In the first instance Hesione says, "Come good Anchises, binde me to this rocke" (E4v). She is bound to the rock, according to the dialogue, and released upon Hercules' order: "Take along/ This beauteous Lady, if he must have pray,/ Instead of her Alcides here will stay" (F1). Later in *The Brazen Age* (L2) a rock, probably the same property, is called for in a stage direction reading "*Enter Hercules from a rocke above tearing down trees.*"

i Hell mought (p. 319, line 56)

Holaday believes (p. 436) that the hellmouth is used in *The Silver Age*. Such a property seems to be mentioned twice: "*Phi.* We have arriv'd/ At Tenaros; this is the mouth of hell" (K1v), and "*Peri.* . . . Let's rouze the hell-hound, call him from his lodge,/ and (maugre *Cerberus*) enter helsmouth" (K2). Later, on the same page, a stage direction reads: "*They beate against the gates. Enter Cerberus.*"

i globe, & i golden scepter (p. 319, line 61)

Neither the "globe" nor the "scepter" have been cited to support the identification of *The Golden Age* with the Rose. And while these properties may be associated with other plays, it should be noted that they appear together in the inventory on the same line and are likewise called for in a stage direction in Heywood's play (K2v): "*Sound a dumbe shew. Enter the three fatall sisters . . . bringing in a Gloabe, in which they put three lots. Jupiter draws heaven: at which Iris descends and presents him with his Eagle, Crowne and Scepter, and his thunderbolt.*"

i gowlden flece (p. 319, line 63)

"*Two fiery Buls are discovered, the Fleece hanging over them*" (*Brazen Age*, G2). "*Enter Jason with the Fleece, and all the Greekes muffled*" (*Brazen Age*, G3v).

i baye tree (p. 319, line 63)

Holaday believes (p. 436) that the bay tree found on the same line in the inventory with the golden fleece was used in *The Brazen Age* (G2) as a property on which to hang the fleece.

i lyone skin (p. 319, line 66); *ii lyon heades* (p. 320, line 85)

"*Enter to them at one doore, Euristeus, and the Kings of Greece: at the other Hercules, with the Lyons head and skinne*" (*Silver Age*, G1v). "*He burns his Club, & Lyons Skin*" (*Brazen Age*, L2v).

Ierosses head, & raynbowe (p. 320, line 70)

Presumably Iris wore a distinctive headdress or mask of some kind. She is an important character in *The Silver Age* and on two occasions appears above the stage in a cloud. "*Windhornes. Enter Juno and Iris above in a cloud*" (G1). "*Juno and Iris plac'd in a cloud above*" (I4).

The "raynbowe" is clearly associated with Iris. Juno says,

> Iris my Raine-bow threw her circle round,
> If he had beene on earth, to have clasp't him in
> And kept him in the circle of her armes
> Till she had cal'd for Juno.

Iris is successful in her efforts to capture Jupiter: "*Thunder and light-ning. . . . Jupiter appeares in his glory under a Raine-bow, to whom they all kneele*" (*Silver Age*, F1v).

i littell alter (p. 320, line 70)

Tatlock (pp. 710–11) identifies the altar with the properties used in staging the *Brazen Age*: "*Enter Busyris . . . and kils them upon the Altar: enter Hercules . . . kils Busyris and sacrificeth him upon the Altar*" (C2v). "*Enter to the sacrifice two Priests to the Altar*" (K3v). "*All the Princes knele to the Altar*" (K4). At first glance the altar appears to be the kind of property that may be called for in any number of plays. Thus far, however, no one seems to have suggested another play with which it may have been associated.

the cloth of the Sone & Mone (p. 320, line 72)

Holaday believes "The cloth of the sun and moon apparently were used to costume Phoebus, particularly in his scenes with Mars and Venus [*Brazen Age*, H2–I3v], and Persephone, who in the play [*Silver Age*, G3] is identified with the moon even before her episode in hell. The stage direction tells us of her attire: '*Enter Ceres and Proserpine attired like the Moone*'" (p. 437).

i bores heade (p. 320, line 73)

"*The fall of the Boare being winded, [Enter] Meleager with the head of the Boare*" (*Brazen Age*, D3v).

Serberosse iii heades (p. 320, line 73)

"*They beate against the gates. Enter Cerberus Cerb.* These my three empty throats you three shall gorge. . . . And with your bloods Il'e smeare my triple chaps,/ Your number fits my heads, and your three bodies/ Shall all my three-throates set aworke at once" (*Silver Age*, K2).

i Cadeseus (p. 320, line 74); *Mercures wings* (p. 320, line 80)

Mercury is a character in both *The Silver Age* and *The Brazen Age*. In *The Silver Age* (H1), "*Mercury flies from above.*"

i snake (p. 320, line 74)

This snake could be one of the two that Hercules strangles while still a child in his cradle: "*The Nurses bring yong Hercules in his Cradle, and leave him. Enter Juno and Iris with two snakes, put them to the childe and part: Hercules strangles them: to them Amphitrio, admiring the accident*" (*Silver Age*, F3v). It is more likely, however, to be "that wakefull snake that guards the Fleece" (*Silver Age*, G1), which is described in a stage direction as "*the Dragon sleeping*" beneath the "*Two fiery Buls*" and then killed by Jason following Medea's command "now kill the sleeping snake/ Which I have charm'd, and thence the Trophy take" (G2v).

i eleme bowle (p. 320, line 81)

The "eleme bowle" may be the "standing bowl" that Amphitrio locks in a casket in the Alcmena-Jupiter episode in *The Silver Age*. There it is described as "A golden cup . . . the choice boule" (C4v), "this rich boule" (D1), "the standing cup," "the cup," "the bowle" (E1v) and "this golden bowle" (E2). Possibly the "eleme bowle" is a survivor of Hercules' banquet with the centaurs, which ends in "*A confused fray with stooles, cups & bowles*" (H3).

i chayne of dragons (p. 320, line 82)

Fleay assigns this property to Medea. Both Tatlock and Holaday include it in their lists. The item, however, is not mentioned in the dialogue or noted in the stage directions in *The Brazen Age* (F2–G4) where the story is told of Medea and Jason's courtship and of the winning of the golden fleece.

i bulles head (p. 320, line 83)

The "bulles head" has been cited regularly, since Greg noted it, as one of the properties in the *Diary* required in staging the *Ages*: "*When the Fury sinkes, a Buls head appeares. . . He tugs with the Bull, and pluckes off one of his horns. Enter from the same place Achelous with his fore-head all bloudy"* (*Brazen Age*, B3).

Junoes cotte (p. 321, line 122)

Juno is a character in all of the first three *Ages*, appearing, for instance, in *The Golden Age* (E4), *The Silver Age* (F1v), and *The Brazen Age* (I3). Holaday suggests (p. 437) that the costume or coat in the inventory may be the one involved in *The Silver Age* when Juno commands: "Pull me from heaven (faire *Iris*) a blacke cloud,/ From which Il'e fashion me a beldams shape." Iris leaves the stage and returns a few lines later with a garment of some kind (F1v): "*Enter Iris with a habit.*" Apparently Juno puts on the garment and leaves the stage, reentering (F2) as a "Beldame."

The properties and costumes in the inventories do not speak conclusively about *The Golden Age*. The "sewtt for Nepton" and "Nepun forcke & garland" were required for *The Brazen Age* as well as *The Golden Age*. And "Junoes cotte" and Jupiter's "golden scepter" may have been used in all three of the *Ages* plays. Only the "globe" mentioned at the end of the play (K2v) seems to be particular to *The Golden Age*, and one cannot be sure of that. Theatrical properties and costumes, of course, are transitory things, quickly cannibalized for new shows when an old play ends its run. The absence from the inventories of all but a few items that may be related to *The Golden Age* can be explained by the disappearance from the Rose, early in 1596, of "seleo & olempo," the play with which Fleay has identified *The Golden Age* (*Chronicle History*, p. 114). On the other hand, the many items in the inventories assignable to *The Silver Age* and *The Brazen Age* can be accounted for by the fact that the popular Hercules plays were revived at the Rose in 1598, at the time when the inventories were made (Foakes and Rickert, pp. 324 and 93). Of course, it is not certain if the properties listed were assembled prior to the revival, were on hand during the performances, or were in stock shortly after the run of the plays, because the inventories with their dates of 10 and 13 March 1598 are extant only in Malone's transcript and we cannot be sure of the accuracy of the dates. Foakes and Rickert believe that "it is just possible that they [Henslowe's lists] were made in 1599, when there was no playing during most of March" (pp. 316–17).

The dialogue and stage directions in the plays show that most of the costumes and properties identified with *The Silver Age* and *The Brazen Age* were called for and used. Often two or more items used in the same scene appear together in the same line in the lists, suggesting that the items were stowed as they had come from the stage and were ready for use again. The appearance of the golden fleece in the same line with the bay tree supports

Holaday's belief that the fleece was hung on that tree (p. 436). Neptune's fork and garland, which may have come from *The Golden Age*, are together, possibly for use in the Mars and Venus episode in *The Brazen Age*. Iris's head and the rainbow are in place for the spectacular scene that ends the Jupiter and Alcmena story, with which *The Silver Age* begins. And with the costumes are the distinctive gown and hood, for the centaur, Nessus, with exactly "5 senetores capes" for Nessus's five "doubly shap't" followers who do battle with Hercules in *The Silver Age* (H2–H3v).

Frequently, the same costumes and properties are called for in both of the Hercules plays. Nessus, for instance, survives the first battle with Hercules and needs his costume when he is finally slain in *The Brazen Age* (C1v). Most of the items identified with Hercules, Juno, Jupiter, and Mercury are required for both plays. It is probable that the boar's head used in the Meleager story in *The Brazen Age* (D3v) was also used earlier in *The Silver Age* when Hercules entertained the centaurs: "*Herc*. To grace thy feast faire Hypodamia, / The Eremanthian forrest we have rob'd / Of that huge Boare" (H2). And some of the properties mentioned in *The Silver Age*, such as Cerberus's three heads (K2) and the lion's head (G1v), are certainly used in *The Brazen Age* (I4 and K3v) where the trophies representing Hercules' labors are displayed. At least one of the properties, the rock, is called for twice in different episodes in the same play: Hesione is bound to the rock and later Hercules jumps down from it (*Brazen Age*, E4v and L2).

The items in the inventories link *The Silver Age* and *The Brazen Age*, in the form in which they are extant, directly to production at the Rose theater in 1598 as "1 pᵗ of Hercules" and "2 pᵗᵉ of Hercoles," the titles under which they were entered by Henslowe in the list of playbooks purchased by him at some point after 3 March 1598 (Foakes and Rickert, pp. 322–24). And surely these are the "ne" pieces, "the firste pte of herculous" and the "2 p of hercolas," given originally at the Rose on 7 and 23 May 1595.

The identification of *The Silver Age* and *The Brazen Age* as the new Hercules plays given at the Rose in May 1595 indicates that *The Golden Age*, also written by Heywood, was presented in Henslowe's theater sometime before May 1595. Heywood was certainly writing plays at the Rose by that time. Greg believes he began working for Henslowe in 1594 (2:284), while Chambers entertains the idea that Heywood began working for Henslowe as early as 1592 (*ES* 3:341). The clearest indication that *The Golden Age* was written for the Rose and presented there before the two Hercules plays is to be found, however, in the texts of the extant plays.

Homer serves as the chorus and addresses the audience at the beginning and at the end of each of the three *Ages*. His remarks show that *The Golden Age* (K2–K2v) was written first:

Of Hercules, and of his famous deeds:

. . . .

Of these my Muse (now trauel'd) next proceedes.

. . . .

But if you send me hence uncheckt with feare,
Once more I'l dare upon this Stage t'appeare.

The Golden Age was followed on the same stage by *The Silver Age*, in which Homer says (B1v):

The Golden past, The Silver age begins

. . . .

We enter where we left, and so proceed.

Provisions are made at the end of *The Silver Age* (L1v) for its sequel, *The Brazen Age*, when Homer promises:

The acts of Hercules I shall pursue,
And bring him to the thrice-raz'd wals of Troy
His labours and his death Ile shew you.

And, clearly, Homer picks up the story of Hercules at the beginning of *The Brazen Age* (B1) and continues it from the point where he left off at the end of *The Silver Age:*

Still with our history we shall proceed,
And Hercules vi[c]torious acts relate:
His marriage first, next many a noble deed
Perform'd by him: last how he yeelds to Fate.

Unfortunately, *The Golden Age* cannot be identified in Henslowe's records as readily as its sequels, the Hercules plays. The only title in the *Diary* that has been suggested for identification with the first play in the *Ages* series is "seleo & olempo," presented at the Rose as a new piece on 5 March 1595. Fleay believes (*Chronicle History*, p. 114) that Henslowe knew the play as "Coelo et Olympo," a piece recorded in the *Diary* with Henslowe's characteristic indifference to spelling as "seleo & olempa," "seleo & olympo," "olimpo" (twice), "olimpio," "olempeo & Heugenyo," "olempeo" (twice), and "olempo" (Foakes and Rickert, pp. 28–34). We need not hesitate, as Greg does (2:175), "over what appears a rather fantastic title," that is, Fleay's identification of "Coelo et Olympo" as the original title of *The Golden Age*. Henslowe's titles in the *Diary* are often "fantastic." Actually, "Coelo et Olympo" is a likely title for the extant play. It suggests a piece that has something to do with the heavens, Olympus, or the Olympians—certainly the subject matter of Heywood's *Golden Age*. And we know from Heywood's address "To the Reader" that *The Golden Age* fell "accidentally" into the hands of the printer, in 1611, without a title. It seems likely that Henslowe, in the absence of a title on the original manuscript, recorded the play as "Coelo et Olympo" in 1595. Presumably the original manuscript passed finally into the hands of the printer, Nicholas Okes, who published it in 1611 after Heywood had assigned the present title, *The Golden Age*, and provided "an Epistle for ornament."

A digest of entries in the *Diary* (Foakes and Rickert, pp. 28–34) shows that "seleo & olempo" and the Hercules plays were presented at the Rose as "ne" plays in the same order that *The Golden Age*, *The Silver Age*, and *The Brazen Age* were written and originally staged.

5 March 1595	ne—Rd at seleo & olempo	[£3.]
2 May 1595	Rd at seleo & olempa	[£1.]
7 May 1595	ne—Rd at the firste pte of herculous	[£3.13s]
9 May 1595	Rd at selyo & olympo	[26s]
19 May 1595	Rd at olimpo	[23s]
20 May 1595	Rd at hercolas	[£3.9s]
23 May 1595	ne—Rd at 2 p of hercolas	[£3.10s]
27 May 1595	Rd at i pte of herculos	[£3.]
28 May 1595	Rd at 2 pte of herculas	[£3.2s]
29 May 1595	Rd at olimpo	[29s]
7 June 1595	Rd at olimpio	[15s]
12 June 1595	Rd at the i pt of herculos	[£3.1s]
13 June 1595	Rd at the 2 pt of herculos	[£3.2s]
1 Sept. 1595	Rd at i pte of herculos	[£3.4s]
2 Sept. 1595	Rd at 2 pte of herculos	[£3.]
4 Sept. 1595	Rd at olempeo & heugenyo	[18s]
22 Sept. 1595	Rd at i pte of herculos	[31s]
23 Sept. 1595	Rd at 2 pt of herculos	[23s]
3 Oct. 1595	Rd at olempeo	[15s]
12 Oct. 1595	Rd at i pte of herculos	[29s]
13 Oct. 1595	Rd at 2 pte of herculus	[25s]
25 Oct. 1595	Rd at i pt of herculos	[32s]
2 Nov. 1595	Rd at 2 pt of hercolas	[28s]
22 Nov. 1595	Rd at olempo	[4s.6d]
24 Nov. 1595	Rd at i herculos	[20s]
25 Nov. 1595	Rd at 2 pt of herculos	[16s]
18 Dec. 1595	mʳpd—Rd at i pt of herculos	[13s]
6 Jan. 1596	Rd at hurculos the i pte	[£3]
18 Feb. 1596	Rd at olempeo	[10s]

The digest shown above of entries in the *Diary* indicates that "seleo & olempo" and the Hercules plays were treated by Henslowe as a trilogy as long as they were together in the repertory of the company. "Seleo & olempo" earned £3 for Henslowe at its first performance and £1 when it was given for the second time, 2 May 1595. After the first performance of the Hercules plays, Henslowe's earnings for "seleo & olempo" are regularly recorded in shillings. Despite its meager earnings, or perhaps to take advantage of its relationship with the profitable Hercules plays, "seleo & olempo" either precedes performances of the Hercules pair or follows closely on four occasions.

"Seleo & olempo" was given on 19 May, followed on 20 May by *The Silver Age* and on 23 May by the initial performance of *The Brazen Age*. "Seleo & olempo" follows the Hercules plays in successive performances dated 27, 28 and 29 May, earning shillings while they earned pounds. It follows the pair again, with the lapse of a single day, in performances given on 1, 2 and 4 September and again earns but shillings while the other two plays earn pounds. "Seleo & olempo" precedes the Hercules plays in consecutive performances on 22 (no play recorded for the 23rd), 24 and 25 November, marking the last time that all three plays were known to be together in the repertory of the Rose. The poor returns of 4s. 6d., 20s., and 16s. indicate that the trilogy was no longer profitable, and presumably account for the fact that it was split up at about this time.

On the first and last time that these plays were together at the Rose, they were presented as a trilogy in the same order as the extant *Ages* trilogy. And if one can believe that the performances of the less profitable "seleo & olempo" were spaced to take advantage of the more profitable Hercules plays, the pieces were handled as a trilogy during the entire time that they were together at the Rose.

An entry in the *Diary* shows that the "lift" was modified in 1595 (Foakes and Rickert, p. 7), apparently between the first performance of "seleo & olempo" and the first performance of *I Hercules*. On the basis of what can be found out about the lift at the Rose and the requirements made on that piece of stage machinery by *The Golden Age* and *The Silver Age*, it seems reasonable to believe that "seleo & olempo" was *The Golden Age* and that experiments with the lift in staging that play prompted Heywood to make even greater demands on the lift in the sequel *The Silver Age*. Consequently, Henslowe had the lift modified while the theater was closed during Lent, paying £7.2 "for carpenters worke & mackinge the throne In the hevenes." The work was undertaken, it appears, to make it easier to lower actors onto the stage and especially to take them up to the heavens from the stage.

No play known to have been given at the Rose before "seleo & olempo" requires that an actor be raised from the stage to the heavens in a lift. An actor may have been lowered from the heavens at the Rose in *Alphonsus of Aragon*, an old play given on 16 August 1594, which begins with the stage direction: "*After you have sounded thrise, let Venus be let downe from the top of the Stage.*" And the author of *Alphonsus* suggests the possibility of having Venus taken up to the heavens from the stage: "*Exit Venus. Or if you can conveniently, let a chaire come downe from the top of the stage, and draw her up*" (2109–10). A little more than six months after *Alphonsus* was given at the Rose, *The Golden Age*, which I believe was given at the Rose as "seleo & olempo" on 5 March 1595, called for an actor to be lowered onto the stage and for two actors to be taken from the stage up to the heavens. "*Sound a dumbe shew. . . . Jupiter drawes heaven; at which Iris descends and presents him his Eagle, Crowne and Scepter, and his thunder-bolt. Jupiter first ascends upon the Eagle, and after him Ganimead*" (*Golden Age*, K2v). *The Silver Age*, which was given at the Rose as *I Hercules*, for the first time on 7 May 1595, contains directions calling for the lift to be used at least seven and possibly nine or more times. Two of the stage directions calling for the lift require more than one actor to be raised up to the heavens: "*Jupiter taking up the Infant, Speaks as he ascends in his cloud*" (K1); "*Jupiter, the Gods and Planets ascend to heaven*" (L1). In addition to Jupiter, "the Gods and Planets" on stage to be taken up to heaven include: Saturn, Juno, Mars, Phoebus, Venus and Mercury.

While we do not know exactly when the work on the lift was started or completed, the entry for "mackinge the throne In the hevenes" follows a list of expenses totaling £108.9 for "Repracyones" made "about my playhowsse" during Lent in 1595—after "seleo & olempo" made its initial appearance at the Rose. The theater was closed for Lent from 15 March to 22 April. Presumably the work on the lift began while the theater was closed and was completed before Henslowe paid for it on 4 June 1595. The work was probably finished by 7 May 1595, in time for the opening performance of Heywood's "ne" play, "the firste pte of herculous," which is clearly *The Silver Age*.

Thus far, I have offered evidence from the plays and the *Diary* that establishes with a reasonable degree of certainty Fleay's identifications of the first three of Heywood's *Ages* as plays written for production at the Rose and given there as new plays for the first time in 1595. Now, by tracing the history of these plays up to the time that they were printed, I will offer evidence that the plays were not revised for production in other theaters after they left the Rose.

The *Ages* trilogy was broken up at the Rose at some time after the performance there of *The Brazen Age* on 25 November 1595. *The Golden Age* was given on 18 February 1596, and, except for a few properties and costumes that may have survived from this time, it disappears from Henslowe's records. Dekker's observation, that "The Golden Age is moulding new again," in his *If it be not Good* (1.1), may allude to a production of Heywood's play in about 1610; Chambers, however, is skeptical (*ES* 3:344). No more is heard of it until it is published in 1611 marked with Nicholas Okes's device on the title page and described as "acted at the Red Bull" by the Queen's men.

   The Silver Age was given at the Rose on 6 January 1596 and apparently became, shortly after that performance, the property of Martin Slater who left the Admiral's company on 18 July 1597. Slater also obtained *The Brazen Age* and resold both plays to the Admiral's men in May 1598 (Foakes and Rickert, p. 89). The plays were revived that summer when Henslowe lent 30s to Thomas Downton on 16 July "for to bye A Robe to playe hercolas in" (Foakes and Rickert, p. 93). *The Silver Age* and *The Brazen Age* are also listed by Henslowe as "I p^t of Hercules" and 2 p^{te} of Hercoles" under "A Note of all suche bookes as belong to the Stocke, and such as I have bought since the 3d of March 1598" (Foakes and Rickert, p. 323).

   The *Diary* contains two other entries that may be related to a revival of *The Silver Age* or *The Brazen Age*, or both, in 1601 at the Fortune (Foakes and Rickert, p. 185):

> [p]d unto the little tayller to bye . . . .
> for the play of hercollas the 14 of december
> 1601 the some of . . . . [20s]

and

> pd unto the littell tayller 18 of december 1601
> for divers thinges for the playe of hercolas the
> some of . . . . [5s]

   Following this possible revival of *The Silver Age* at the Fortune in 1601, the play is next mentioned in the Revels Accounts of 12 and 13 January 1612: "By the Queens players and the Kings Men. The Sunday following [Twelfth Night] att grinwidg before the Queen and the Prince was playd the Silver Aiedg: and ye next night following Lucrecia" (*ES* 4:126 and 178). Chambers infers from the Accounts that both plays were given by the two companies acting together. But, as Reynolds points out (p. 10), "This item has been questioned as forged." Printed in 1613 by Okes for

Benjamin Lightfoot, the title page of *The Silver Age* gives no information about the company that owned it or where or when it was produced.

No trace can be found of *The Brazen Age* after its possible revival at the Fortune in 1601 until it was printed in 1613 by Okes for Samuel Rand. Again, the title page gives no information about the company that controlled the play or the time or place in which it was staged.

Nothing in the history of the *Ages* trilogy indicates that the extant plays were revised to accommodate them to the stage of the Red Bull or to the stage of any other playhouse in which they may have been presented after they left the Rose. Indeed it is doubtful if *The Silver Age* and *The Brazen Age* were ever staged at the Red Bull. Heywood points to the conditions that would have made it difficult to bring the trilogy together for a revival. In the Epistle to *The English Traveller*, in 1633, the playwright says his plays were never published as his works because "many of them by shifting and change of Companies, have been negligently lost, Others of them are still retained in the hands of some Actors, who think it against their peculiar profit to have them come in Print." Certainly the trilogy was not in Heywood's control when he wrote his address "To the Reader" for the publication of *The Golden Age* in 1611. And it seems unlikely that all three plays were the property of Okes in 1611, although Heywood suggests that the other two plays would be published if *The Golden Age* were well received. If either Okes or Heywood controlled all three plays in 1611, *The Golden Age* must have been poorly received because *The Silver Age* and *The Brazen Age* were not printed until two years later, in 1613. It does not seem reasonable to believe that publication of *The Silver Age* and *Brazen Age* was held up for performances of the plays at the Red Bull between 1611 and 1613. If they were given there, one assumes that Okes would have included the fact on the title page of those two plays, as he does on the title page of *The Golden Age*, hoping to profit from the popularity of the pieces that might have resulted from production on stage. And presumably Okes would have noted, for the same reason, that *The Silver Age* had been presented at court in 1612, if it had been given there. The fact that the first play in the *Ages* trilogy, *The Golden Age*, was revived at the Red Bull simply does not prove that the other two plays were also revived at that theater.

Of course it is possible that the trilogy was reassembled and presented at the Red Bull before the three plays were printed. Even so, there is no evidence to show that the extant pieces were revised. While Okes printed *The Golden Age* "as it hath beene sundry times acted at the Red Bull, by the Queenes Majesties Servants," there is no indication that the play was altered for production at the Red Bull. In his address "To the Reader," Heywood is explicit about the extent of his work on the piece: "I have fixt these few lines in the front of my Booke." He does not claim to have revised or amended the play or to be aware of any changes made to the play upon "finding it mine owne."

On the basis of information provided by Henslowe's *Diary* and by the plays themselves, it may be concluded that *The Golden Age*, *The Silver Age*, and *The Brazen Age* were written for the stage of the Rose theater where they were presented as new plays in 1595 and that there is no evidence to support the general assumption that they were revised to accommodate them to the stages on which they were later played.

Obviously, it is of importance to those interested in Heywood's work that Fleay's identification of these three plays be clearly reestablished. For one thing, the identification of the pieces with the Rose dates the plays, which must now be considered among Heywood's earliest works. And it is of especial interest to the historian concerned with the physical stage to know that these plays exist today apparently in the form in which they were written for production at the Rose theater. Demanding such spectacular staging, the trilogy must have something to reveal about the stage in the playhouse for which they were written. At the very least, a cursory inspection of the plays will suggest that the stage of the Rose was far more complex in its arrangements than the platform stage shown in Arend Van Buchell's rough sketch of the Swan.

75 *Edward I* (b–9)
    THE Famous Chronicle of king Edwarde the first, sirnamed Edward Longshankes. . . . Imprinted at London by W. White dwelling in Cow-lane. 1599. Photocopy. Ann Arbor, Mich.: University Microfilms.
    Greg (2:176) points out that a "ne" piece was presented by the Admiral's men for Henslowe fourteen times between 29 August 1595 and 9 July 1596, as "longeshancke" or "prynce longschanckes." Greg observes that "the only known play on the subject is Peele's *Edward I surnamed Long-shankes*, entered S.R. 8 Oct. 1593 and printed the same year." Chambers (3:460–61) notes that "'Longeshanckes sewte' is in the Admiral's inventory of 10 March 1598," and records the fact that on 8 August 1602, Alleyn sold the book of the play to the Admiral's with another play for four pounds. The earliest extant edition of the play was printed in 1593 before it was given at the Rose and the edition printed in 1599, which is used here, is described by Greg as a "reprint" of the one made in 1593 (2:176). Kirschbaum labels the edition printed in 1593 as a "bad quarto" (*RES* 14:36–38), and Jewkes (p. 129) says that some of the stage directions "certainly are of the abrupt type found in the theatrical copy."

82 *The Famous Victories* (b-3)

THE FAMOUS VICtories *of Henry the fifth. . . . As it was plaide by the Queenes Majesties Players. LONDON Printed by Thomas Creede, 1598.* Photocopy. Ann Arbor, Mich.: University Microfilms.

Chambers (4:17) is of the opinion that this play is "obviously too early to be the new play of 'harey the V' given thirteen times for Henslowe between 28 Nov. 1595 and 15 July 1596 by the Admiral's in whose inventories of March 1598 Harry the Fifth's doublet and gown appear." Elsewhere (2:144–45), Chambers says, "One would be more willing to identify *Henry V* with *The Famous Victories*, if the latter had not been printed in 1598 with the name of the Queen's men on its title-page." Greg (2:177) believes the Queen's men sold the manuscript of *The Famous Victories* to Creede in 1594, "but the Admiral's men appropriated and revised the play and stayed the publication till 1598 when Creede printed it from the original MS." On the other hand Kirschbaum lists the piece with the "bad quartos" (*RES* 14:33), and Jewkes believes (p. 199) "the copy for this play was probably a prompt-book which had been discarded after a revision or a revival, or an author's manuscript which had been prepared for the stage."

88 *The Blind Beggar of Alexandria* (b-3)

THE BLINDE begger *of Alexandria. . . . As it hath beene sundry times publickly acted in London. by the right honorable the Earle of Nottingham, Lord high Admirall his servantes. By George Chapman: Gentleman. Imprinted at London for William Jones. . . . 1598.* Edited by W. W. Greg. Malone Society Reprints. Oxford: University Press, 1928.

According to Greg (2:179), this play was given at the Rose on twenty-two occasions between 12 February 1596 and 1 April 1597. Chambers (3.251) agrees with Greg. It was entered in the *Stationers' Register* 15 August 1598, and printed the same year for William Jones. Jewkes (p. 345) describes the text of 1598 as a "bad quarto" and sums up the scholarship on the text (p. 252) by quoting Greg. In the edition of the play for the Malone Society in 1928, Greg says (p. vi): "there is reason to suppose that the play has not come down to us in anything like the state in which it left the author's hand. . . . The text . . . runs to 1612 lines only." Greg also contests Chambers's view (3:251) that the text is a "'cut' stage copy," holding that "the directions are no more than what might be supplied from memory of a performance." Greg concludes that "in spite of its apparent regular publication, the piece if not surreptitiously obtained had at least a somewhat irregular history."

96 *Captain Stukley* (a-3)
THE Famous Historye of the life and death of Captaine Thomas Stukeley. . . .
As it hath beene Acted. Printed for Thomas Pavyer . . . 1605. Photocopy of
Huntington Library copy. Ann Arbor, Mich.: University Microfilms.

Chambers says (4:47) that "the present play is probably the *Stewtley*
produced by the Admiral's on 11 Dec. 1596," as a "ne" piece. Jewkes says
(p. 218), "the text looks very much as if it had seen service in the playhouse,
and it may even have been the official prompt-book, or a transcript from
it." It was entered in the *Stationers' Register* on 11 August 1600. However,
the earliest edition is dated 1605.

103 *Jupiter and Io* (b-8)
In *PLEASANT DIALOGUES AND DRAMMAS. . . . By Tho. Heywood.*
LONDON, Printed by R. O. for R. H. . . . to be sold by Thomas Slater . . .
1637. Photocopy of Huntington Library copy. Ann Arbor, Mich.: University Microfilms.

Greg (2:183) seems to support Fleay's identification of this play as one of
the "v playes in one" done as "ne" by the Admiral's men for Henslowe on 7
April 1597. Fleay (1:286) points out that the "Argosse heade" mentioned in
the Admiral's inventory of 10 March 1598 is required for no known play
except *Jupiter and Io*. Chambers (3:346–47) concedes the possibility of the
identification. The earliest extant text is that printed in *Pleasant Dialogues
and Drammas*, 1637, as "never before published." Jewkes does not concern
himself with this short play (743 lines); I find, however, that the piece
contains a number of abrupt directions in the margin that are characteristic
of texts derived from playhouses: "*A great damp ariseth.*" "*Exeunt*" and "*Exit*"
are found frequently in the margin on the right, one line above centered
stage directions, presumably the playwright's, calling for other characters
to "*Enter.*" "Aside" appears regularly, with one direction marked "*Spoken
aside.*" At one place "*Jupiter starts,*" and in another "*Musicke*" is jotted in the
margin beside dialogue asking, "But ha, what musick/ Was that strooke
up?" Near the end of the play Mercury charms Argus's eyes to sleep and
according to a stage direction in the margin "(cuts off his head. Exit."

106 *Humorous Day's Mirth* (a-3)
A pleasant Comedy entituled: An Humerous dayes Myrth . . . . By G. C. . . .
LONDON Printed by Valentine Syms: 1599. Edited by W. W. Greg and
David Nichol Smith. Malone Society Reprints. Oxford: University Press,
1937.

Chambers (3:251) says, "The 1598 inventories of the Admiral's (Greg,
Henslowe Papers, 115, 119) include Verone's son's hose and Labesha's cloak,

which justifies Fleay, i. 55, in identifying the play with the comedy of *Humours* produced by that company on 1 May 1597." The play cannot be found in the *Stationers' Register*, and the earliest extant edition was printed by Valentine Syms in 1599. Greg says in his edition of the play for the Malone Society, 1937 (p. vii), that "the copy may have been surreptitiously obtained." He observes, however, that "it was, nevertheless, printed from a theatrical manuscript of some sort and not from a pirated report, for however confused in places, the text is in essence sound. Its worst feature is the rendering of the whole as prose, whereas a considerable portion is obviously intended to be in verse."

108 *Frederick and Basilea*, plot (a1)
    The plott of Frederick & Basilea. W. W. Greg's reproduction and transcript in *Dramatic Documents from the Elizabethan Playhouses*. Oxford: Clarendon Press [1931].
    Greg (3:135) says that "*Frederick and Basilea* was performed by the Admiral's men at the Rose as a new play, on 3 June 1597, and the present plot belongs to that occasion." Chambers (4:14) does not contest this assertion.

125 *The Downfall of Robert* (a-2)
    THE DOWNFALL OF ROBERT, Earle of Huntington, AFTERWARD CALLED Robin Hood . . . . Acted by the Right Honourable, The Earle of Notingham, Lord high Admirall of England, his servants . . . . Imprinted at London, for William Leake, 1601. Edited by Arthur Brown and John C. Meagher. Malone Society Reprints. Oxford: University Press, 1964.
    Entries in the *Diary* (Foakes and Rickert, pp. 86–87) show that *The Downfall of Robert* and its sequel *The Death of Robert* were both written for the Admiral's men and licensed for presentation while the company was playing at the Rose. The title pages indicate that both parts were acted by the same company. Anthony Munday was paid five pounds for the first part on 15 February 1598, and he was lent ten shillings on 20 February "upon his seconde part of the downefall of earlle huntyngton surnamed Roben Hoode." Henry Chettle was lent twenty shillings on 25 February "in pt of paymente of the second pte of Robart hoode." The second part was apparently finished about 8 March 1598 when Henslowe lent Robert Shaw, for the Admiral's men, £3.5 "in full paymente of the seconde pte . . . of Roben hoode." On 28 March the Master of Revels was paid fourteen shillings for licensing "the ii ptes of Robart hoode" (Foakes and Rickert, p. 88). The plays, apparel, and properties are listed in the Admiral's inventories for March 1598; both were entered in the *Stationers' Register* on 1 December 1600 and printed in 1601. Greg identifies the plays as those

given at court by the Admiral's men during the Christmas season of 1598. Arthur Brown, in the edition of *The Death of Robert* for the Malone Society, 1965 (p. vi), doubts that the alterations which may have been made in November 1598 for the presentation of one or both of these plays at court will be found in the extant texts because "the text of *The Death*, like that of *The Downfall*, represents an unsettled and intermediate stage of composition and was probably printed from foul papers dating from early March 1598." If Brown is correct both plays are extant in texts designed specifically for presentations on the stage of the Rose.

126 *Englishmen for My Money* (a-2)
   ENGLISH-MEN For my Money. . . . Imprinted at London by W. White . . . 1616. Edited by W. W. Greg. Malone Society Reprints. Oxford: University Press, 1912.
   The identification of this play with a piece for which Henslowe paid Haughton a total of two pounds is uncontested by Greg (2:191) and Chambers (3:335). The payments were entered in the *Diary* on 18 February and early in May 1598. The play was entered in the *Stationers' Register* 3 August 1601, but the earliest extant edition dates from 1616. Greg in his introduction to the Malone Society Reprint of the play says, "It has been suggested, not unreasonably, that the mention of 'the Kings English' at l. 319 points to a revision after the accession of James I. Since, however, the manuscript was presumably in White's hands as early as 1601, there is no reason to suppose that the alteration amounted to more than what a compositor might feel impelled to make in his copy." The play, like many of the new pieces mentioned in the *Diary* after 1597, was paid for in installments—the authors were given advances, loans, payment in earnest while working on plays. Since Haughton was paid in installments for this play it seems likely that the piece was written specifically for production at the Rose where the Admiral's men were playing. The extant text, therefore, speaks with authority about the stage of the Rose. Jewkes says (p. 219) that "an author's copy in good condition or a transcript from it seems likely to be the kind of copy from which this play was printed."

127 *The Death of Robert* (a-2)
   THE DEATH OF ROBERT, EARLE OF HUNTINGTON. OTHERWISE CALLED Robin Hood. . . . Acted by the Right Honourable, the Earle of Notingham, Lord high Admirall of England, his servants. . . . Imprinted at London, for William Leake, 1601. Edited by Arthur Brown and John C. Meagher. Malone Society Reprints. Oxford: University Press, 1965.
   See above, 125.

136 *The Two Angry Women* (a-2)

THE PLEASANT HISTORIE OF the two angrie women of Abington. . . .
As it was lately playde by the right Honorable the Earle of Nottingham, Lord high Admirall, his servants. By Henry Porter Gent. . . . Imprinted at London for Joseph Hunt, and William Ferbrand . . . 1599. Edited by W. W. Greg.
Malone Society Reprints. Oxford: University Press, 1912.

There is some question about which of the pieces mentioned in the
Diary is to be identified with *The Two Angry Women*. Greg (2:193) agrees
with Fleay that the play is Porter's *Love Prevented*. And Chambers says
(3:467) that "of the plays named as his [Porter's] by Henslowe, *Love
Prevented* seems the only likely title." Published in 1599 "*as it was lately
playde by the right Honorable Earle of Nottingham, Lord high Admirall, his
servants*," the extant text seems to Jewkes (p. 216) to have been based on "an
author's manuscript or a non-theatrical transcript of it." Porter's work as a
playwright appears to have been limited to the Rose from about 1596 to
1600, and one can be almost certain that the play was written specifically
for production on the stage of the Rose.

172 *Troilus and Cressida*, plot (a-1)

A fragmentary plot without a title. W. W. Greg's reproduction and
transcript in *Dramatic Documents from the Elizabethan Playhouses*. Oxford:
Clarendon Press [1933].

Greg (3:144) believes this plot may be assigned to the *Troilus and Cressida*
on which Dekker and Chettle were working in April 1599, and Chambers
(*ES* 4:51) agrees that "the few names of actors are not inconsistent" with
Greg's identification of the fragment.

176 *The Shoemakers' Holiday* (a-2)

*THE SHOEMAKERS Holiday OR The Gentle Craft. . . . As it was acted
before the Queenes most excellent Majestie on New-yeares day at night last, by the
right honourable the Earle of Notingham, Lord high Admirall of England, his
servants. Printed by Valentine Sims. . . . 1600*. Edited by Fredson Bowers in
The Dramatic Works of Thomas Dekker. Cambridge: University Press, 1953.
1:7–104.

Thomas Deloney's prose tract *The Gentle Craft* was published in 1598
and Henslowe lent the Admiral's men three pounds on 15 July 1599
(Foakes and Rickert, p. 122) "to bye A Boocke of thomas dickers Called the
gentle Craft." Based on Deloney's tract, Dekker's play, *The Shoemakers'
Holiday or the Gentle Craft* was printed in 1600 by Valentine Sims as acted
for the queen by the Admiral's men "*on New-yeares day at night last*." In the
introduction to his edition of the play (1:9), Fredson Bowers says the 1600

quarto "appears to have been completely authorized." Bowers is not as certain about the printer's copy, pointing out that "there are no definite signs of theatrical, or prompt, copy, and some indication that the author's papers may have been used, possibly the 'foul papers,' although a transcript of these cannot be ruled out of the question." On the basis of what is known about the play, it may be classified with those written for the Rose and extant in a nontheatrical copy close to the author's manuscript.

179 *Look about You* (a-4)

A PLEASANT COMMODIE, CALLED Looke about you. As it was lately played by the right honourable the Lord High Admirall his servants. . . . London, Printed for William Ferbrand . . . 1600. Edited by W. W. Greg. Malone Society Reprints. Oxford: University Press, 1913.

Chambers says (4:28), "The play ought itself to appear somewhere in Henslowe's diary, and Fleay may be right in identifying it with the *Bear a Brain* of 1599, although the only recorded payment for that play was not to Wadeson, but to Dekker." Greg (2:204) is "inclined to believe that *Bear a Brain* may possibly have been another title of the *Gentle Craft*." Despite the difficulty about the identification of *Look about You* with entries in the *Diary*, the title page of the play printed in 1600 describes it as "lately played" by the Lord Admiral's men, who were then at the Rose theater. According to Jewkes "the most likely origin of the copy for this text is an author's manuscript, with little evidence of any preparation for the stage" (p. 222).

185 *Sir John Oldcastle* (a-1)

The first part Of the true and hono-rable historie, of the life of Sir John Old-castle, the good Lord Cobham. As it hath been lately acted by the right honorable the Earle of Notingham Lord high Admirall of England his servants. . . . LONDON Printed by V. S. For Thomas Pavier . . . 1600. Edited by W. W. Greg and Percy Simpson. Malone Society Reprints. N.p.: Chiswick Press, 1908.

The identification of this play with the Rose is uncontested by Greg (2:206) and Chambers (3:306). It is mentioned, sometimes with a sequel, at several places in the *Diary* (Foakes and Rickert, pp. 125, 126, 129, 132, 213, and 216). Entered in the *Stationers' Register* 11 August 1600, it was printed the same year as "*lately acted*" by the Admiral's men. The entries in the *Diary* show that the play later passed to Worcester's men who paid Dekker for additions to the piece and presumably revived it at the Rose in 1602. Jewkes thinks (p. 221) that the text printed in 1600 "looks as if it were prepared from an authorial manuscript which had been prepared by a stage adapter or prompter for performance, and from which the prompt-book had probably been transcribed."

187 *Patient Grissil* (a-1)

THE PLEASANT COMODIE OF Patient Grissill. As it hath beene sundrie times lately plaid by the right honorable the Earle of Nottingham (Lord high Admirall) his servants. . . . LONDON. Imprinted for Henry Rocket . . . 1603. Edited by Fredson Bowers in *The Dramatic Works of Thomas Dekker*. Cambridge: University Press, 1953. 1:207–98.

Five entries in the *Diary* (Foakes and Rickert, pp. 65, 125, 128 and 129) record payments made between 16 October and 29 December 1599 to Thomas Dekker, Harry Chettle, and William Haughton, "in earnest" for *Patient Grissil*. Clearly, the play was written specifically for production at the Rose and given there, where another entry (Foakes and Rickert, p. 130) records the payment of one pound on 26 January 1600 "to buy a grey gowne for gryssell." And finally Henslowe records the payment of two pounds on 18 March 1600 (Foakes and Rickert, p. 132) "to staye the printinge of patient gresell." The play was entered in the *Stationers' Register* 28 March 1600 but not printed until 1603. Jewkes is of the opinion that "internal evidence of playhouse use is almost non-existent" in the extant text (p. 139). Bowers says (p. 210): "The nature of the manuscript which served as printer's copy is not altogether certain," and points out that "there is some evidence for prompt copy." Dekker's editor concludes of the text of this play written specifically for production at the Rose (p. 210) that "in the nature of the case it might be plausible to conjecture that the actual copy was a transcript of the book rather than the prompt-book itself."

189a *Fortunatus* (b-1)

THE Pleasant Comedie of Old Fortunatus. As it was plaied before the <u>Queenes</u> *Majestie this Christmas, by the Right Honourable the Earle of Nottingham, Lord high Admirall of England his Servants. . . . LONDON Printed by S. S. for William Aspley. . . . 1600.* Edited by Fredson Bowers in *The Dramatic Works of Thomas Dekker*. Cambridge: University Press, 1953. 1:105–205.

The identification of *Fortunatus* with the Rose is uncontested. Entries in the *Diary* under various dates suggest that *Fortunatus* was part I of an old play when it was performed by the Admiral's men on six occasions between 3 February and 24 May 1596. Dekker received a total of six pounds in payments made between 9 November and 30 November 1599 for the "hole history of Ffortunatus." He received another pound on 1 December 1599 for "altrenge of the boocke of the wholl history of fortewnatus," and was paid two pounds more on 12 December 1599 "for the eande of fortew-natus for the corte." The Admiral's company paid ten pounds, borrowed from Henslowe, on 6 December 1599, "for to by thinges for ffortunatus." The play, according to Chambers (3:291), was presented at court on 27 December 1599. It was entered in the *Stationers' Register* 20 February 1600, and printed in the same year "*as it was plaied before the Queenes Majestie this Christmas.*" Jewkes says of the extant text (p. 138), "There is little doubt that the play was printed from a manuscript which had been prepared for production." Bowers finds conflicting evidence about the nature of the text which he believes can be reconciled (p. 108) "by the conjecture that no formal prompt-book for public performance was made up before the court presentation, that this court performance was regulated by Dekker's pa-pers with some prompt markings—only one of which has been preserved or can be recognized in the printed text—and that subsequently when a prompt copy was transcribed for ordinary use these original papers were handed to the printer." Following Bowers, it may be concluded that while *Fortunatus* was written for the Rose and presented there, the extant text bears marks of presentation of the play at court. At the very least, the prologue and the epilogue for the court performance are preserved along with the prologue for the production at the Rose. Greg believes (2:179) the alterations for court include "the Virtue and Vice scenes . . . and such modifications as were necessary to make these fit into the general scheme."

269a *David and Bathsheba* (b-9)
   THE LOVE OF KING DAVID AND FAIR BETHSABE. With the Tragedie of Absalon. As it hath ben divers times plaied on the stage. Written by George Peele. . . . LONDON, Printed by Adam Islip. 1599. Edited by W. W. Greg. Malone Society Reprints. Oxford: University Press, 1912.
   Greg (2:232) and Chambers (3:461) contest Fleay's identification (2:153) of Peele's *David and Bethsabe* as the play for which Henslowe laid out four-teen pence in October 1602 "for poleyes & worckmanshipp for to hange absolome." The play was entered in the *Stationers' Register* on 14 May 1594 and printed in 1599. The title page does not indicate the company to whom the play belonged but it does claim that the piece "*hath ben divers times plaied on the stage.*" The stage direction at the beginning of scene 15 in the Malone Society Reprint of the play reads, "*The battell, and Absalon hangs by the haire.*" He hangs while more than a hundred lines are spoken. This unusual stage business, supported by the entry in the *Diary* recording the payment of money for the "worckmanshipp" and "poleyes" to effect it, must, I think, outweigh Chambers's and Greg's opposition. Peele's play, printed in 1599, would not have been the first that fell into the hands of a

printer and was revived by a company other than the one for which it was written. *Titus Andronicus* can be cited as an example. *David and Bathsheba* was almost certainly revived by Worcester's men at the Rose in 1602. Jewkes says of the extant text that it "shows connection with the playhouse" (p. 128), and adds that "the text has suffered considerable mutilation." These mutilations and marks of transmission through the playhouse were made before the piece was presented at the Rose.

278 *Woman Killed with Kindness* (a-2)

A WOMAN KILDE with Kindnesse. Written by Tho: Heywood. . . . LON-DON Printed by William Jaggard . . . to be sold . . . by John Hodgets. 1607. Photocopy of British Museum copy. Ann Arbor, Mich.: University Microfilms.

Henslowe's records show that Heywood's *Woman Killed with Kindness* was written for Worcester's men while they were at the Rose theater in February and March of 1603. Heywood received £6.13 on 5 February to purchase a gown for the play (Foakes and Rickert, p. 223). On 12 February he received £3 "in part payment for his playe called A womon kylled with kyndness," and on 6 March another £3 "in fulle payment for his playe called a womon kyld with kyndness" (Foakes and Rickert, p. 224). Jewkes believes (p. 132) that the text of this play printed in 1607 "was closer to Heywood's manuscript than to a playhouse prompt-book."

B

Introduction of Properties onto the Stage

	Trap	Discovery	Heavens	Carried [a]	Undesignated: Prop. Indicated	Undesignated: Prop. Suggested	Total
Bushes					2	2	4
Trees				1	9	7	17
Arbours	1				2	3	6
Bankes		1				3	4
Rocks					1	1	2
Tents					6	1	7
Beds		2[b]		5	3		12
Thrones		1	1	2[b]	21	5	28
Seats		1		2	16	20	39
"The bench"						3	3
"The barre"						2	2
Seats at tables				3	1	4	8
Tables				3	2	4	9
Banquets				10 / 2[b]	6		18
Canopies				2			2
Litters, chairs				5			5
Coffins, hearses				3 / 2[b]			5
Chariots				2 / 2[b]		1	5

	Trap	Discovery	Heavens	Carried[a]	Undesignated: Prop. Indicated	Undesignated: Prop. Suggested	Total
Ladders				1	1	2	4
Miscellaneous	3[b]	5	4	8	6	6	39
			4[b]	3[b]			
Total	1	8	5	45			
	3[b]	2[b]	4[b]	11[b]			
	4	10	9	56	76	64	219

[a] This includes properties brought, thrust, or carried onto the stage.
[b] Removed from stage in same manner as introduced.

C

References to Parts of the Rose

THE TRAPDOOR

Friar Bacon (b-4)

The dialogue and stage directions (1191–203) suggest that a tree is pushed up from below: *"Heere Bungay conjures and the tree appeares with the dragon shooting fire."*

The dialogue and stage directions (1203–08) suggest that an actor comes on stage through a trapdoor: *"Hercules appeares in his Lions skin."*

Actors and properties are apparently removed from the stage through the trapdoor (1275–80): *"Exit the spirit with Vandermast and the Tree."*

1 Henry VI (b-8)

The dialogue and stage directions (5.3) suggest that "Fiends" enter and exit through the trapdoor:

> *Puc.* . . . . This speedy and quicke appearance argues proofe
> Of your accustom'd diligence to me.
> Now ye Familiar Spirits, that are cull'd
> Out of the powerfull Regions under earth,
> Helpe me this once.

A Looking Glass for London (b-6)

A large property is brought on stage through the trap (517–25): *"The Magi with their rods beate the ground, and from under the same riseth a brave Arbour."*

The dialogue and stage directions (1223–31) indicate that an actor sinks down to hell: *"Upon this praier she departeth, and a flame of fire appeareth from beneath, and Radagon is swallowed."*

The dialogue and stage directions suggest (1460–66) that an actor is thrust on stage through the trapdoor: *"Jonas the Prophet cast out of the Whales belly upon the Stage."*

A Knack to Know a Knave (a-4)

The dialogue and stage directions (1582–83) suggest that a devil enters through the trap: *"Asmoroth ascende, veni Asmoroth, Asmoroth veni. Enter the Devill."*

The dialogue and stage directions (1714–17) suggest that two people enter through the trap: "*Dun.* . . . Veni Asmoroth, in good time see where he comes. *Here enter Alfrida disguised with the devil.*"

George a Green (b-3)

The dialogue and stage directions (795) indicate that the trap was opened from below: "*He throwes the ground in, and she comes out.*"

Titus Andronicus (a-4)

The dialogue and stage directions indicate (D4–E) that the trap is a pit into which two men fall.

The Four Prentices of London (b-8)

A stage direction (C2) indicates that the trap is used as a grave: "*Enter a Coarse after it Irishmen mourning, in a dead March: to them enters Eustace, and talkes with the chiefe mourner, who makes signes of consent, after buriall of the Coarse, and so Exeunt.*"

Alphonsus of Aragon (b-6)

The dialogue and stage directions indicate (951–70) that an actor comes on stage through a trap and later exits through the same trap: "*Rise Calchas up in a white Cirples and a Cardinals Myter.* . . . *Calchas sinke downe where you came up.*"

Faustus (b-5)

The dialogue and stage directions suggest (225–72) that a trap is used for an entrance and for an exit.

Wagner raises up two devils (370–77) who may enter and exit through the trap.

The dialogue and stage directions suggest that a devil enters through a trap (417): "Veni veni Mephostophile. *Enter Mephosto.*"

The use of a trap is suggested by the dialogue and stage directions (1154–62).

The dialogue suggests (1345–53) the threatened use of a trap or traps to call up devils.

The dialogue suggests that three devils enter through the trap (1894–96): "*Thunder. Enter Lucifer, Belzebub, and Mephostophilis. Lucif.* Thus from infernall *Dis* do we ascend to view the subjects of our Monarchy."

John a Kent (b-7)

The use of the trap is suggested by a stage direction (819): "*ffrom under the Stage the third Antique.*"

The Silver Age (b-2)

The dialogue indicates (G4v) that a trap is used for the exit of Pluto, with Proserpine, in his chariot drawn by devils: "*Pluto*. Cleave earth, and when I stampe upon thy breast/ Sinke me, my brasse-shod wagon, and my-selfe,/ My Coach-steeds, and their traces altogether."

Stage directions (H1v) indicate that an actor makes an entrance and an exit through a trap: "*Earth riseth from under the stage. . . . Earth sinkes.*"

Stage directions suggest the possible use of a trap (H2) for an entrance and an exit: "*The river Arethusa riseth from the stage. . . . Exit Are.*" Probably the actor playing Arethuse just "flowed" through one of the stage doors.

An actor exists (K2v) through a trapdoor: "*Hercules sinkes himselfe.*"

A stage direction and the situation indicate that several actors use a trap or traps (L1) to exit: "*Pluto, hels Judges, the Fates and Furies downe to hell.*"

The Brazen Age (b-2)

The dialogue and stage directions (B3) indicate that a trap is used for an exit, then for putting a property on stage, and finally for the entrance of an actor: "*When the Fury sinkes, a Buls head appeares. . . . He tugs with the Bull, and pluckes off one of his horns. Enter from the same place Achelous with his fore-head all bloudy.*"

The dialogue (G2v) indicates that Medea sows dragons' teeth, and armed men enter through a trap to assist Jason.

A stage direction indicates (H4v) that an actor exits through a trap and that another enters through the same trap: "*Gallus sinkes, and in his place riseth a Cocke and crowes.*"

A stage direction indicates that an actor exits through a trap (L3): ". . . *his body sinkes.*"

Edward I (b-9)

The dialogue indicates that an actor exits through a trapdoor (H2v), which opens from below: "*Queene*. Gape earth and swallow me, and let my soule sinke downe to hell. . . . *Jone*. . . . oh she is suncke, and here the earth is new closde up againe."

The dialogue indicates that an actor enters through a trapdoor (H3v): "*Potters wife*. . . . but stay John, what's that riseth out of the ground Jesus blesse us; John look how it riseth higher and higher."

Look about You (a-4)

The dialogue indicates that two men fall into a hole in the ground and are robbed by a third (2043–70). They are able to crawl out. Note that the hole is described (2043) as a cave.

SEATS FOR THE AUDIENCE

The Battle of Alcazar (b-4)

The presenter speaks to the audience (30): "Sit downe and see what hainous stratagems/ These damned wits contrive."

Again (63) the Presenter speaks to the audience: "Sit you and see this true and tragicke warre."

The Brazen Age (b-2)

Homer as the chorus addresses the audience (B1v): "And these, I hope, may (with some mixtures) passe,/ So you sit pleas'd in this our Age of Brasse."

Captain Stukley (a-3)

The chorus (L3) addresses the audience: "Sit now and see unto our stories end,/ all those mishaps that this poore Prince attend."

The Downfall of Robert (a-2)

Skelton who serves as the prologue begins his final remarks (118–21) as follows: "Therefore I pray yee,/ Contentedly stay yee,/ And take no offending,/ But sit to the ending."

The friar, who also takes the role of Skelton and serves as the prologue, makes two references (2242–47) in a single speech to the audience as seated: "Wherefore still sit you, doth Skelton intreat you . . . be rul'd by me, sit patiently, & give a plaudite, if anything please yee."

The Death of Robert (a-2)

Friar Tuck addressed the audience (17–18): "Blithe sit yee all, and winke at our rude cry,/ Minde where wee left, in Sheerewod merrily."

THE GATES

I Henry VI (b-8)

A scene (1.3) is set before the gates to the Tower of London: "*Glos.* I am come to survey the Tower this day. . . . Where be these Warders, that they waite not here?/ Open the Gates, tis Gloster that calls." A person inside the gates calls out: "*Warder.* Who's there, that knocks so imperiously." The gates are not opened. A rival group comes onto the stage: "*Enter to the Protector at the Tower Gates Winchester and his men in Tawney Coates.*" A fight takes place. Flanking entrances are apparently used.

A scene (3.2) is played before the gates of "Roan": "*Pucell.* These are the Citie Gates, the Gates of Roan. . . . [Soldier] Therefore wee'le knock." A person inside the gates calls out: *"Watch. Che la."* Pucell answers: *"Pea-sauns la pouure gens de Fraunce."* The gates are opened: *"Watch.* Enter, goe in, the Market Bell is rung." The town is assaulted later by the English forces and flanking doors are obviously used.

A scene (4.2) is played before the gates of "Burdeaux": *"Talb.* Go to the Gates of Burdeaux Trumpeter, Summon their Generall unto the Wall. *Sounds."* A stage direction reads: *"Enter Generall aloft."* The Captain describes Talbot's situation in such a way as to suggest entrances to the right and the left of the "Gates of Burdeaux":

> *Cap.* . . . On us thou canst not enter but by death;
> For I protest we are well fortified,
> And strong enough to issue out and fight.
> If thou retire, the Dolphin well appointed,
> Stands with the snares of Warre to tangle thee.
> On either hand thee, there are squadrons pitcht,
> To wall thee from the liberty of Flight.

Talbot observes:

> O negligent and heedless Discipline,
> How are we park'd and bounded in a pale?
> A little Heard of Englands timorous Deere,
> Maz'd with a yelping kennell of French Curres.

George a Green (b-3)

George a Green contains an episode (295–99) in which people meet before a house or castle:

> *James.* . . . Tell me, Ned, who is within with thy mother.
> *Ned.* Not but herselfe and houshold servants, sir:
> If you would speake with her, knocke at this gate.
> *James.* Johnie, knocke at that gate.
> *Enter Jane a Barley upon the walles.*

Entrance is refused to James until the end of the scene.

Titus Andronicus (a-4)

Two contending parties meet and clamor at the gates for entrance to the "Senate house" (A4):

> *Saturninus.* . . . Open the gates and let me in.
> *Bassianus.* Tribunes and me a poore Competitor.
> *They goe up into the Senate house.*

The Four Prentices (b-8)

Several references are made to gates (I2v) by people inside a stronghold:

> *Sop.* . . . Let's ope the gates and boldly issue out. . . .
> *Sol.* And so expose us to the generall spoyle.
> Keep the gates shut, defend them manfully.
> These Christians fight like devils; keepe fast the gates.

John a Kent (b-7)

Four scenes (740–1030, 1187–491, 1492–518, and 1577–618) are set about castle gates and abbey gates, and flanking entrances are used or their use is strongly implied. In each scene the gates are locked or guarded against intruders.

The Golden Age (b-2)

A scene is played in the Fort of Brass where Danaë is kept by her father (H1):

> *Beld.* The larme bell rings,
> It should be K. Acrisius by the sound of the clapper.
> *4. Beld.* Then clap close to the gate and let him in.
> *Enter Acrisius.*

Later Jupiter and his man enter and apply for admission to the Fort of Brass (H2v–H3). They are admitted.

Jupiter and his man spend the night in the Fort of Brass (I2v–I3) and experience some difficulty in getting out. The gates are obviously centered between flanking doors.

The Silver Age (b-2)

Jupiter descends (C3–D3) to the gates before Amphitrio's house in Thebes. Ganimed is disgusted as Socia and assigned to guard the gate. A procession within this scene suggests that flanking doors were used.

Amphitrio attempts (D4–F2) to gain entrance to his house through the gates guarded by Ganimed. Flanking entrances are obviously used.

Hercules and his friends battle Cerberus at the gates of hell (K1v–K2v): "*They beate against the gates. Enter Cerberus.*"

The Brazen Age (b-2)

A scene (E4–F2) is played before the gates of Troy, which are located between two flanking entrances. The gates are practical because Hercules and his friends are shut out:

> *Herc*. Laomedon, Il'e toss thee from thy walles,
> Batter thy gates to shivers with my Club.

The gates flanked by two entrances are used (G1v–G2v) to discover the place where the Golden Fleece is kept. The action in this scene begins: "*Sownd: Enter King Oetes, Absyrtus, and Lords*." Oetes remarks:

> The howre draws nigh, the people throng on heapes
> To this adventure in the field of Mars,
> And noble Jason arm'd with his good shield,
> Is up already and demands the field.
> *Enter Jason, Hercules, and the Argonauts.*

Here a procession meets another procession coming on stage from the opposite side. Jason addresses his host:

> Oetes, I come thus arm'd, demanding combat
> Of all those monsters that defend thy Fleece:
> And to these dangers singly, I oppose
> My person as thou seest, when setst thou ope
> The gates of hell to let thy devils out?

After twenty-four lines in which Oetes attempts to change Jason's mind, Jason refuses and the gates are opened: "*Oetes*. Discover them." "Discover them" is written as dialogue; however, the term "Discover" is a technical theatrical term and it may well be a part of a stage direction. In any case, the gates are either opened by Oetes or are opened by someone in response to a command delivered by him, because "*Two firey Buls are discovered, the Fleece hanging over them, and the Dragon sleeping beneath them: Medea with strange fiery-workes, hangs above in the Aire in the strange habite of a Conjuresse.*" This scene (G1v–G2v) is significant because it shows the "gates" at the Rose theater used for a discovery episode.

Edward I (b-9)
Longshanks besieges a castle held by "Lluellen" who speaks to the attackers from the walls (C4v–D3). The castle gates are opened at the end of the scene: "*Longs*. . . . Lluellen open the gates. *Lluel*. The gates are opened, enter thee and thine." "*Exeunt*" Longshanks and his forces, apparently through the gates into the castle.

Captain Stukley (a-3)
Three men creep near the gates of Dundalke castle at night and are frightened away by the coughing of someone inside the castle (D2v–D4):

"*Mack.* Be whist I heare one stir. *On Coughs within.*" A few lines later Oneale remarks, "One coughes againe, lets slip aside unseene, tomorrow we will ease them of their spleen."

The same incident is repeated in a second version, representing an attempt at dialect: "*One coughs within. Han.* Cresh blesh us, so ish tat ishe coughes." Oneale remarks, "No matter come, no noyse tis almost day, softly let us creape aboote by the valles seed ane awan sene at night Even at shuttene of the gates fan Ocane and Magennis Come from Carlingford, we will Enter lustily the town." Obviously the gates of the castle are provided with a grate or opening of some kind through which people on the inside of the gate can be heard.

The scene (D4–D4v) which follows the two versions of the coughing episode shows plainly that the gates were flanked by at least two doors: "*Enter Herbart at one dore with soldiors, and Vernon at another.*"

Herbert appears on the walls (E2v–E3) and orders the gates closed: "*har.* Are all the gates and Posternes closed againe." A few lines later Stukley appears at the gates and demands entrance but is denied by Herbert on the walls:

> *stuk.* Are the gates shut alreadie? open how
> *herb.* Who knocks so boldly?
> *stuk.* Ha: who's that above?
> *her.* Herbart the Governor, who is that below:
> *Stuk.* Stuley the captaine, knocks to be let in
> *herb.* Stukley the captains comes not in to night.

The Death of Robert (a-2)

A company comes on stage and seeks to enter the gates to a castle but is denied permission (1566–69):

> *Enter Bruse, Richmond, Souldiers.*
> *Rich.* The Castle gates are shut. what ho? what ho?
> You that are servants to the Lady Bruse,
> Arise, make entrance for your Lord and friends.

Another episode like that above is found in the same play (2123–25): "*Enter, on the wall, Abbesse, Matilda. Hu.* Matilda is afraid to leave the house:/ But loe, on yonder battlement she stands." King John who has been pursuing Matilda calls up to the people on the walls, "Speake Ladie: wherefore shut you up your gates?"

A typical instance in a scene taking place before a stronghold contains a reference to the gates (2702–80) which suggests that they were double doors. The reference is found in an episode that begins with the stage direction: "*Enter Bruse, upon the walles.*" Two flanking doors are indicated by another stage direction: "*Drum. Enter Chester, Mowbray, Souldiers: Lester, Richmond at an other: Souldiers.*" After about nineteen lines a third stage direction reads: "*Drum: Enter King, Hubert, Souldiers.*" The forces have assembled at the gates to Windsor Castle which has been seized by "young Bruse." The King calls to Bruce on the walls: "Come downe young Bruse, set ope the castle gates." Bruce replies:

> I will not ope the gates, the gate I will:
> The gate where thy shame, and my sorrow sits.
> See my dead mother and her famisht sonne:
> Open thy tyrants eyes: for to the world,
> I will lay open thy fell cruelties.

The distinction Bruce draws between "gates" and "gate" (apparently the shutter to a window above the main stage) indicates that the "gates" had two shutters.

Sir John Oldcastle (a-1)

Cobham admits a crew of hungry people through his gate (359–406): "a crue of seely knaves, / And sturdy rogues, still feeding at my gate. . . . go in poore men into the inner court, and take such alms as there is to be had."

A Woman Killed with Kindness (a-2)

Charles and his sister enter and go to the gate in front of Acton's house (G3), but Acton enters with Malbie before Charles knocks at the gate. One does not know whether Acton comes on stage through the gate or at another place.

PRACTICAL DOORS

Friar Bacon (b-4)

A practical door is suggested by stage directions and dialogue (1797–801):

> *Enter two Schollers, Sonnes to Lambert and Serlby.*
> *Knocke.*
> *Bacon*. Whose that knockes.
> *Bungay*. Two schollers that desires to speake with you.
> *Bac*. Bid thē come in, Now my youths what would you have.

The Jew of Malta (b-5)

Abigall apparently opens a practical door and comes through it (E2v):

Bar. . . . What, ho, Abigall; open the doore I say,
Enter Abigall.
Abig. In good time, father, here are letters come.

The Spanish Tragedy (a-3)

An actor knocks at a door "within" and is admitted onto the stage (2137–40):

> *One knockes within at the doore.*
> *Hier.* . . . See who knocke there.
> *Pedro.* It is a painter sir.
> *Hie.* Bid him come in, and paint some comfort.

At line 2146 the painter enters: "*Enter the Painter.*"

In the same play, Hieronimo apparently locks a door between the main stage and the gallery (2921–23):

> *Hier.* Let me entreate your grace,
> That when the trains are past into the gallerie,
> You would vouchsafe to throw me down the key.
> *Cast.* I will *Hieronimo.*   *Exit. Cas.*

At lines 3114–15, the royal party apparently breaks this door open and enters: "*Vice.* . . . Breake ope the dores, run, save *Hieronimo. They breake in, and hold Hieronimo.*"

The Massacre at Paris (b-3)

The use of a practical door is suggested (417–22):

> *Enter Mountsorrell and knocks at Serouns doore.*
> *Serouns wife.* Who is that which knocks there?
> *Mount.* Mountsorrell from the Duke of Guise.
> *Wife.* Husband come down, heer's one would
> speak with you from the Duke of Guise.
> *Enter Seroune.*

The use of a practical door is suggested at a later place in the same scene (519–20): "*He knocketh, and enter the king of Navarre and Prince of Condy, with their scholmaisters.*"

George a Green (b-3)

A stage direction (622–23) suggests the use of a practical door: "*He knocks at the doore. Enter Grime.*"

Titus Andronicus (a-4)

A stage direction and the dialogue that follows (I3–K1) suggest that an actor knocks on a door on the main stage and that another actor comes through a door onto the gallery and speaks to the actors below.

> *They knocke and Titus opens his studie doore.*
> *Titus.* Who doth molest my contemplation?
> Is it your tricke to make me ope the dore,
> That so my saddecrees may flie away,
> And all my studie be to no effect.

This speech must be delivered from the balcony because Tamora urges Titus to come down (I3v):

> *Tamora.* . . . . come downe and welcome mee.
> *Titus.* Doe me some service ere I come to thee.

About twenty lines later, Titus agrees to come down from the balcony (I3v):

> Oh sweete Revenge, now doe I come to thee,
> And if one armes imbracement will content thee,
> I will imbrace thee in it by and by.

Tamora's speech that follows is one that Titus should not hear. It takes about eleven lines and ends (I4): "See here he comes, and I must plie my theame."

Faustus (b-5)

A stage direction (1485–88) indicates the use of a practical door: "*Faustus strikes the dore, and enter a devill playing on a Drum, after him another bearing an Ensigne: and divers with weapons, Mephotophilis with fire-workes; they set upon the Souldiers and drive them out.*"

A Knack to Know an Honest Man (b-3)

A stage direction (80) calls for Lelio to enter with his sword drawn and knock at his door. Gnatto answers from "within" and later (103) Annetta and Lucida come on stage from inside the house.

Marchetto knocks at Lelio's door (397). Gnatto answers from "within" and Annetta and Lucida come onto the stage from inside the house.

A besieging scene is staged before the door of Lelio's house. Soldiers bent upon defending the house "stand close"—conceal themselves—and are instructed to kill anyone that "shall attempt to scale these walles"

(993–95). Gnatto speaks from within and Annetta and Lucida appear on the balcony and speak to the men besieging the house.

A stage direction reads (1081): *"Here open the doore, and Enter the two brethren."* The brethren are prisoners kept by Phillida who loves one of them, and she is setting them free. Phillida was instructed in an earlier scene (1060–61) to

> Go take these prisoners, & see thou keep them close
> Locke them in the upper loft till I returne.

Presumably the door she unlocks to free the prisoners is located on the level with the gallery.

A practical door is opened and people come out of Lelio's house (1386–89):

> Silence Lelio, me thinkes my doore doth ope,
> Ah yonder comes my wife and daughter forth,
> How fares Annetta, how doth Lucida.

The Blind Beggar of Alexandria (b-3)

An actor knocks for admission from within (1020–80): *"Count knocke within."* He apparently talks to the people through a grate in a door for about sixty lines before he is admitted onto the stage.

Captain Stukley (a-3)

A practical door is suggested (A4v) at the entrance to a chamber: *"He knocks."* *"Enter the Page."* Within the chamber is another door (B1):

> *Old Stuk.* Sirra heare yee me, give me the key of his studdy.
> *Page.* Sir he ever carries it about him,
> *Old Stuk.* how let me see methinks the doore stands open.

The same scene contains yet another reference to a door (B3):

> *Stuk.* I pray you let it be so: Sirra Boye
> Locke the door, and bring my sword;
> *Page.* I will Sir.

Humorous Day's Mirth (a-3)

Actors exit through a door and it is shut behind them (1371–76):

> *Enter Lemot.*
> *Le.* My lorde, the roome is neate and fine, wilt please
> you go in?

Ve. Gentlemen, your dinner is ready.
All. And we are ready for it.
Le. Jaquis, shut the doores let no body come in.

Exeunt omnes

The Downfall of Robert (a-2)

A practical door is used (1–4): "*Enter sir John Eltam, and knocke at Skeltons doore*." Two lines later a stage direction indicates that someone "*Opens the doore*."

The dialogue suggests that a practical door is used later in the same play (2329–31):

War. . . . Ho goodwife Tomson?
Wo. What a noyse is there?
A foule shame on yee: is it you that knockt?

Englishmen for My Money (a-2)

A practical door opens onto a street (253–307). Walgrave orders someone to "Knocke for the Churle bid him bring out his Daughter." Anthony, who cannot afford to be seen by the people in the house, comes by on the street. He remarks (307) that "The Doore doth ope, I dare not stay reply,/ Least beeing discride." He leaves and a stage direction calls for Frisco and the Clowne to enter.

A stage direction and the dialogue suggest that a practical door is used to admit someone who knocks within (795–97):

(knock within
Pisa. . . . Stirre and see who knocks?
Enter Harvie, Walgrave, and Heigham.

A stage direction suggests the presence of a practical door at which two people knock but are not admitted: Alvaro knocks on the door (1464), and later Delion knocks (1500).

The door to Pisaro's house, around which much of the action is centered in a long scene, was apparently a practical door (1964–65): "*Exeunt Pisaro and Daughters. Pisa*. . . . In baggages, Mowche make fast the doore."

A practical door is suggested by the dialogue (2247): "*Pisa*. Stay Frisco, see who ringes: looke to the Dore." A stage direction reads (2256): "*Enter Walgrave in Woman's attire*."

A practical door is suggested by the fact that on three occasions people knock at a door; someone goes to the door; and people enter onto the stage (2423, 2431, and 2546). The action takes place inside Pisaro's house, which suggests that the knocking takes place "within"—inside the tiring-house

—and that the actors come onto the stage through a door opened for them by someone on the stage.

The Death of Robert (a-2)
  A practical door is used (H1–H1v):

> Brand. . . . You must remove your lodging; this is all.
> Be not afeard; come come, here is the doore.
> L. O God how darke it is
> Brand Goe in goe in; its higher up the staires.

After about twenty lines the Lady Bruce and her son go through the door (H1v): "*Exit*" and "*He seemes to locke a doore.*"

David and Bathsheba (b-9)
  An actor is thrust upon the stage and a door closed to indicate the use of a practical door to bar someone from a house (321–34):

> *Ammon thrusting out Thamar. . . .*
> *Jethray.* Go madame goe, away, you must be gone,
> My lord hath done with you, I pray depart. *He shuts her out.*
> *Tham.* Whether alasse, ah whether shall I flie.

A Woman Killed with Kindness (a-2)
  Frankford apparently uses a key to open a practical door to the bedroom in which he surprises Wendoll and Mrs. Frankford (F3–F3v).

"ONE DOORE" AND "THE OTHER DOORE"

Titus Andronicus (a-4)
  "*Enter Aron . . . at one doore, and at the other doore young Lucius*" (G1v).

The Four Prentices of London (b-8)
  "*Enter severally Godfrey, and Tancred*" (H1v).
  "*Enter at two severall dores, Guy and Eustace*" (I2v).
  "*Enter at one dore Robert . . . Enter at another dore Godfrey*" (I3).

Alphonsus of Aragon (b-6)
  "*Enter Flaminius at one doore, Alphonsus at an other*" (392).

Faustus (b-5)
  "*Enter at one the Emperour Alexander, at the other Darius; they meete*" (1293).

A Knack to Know an Honest Man (b-3)
"*Enter Forsa . . . Enter Medesa . . . at the other doore*" (901).

John a Kent (b-7)
"*Enter at one doore Ranulphe. . . . At another doore enter the Earles*" (137–39).
"*Enter at one doore John a Kent . . . at anoth[er] enter the Countess*" (406).

The Golden Age (b-2)
"*Enter at one doore Saturne . . . at the other Vesta*" (C4).

The Silver Age (b-2)
"*Enter at one dore Alcmena . . . at the other Jupiter*" (C4).
"*Enter Homer one way, Juno another*" (F2).
"*Enter to them at one doore, Euristeus . . . at the other Hercules*" (G1v).

The Brazen Age (b-2)
"*Enter at one doore the river Achelous. . . . At the other Hercules*" (B2).
"*Enter K. Oeneus and Althea, meeting the bodies of their two brothers borne*" (E1).

Captain Stukley (a-3)
"*Enter at one doore Crosse . . . at another spring the Vintyner*" (B3).
"*Enter Herbart at one dore . . . Vernon at another*" (D4).
"*Enter at one doore Phillip . . . then Enter another way sebastian*" (K1).

The Downfall of Robert (a-2)
"*Enter Robin Hoode . . . at one doore, little John . . . at another doore*" (782).
"*Enter Scathlocke and Scarlet . . . at severall doores. To them enter Robin Hoode*" (F4).

The Death of Robert (a-2)
"*Drum. Enter Chester, Mowbray, Souldiers: Lester, Richmond at an other: Souldiers*" (L1v).

Look about You (a-4)
"*Enter Lancaster & Huntsmen at one doore, Leyster & Huntsmen at another*" (2641).

Fortunatus (b-1)
"*Enter Athelstane . . . at one dore: Fortune, Vice . . . at another dore*" (187–88).

"ONE SIDE" AND "THE OTHER SIDE"

The Four Prentices of London (b-8)
"*Enter with a Drumme on one side certaine Spaniards; on the other side certaine Citizens of Bullen*" (C1).
"*Alarum. The foure brethren each of them kill a Pagan King, take of their Crownes, and exeunt: two one way, and two another way*" (K4).

The Golden Age (b-2)
"*Enter at one doore Saturne . . . at the other Vesta . . . The King departs one way . . . the Ladies the other way*" (C4).

Captain Stukley (a-3)
"*Enter stuklie at the further end of the stage*" (B1v).
"*Enter at one doore Phillip . . . then Enter another way, sebastian*" (K1).
"*Two trumpets sound at either end: Enter Mully hamet and Antonio*" (K3).

Look about You (a-4)
"*Sound Trumpets, enter with a Harrald on the one side, Henry the second Crowned . . . on the other part, K. Henry the Sonne crowned*" (76–78).

THE DISCOVERY SPACES

Friar Bacon (b-4)
An episode suggests the use of a discovery space (633–811): "*Bacon and Edward goes into the study. Bacon. . . .* welcome to my Cell . . . Within this glasse prospective thou shalt see/ This day whats done in merry Fresingfield, / Twixt lovely Peggie and the Lincolne earle . . . Stand there and looke directly in the glasse." Apparently the cell contains a table and a chair because Bacon says (649), "Sit still and keepe the cristall in your eye." Again (683 and 766) Bacon tells Edward to "sit still." The cell is located between flanking doors because the scene ends (811) with Bacon and Edward watching Bungay being carried off the stage through one door on the back of a devil and Margaret and Lacie fleeing through another door.

The action in the episode in which the Brazen Head speaks and is destroyed (1561–694) should be blocked, that is, traced in detail: "*Enter Frier Bacon drawing the courtaines with a white sticke, a booke in his hand, and a lampe lighted by him and the brazen head and miles, with weapons by him.*" Bacon apparently comes onto the stage through a discovery space; the brazen head is placed in such a way that a hand can be thrust through an opening and break the head with a hammer. Bacon commands (1600), "Draw closse the courtaines Miles now for thy life be watchful and *Here he falleth asleepe.*" Miles apparently goes to sleep, while Bacon sits at a table asleep. "*The Head Speakes*" (1615) and then is destroyed (1635): "*Heere the Head Speakes and a lightning flasheth forth, and a hand appeares that breaketh down the Head with a Hammer.*"

The scene in which Bacon destroys the "glasse" (1779–894) apparently takes place in or before a discovery space: "*Enter frier Bacon with frier Bungay to his cell.*" I am inclined to think that the stage direction (1797): "*Enter two schollers, sonnes to Lambert and Serlby*" is a cue for them to come onto the stage from a discovery space. The action is as follows (1798–801):

> *Knocke.*
> *Bacon.* Whose that knockes.
> *Bungay.* Two schollers that desires to speake with you.
> *Bac.* Bid thē come in, Now my youths what would you have.

A table and chairs are used in this scene because Bacon asks the scholars to "sit downe" (1813) and again asks them (1846) to "sit still" while they watch the "glasse" showing the fight in which their fathers kill each other.

The Battle of Alcazar (b-5)

Two dumb shows (24–40), because of the properties and the curtains, seem to have been played in or near a discovery space:

> *The first dumbe show.*
> *Enter Muly Mahamet and his sonne, and his two young brethren, the Moore sheweth them the bed, and then takes his leave of them, and they betake them to their rest. And then the presenter speaketh.*

The second dumb show begins as soon as the presenter ends his speech.

> *Enter the Moore and two murderers bringing in his unkle Abdelmunen, then they draw the curtains and smoother the young princes in the bed. Which done, in sight of the unkle they strangle him in his chaire, and then goe forth.*

The extant "plot" of this play (Greg's *Dramatic Documents*, 23–28), does not indicate the place in which the first dumb show was played; however, the reference to curtains in that portion of the plot concerned with the second dumb show indicates that a discovery space was used:

> E[n]ter the Presenter   :   to him
>   2 domb shew
> En[te]r abovė Nemesis, Tho : Dro[m] to
> them 3 · ghosts w · kendall Dab · [& Harry:]

[t]o them [l]ying behind the Curt[a]ines   3·
Furies: Parsons ; George & Ro : T[ail]or

Orlando Furioso (b-3)

Reference is made (700) to a cave which is apparently offstage: "*Sh.* . . .
Yon cave beares witnes of their kind content."

The Jew of Malta (b-5)

I do not place the action of the opening scene (B1v) in a discovery space:
"*Enter Barabas in his Counting-house with heapes of gold before him.*" Allusions to
the counting-house (F1 and H3) strongly suggest that it was on the gallery
level.

A discovery space may have been used (B4–C3v) for that part of the
scene which apparently takes place in a council chamber in Malta; the
scene seems to shift, however, to the street and is too confusing for one to
say with certainty just what parts of the stage, other than the doors at
either end, were used in presenting it.

A discovery space may have been used (G4–G4v) as the place in which
the "Fryar Bernardine" is murdered.

A discovery space is used (K2) to present the episode in which Barabas is
shown in the caldron.

A Looking Glass for London (b-6)

A discovery space is used for the following episode which begins with a
speech by Remilia (503–11):

> Shut close these Curtaines straight and shadow me,
> For fear Apollo spie me in his walkes,
> And scorne all eyes, to see Remilias eyes.
> Nymphes, Knancks, sing, for Mavors draweth nigh,
> Hide me in Closure, let him long to looke,
> For were a Goddess fairer than am I,
> Ile scale the heavens to pull her from the place.
> *They draw the Curtaines and Musicke plaies.*

This episode is followed by another in which the same discovery space is
used (552–53): "*He drawes the Curtaines and findes her* [Remilia] *stroken with
Thunder, blacke.*"

The Spanish Tragedy (a-3)

Hieronimo indicates (2852–53) that he is going to cover an opening of
some kind with a curtain in order to present a discovery episode: "A

strange and wonderous shew besides/ That I will have there behinde a curtaine."

A stage direction indicates that Hieronimo prepares for a discovery episode (2909): *"Enter Hieronimo, he knocks up the curtaine."*

Hieronimo presents his discovery episode (3045): *"Hier. . . . .* Behold the reason urging me to this. *He Shewes his dead sonne."* He apparently opens the curtain that he *"knocks up"* in the preceding scene.

George a Green (b-3)

The dialogue (593–97) suggests a future scene (670–814) will be played before a cave: *"George. . . .* Here in a wood not farre from hence,/ There dwels an old man in a cave alone. . . . Go you three to him early in the morning."

Alphonsus of Aragon (b-6)

The clearest reference to the use of the area behind the practical door as a discovery space at the Rose theater is contained in the stage direction (1246) which follows: *"Let there be a brazen Head set in the middle of the place behind the Stage, out of which, cast flames of fire, drums rumble within, Enter two Priests."*

Faustus (b-5)

The dialogue and a stage direction indicate that Faustus (28–29) may have been in a discovery space: *"Chorus. . . .* And this the man that in his study sits. *Faustus in his study."*

A stage direction (389) indicates that a discovery space is used (28–29): *"Enter Faustus in his Study."*

A stage direction (1774–76) indicates that Faustus's study was in or before a discovery space: *"Thunder and lightning: Enter devils with cover'd dishes; Mephostophilis leades them into Faustus Study: Then enter Wagner."*

A stage direction (2017) indicates that a discovery space is used: *"Hell is discovered."* Faustus may make his exit through a discovery space to go to hell (2092), and if this is the case, then the curtain was closed briefly to be reopened by the "Schollers" (2099) who discover Faustus's torn limbs.

A Knack to Know an Honest Man (b-3)

A cell is mentioned (70–77):

> *Enter olde Phillip an hermit.*
> *Phil*: What noise is this before my hold of peace?
> A little breach of peace to men of zeale,
> Is held a world of griefe to cross his minde:

Behold a young man weltering in his bloud.
Hie thee olde Phillip, shew thy charitie
Bear him to thy cell, and if thou canst recure his wounds,
If not, goe burie him, the badge of contemplations charitie. *Exit.*

II Tamburlaine (b-6)

An episode is presented in or before a discovery space (H2) with ten
people around a woman in bed: *"The Arras is drawne, and zenocrate lies in her
bed of state, Tamburlaine sitting by her: three Physitians about her bed, tempering
potions. Theridimas, Techelles, Usumcasane, and the three sonnes."* The scene
ends (H4v) with the stage direction: *"The Arras is drawne."*

The episode (I2–I3) in which the wife of the "Captaine of Balsera"
throws the bodies of her husband and son into the fire, after they have died
in an unsuccessful attempt to flee "Along the cave that leads beyond the
foe," suggests that a discovery space was used, although a trapdoor could
have been employed.

A discovery space is used to represent a tent (I6v–K2) which is apparently opened as the scene begins: *"Alarme: Amyras and Celebinus issues from
the tent where Caliphas sits asleep."* Amyras and Celebinus call Caliphas to
join them in the battle (I7): *"Alarme and Amy. and Celeb. run in."* Caliphas
and Perdicas play cards (I8), and comment on the battle raging offstage:
"Cal. What a coyle they keep, I beleeve there will be some hurt done anon
amongst them." Tamburlaine enters with a procession onto the stage, and
(I8v) *"He goes in and brings him out."*

The Golden Age (b-2)

A bed is apparently thrust onto the stage through a discovery space (C2):
"Enter Sibilla lying in child-bed, with her child lying by her, and her Nurse, & c."

An episode in the same play (I1v) calls for a bed to be used: *"Enter the
foure old Beldams, drawing out Dana's bed."*

The Silver Age (b-2)

A bed scene (I4v) suggests that a discovery space was used: *"Enter Semele
drawne out in her bed."*

The Brazen Age (b-2)

A discovery space is used as a cave by Venus and Mars (H2v–H3):
*"Venus. . . . Here is a place remote, / An obscure cave, fit for our amorous
sport."* Mars describes the cave in more detail (H3) suggesting, possibly,
that the space behind the practical door was used:

> *Mars.* Syrrah attend, this night yon Queen and I
> Must have some private conference, in yon cave,

Where whilst we stay, 'tmust be thy care to watch
That no suspicious eye pry through these chinks,
Especially I warn thee of the Sunnes.
Gallus. I smell knavery, if my Lady Venus play the whoore
What am I that keepe the doore?

Edward I (b-9)

No provisions are made for the removal of the "Maris" after she is bound in a chair and murdered (H1). Possibly the curtains before a discovery space were closed at the end of the scene.

Apparently a discovery space is used (I1) where a stage direction reads: *"Elinor in child-bed, with her daughter Jone, and other Ladyes."*

The Famous Victories (b-3)

The use of a discovery space, with a throne in or before that space, is suggested by the dialogue in which the king twice orders curtains drawn (C3v–D1):

> *Hen.* 4. . . . Draw the Curtaines and depart my chamber
> a while, And cause some Musicke to rocke me asleepe.
> *He sleepeth.*   *Exeunt Lords.*
>   *Enter the Prince.*

The prince finds his father sleeping and, thinking he is dead, takes the crown. A direction calls for the prince to *"exit,"* possibly into another discovery space. In any case, he is found with the crown in his possession and is brought back into the chamber to face his dying father. The king dies (D1) after requesting again, "Draw the Curtaines, depart my Chamber, / And cause some Musicke to rocke me a sleepe." The retainers and the prince evidently enter and leave the stage at different places in this scene, which indicates the use of two openings flanking a discovery space. The king's body is probably removed from behind the curtains, because no provisions are made in the stage directions or the dialogue for the removal either of his body or of the chair.

The Blind Beggar (b-3)

Reference is made to a "cave" (4): *"Aegiale.* . . . Leave me a while my Lords. . . . Ile walke alone to holy Irus cave."

"Irus cave" is described (797–802) as having an iron door which suggests the practical door may possibly have been used:

> *Euri.* But he is now they say lockt in his cave,
> Fasting and praying talking with the Gods,

And hath an Iron doore twixt him and you,
How will you then come at him.
Count. Ile fetch him from his cave in spight of all
his Gods and Iron dores, or beate him blinde.

Captain Stukley (a-3)

A discovery space is set between two flanking openings, (A3v–B1v). Stukley's father enters from old Newton's house, Old Stukley and Newton walk along the street till they reach Tom Stukley's "chamber" at Temple Inn. Stukley senior knocks and is finally admitted by a servant into his son's quarters. He returns to meet his son who apparently comes onto the stage through some entrance other than the door to old Newton's house.

Humorous Day's Mirth (a-3)

The action (1013–347) suggests that a discovery space and possibly the gallery were used in presenting this scene.

A discovery space and the gallery may possibly be used (1465–536).

The Downfall of Robert (a-2)

A discovery space is provided with a curtain, which is opened and closed, on a stage with an entrance and a practical door (1–141). The scene begins with a stage direction: "Enter sir John Eltam, and knocke at Skeltons doore." Another direction follows: *"Opens the doore."* A part of a stage direction (52–56) reads: *"They infolde each other, and sit downe within the curteines, Warman with the Prior, sir Hugh Lacy, Lord Sentloe, & sir Gilbert Broghton folde hands, and drawing the curteins, all (but the Prior) enter and are kindely received by Robin Hoode. The curteins are againe shut."*

A discovery episode is indicated (1490) by the following stage direction: *"Curtaines open, Robin Hoode sleeps on a greene banke, and Marian strewing flowers on him."*

It is possible that the curtains before a discovery space are closed with Jenny's exit (1586) in order for properties used in the next scene (1629) to be placed. An elevated throne and seats for at least four others must be provided. More likely, however, is the use of another discovery space.

The Death of Robert (a-2)

Possibly a throne is provided with a curtain (923–25), but more probably a discovery space is used here: *"Fri. . . . draw but that vaile,/ And there king John sits sleeping in his chaire. Drawe the curten, the king sits sleeping, his sworde by his side."*

The place behind the window located above the stage is used as a discovery space (2224–941):

> *Mess.* Yoūg Bruse, my Lord, hath gotten Windsor castle,
> Slaine Blunt your Constable, and those that kept it:
> And finding in a tower his mother dead,
> With his young brother starv'd and famished:
> That every one may see the rufull sight,
> In the thick wall he a wide windowe makes:
> And as he found them, so he lets them be
> A spectacle to every commer by
> That heaven and earth, your tyrant shame may see.
> ....
> *Bru.* Say, shall I open shop, and shewe my wares?
> *Lest.* No, good Lord Bruse, we have enough of that (2754–55).
> ....
> *Ki.* Come downe young Bruse, set ope the castle gates (2770)
> ....
> *Br.* I will not ope the gates, the gate I will:
> The gate where thy shame, and my sorrowe sits.
> See my dead mother, and her famisht sonne:
> Open thy tyrants eyes: for to the world,
> I will lay open thy fell cruelties (2776–80).

Bruce apparently opens the shutter before a window located in the gallery to reveal a tableau representing a starved woman seated and holding her starved child. The tableau is referred to again:

> *Qu.* Whose turne is next now to be murdered?
> The famisht Bruses are on yonder side. . . .
> Looke up king John, see, yonder sits thy shame (2936–41).

I Troilus and Cressida, plot (a-1)
   Reference is made to a tent (38): "To them Achillis in his Tent."

The Shoemakers' Holiday (a-2)
   A discovery space represents a "shop" (3.4.1–2):

> *Enter Jane in a Semsters shop working, and Hamond muffled at another doore, he stands aloofe.*
>
> *Ham.* Yonders the shop, and there my faire love sits. . . .
> Unseene to see her, thus I out have stood,
> In frostie evenings, a light burning by her,

> Enduring biting cold, only to eie her. . . .
> Muffled Ile passe along and by that trie
> whether she know me.
> *Jane*.   Sir, what ist you buy?

All the properties except the chair on which Jane sits and the light by her are articles of clothing. It should be noticed that the stage direction above places Hamond's entrance *"at another doore."*

The "Semsters shop" scene (3.4) is followed (4.1) with another shop scene: *"Enter Hodge at his shop boord, Rafe, Firk, Hans, and a boy at work."*

Eyre orders his men to "Shutte up the shop knaves, and make holiday" (3.2.149); the action appears to take place in the street before Eyre's shop.

Look about You (a-4)

A scene (1–75) is played before a hermit's cell: *"Robert*. Goe, walke the horses, wayte me on the hill, / This is the Hermits Cell, goe out of sight."

A scene (1845–2028) is played before a hermit's cell and a person looks into the cell (2026–27): *"La*. . . . Jesus defend me I will fly this denne, / It's some theeves cave, no haunt for holy men."

The "Hermits Cell" or "cave" (2071–169) is located between flanking doors. Gloster enters from the cell at the beginning of the scene and Skink enters at another door fleeing from John and Faukenbridge. Skink sees Gloster near the cell and therefore cannot take refuge in that place; so he must exit through a third door because it would not be logical for him to turn back in the direction from which he is fleeing.

Fortunatus (b-1)

A curtain is drawn (2.1.64–70) to discover the casket in which the wishing hat is kept.

An episode is played in and before a discovery space (3.1.356–57): · *"Musicke sounding still: A curtaine being drawne, where Andelocia lies sleeping in Agripines lap, shee has his purse, and herselfe and another Lady tye another (like it) in the place, and then rise from him."*

David and Bathsheba (b-9)

The play begins with an episode which indicates the use of a discovery space (25–27): *"He [The Prologue] drawes a curtaine, and discovers Bethsabe with her maid bathing over a spring: she sings, and David sits above vewing her."*

Stage directions and dialogue (1911–67) indicate the use of a discovery space or else a stage property of some kind which was provided with a curtain capable of being opened and closed: *"He goes to his pavillion, and sits close a while"* (1911). *"He lookes forth, and at the end sits close againe"* (1929). *"Joab. . . .* Advance thee from thy melancholy denne" (1967).

OBSTRUCTIONS ON THE STAGE

Friar Bacon (b-4)

An unusual direction is found in the margin (1611–14): *"Sit down and knocke your head."* The direction obviously refers to a post because Miles's speech which accompanies the direction reads in part, "Now sir I will set me downe by a post, and make it as good a watch-man to wake me if I chaunce to slumber."

The Spanish Tragedy (a-3)

A man is bound to a stake, presumably one of the columns supporting the heavens, to be burned to death: *"They binde him to the stake"* (1134). Later, however, *"They unbinde him"* (1169).

Englishmen for My Money (a-2)

Reference is made to a post (1406–07): *"Frisc. . . . take heede sir hers a post."*

An episode involving the use of two posts is indicated by the dialogue (1654–61):

> *Delio.* Dats good: but watt be dis Post?
> *Frisc.* This Post; why tis the May-pole on *Ivie-bridge*
> going to *Westminster.*
> *Delio.* Ho *Wesmistere,* how come we to *Wesmistere?*
> *Frisc.* Why on your Legges folles, how should you
> goe? Soft, heere's an other: Oh now I know in deede
> Where I am; wee are now at the fardest end of *Shoredich,*
> for this is the May-pole.

The episode above was apparently worth repeating (1700–1702):

> *Vand.* Oh de skellam Frisco, ic weit neit waer dat
> ic be, ic goe and hit my nose op dit post, and ic
> goe and hit my nose op danden post.

The Two Angry Women (a-2)

An incident involving a post reads like a reaction to an accident which was retained because it was considered funny (2249–51). Two men are wandering about in a field at night; one of them runs into a column on stage and apparently breaks character for a moment:

Coom. Nay, Ile grope sure, where are yee? *Hodge*. Heere.
Coom. A plague on this poast, I would the Carpenter had
bin hangd that set it up for me, where are yee now?

THE STAIRS

The Jew of Malta (b-5)
Barabas calls down from the gallery (K1v): "Will't please thee, mighty
Selim Calymath, / To ascend our homely stayres?" Calymath, however,
does not ascend the stairs.

Titus Andronicus (a-4)
Stairs are indicated by the action (A4) as being located behind the gates
on which Saturninus and Bassianus pound for admission and through
which they enter to *"goe up into the Senate house."*
An episode indicates that stairs are located behind the stage wall.
Tamora knocks at Titus's door and he enters above (I3). Titus comes down
the stairs (I3v–I4), while Tamora delivers a speech of eleven lines which
plainly must not be heard by Titus.

John a Kent (b-7)
Several people in the gallery start down to those below "uppon this
Castell greene." A direction (980) reads *"they discend,"* but none of them
enters or speaks for fifty-one lines; the dialogue which ensues must not be
heard by those coming down from the gallery.

The Blind Beggar of Alexandria (b-3)
The count's lines (371–73) must not be heard by Elimine as she descends from her father's tower, apparently using stairs located behind the
wall at the rear of the stage.

Englishmen for My Money (a-2)
An episode (1333–76) which is played above indicates that the stairs to
the gallery are located behind the walls of the main stage.
The entire scene (1699–2167) indicates that the stairs are behind the
walls of the main stage.

The Death of Robert (a-2)
An episode (1891–94) suggests that the stairs are behind the gates and
the walls of the main stage:

> *Brand.* . . . You must remove your lodging: this is all.
> Be not afeard: come come, here is the doore.

L. O God how darke it is!
Brand. Goe in goe in: its higher up the staires.

After about twelve lines the Lady speaks again and says (1907–08):

I will not in: help us, assist us Blunt,
We shall be murdred in a dungeon.

Again, after about twelve lines the lady speaks and says (1919–21):

I will goe in: but very much I doubt,
Nor I, nor my poore boy shall ere come out. *Exit*.
Hee seemes to locke a doore.

THE GALLERY

Orlando Furioso (b-3)
A stage direction reads (394): "*Sound a Parle, and one comes upon the walls*."

The Jew of Malta (b-5)
It does not seem likely that Barabas was actually thrown from the walls when the governor directed (I2): "For the Jewes body, throw that O're the wals." The walls were about fourteen feet above the main stage. Admittedly, the descent was speedy; after one line is spoken, Barabas speaks and we know from what follows that he is on the main stage outside of the town. One suspects that Barabas was carried off the walls and made his way down the stairs to the main stage. He then apparently stumbled onto the stage, shaking off the effects of the drug he had presumably taken to persuade his enemies that he was dead.

The height of the gallery above the main stage also precludes the use of the trapdoor, presumably cut in the floor of the gallery by Barabas (K1–K2v). One may believe that in the confusion caused by "*A charge, the cable cut*" that Barabas sank to the floor of the gallery, crawled to the stairs, descended, and took his place in the "Caldron" to be discovered: caught in his own trap.

A distinction is made between the places above the stage referred to as the gallery and the tower (K1v): "*Bar*. . . . Here have I made a dainty Gallery, / The floore whereof, this Cable being cut, / Doth fall asunder." (Barabas is here referring to a trap in the floor of the gallery.) A few lines later he explains in connection with his plot against the Turks that "A warning-peece shall be shot off from the Tower, / To give thee knowledge when to cut the cord."

I Henry VI (b-8)

At least six people appear on the walls at one time (1.5.639–40): "*Enter on the Walls, Puzel, Dolphin, Reigneir, Alanson, and Souldiers.*"

Colors are placed on the walls (1.5.641): "*Puzel*. Advance our waving Colours on the walls."

The walls are scaled by the English with ladders and the French inside the town "*leape ore the walles*" (2.1).

Dialogue and stage directions refer to the wall aloft (4.2): "Summon their Generall unto the Wall. *Sounds. Enter General aloft.*"

An episode (5.3) involves people on the walls and their descent from the walls, which is speedily made!

The Spanish Tragedy (a-3)

"*Balthazar above*" (769), along with Lorenzo, spies on Horatio and Belimperia.

An audience for a "play within a play" is seated in the "gallerie" above the main stage (2921–24).

The Massacre at Paris (b-3)

The Guise's command to those who have murdered the admiral (362–69), to "throw him down," suggests that the bed in which the admiral was killed was located above the main stage. The body of the admiral is thrown down and then inspected to see if he is the man the murderers were seeking.

George a Green (b-3)

A stage direction reads (299): "*Enter Jane a Barley upon the walles.*"

Titus Andronicus (a-4)

This play begins (A3) with a stage direction "*Enter the Tribunes and Senatours aloft.*"

A stage direction reads (B3v): "*Enter aloft the Emperour with Tamora and her two sonnes and Aron the moore.*"

Titus's study (I3–I4) is apparently located above the stage, and he comes down to speak with Tamora.

The Four Prentices of London (b-8)

Several people enter and place crowns and standards on the walls of "hierusalem" (I1–I2v). These are taken down by Guy and Eustace, who climb the walls.

Faustus (b-4)

Reference is made to a place above the stage (4.6.1593): "*Host.* . . . looke up into th'hall there ho."

A Knack to Know an Honest Man (b-3)

Reference is made to a possible attempt to scale the walls of a house. Two people also appear on these walls (993–1048).

An "upper loft" is used as a temporary prison (1060–61): "*Se.* Goe take these prisoners, & see thou keep them close, / Locke them in the upper loft till I return."

The gallery is apparently used (1071–110) as a passage way between Phillida's room and the "upper loft" in which two men are imprisoned.

The gallery continues to be used (1111–83) as a passage to the "upper loft."

John a Kent (b-7)

A stage direction reads (900): "*Enter John a Cumber on the walles lyke John a Kent.*"

Another stage direction (918–20) indicates that ten people are on the walls at the same time: "*Whyle the musique playes, enters on the walles Llwellen Chester wth his Countesse, Moorton with Sydanen, Pemb. with Marian, Oswen and Amerye.*" Cumber is also on the walls at this time.

Still another direction (1447–48) indicates that nine people are on the walls: "*John a Kent in his owne habit, denvyle, Griffin, Powesse, Evan, Countesse, Sydanen, Marian, and Shrimp on the walles.*"

II Tamburlaine (b-6)

Three people appear on the walls of a town (I1): "*Captaine with his wife and sonne.*"

Several references are contained to the walls of Babylon: "*Enter the Governour of Babylon upon the walles, with others*" (K6v). "*Alarme, and they scale the walles*" (K7). "*tam.* . . . Hang him up in chaines upon the citie walles, And let my souldiers shoot the slave to death" (K8v).

The dialogue which follows (L1 and L1v) suggests that the people shooting the governor of Babylon stand on stage and that the man being executed is actually offstage.

The Golden Age (b-2)

The dialogue (H1v) indicates that Danaë's quarters are above the stage: "*Acri.* . . . See! Danae is descended."

The episode portraying the mating of Danaë and Jupiter (I1v–I2v) apparently takes place in a bed above the main stage. Jupiter enters onto the main stage and must leave it to reach Danaë. "Yon is the doore, that in forbidding me/ She bad me enter." After a speech of about nineteen lines he enters the door leading, probably, up to the gallery: "Heavens gates stand ope, and Jupiter will in." He apparently knocks at a door leading to the gallery: "*Dan.* Who's that?" "*Jup.* 'Tis I, K. Jupiter."

It seems a reasonable assumption that Jupiter and Danaë part (I3) in an episode played above the main stage, but one cannot be sure from the stage directions or dialogue.

The Silver Age (b-2)

A stage direction indicates that Amphitrio knocks at his gates and Ganimed enters above (E3v): "*Knockes, enter Ganimed above.*"

A stage direction and the dialogue (G1–G1v) suggests that an actor is placed "*above in a cloud.*" I do not think the lift is used here or later (I4) where a stage direction reads: "*Juno and Iris plac'd in a cloud above.*" It seems more likely that a lords' room was used, because Jupiter descends in the lift as Juno and Iris watch from their "*cloud above.*"

The Brazen Age (b-2)

The people of Troy appear on the walls after barring the gates against Hercules (F1v–F2).

The Trojans appear on their walls (H1) and Hercules and his friends scale the walls.

A stage direction (I3) indicates that several people appear above to laugh at Venus and Mars: "*All the Gods appeare above, and laugh, Jupiter, Juno, Phoebus, Mercury, Neptune.*"

A stage direction (L2) reads: "*Enter Hercules from a rocke above.*"

Edward I (b-9)

A stage direction (D1) reads: "*On the walles enter Longshankes, Sussex, Mortimer.*"

A stage direction (H1) reads: "*Then make the proclamation upon the walles. Sound Trumpets.*"

The Blind Beggar of Alexandria (b-3)

A stage direction (354) reads: "*Enter Elimine above the walles.*" Later (358 and 372) the place where Elimine appears is referred to as "this tower" and "the tower."

The count speaks only three lines (371–73) while Elimine descends from "the tower" and comes on stage with "*A Spaniard following her.*"

Captain Stukley (a-3)

A stage direction (E2v) reads: "*Enter Harbart, Gainsford, and some souldiers on the walles.*" Later during the same scene (E3–E4) people before the gates talk to people on the walls.

Frederick and Basilea, plot (a-1)

Reference is made to the walls and an actor descending from them (Greg's *Dramatic Documents*): "*To them Pedro Basilea upon the walls. come downe Pedro Basilea. ledb: Dick.*"

Englishmen for My Money (a-2)

The dialogue (955–1403) suggests that the gallery was used to represent the upstairs in Pisaro's house.

A stage direction (1706) reads: "*Enter Laurentia, Marina, Mathea, above.*"

A man is pulled up from the main stage and suspended in a basket (1751–2143). Possibly the machinery in the hut was used in staging this episode.

The dialogue and stage directions indicate the use of the gallery in three scenes (2168–685).

The Death of Robert (a-2)

A stage direction (1570): "*Enter, or above, Hugh, Winchester*," suggests that the playwright wrote this episode so it could be played either above or on a stage without a gallery.

The walls are described as "yonder battlement" in a stage direction and the dialogue (2123–25):

> *Enter, on the wall, Abbesse, Matilda.*
> *Hu.* Matilda is afraid to leave the house:
> But loe, on yonder battlement she stands.

The dialogue and stage directions (2702–3040) indicate that a man appears on the walls, discovers a scene behind a window, descends, and comes onto the stage through the gates.

The Two Angry Women (a-2)

The dialogue indicates that the gallery may have been used to represent a high place (2029): "*Phil.* . . . I did appoynt my sister, / To meete me at the cunnie berrie below."

The dialogue (2681–86) indicates that the gallery may have been used in a second instance to represent a high place: "*Mis. Bar.* . . . Then here Ile set my torch upon this hill . . . here Ile lie unseene, / And looke who comes, and chuse my companie."

1 Troilus and Cressida, plot (a-1)

A direction calls for people to appear on the walls and to descend (Greg's *Dramatic Documents*):

> Enter D[io]med & Troylus to them
> Achillis [t]o them Hector & Deiphobus
> to them on the walls Priam Paris
> Hellen Polixina & Cassandra to them
> Ulisses Ajax menalay & Hea[ralds]
> Priam & they on the wall descend to them.

Fortunatus (b-1)

The dialogue indicates that a pair of stocks is located above the stage in a place which is referred to as "yonder towre," "this prison," and "this towre" (5.2.86–183).

David and Bathsheba (b-9)

A stage direction indicates (25–27) that an actor is placed above the stage in a position to overlook action in a discovery space: "*He [The Prologue] drawes a curtaine, and discovers Bethsabe with her maid bathing over a spring: she sings, and David sits above vewing her.*" Later in this scene Bathsheba goes up to David (120–34).

People appear on the walls (195): "*Hanon with King Machaas and others, upon the wals.*"

People appear on the walls (802–50) and "Rabba" which is also called "Hannons Towne" is assaulted. It is taken in the scene that follows.

A Woman Killed with Kindness (a-2)

The situation and dialogue suggest that people pass across the stage in the gallery and that it is later used by a person who overlooks action taking place on the main stage (C2v–D1).

THE PENTHOUSE AND THE WINDOW

The Jew of Malta (b-5)

A window is located in a "house" above the main stage (B1v): "*Enter Barabas in his Counting-house, with heapes of gold before him.*"

Barabas refers to gold (C4v), which he has "hid close underneath the plancke/ That runs along the upper chamber floor"—the floor of the countinghouse.

"*Enter Abigall above*" (D2) and "*Throwes downe bags*" of gold to Barabas (D2v).

Pilia-borza locates the countinghouse (F1): "I chanc'd to cast mine eye up to the Jewes counting-house/ Where I saw some bags of mony, and in the night I/ Clamber'd up with my hooks."

Barabas refers to the countinghouse as being above the stage (H3): "Or climbe up to my Counting-house window:/ You know my meaning."

Barabas mentions "the tower" which is clearly a different place from the "gallery" (K1v) when he explains in connection with his trapdoor in the floor of the gallery that "A warning-peece shall be shot off from the Tower,/ To give thee knowledge when to cut the cord." The "warning-peece" is fired, presumably from the window in the tower, according to a stage direction (K2): "*A charge, the cable cut, A Caldron discovered.*"

I Henry VI (b-8)

Reference is made to a "Grate" in "this Turrets top," which may point to a window located above the stage (1.4):

> *Salisb.* . . . . by what means got's thou to be releas'd?
> Discourse I prethee on this Turrets top.

The English leader, Salisbury, is shot and mortally wounded while he looks through the "Grate," spying on the French inside of Orleans.

An area above the main stage is referred to as a "Tower" and "the top." Pucell is to indicate the best way into the city "By thrusting out a Torch from yonder Tower" (3.2); this she does according to a stage direction a few lines later: "*Enter Pucell on the top, thrusting out a Torch burning.*" The French are successful in expelling the English according to another stage direction reading: "*Enter Talbot and Burgonie without: within, Pucell, Charles, Bastard, and Regneir on the Walls.*"

A Looking Glass for London (b-6)

Oseas is seated over the stage in a throne (159–60): "*Enters brought in by an Angell Oseas the Prophet, and set downe over the Stage in a Throne.*" Oseas comments upon the action at the end of each scene until the angel returns and leads him away (1846).

The Spanish Tragedy (a-3)

"*A letter falleth*" (1225), presumably from a window above the main stage because it is written by Bel-imperia who reports that "Me hath my haples brother hid from thee [Hieronimo];" and later (1724) a stage direction calls for her to appear *"at a window,"* where she continues to complain about being "sequestred from the Court."

A stage direction (1724) calls for *"Bel-imperia, at a window,"* the one behind which she is imprisoned and from which she earlier dropped her letter to Hieronimo.

The Massacre at Paris (b-3)

A window is used as a place from which to shoot a man as he passes along the street (103–05):

> Stand in some window opening neere the street
> And when thou seest the Admirall ride by,
> Discharge thy musket and perfourme his death.

These instructions are carried out (227–28): *"As they are going, the Souldier dischargeth his Musket at the Lord Admirall."*

A man threatens to jump out of a window (446–48). However it is not certain that this window is visible to the audience or even that it is eventually used:

> *Taleus.* The Guisians are hard at thy doore, and
> meane to murder us: harke, harke they come, Ile
> leap out at the window.

The episode in which the Duke of Guise is murdered (1130–247) refers to the king (1169) as having "Mounted his royal Cabonet," which suggests the use of a place above the stage; however, the "cabonet" is more likely an elevated throne provided with curtains.

Titus Andronicus (a-4)

Two men seek admission at the gates, are admitted, and according to a stage direction (A4): *"They goe up into the Senate house."*

Titus's study (I3–I4) is apparently located above the stage and he comes down to speak with Tamora and her sons.

Faustus (b-5)

A window is located above the stage (4.1.1203–06):

> *Fre.* See, see his window's ope, we'l call to him
> *Mart.* What hoe, Benvolio.
> > *Enter Benvolio above at a window,*
> > *in his nightcap: buttoning.*

Benvolio can stand and thrust his head through the window (1223–31): "And I fall not asleepe. . . . I am content this once to thrust my head out at a window."

In the scene that follows (4.2), Benvolio goes to sleep lolling in the window and Mephistopheles apparently fastens two "spreading hornes" on his head. Benvolio is trapped in the window, unable to draw his head through it, until Faustus directs Mephistopheles "to remove his hornes" (1322–59).

A possible reference to an area above the main stage is suggested by the Hostess's call (4.5.1593): "Looke up into th'hall there ho."

A Knack to Know an Honest Man (b-3)

An "upper loft" is used as a temporary prison (1060–61): "Goe take these prisoners, & see thou keep them close, / Locke them in the upper loft till I return."

The Blind Beggar of Alexandria (b-3)

Irus directs Elimine to go home and ascend to her father's "tower" (252) and to come down to a man wearing a velvet patch over one eye. A stage direction reads (354): *"Enter Elimine above on the walles."* She refers to "this tower" (358), sees the man with a patch on his eye, and descends (370). It is difficult to know whether the gallery or the penthouse was used in this episode. While she is coming down the count has three lines which must not be heard by her, if the plot is to go forward. She enters (374) with *"Bragadino A Spaniard following her."*

Englishmen for My Money (a-2)

Reference is made to a window, apparently above the main stage (1827–28): "Come backe, come backe, for wee are past the house, / Yonder's Matheas Chamber with the light."

Actors on the main stage (1998–99) are aware of someone watching them from a window above the stage: "I hear him at the Window, there he is. / *Enter Pisaro above.*"

Possibly glass was used in stage windows (2097–98):

> *Frisc.* . . . Is there nere a Stone to hurle at his Nose.
> *Pisa.* What, wouldst thou breake my Windowes with a Stone?

The Death of Robert (a-2)

A window is used in a place above the stage to discover a Senecan tableau (2776–78).

The Two Angry Women (a-2)

A window with a light in it is mentioned (1491). An actor appears in the window (1495): "*Enter Mall in the window.*" The dialogue indicates that Mall is above the main stage and that as she descends (1588–95) lines are spoken that she ought not hear for the sake of the plot.

The Shoemakers' Holiday (a-2)

Shop windows are mentioned but there is no indication that they are located above the stage or are visible or used (1.4.8): "*Eyre. . . . open my shop windowes.*"

Look about You (a-4)

Prince Richard brings a musician to play at the window of Lady Faukenbridge but apparently the lady is not at home (2174–79).

Sir John Oldcastle (a-1)

A window is mentioned but it is apparently not visible to the audience (2016–17).

Fortunatus (b-1)

The dialogue indicates that stocks are located above the stage in a place referred to as "yonder towre," "this prison," and "this towre" (5.2.86–183). Two men are taken at different times and placed in the stocks. They must be seen by the audience.

David and Bathsheba (b-9)

The assault upon Rabath involves scaling walls on which people appear and capturing a "kingly Tower/ Where all their conduits and fountaines are" (188–89). Joab describes the situation while he is on the walls (238–44):

> Tell my lord the King that I have fought
> Against the citie Rabath with successe,
> And skaled where the royal pallace is
> The conduit heads and all their sweetest springs,
> Then let him come in person to these wals,
> With all the souldiers he can bring besides,
> And take the city as his owne exploit.

A few lines later Abisay says (252):

> Let us descend, and ope the pallace gate
> Taking our souldiors in to keepe the hold.

THE HEAVENS

A Looking Glass for London (b-6)

This play contains the first suggestion of the use of the heavens in a play staged at the Rose (1636–38):

> *A hand from out a cloud, threatneth a burning sword.*
> K. *Cill.* Behold dread Prince, a burning sword from heaven,
> Which by a threatning arme is brandished.

Alphonsus of Aragon (a-6)

This play contains the first stage direction calling for a god to be lowered from the heavens (1–2):

> *After you have sounded thrise, let Venus be let downe*
> *from the top of the Stage, and when she is downe, Say.*

Venus is not removed from the stage by a throne let down from the heavens at the end of the Induction:

> "*Ven.* Then sound your pipes, and let us bend our steps
> unto the top of high Pernassus hill. . . . *Exeunt.*"

The author's directions suggest that Venus be removed from the stage at the end of the play (2109–10) in a "chair" if it is possible:

> *Exit Venus. Or if you can conveniently, let a chaire come*
> *downe from the top of the stage, and draw her up.*

Faustus (b-5)

An episode calls for "*Musicke while the Throne descends,*" providing the magician with a glimpse of the heavens he has lost (5.2.2006).

The Golden Age (b-2)

A stage direction calls for an actor to be lowered onto the stage and for two others to be raised to the heavens in the "lift" (K2v). This action occurs in a dumb show: "*Sound a dumbe shew. . . . Jupiter drawes heaven; at which Iris descends and presents him with his Eagle, Crowne and Scepter, and his thunder-bolt. Jupiter first ascends upon the Eagle, and after him Ganimed.*"

The Silver Age (b-2)

Actors are apparently lowered onto the stage or raised to the heavens in the lift on several occasions: "*Homer. . . . but Jove himselfe discends. . . . Thunder and lightning. Jupiter discends in a cloude*" (C3). "*Juno and Iris descend from the heavens* " (F1). "*Thunder and lightning. . . . Jupiter appeares in his glory under a Raine-bow, to whom they all kneele*" (F1v). "*Windhornes. Enter Juno and Iris above in a cloud*" (G1). The dialogue which follows this last stage direction (G1) indicates that only Iris is "*in a cloud:*" "*Juno. . . .* Where art thou Iris? tell me from the cloud, / Where I have plac'd thee to behold the Chace." A stage direction accompanying Iris's reply reads: "*Iris aloft.*" A few lines later Juno commands: "*Iris discend*" (G1v). "*Mercury flies from above. Mer. . . .* I search't the regions of the upper world . . . Yet no where can I finde faire Proserpine. *Exit Mercury*" (H1). "*Juno and Iris plac'd in a cloud above*" (I4) "*Thunder, Lightnings, Jupiter descends in his majesty, his Thunderbolt burning*" (I4v). "*Jupiter taking up the Infant, Speaks as he ascends in his cloud*" (K1). "*Jupiter, the Gods and Planets ascend to heaven*" (L1).

The Brazen Age (b-2)

The lift is used (G2v) to suspend Medea above the stage: "*Medea with fiery-workes, hangs above in the Aire in the strange habite of a Conjuresse.*"

The lift is used in staging the following episode (L3): "*Jupiter above strikes him with a thunder-bolt, his body sinkes, and from the heavens discends a hand in a cloud that from the place where Hercules was burnt, brings up a starre, and fixeth it in the firmament.*"

Jupiter and Io (b-8)

The following stage direction suggests the use of a lift (p. 158): "*A noise of thunder. Enter Jupiter in his glory, his Trisull in his hand burning; at sight of whom they stand afrighted.*"

David and Bathsheba (b-9)

The lift, or part of the machinery in the heavens, may have been employed (1536–645): "*The battell, and Absalon hangs by the haire.*" Absalom is suspended until he is taken down at Joab's command (1634): "Well done tall souldiers take the Traitor downe, / And in this myerie ditch interr his bones." One cannot be sure whether the reference in the *Diary* (Foakes and Rickert, p. 217), "pd for poleyes & worckmanshipp for to hange ab-solome," indicates alteration to the lift or is related to work upon a special device that had no connection with the lift. The "poleyes" and the labor cost only fourteen pence, which suggests that the task involved little more than minor alterations to the lift. If this entry in the *Diary* does show that the lift was altered and employed, it is the last record we have of its use at the Rose.

D
Dimensions for Reconstruction

THE DIMENSIONS used for the reconstruction of the Rose (plates 1, 14, and 15) are given below. Most of the horizontal measurements are based on the argument that the outside diameter of the Rose was fixed by the Henslowe-Cholmley deed of partnership as "fforescore and fourteene foote of assize little more or lesse" (chap. 1). I estimate that the outside wall of the theater was about eighteen inches thick. Thus the inside diameter of the theater on which I base the Vitruvian plan for the reconstruction was ninety-one feet. And, of course, if either the outside diameter or the thickness of the exterior walls were a "little more or lesse," the size of the stage and the depth of the galleries would have been proportionally a "little more or lesse." Also, according to the Vitruvian plan (plate 17), the several openings on the stage would not have been located precisely where I have centered them. The vertical measurements are taken from the contract for the Fortune; and while they may have been drawn from Henslowe's earlier playhouse, it is equally possible that they represent changes he made when he built the square theater. Some of the measurements—the height of the stage and the size of the doors, for example—have been deduced from the demands seemingly made upon the stage by the extant plays known to have been given at the Rose. The measurements for other parts of the reconstruction, such as the windows in the huts and the openings in the lords' rooms, correspond to the estimated dimensions of those parts of Jonson's *Theatrum*.

Building

Outside diameter   94′
Thickness of exterior walls   1′ 6″
Inside diameter   91′
"Breadth throughoute"—galleries in the
   auditorium, without "Juttey forwarde"   13′ 3″
Height of foundation   1′
Height of first gallery   12′
Height of second gallery   11′

Height of third gallery 9'

Height, ground to underside of the shadow 33'

Height, ground to ridgepoles of huts above
lords' rooms 43'

Height, ground to ridgepole of the hut above
the shadow 49'

Pitch, all roofs 6" drop in 1'

Stage

Width 45' 6"

Depth 22' 9"

Height above ground 5'

Trap

Length 12'

Width 3' 6"

Centered at a point 6' 6" downstage from the gates and equidistant (22' 9")
from the walls at each side of the stage

Openings in the Walls around the Stage

The gates, centered in wall at rear of stage 8' x 9' 6"

One door and the other door, one in each wall at the side of the stage,
centered 13' 3" from front of the stage 5' x 7' 6"

Discovery spaces, two, centered 13' 3" from each side of the center of the
gates in the wall at the rear of the stage 6' x 8' 6"

Gallery

Width 45' 6"

Depth of playing area behind wall 5'

Height of floor of gallery above the stage 15'

Height of wall at front of gallery 3' 6"

Penthouse "at the tyeringe howsse doore," bay-window-like structure,
centered in the wall at the front of the gallery, above the gates (see plate
15) 12' x 13'

Hinged window, set 17' above the floor of the stage and centered in the
front of the penthouse 3' x 5' 6"

Windows, flanking the hinged window, two (see plate 15) 1' 6" x 5' 6"

Lords' Rooms

Floor space in each of the lords' rooms   9′ 6″ x 27′ 9″
Height of floors above the stage   15′
Height of lords' rooms, floor to ceiling   13′
Height of walls running along front and sides of lords' rooms   3′ 6″
Height of the openings in front and sides of the lords' rooms   5′
Width of openings overlooking the stage   22′ 9″
Width of openings facing the auditorium   9′ 6″

Huts above Lords' Rooms

Floor space in each hut   9′ 6″ x 22′ 9″
Height from ceilings in lords' rooms to eaves of huts   8′
Height from ceilings in lords' rooms to ridgepole of huts   10′
Center windows facing auditorium, set on a line 3′ above the ceilings in the
    lords' rooms   2′ x 3′
Flanking windows facing auditorium, set on a line 3′ above the ceilings in
    the lords' rooms   18″ x 3′
Windows overlooking the stage, set on a line 18″ above the ceilings in the
    lords' rooms   18″ x 5′

Hut above the Shadow

Floor space   45′ 6″ x 22′ 9″
Placed on line 9′ 6″ behind the front of the stage
Height, shadow to eaves of the hut   10′
Height, shadow to ridgepole   16′
Windows (five), set on a line 5′ 6″ above the shadow   3′ x 3′ 6″
Windows (two), centered in each end of the hut on a line 10′ above the
    shadow   3′ x 3′ 6″

Columns Supporting Hut

Diameter   2′
Height, floor of stage to shadow   28′
Centered on a line 12′ from the front of the stage, equidistant (15′ 2″) from
    each other and from the nearest wall

Notes

INTRODUCTION

1. Shakespeare's *Titus Andronicus* and *I Henry VI* were given at the Rose, and Ben Jonson was twice paid for additions to be made to Thomas Kyd's *Spanish Tragedy*. Others who wrote plays given for Henslowe included: Christopher Marlowe, *I and II Tamburlaine*, *The Jew of Malta*, *Faustus*, and *Massacre at Paris*; Thomas Dekker, *The Shoemaker's Holiday*, *Fortunatus*, *Patient Grissil* (with Henry Chettle and William Haughton); Robert Greene, *Friar Bacon*; George Chapman, *Blind Beggar of Alexandria* and *Humourous Day's Mirth*; and Thomas Heywood, *A Woman Killed with Kindness*, *The Golden Age*, *The Silver Age*, and *The Brazen Age*.

2. George Fullmer Reynolds, *The Staging of Elizabethan Plays at the Red Bull Theater 1605–1625* (New York: Modern Language Association of America, 1940), p. 2.

3. *ES* 3:50. For list of abbreviations see p. xxx.

4. "Studies in the Elizabethan Stage Since 1900," *SS* 1(1948):15.

5. *Theatre of the World* (London: Routledge & Kegan Paul, 1969), p. xii.

6. *EES* 1:309.

7. *The Globe Playhouse: Its Design and Equipment*, 2d ed. (New York: Barnes & Noble, 1961), pp. 15–30.

8. *The Globe Restored: A Study of the Elizabethan Theatre* (New York: Coward-McCann, 1954), p. 16.

9. "On Reconstructing a Practicable Elizabethan Public Playhouse," *SS* 12(1959):22–34.

10. A. M. Nagler, *Shakespeare's Stage* (New Haven, Conn.: Yale University Press, 1958), p. 12.

11. *Shakespeare's Wooden O* (London: Rupert Hart-Davis, 1960), p. 91.

12. *The Drama Review* 12, no. 2 (Winter, 1968):28.

13. *The Shakespearean Stage 1574–1642* (Cambridge: University Press, 1970), p. 89.

14. *Shakespearean Staging, 1599–1642* (Cambridge, Mass.: Harvard University Press, 1971), p. 3.

15. *The Art of Memory* (Chicago: University of Chicago Press, 1966) pp. 336–37, plates 16, 17, 18a and 18b.

16. "Another Globe Theatre," *SQ* 9(1958):19–29.

17. "Robert Fludd's Stage-Illustration," *SSt* 2(1966):192–209.

18. "The Stage in Robert Fludd's Memory System," *SSt* 3(1967):138–66.

19. *SSt* 3(1967):11–21.

20. Glynne Wickham believes that alterations made to the stage and tiring-house by Henslowe in 1592 "spells the translation of the house [the Rose] from a gamehouse that could be hired by actors for stage-plays into a playhouse for a resident company that could still be used for games if not needed by the actors." *EES* vol. 2, pt. 2, pp. 60–61.

21. *Shakespeare at the Globe 1599–1609* (New York: Macmillan Co., 1962), p. 100.

22. "The Staging of Elizabethan Plays at the Rose Theater 1592–1603," (Ph.D. diss., University of Kentucky, 1958), facing p. 1. "Elevation View Rose Theater."

23. "The Fortune Contract and Vitruvian Symmetry," *SSt* 6(1970):311.

24. R. A. Foakes and R. T. Rickert, eds., *Henslowe's Diary, Edited with Supplementary Material, Introduction, and Notes* (New York: Cambridge University Press, 1961), p. ix. This edition is cited hereafter as Foakes and Rickert. Walter W. Greg's edition (1904), which includes the text of the *Diary*, his *Commentary* on it, and the Henslowe *Papers*, is cited as Greg 1, 2, or 3.

25. Only two full-length studies have been made of the Rose, both unpublished Ph.D. dissertations: mine in 1958 and that of Harvey S. McMillin, Jr., also with the title "The Staging of Elizabethan Plays at the Rose Theatre," (Stanford, Calif., 1965).

26. For Greg's discussion of the use he makes of Fleay's work, *see* 2:viii–ix).

27. Fredson Bowers, ed., *The Dramatic Works of Thomas Dekker*, 4 vols. (Cambridge: University Press, 1953–61).

28. Wilfred T. Jewkes, *Act Division in Elizabethan and Jacobean Plays 1583–1616* (Hamden, Conn.: Shoe String Press, 1958).

1: THE THEATER BUILDING

1. Three accounts of the Rose have been written: Greg's (2:42–56) is the earliest; J. G. Adams's (*Shakespearean Playhouses*, pp. 142–60) is next; and E. K. Chambers's (2:405–10) follows. Chambers draws upon, and amends, the two accounts that precede his. All three, however, rely upon the same primary material, although the accounts by Adams and Chambers contain some new information discovered by C. W. Wallace and reported in the London *Times* (30 April 1914). The three accounts are generally agreed as to the facts about the site of the Rose and the dates related to its existence as a public playhouse.

2. The section which shows the Bankside in Norden's map of 1593 (plate 2) was made before Henslowe completed the hut above the stage of the Rose. The revision, dated 1600, of that section of Norden's map showing the Bankside (plate 3) was made sometime after the erection of the Globe in 1599. See I. A. Shapiro, "The Bankside Theaters: Early Engravings," *SS* 1 (1948):27–31.

3. See below, "The Outside of the Rose," for additional details about these buildings.

4. It may be appropriate here to direct attention to the remarkable degree in which Norden's revised map, discussed by Shapiro (*SS* 1:25–37), corroborates the evidence in the earlier map and in the Henslowe material. See below, "The Outside of the Rose."

5. Greg says (2:44), "The partnership is in some respects curious. Henslowe was to find the capital, Cholmley to pay £102 a year and to receive half the profits. . . . He [Henslowe] seems to have been anxious to insure himself up to a point, and the £816 very likely represented his outlay on the concern, he being willing to forego half the profits for the certainty of getting his capital back in the course of the next eight years."

6. The property consisted of "All that her messuage or Tennement then Called the little rose with Twoe gardens to the same adioyinge" (Greg 3:1–2), that is, three distinct parcels of land.

7. This structure is described as "standinge at the sowthe ende or syde" of the plot on which the playhouse was then being erected. The building is shown in Norden's map of 1593 (plate 2) at the southeast corner of the property and should not be confused with the "little rose" which is shown in the same map at the southwest corner.

8. I do not argue that the Rose was a fully round structure whose outside wall rested on a foundation that formed a perfect circle. It is possible that the wall consisted of many short sides giving the theater the appearance of a circular or round building. The terms *circular* and *round* are employed here loosely and interchangeably to emphasize a point that I wish to make: the Rose was not an obviously polygonal structure. The building in which I house my

reconstructed stage is represented, for the sake of convenience, as having a wall erected on a foundation that is a "perfect circle" (plates 1, 14, and 15).

9. Plates 2–4, and 23–27 show the exteriors of theaters located on the Bankside. Henslowe's Rose is "certainly" shown in three of these maps and engravings and may possibly appear in the others. These maps and engravings are listed and discussed in Appendix A, "Pictures of the Rose."

10. Shapiro includes the Visscher engraving with those derived from the *Civitas Londini*, a rather solid blow at the cornerstone on which John C. Adams's octagonal Globe playhouse rests.

11. "The Bear howse," the Beargarden, is shown also as an unfinished shell in the first map. Does the fact that Alleyn invested £450 in the Beargarden in 1594 (Foakes and Rickert, p. 301) explain the extra row of windows, thatching, hut, flagstaff, and flag that appear on the building in Norden's revised map?

12. *EES*, vol. 2, pt. 2, pp. 60–61.

2: THE TRAPDOOR

1. The *Diary* and *Papers* show that wood and plaster were used in the construction and repair of the Rose (Foakes and Rickert, pp. 6–7, 9–13, and 304).

2. Reynolds treats these plays, and *The Brazen Age*, as representative of production at the Red Bull (p. 20). I argue that the extant texts of all three plays are even more surely representative of production at the Rose theater (Appendix A, "A Repertory of Extant Plays of the Rose," nos. 70, 71, and 72).

3: THE STAGE OF THE ROSE THEATER

1. Chambers (2:405) is relying here on W. Rendel's *Antiquarian*, 8:60.

2. C. Walter Hodges, *The Globe Restored*, 2d ed. (London: Oxford University Press, 1968), pp. 35–36.

3. Platter was in England from 18 September to 20 October 1599, and wrote his account in 1604 or 1605. The account is reproduced and translated by Chambers (2:364–65). It begins with a report of a visit on 21 September, at about two o'clock in the afternoon, to a performance of *Julius Caesar* at the theater "over the water," which it seems certain was the Globe. He then describes a play which he saw on another occasion at a theater which Chambers says "must be the Curtain." Chambers's translation of the account continues:

The places are so built, that they play on a raised platform, and everyone can well see it all. There are, however, separate galleries and there one stands more comfortably and moreover can sit, but one pays more for it. Thus anyone who remains on the level standing pays only one English penny: But if he wants to sit, he is let in at a further door, and there he gives another penny. If he desires to sit on a cushion in the most comfortable place of all, where he not only sees everything well, but can also be seen, then he gives yet another English penny at another door.

4. Carleton Coon, *The Races of Europe* (New York, 1939), pp. 373–75.

5. I have found nothing to suggest that the stage at the Rose was enclosed by a rail that would hinder the view of the groundling. Nor have I found anything to suggest that the yard was sloped so that he could have a better view of the stage.

6. Frank Granger, ed., *Vitruvius on Architecture* (Cambridge, Mass.: Harvard University Press, 1931), 1:283.

7. *The Development of the Theatre*, 4th ed. rev. (New York: Harcourt, Brace & World, 1957), p. 123.

8. "The Fortune Contract and Vitruvian Symmetry," *SSt* 6(1970):311.

9. Kohler believes the Rose was about 85 or 86 feet in diameter. *SSt* 6(1970):322.

10. Miss Yates explains the Renaissance interpretation of the Vitruvian plan in her *Theatre of the World*, pp. 114–18. See also Kohler's discussion, *SSt* 6(1970):313–16.

4: FIVE OPENINGS IN THE WALLS

1. "The Origins of the So-called Elizabethan Multiple Stage," *The Drama Review* 12, no. 2 (Winter 1968):28.

2. "The Discovery-Space in Shakespeare's Globe," *SS* 12(1959):35.

3. *Shakespeare at the Globe 1599–1609* (New York: Macmillan Co., 1962), p. 100.

4. "Passing over the Stage," *SS* 12(1959):53.

5. "Staging at the Globe, 1599–1613," *SQ* 11(Autumn 1960):401–25.

6. "The Five-entry Stage at Blackfriars," *Theatre Research* 8(1967):130–38.

7. Allardyce Nicoll, *The Development of the Theatre*, 4th ed. rev. (New York: Harcourt, Brace & World, 1957), p. 122.

8. Ibid., p. 123.

9. Frank Granger, ed., *Vitruvius on Architecture* (Cambridge, Mass.: Harvard University Press, 1931), 5.6.7.

10. "The Staging of Elizabethan Plays at the Rose Theater 1592–1603" (Ph.D. diss., University of Kentucky, 1958), facing p. 1, "Elevation View Rose Theater."

11. These scenes include *The Jew of Malta* (b-5) (K1–K2v), *The Spanish Tragedy* (a-3) (1864–1947), *Faustus* (b-5) (4.5), *A Knack to Know an Honest Man* (b-3) (scenes 1 and 2), *The Four Prentices of London* (b-8) (G4–G4v), *A Humorous Day's Mirth* (a-3) (1640–79), *The Downfall of Robert* (a-2) (A2–A4v).

12. George R. Kernodle, *From Art to Theatre: Form and Convention in the Renaissance* (Chicago: University of Chicago Press, 1944), p. 149.

13. *The Massacre at Paris* (b-3) (323–543), *A Knack to Know an Honest Man* (b-3) (600–900), *The Golden Age* (b-2) (H1–I3v), *Humorous Day's Mirth* (a-3) (639–1992), *Look about You* (a-4) (782–967 and 1463–1746), *Patient Grissil* (a-1) (3.2), *David and Bathsheba* (b-9) (321–571).

14. See Miss Yates's *Theatre of the World*, pp. 114–16, for a discussion of the Renaissance interpretation of the Vitruvian plan.

5: THE GATES

1. "The gates" are mentioned and their use indicated in ten episodes found in five a-plays and seventeen episodes in eight b-plays (Appendix C, "The Gates"). The presence and use of a practical door is indicated in eight episodes in six a-plays and five episodes in five b-plays. The presence and use of a practical door is suggested in ten episodes in four a-plays and four episodes in three b-plays (Appendix C, "Practical Doors").

2. George R. Kernodle, *From Art to Theatre: Form and Convention in the Renaissance* (Chicago: University of Chicago Press, 1949), pp. 109–10.

6: ONE DOOR AND THE OTHER DOOR

1. *The Development of the Theatre*, 4th ed. rev. (New York: Harcourt, Brace & World, 1957), p. 123.

2. *The Art of Memory* (Chicago: University of Chicago Press, 1966), pp. 336–37.

3. *SSt* 3(1967):11–21.

4. If we may define a procession as the orderly entrance or exit of a party of five or more persons, almost half of the scenes in the plays given at the Rose begin with a procession or call for a procession to come onto the stage during the scene. However, few exits of groups of five or more persons in a procession are called for by stage directions more explicit than "*Exeunt*." Even so, groups of five or more people usually left the stage in some kind of order—especially when royalty and military leaders were present at the end of a scene. King Henry, for instance, calls for his party to form a procession in *Friar Bacon* (b-4) (2148–55) to clear the stage: "Lets march, the tables all are spread." Slain kings and military leaders, even enemies, were regularly honored with a procession, as in *The Battle of Alcazar* (b-4) (1587–92) where Muly gives directions for honors to be paid to the slain Sebastian:

> My Lord Zareo, let it be your charge,
> To see the souldiers tread a solempne march,
> Trailing their pikes and Ensignes on the ground,
> So to performe the princes funeralls.
> *Here endeth the tragicall battell of Alcazar.*

Perhaps Raphe Simnell, the Fool—disguised as the Prince of Wales in *Friar Bacon* (938–44)—best illustrates that retirement of a group of five or more people from the stage was usually made in processionlike order at the Rose. Raphe's joke pointed at Bacon's stupid servant, Miles, unconsciously mimics court and military usage:

> *Warren.* . . . I must desire you to imagine him all
> this forenoon the prince of Wales.
> *Mason.* I will sir.
> *Raphe.* And upon that I will lead the way, onely I will
> have Miles go before me, because I have heard Henrie say,
> that wisedome must go before Majestie.   *Exeunt omnes.*

To this day, our military follows the practice of having juniors in rank enter a place before and leave after seniors. I am inclined to believe that rigid order likewise was observed as a matter of form in exits from the Elizabethan stage, and that when royal persons and military men were present at the end of a scene one may translate the usual stage direction "*Exeunt*" to read: "Here a procession is formed and the stage is cleared." Some instances in which stage directions and the dialogue suggest that processions were formed at the end of a scene: *I Tamburlaine* (b-6) (C6v), *King Leir* (b-6) (2665), *The Four Prentices* (b-8) (F1v and K3), *Alphonsus of Aragon* (b-6) (1722–23 and 2083–86).

5. In lieu of a more exhaustive list, a few instances may be cited to show that processions often met on the stage of the Rose: *Titus Andronicus* (a-4) (A3), *A Knack to Know an Honest Man* (b-3) (901–93 and 1465–69), *The Downfall of Robert* (a-2) (1659–67, 1978–2006, and 2735–36), *The Shoemakers' Holiday* (a-2) (5.2.1–21), *Look about You* (a-4) (76–81 and 2641–42), *Fortunatus* (b-1) (5.2.187).

6. I discuss the movement in besieging episodes in chapter 5.

7. Included in this group are eighty-six scenes set inside houses, twelve scenes inside taverns, two scenes in a trial court room, five scenes inside a council chamber, five scenes inside a prison, and eighteen scenes in a garden. Also included with the scenes which follow no discernible pattern of action are thirty-one "complex" scenes which cannot be classified

with any of those considered thus far. These complex scenes include a number which may be called "traveling" or "shifting" scenes because the location of the action being depicted shifts from one place to another without any break in the action on stage. Such a scene is the one depicting the Saint Bartholomew's Day massacre in *The Massacre at Paris* (b-3) (323–543). With the "complex" scenes I also put several "split" scenes in which action occurring at two different places is staged simultaneously, as in the "prospective glasse" scenes in *Friar Bacon* (b-4) (scenes 5 and 12).

7: THE DISCOVERY SPACES

1. W. W. Greg's observations about this play should be noted (MSR, p. x.): "Even among admittedly garbled versions it has an evil distinction, and must for shortness and fatuity be classed with such pieces as *The Famous Victories of Henry V* and *Orlando Furioso*." However, the shortness of the text of *The Massacre at Paris*, or any other play, does not necessarily negate the value of the evidence the play may offer about the stage. Moreover, the number of lines in a text does not always give a clear indication of the length of the time required to stage a play. The 220 lines in scene 5 of *The Massacre at Paris* involve stage action requiring much more playing time than would be required by 220 lines of verbal repartee. The 1587 lines in the Malone Society reprint of the play contain enough action to permit one to classify *The Massacre* as a full-length play, albeit a short one. Aside from his objection to the shortness of the play, Greg's chief complaints are that "it is at times so confused as to be hardly intelligible, while the structure of the verse is frequently lost." As to the structure of the verse, it may be so. As to the intelligibility of the play—if I understood him correctly—Greg objects to the seemingly confused action of the play. He was unable to follow what was going on, and understandably so. The play is unintelligible when one attempts to trace the action on a stage provided with only three openings. Leslie Hotson uses three houses, a study, and two doors in tracing the movement of this scene in *Shakespeare's Wooden O* (London: Rupert Hart-Davis, 1960), pp. 144–51.

2. Banquets are served in *Friar Bacon* (b-4) (1325–87), *Battle of Alcazar*, plot (b-4) (91–101), *Looking Glass for London* (b-6) (1847–2040), *Spanish Tragedy* (a-3) (521–93), *George a Green* (b-3) (1176–342), *Titus Andronicus* (a-4) (K2–K4v), *King Leir* (b-6) (2091–355), *I Tamburlaine* (b-6) (D8v–E3), *Faustus* (b-5) (1008–126), *Golden Age* (b-2) (D1–D1v), *Silver Age* (b-2) (C4–D1, also H2–H3), *Brazen Age* (b-2) (E1v–E3v), *The Blind Beggar* (b-3) (542–646), *Patient Grissil* (a-1) (4.3.1–279), *David and Bathsheba* (b-9) (706–53, also 753–801), *Woman Killed with Kindness* (a-2) (D2v–D3).

3. Curtains are mentioned and apparently used before openings in the following episodes: *Friar Bacon* (b-4) (1561), *Battle of Alcazar* (b-4) (37), *Battle of Alcazar*, plot (b-4) (27, 84), *Looking Glass for London* (b-6) (503–10, 552), *Spanish Tragedy* (a-3) (2853, 2909, 3045), *II Tamburlaine* (b-6) (H2, H4v), *Golden Age* (b-2) (I2v), *Edward I* (b-9) (F1, F2, F2v, F4, references to opening and closing a tent), *Famous Victories* (a-3) (C3v, D1), *Downfall of Robert* (a-2) (53, 55, 56, 85, 1490), *Death of Robert* (a-2) (923–25), *Fortunatus* (b-1) (2.1.64–70, 3.1.356–57), *David and Bathsheba* (b-9) (25–27, 1911–67).

4. It is possible that these thrones were provided with curtains, but a more reasonable supposition is that thrones were regularly "discovered" or else "thrust out" onto the stage through one of the discovery spaces or through the gates. If the three thrones demanded by a stage direction in *Edward I* (b-9) (A3v) were placed side by side, they may well have been placed in each of the three openings located in the rear wall of the stage of the Rose. The importance of royalty suggests also that thrones may frequently have been thrust out through the gates centered in the wall at the rear of the stage.

8: LINKS BETWEEN THE HEAVENS AND HELL

1. Richard Hosley, "Was There a Music-room in Shakespeare's Globe?" *SS* 13(1960):116.

2. "Sellynge"—that is "ceiling"—is defined in the *Oxford English Dictionary* as "the lining of the roof of a room with woodwork, plaster or the like; now usually with lath and plaster."

3. Henslowe paid his workmen about a shilling a day. An entry in the *Diary* (Foakes and Rickert, p. 10) reads: "Itm pd for iii dayes for A workman. . . . . . iii^s vi^d." Another entry on the same page reads: "Itm pd for A[nail]er for iiii dayes. . . . . iii^s 4^d."

4. Unfortunately a portion of the bottom of the leaf on which these entries appear has been torn from the *Diary* and other entries which could have been related to the project have been lost.

5. The external arrangement of the door and the windows is the same for both the Rose and the Globe, which appear in the map of 1600. One doubts if this is a mere coincidence; the Bear Garden and the Swan are also shown in the same map with arrangements of doors and windows differing from each other and from the Rose and the Globe. I believe the map is important pictorial evidence indicating that the facade of the Globe was also limited to two levels.

6. While I find that the maps seem to be consistent on almost every point about which we have similar or related information concerning theaters, it should be noted here that I have been concerned with these maps mainly in connection with the Rose theater (see chapter 1). It should also be noted that the maps do not properly label the Rose; it appears as "The play howse" in the map of 1593 and as "The Stare" in the map of 1600. Here one wonders if Norden confused a rose in the theater's flag for a multipointed star. Also, the Bear Garden appears in the map of 1593 without a hut and thatching and with only a single row of windows near the top of the building. In the map of 1600 it has a hut, thatching, and two rows of windows. Are we to assume that extensive alterations were made to the building between 1593 and 1600? It is entirely possible. Alleyn spent £450 on the Bear Garden in December 1594: "first to mr: Burnabye. . . . 200," and "Then for the patten . . . . 250." These expenditures were made during the time when three other theaters provided with huts appeared on the Bankside. One might also question the representation of the Swan in the map of 1600. Unfortunately the theater is so far away that one cannot be sure if it has the hut with which it was provided in the De Witt drawing. In general, I am conscious of the risks involved in overstressing the evidence that is derived from sketches, engravings, and maps; even so, I am convinced that Norden's maps are reliable in the information they give about the exteriors of the playhouses on the Bankside.

7. *Friar Bacon* (b-4) (634–811, 1800–69), *Orlando Furioso* (b-3) (325–42), *Jew of Malta* (b-5) (C4v–D1, E3v–E4, K1v), *Spanish Tragedy* (a-3) (749–809, 2072–3028), *Knack to Know a Knave* (a-4) (597–647, 1753–832), *George a Green* (b-3) (450–83), *King Leir* (b-6) (597–634, 1473–1502, 2107–73), *Alphonsus of Aragon* (b-6) (280–329, 448–75, 690–718), *I Tamburlaine* (b-6) (C5–C6), *Faustus* (b-5) (1402–14, 1904–83), *Knack to Know an Honest Man* (b-3) (20–59, 318–48, 794–852, 993–1035), *John a Kent* (b-7) (408–474, 773–857, 1047–96, 1131–56), *Silver Age* (b-2) (C4, I4–K1), *Brazen Age* (b-2) (E2–E3, I2v–I3), *Edward I* (b-9) (E1–E2, G1–G2), *Blind Beggar* (b-3) (918–1001), *Captain Stukley* (a-3) (C2–C4), *Humorous Day's Mirth* (a-3) (820–1012, 1482–1536), *Downfall of Robert* (a-2) (1414–50, 1577–628), *Englishmen for My Money* (a-2) (31–129, 1454–599, 1796–961), *Death of Robert* (a-2) (1819–35, 2428–526), *Two Angry Women* (a-2) (1613–19, 2361–405, 2680–730), *Shoemakers' Holiday* (a-2) (3.1.3–27, 3.4.1–21), *Look about You* (a-4) (663–725), *Sir John Oldcastle* (a-1) (2086–117, 2310–20), *Patient Grissil* (a-1) (3.2.1–63, 4.1.111–65), *Fortunatus* (b-1) (3.1.186–208), *Woman Killed with Kindness* (a-2) (C2v–C3, D1, H–H1v).

9: THE PLACES ABOVE THE STAGE

1. "Shakespeare's Use of a Gallery over the Stage," *SS* 10(1957):77–89.

2. *SS* 10(1957):77. See also his "Origins of the So-called Elizabethan Multiple Stage," *The Drama Review* 12, no. 2 (Winter 1968):28–50.

3. George Riley Kernodle, *From Art to Theatre* (Chicago: University of Chicago Press, 1944), p. 149.

4. It does not seem likely that this action, or action occurring later in *I Henry VI* (b-8)(3.2) when Pucell enters "*on the top, thrusting out a Torch burning*," involves the use of a window in the "hut." And aside from the possibility that "on the top" in *I Henry VI* may refer to the hut, I find nothing to suggest the use of that part of the stage for anything except the lift.

5. Richard Hosley refers to the gallery as the Lords' room at the Swan in "Shakespeare's Use of a Gallery over the Stage," *SS* 10 (1957):77.

6. Thomas Heywood, *An Apology for Actors* (London: Shakespeare Society, 1841), pp. 34–35.

7. Payments for "makenge the penthowse shed at the tyeringe howse doore" are recorded in the *Diary* following an unrelated entry dated 13 April 1592 (Foakes and Rickert, p. 13).

8. See Appendix A, "Repertory of Extant Plays of the Rose," nos. 70, 71, and 72.

9. See Appendix C, "The Heavens." In the absence of other evidence for two lifts at the Rose, one doubts that the stage direction calling for "*Juno and Iris plac'd in a cloud above*" (I4) involves a lift. They are in the "*cloud*" watching as Jupiter "*descends*" from the heavens (I4v). It is also unlikely that a lift was used in connection with a direction calling for Jupiter, the gods, and the planets to "*ascend to heaven*" (L1). Nine persons are in the group; they do not come on stage in the lift; and in no instance are two people raised to the heavens together. In *The Golden Age* (b-2) (K2v) two separate trips are required: "*Jupiter first ascends upon the Eagle, and after him Ganimed.*" Possibly the fact that directions call for so many people to be taken from the stage in the lift in *The Silver Age* (b-2) (L1) remains to show something of the author's intent after the success of the device in *The Golden Age*.

Index

Gods above the stage, 25

Gods from heavens, 90–92. *See also* Heavens; Lift

Golden Age, 199–214; trapdoor, 16; openings in walls, 30; movement of actors about the stage, 45; discovery spaces, 59, 68; beds, 68, 82; stairs to gallery, 77–78; lords' rooms, 88–89; lift, 91–92, 123; chorus, 98; "*knock and enter*," 112–13; Jupiter's eagle, 119, 123; arbor, 133; beds, 136–40; elevated throne, 144; banquet, 150; porter's lodge, 171; identified with "seleo & olympo," 201, 206, 208–12

"Grate" in "this turrets top," 87

Greek theater, 174

Greene, Robert, 190, 193, 195, 197

Greg, Sir Walter W., 114, 142, 157, 179, 182, 184; on identification of plays, xxv–xxvii; on Rose, 1–4, 7, 10, 73; on identification of Bankside theaters, 7; on Henslowe-Cholmley partnership, 10; on operation of trapdoor, 18; on *Fortunatus*, 186; editor of Malone Society Reprints, 196–99, 201, 205, 214–20, 222

Grille or grate in gates, 39–40

"Groundlings," 21, 23, 24

Gurr, Andrew, xxi

Hamlet, 22, 49

Haughton, William, 218, 221

Heavens, 53, 70, 79, 89–91, 109, 173–74, 176, 262–63; decorated, 90; trapdoor in, 90; machinery in, 90–91; alterations and repairs to, 91; throne let down from, 142; thrones manipulated from, 142–43, 145; seats lowered from, 153. *See also* Lift

Hell, 14, 53, 176; openings to, 14; size and shape, 19–20. *See also* Trapdoor

Henry V, 4, 192; prologue, 106, 156, 159

I Henry VI, 70, 93–94, 192–93; walls of stage, 25; court of guard, 32, 171; openings in walls, 32–34; gates, 39, 172; gallery, 81; penthouse, 86–87; "Turrets top," 87; messenger, 99; symmetry in staging, 112; "Woodden Coffin," 121; bushes, 124; couplet to end scenes, 158; allusions and reports, 160; dialogue to indicate place, 161; disguise, 167–68; offstage sounds, 169

Henslowe, Philip, xvii–xxv, 1–6, 24, 26–30, 38, 43–44, 71, 73–74, 84, 115, 117, 124, 133, 142, 153, 166, 174; partnership agreement with John Cholmley, 179, 264; sketch on letter, 181–82, plate 28. *See also* Admiral's inventories (1598); Cholmley, John; *Diary*; Documents of the Rose; Greg, Sir Walter W.

Heywood, Thomas: *Woman Killed with Kindness*, 101–2,138, 223; *Four Prentices of London*, 196; *Jupiter and Io*, 216

Heywood's *Ages*, 15–16, 89–92, 136, 138, 186–87, 199–214; identified with Red Bull, 200; presented at Rose (1595), 200; and Admiral's inventories, 201–12; *Golden Age* identified with "seleo & olempo," 201, 208–12; identification of *Golden Age* contested (1923), 201; *Silver Age* and *Brazen Age* identified as "I and II Hercules," 201, 207–12; "seleo & olempo" disappears from repertory of Rose (1596), 206; and *Diary*, 207–11; and work on throne in the heavens (1595), 210–11; history of Hercules plays after revival at Rose, 211–14; author's role in printing of, 212–14

Hodges, C. Walter, xx, 21, 23

Holaday, Allan, 201, 203–7

Holland view of Bankside, 6, plate 25

Hondius view of Bankside, 6–7, plate 23

Hope playhouse, 1, 70; contract for, xxiii, xxv

Horrror in plays of the Rose, 103–4

Hosley, Richard, xxi, 28, 54–55, 70, 79, 141, 146–47

Hotson, Leslie, xxi

Humorous Day's Mirth, 216–17

Hut, 11–13, 73–76, 82, 84, 90; thrones stored in, 142. *See also* Heavens; Lift

If it be not Good, 212

Imagination, direct appeals to, 156, 159

Indicative evidence, defined, xxvii

Ingressus, 29

Inner stage, 54, 56–57. *See also* Curtained framework

Invisibility, 167

Jeronimo, 194

Jerusalem, 196